*TWENTIETH CENTURY STUDIES*
edited by
Donald Tyerman

ECONOMICS AND POLICY

*Twentieth Century Studies*

# ECONOMICS AND POLICY
## *A Historical Study*

by

# DONALD WINCH

HODDER AND STOUGHTON

Copyright © 1969 by Donald Winch

First Printed 1969

SBN 340 10972 6

Printed in Great Britain for Hodder and Stoughton Limited, St. Paul's House, Warwick
Lane, London E.C.4 by C. Tinling & Co. Ltd., London and Prescot

For
Robert and Mary

# Editor's Preface

*Economics and Policy* is conspicuously a Twentieth Century Study as we have conceived the series. It is not just an account of the changes in economic thought since the time of Queen Victoria and Alfred Marshall. It is not just an account of the changes until today in the economic policies and attitudes of politicians and governments in Britain and the United States. It is also, primarily and distinctively, an account of the constant interchanges between the two, between economic thought and economic policy, between the professional economists and the professional politicians, between intellectual propositions and enquiries of the political economists and the problems of society itself.

This is precisely the purpose of these Twentieth Century Studies: to show, in each book's separate and independent field, the interplay between what men have thought and thought out, during this century so far, and what they have done or tried to do about it. This is the common theme or approach of all the Studies, though each is its author's own responsibility. This is the theme of David Edwards's *Religion and Change*, which looks at the role of religious belief in a secularised society. This is the theme of Alan Norton's *The New Dimensions of Medicine* which looks at the impact of scientific revolution and social transformation on the theory and practice of medicine, on concepts of health and disease and the prospects of life and death. Just as much as these, Donald Winch's book, the third of our Twentieth Century Studies, is concerned with the connection between ideas and events, with the struggle of modern societies, furnished with new knowledge, new techniques and new modes of organisation, but faced with new problems and new dilemmas as well as still the old ones, to control their destiny and better their lot. If it is concerned first with the pursuit of wealth and welfare, it is concerned equally with the pursuit of happiness and the abatement of misery—goals, now as always, just beyond the horizon, however the material standards of many may go up.

*Economics and Policy* takes as its frame one distinctive trend of this century, the widening scope of the state's responsibilities for economic affairs, not only in Britain but also in America. Professor Winch has set out to describe the contribution made by economists to the ways in which the politicians have sought to discharge these responsibilities, their contribution to the running debate on the means and ends of economic policy, their contribution to the attempts by governments right up to the present day to combat what Geoffrey Crowther called, just thirty years ago,[1] the "evil trinity" of our economic system—poverty, inequality and irregularity.

If Professor Winch has written a close-knit book fit for the scholars of his subject to read, he has also written a book of the broadest interest to everybody who has a care for the great social and political issues of our times as these have been transmuted but not removed by the transformation of the world as it was before the First World War into the world as it is after the Second World War. It is a dramatic tale, as well as a scholarly one, with its blow-by-blow account of the argument over unemployment and international trade before 1914; of the endeavours between the wars first to re-establish, and re-justify, the old national and international arrangements and then to find new ways of overcoming world depression and mass unemployment; of the historic impact of the ideas of John Maynard Keynes and of the calls of another gigantic war, and its aftermath, on the policies of British and American governments; on the gains and the shortcomings, from the New Deal of the 'thirties to the New Economics of today, of the new techniques of economic management. *Economics and Policy* is not only a crucial chapter in the history of professional economics, from Marshall to Keynes; it is also a crucial chapter in the history of politics—and of social concern.

DONALD TYERMAN

[1] Crowther, G. *Economics for Democrats* (Thomas Nelson and Sons, 1955).

# Preface

I should like to express my thanks to several people who have given me help and encouragement in writing this book. The general editor of the series in which the book appears, Mr Donald Tyerman, has given a great deal of time and thought to the shape and tone of the enterprise; he has also been put to considerable trouble in overcoming doubts that have assailed me at various stages. Professor A. W. Coats read an earlier version with great thoroughness and made a large number of valuable comments. Professor Asa Briggs has helped me by reading through the final version and suggesting ways of improving the book.

Apart from those whose works are cited in the footnotes, many others with whom I have spoken or corresponded in the last two or three years have helped me on specific points and matters of detailed interpretation. I should also like to thank Miss Jane Williams for her services in checking references and in preparing the manuscript for publication. The responsibility for the final product is, of course, mine.

DONALD WINCH

# Acknowledgments

The author is grateful to the following for permission to quote from their publications:

Macmillan and Company Limited, the Estate of the late Lord Keynes and The Macmillan Company of Canada Limited, for material from *General Theory of Employment, Interest and Money* by John Maynard Keynes;

Macmillan and Company Limited, for material from *Principles of Economics* by Alfred Marshall and for material from *The Memorials of Alfred Marshall* edited by A.C. Pigou;

Her Majesty's Stationery Office, for permission to quote from *Hansard*.

The Franklin D. Roosevelt Library for permission to quote from a letter from Keynes to F.D.R.

# Contents

|  | Page |
|---|---|
| EDITOR'S PREFACE | 7 |
| PREFACE | 9 |
| ACKNOWLEDGMENTS | 10 |

*Chapter*

| 1 | ECONOMICS AND POLICY: INTRODUCTION | 13 |

## PART ONE: BEFORE THE WAR

| 2 | THE "SOCIAL QUESTION" AND WELFARE ECONOMICS | 28 |
| 3 | UNEMPLOYMENT AND TARIFF REFORM | 47 |

## PART TWO: BETWEEN THE WARS

| 4 | THE INTER-WAR PERIOD: INTRODUCTION | 67 |
| 5 | £1 = $4.86 | 75 |
| 6 | UNEMPLOYMENT AND PUBLIC SPENDING IN BRITAIN DURING THE 'TWENTIES | 94 |
| 7 | THE POLITICAL ECONOMY OF CRISIS, 1929-1931 | 114 |
| 8 | KEYNES AND THE ACADEMIC COMMUNITY, 1919-1936 | 145 |
| 9 | THE KEYNESIAN REVOLUTION AND THE ACADEMIC COMMUNITY | 167 |
| 10 | BRITAIN IN THE 'THIRTIES: A MANAGED ECONOMY? | 198 |
| 11 | KEYNES AND THE NEW DEAL | 219 |

## PART THREE: THE SECOND WORLD WAR AND AFTER

| 12 | KEYNESIAN WAR ECONOMICS AND POST-WAR PLANS | 255 |
| 13 | THE KEYNESIAN REVOLUTION: FRUITION | 280 |

*Page*

14 Postscript: Economics and Policy in the
Post-Keynesian Era     311

Appendix: Keynes and the British Left in
the Inter-War Period     341

Index     351

# CHAPTER ONE

# Economics and Policy: Introduction

The legitimate role of the state in economic life has always been one of the central concerns of economists. At times they have simply reflected the dominant views on this question of their society or class, while at others they have helped to modify prevailing conceptions of what it was desirable and feasible for governments to attempt. The relationship of changes in the thinking and interests of economists to the methods and aims actually pursued by economic policy-makers in the first half of the twentieth century provides the leitmotiv of this study. The theme is obviously a large one. And since the relationship between thought and policy in a discipline like economics is by no means a straightforward one, it may be helpful to mention at the outset some of the problems involved, and indicate some of the ways in which I have tried to tackle or avoid them.

In the first place I have confined myself to the Anglo-American world. More precisely, I have concentrated on the British debate while attempting to temper provincialism, and provide an essential counterpoint to my argument, by discussing the crucial American experience of the 'thirties and the post-war period. Although this emphasis corresponds closely to the limits of my own knowledge, it was also dictated by the fact that any detailed discussion of policy would have to be confined to one or two political and economic systems. A different story would obviously emerge from other European countries, let alone Russia, where for most of the period the economic experience and political background were different, and diverse traditions of economic thought held sway. Nevertheless, there is plenty of scope for comparative studies of a type which I have flinched from undertaking here. Some of the reasons for making a partial exception in the case of the United States perhaps need to be spelled out in a little more detail.

It was during the first half of the twentieth century that there emerged something which could accurately be described as an Anglo-American school of economic thought, possessing characteristics that marked it off from French, German, or, less decisively, Scandinavian economic thought. Before 1914 non-Marxian economic thought can broadly be divided between the economic theorists, flying under the banner of some version of what we now call neo-classical economics (Marshallian, Austrian or Walrasian), and the economic historians or institutionalists, drawing their chief inspiration from Germany. Representatives of both schools of thought can be found in Britain and the United States, with the theorists more in the ascendancy in the former and gaining it over time in the latter. Although the American tradition is a more eclectic one, with some native roots, it is only slightly unfair to say that the dominant theoretical mode was derived from British writers. In the inter-war period something like parity was established between the British and American contributions to the joint tradition. Just as Alfred Marshall, Professor of Economics at Cambridge until 1906, found some of his ablest exponents in the United States, so was this more emphatically the case with the work of his pupil John Maynard Keynes in the 'thirties. From this time until the present day the exchange of ideas and men across the Atlantic has become a regular feature of the life of the Anglo-American economist. The overwhelming weight of resources, qualitative and quantitative, may now be said to reside in the United States, but the joint tradition, now fed from other channels, remains unbroken.[1]

Economics as a professional pursuit has become a more truly international discipline since the last world war. One of the most interesting developments of recent times, arising mainly out of the increased emphasis on quantitative and mathematical techniques, has been the bridging of the gulf at strategic points between Western and Soviet economics. Again, it is only slightly unfair to say that the consensus has largely formed around the Anglo-American model of economic inquiry as it emerged towards the end of the period considered here. For this reason alone, the story I am concerned with here is important to the understanding of modern economics. Those who write on these matters in the second half of the twentieth century, however, will be more vulnerable to the charge of parochialism if they concentrate as much as this book does on British problems and solutions.

There are other reasons why it is necessary to consider the American experience in this period. After the First World War the United States became one of the world's leading economic powers. What happened there became of vital significance to other countries, and certainly to Britain, the other major financial centre. This was made only too painfully clear when the stock exchange boom on

[1] One of the latest and most revealing examples of the Anglo-American traffic is the study of the British economy recently produced by a group of American economists. See R. E. Caves, (ed.) *Britain's Economic Prospects*, (1968). British reviewers were impressed by the quality of the report and the relative shortness of the time taken to compile it. There was wistful speculation as to whether an equivalent group of British economists could have matched the performance.

Wall Street collapsed in 1929, and was followed by a depression which began in the United States but soon engulfed most of the capitalist world. Of the democratic nations, with the possible exception of Sweden, it was the United States that undertook the boldest experiments in state economic intervention in the 'thirties. Roosevelt's New Deal was the cynosure for all those interested in finding democratic, non-revolutionary solutions for the ills of capitalism. In Britain Keynes was one of the leading spokesmen for the American experiment, and one of the fiercest advocates of a British New Deal. In the United States, Keynes was regarded variously as a sympathetic critic of the New Deal, its guiding light, and its evil genius. A book such as this would be incomplete without a chapter on this remarkable, if somewhat confusing, episode.

When Keynes's ideas became a significant force in the Anglo-American academic world, the battle for their implementation in the field of government policy went on in parallel in both countries. I have therefore tried to indicate the nature of these parallel movements in the chapters dealing with the Second World War and after. Even though I have not attempted to make a full-scale comparative study, some interesting, if tentative, conclusions can be drawn from a consideration of the two cases together.

.     .     .

The student of British debate on economic policy soon begins to notice recurrent themes. This may be due to the fact, as economists are fond of pointing out, that some of the basic problems of all economic systems are the same: every society must find a way of solving *the* economic problem of reconciling limitless wants with scarce resources. But we do not have to retreat to such an Olympian plane: is it not better explained by the fact that the problems faced by a small, highly industrialised country relying heavily on foreign trade have not changed dramatically in the past century? The order of priority may vary but the agenda remains relatively constant. There is even a repetitious note in British debates, uncommonly like a dying fall. It was struck long ago by the anonymous author of a seventeenth-century pamphlet who chose *Britannia Languens* for his title: she has been languishing ever since. Her industries are un-competitive; her rate of innovation and growth is sluggish; her workers and managers are lazy; her economic system is hide-bound. All that seems to change is the country with whom the unfavourable comparisons are made—Holland, France, Germany, the United States, Japan, the Common Market countries. It is perhaps fortunate that, as Adam Smith once remarked, "there is a good deal of ruin in a nation".

Beneath the surface continuities, however, there has been a remarkable sea-change in attitudes to the proper role of the state in economic life, not only in Britain but in most developed societies. The increase in the size of the government contribution to economic activity, and the widening in scope of its responsibilities, is one of the leading themes of twentieth century history. Broadly speaking, at the beginning of the century it was considered unnecessary, unwise, and perhaps even impossible, for governments to exercise detailed control over the direction of the economic machine. Now it is widely accepted that the economic performance of society, both in the large and in the small, is one of the primary responsibilities of the state.

To say that there has been an increase in state intervention in the twentieth century is not—by itself—very enlightening. It is not even strictly true if one bears in mind that the same trend was at work during the latter half of the nineteenth century. A broad movement of this kind virtually subsumes every significant social, economic and political force at work in the period. It could, for example, be accounted for in terms of organic growth; of inherent tendencies towards centralisation in an economy in which increased complexity has favoured the larger decision-units, public as well as private. Or it might be seen as the outcome of a sharper social conscience; of a mixture of egalitarianism and paternalism that has led to the replacement of individual by collective provision of welfare services. It could be depicted as a political phenomenon: the achievement of democracy and the rise of the Labour movement leading to demands for greater security and control over the exercise of private economic power by those who were previously tools of the system. Or again, it might be seen as the result of pragmatic adjustment to the pressure of events in the form of two world wars and a major depression. And so on.

It would be tempting also to speak of a progressive movement away from *laissez-faire* individualism towards state-controlled collectivism. But this too would not be very helpful. *Laissez-faire* has never existed as a conscious system of policy. Even in nineteenth-century Britain, where the principles of *laissez-faire* are supposed to have held greatest sway, there was a steady growth of regulatory and protective activity on the part of the state. It is true, of course, that the *laissez-faire* ideal exercised considerable influence on economic thinking at the popular level, though even here it frequently served merely as a slogan, a term of abuse, or as a rationalisation for a policy of inaction in particular cases. The truth is that while the leading issues of economic policy have often been posed as a choice between individualism and collectivism, the most important discussions have taken place well within the limits set by these slippery terms.

The use of such tags as "the decline of *laissez-faire*" obscures the necessary distinctions that have to be made between the kinds of economic intervention which the state has undertaken. One important distinction is that between measures designed to provide increased protection and security to workers or citizens through collective provision of welfare services, and those measures which have in view the improvement in the overall economic performance of society. Today especially, both types of policy complement each other: unemployment benefits, for example, are simultaneously a feature of the welfare society as well as a stabilising device for the economy as a whole; they prevent incomes and therefore spending from falling as far as they would in their absence during recessions. There may be other, more complex, relationships between welfare and economic stability. It could be argued that welfare services have frequently been pioneered as compensation for the differential hardships imposed by the capitalist system. In the United States, Keynesian ideas on economic stabilisation have frequently been allied with the case for more extensive federal sponsorship of welfare services. Others have depicted them as alternatives: they regard the attainment of full employment and affluence as providing the proper setting for a return to an era of personal rather than state-sponsored provision of welfare services. Finally, for those who believe that the co-operation of various producer groups is an essential feature of modern economic planning, the extension or modification of the welfare services is part of the *quid pro quo* necessary to achieve restraint in other directions.

All of these are intriguing avenues. For the purposes of this study, however, it is useful to separate "welfarist" motives for intervention from those dictated by the needs of overall economic management. It is to be hoped that the significance of making this separation will become clearer later in this study. While economists have frequently supported welfare measures, and have recently pioneered techniques of appraisal that are potentially very useful in this field, they have made a more distinctive contribution to questions of economic management. It is one of the leading characteristics of the twentieth-century revolution in public economic thinking that increasing attention has been paid to the means of controlling the level and growth of economic activity. It is here also that it is possible to speak of a genuine improvement in our understanding of the effects of various economic institutions and policies.

This book deals with one component within a complex and changing pattern of state intervention and policy: the interaction of economic thought, particularly that of professional economists, and

economic policy-making. The story told will be familiar, in outline
at least, to most economists. But this study is not primarily concerned with the history of a professional community, nor is it
exclusively addressed to economists. Those chiefly interested in the
developments in economic *science* in this period will have to look
elsewhere.[1] Nor will the reader find a full and connected account of
the economic events, policies, and institutions of this period, except
where this seems necessary as background to an understanding of
the intellectual debate. My chief concern is with the area of overlap
between professional and policy questions—between developments
that were internal to the discipline and the problems posed by
external demands and circumstance. Clearly, any book that attempts
to cover as much ground as this must be based on a fairly severe
selection from among the large array of contributions by economists
to policy issues. I can only say that I have tried to deal with those
contributions that seemed representative or dominant in the period
in question.

It may be useful at this point to introduce a distinction which is
familiar to all economists but may be less so to others. Economists
distinguish between micro- and macro-economics. Micro-economics
is much older in origin and deals with the central, formal problems
of economics, namely scarcity, value, choice, resource allocation and
efficiency. For the most part it takes the stock of economic resources
and their level of utilisation as given, and concentrates on the means
by which those resources and their rewards are allocated between
different uses and owners, whether by a market process, by a
centralised planning agency, or by some mixture of the two.
Macro-economics is that branch of the subject which derives from
the Keynesian framework of analysis; it uses aggregated variables
such as national income and aggregate demand to explain the general
level of economic activity and employment at any given time and
through time. One of the most important themes running through
this book concerns the way in which the macro-viewpoint was
established as a separable entity. As part of the treatment of this
theme it is necessary to show how micro- and macro-reasoning have
frequently become confused with one another to the detriment of
clear understanding and policy action. But this does not mean that
the two compartments are water-tight: once having made the distinction and established a provisional division of labour, many of the
most important issues can only be explored by a combination of the
two ways of looking at an economic system.

[1] Fortunately, there is at least one recent work which covers a crucial period in this
history: G. L. S. Shackle's *The Years of High Theory; Invention and Tradition in Economic
Thought, 1926-1939* (1967).

I am conscious of the fact that the bias of the middle and latter half of the book leans very much towards macro- rather than micro-economic questions. By the same token, the policy issues connected with micro-economics, notably the economics of the growth in the size of firms, of competition and monopoly, are treated only incidentally. And this in spite of the fact that this was a period of considerable advance in the formal apparatus designed to deal with such questions. Although I have tried to make brief amends for this in my final chapter, I can only record my opinion that the developments in macro-economics in this period were more significant from the point of view of policy-making. Another, and possibly less excusable, gap is the lack of attention paid to issues of international economic policy and diplomacy.

.        .        .

The conceptual snares that lie in wait for those who embark on any study of the relationship of economic thought to policy ought to be faced from the beginning. It would all be much simpler if a series of related distinctions could be sustained with an easy conscience: between means and ends; between questions of what is and what ought to be; between pure science and its applications. Economists have always recognised a dual obligation: to provide scientific explanations of the "normal" working of economic systems, and to furnish guidance as to the "best" policies under any given circumstances. Although economic knowledge alone can never be final in judging what is "best", ideally, the two types of inquiry should complement each other: "normative" economics presupposes a "positive" understanding of the results to be expected from alternative courses of action. But it is not always possible to disentangle the two levels of discourse in economics. There can be a high degree of involvement with politics; a disagreement about the proper ends of policy can easily become confused with a disagreement about the effects of alternative means and their quantitative significance. To add to the confusion, value-judgments can be attached to the choice between means as well as between ends. Small wonder then that economists are notoriously disputatious—though whether they are more so than, say, doctors, whose disputes are more effectively hidden from the public eye, is open to question.

In the light of these difficulties it might be said that even to pose the existence of a relationship between economic thought and policy entails both an over-optimistic conception of the technocratic status of economics, and a naïve view of the processes of political decision-making. There is certainly an element of wishful thinking in Keynes's famous declaration that:

". . . the ideas of economists and political philosophers both when
they are right and when they are wrong are more powerful than is
commonly understood. Indeed the world is ruled by little else.
Practical men, who believe themselves to be quite exempt from any
intellectual influences, are usually the slaves of some defunct
economist. Madmen in authority, who hear voices in the air,
are distilling their frenzy from some academic scribbler of a few
years back."[1]

It is understandable that economists should be biased in favour of
interpreting policy-formation as a rational, intellectual exercise. How
else could they see their task? Keynes, who figures more prominently
in these pages than any other economist, attributed failure to cope
with unemployment in the inter-war period to "muddle", and to
blunders "in the control of a delicate machine, the workings of
which we do not understand". But one must be aware—as Keynes
was not on all occasions—of the rationalist fallacy of believing that
ideas alone are powerful enough to determine the course of events.
All important economic policies require political and moral choices
to be made in a context that is characterised by norms, beliefs,
goals, and pressures which differ from those of an academic community. Even if economic advisers were always unanimous and
relevant in their diagnoses and remedies, there would still be plenty
of scope for slips twixt lip and cup.

An important consequence of this is that compared with the
natural sciences or medicine there is a far greater chance of an
actual retrogression in the application of economic knowledge to
policy problems. Over and above the fact that in economics the
frontier of knowledge may be less clearly marked, so that there is
more room for divisions of professional opinion as to what constitutes
a problem or a solution, there is the possibility that "good" advice
will be ignored or rejected. A similar situation in medicine would be
one in which a well-established remedy for disease was abandoned
in favour of methods whose faults were known. We shall have
occasion to note cases where political doctors have consistently
ignored, or failed to have the courage to apply, remedies proposed
by a significant body of professional economic opinion.

The moral of this for a study of this kind is the need to accept a
certain amount of untidiness and eclecticism. Economic advisers are
only one of the influences that must be considered alongside others
of a more overt political nature as helping to shape economic policy.
Interpreted in a slightly different way, Keynes's dictum concerning
the power of ideas contains an element of truth which supports this

---

[1] *General Theory of Employment, Interest and Money* (1936), p. 383.

approach. Policies that appear to have no conscious basis in economic knowledge may none the less contain an implicit rationale which it is important to distil. In addition to the technocratic application of economic ideas, the connection between economics, political decisions, party alignments, and the broad sweep of ideology must be taken into consideration.

Recognition of these complications should not lead one to the opposite extreme of regarding economics simply as an extension of political debate; to the view that the history of economic thought is a history of ideologies, or one that reflects in a straightforward fashion the dominant interest-groupings or practical problems of society at any particular time. Economists may not be the custodians of a body of undisputed and universally applicable truths which bear no relationship to the conflicting value-schemes of the society at large; but neither are they entirely at the mercy of everyday events and passions. The agenda and timetable set by the internal pressures of the discipline may or may not correspond with that of the external world.[1]

The first half of the twentieth century coincides roughly with the period in which economics emerged as a professionally organised pursuit. The existence of a professional academic community with international ramifications has important consequences for the way in which a discipline conducts its intellectual affairs. Even informal professional standards can diminish the range of disagreement and provide commonly-accepted ways of resolving disputes. Normally this is an advantage; but at times the pressures making for conformity can insulate a professional community from significant social problems. Something like this seems to have happened in the inter-war period over the question of mass unemployment. For this reason, the Keynesian revolution had to be fought out in the pages of learned journals before it could begin to influence policy. Hence the chapters on Keynes's relationship to the academic community in the second part of this study.

Another significant trend recently has been the rise of the official economic adviser employed within the machinery of government. This is bound to modify the relationship between thought and policy in the future. Paradoxically, this change in the channels of communication may simultaneously revive the art of political economy *and* strengthen the technocratic application of economic ideas. A postscript to this study touches on this question.

A further generic problem involved in the study of intellectual history is posed by the gap which may exist between what was

---

[1] This is the theme of a well-argued article by G. J. Stigler, "The Influence of Events and Policies on Economic Theory", reprinted in his *Essays in the History of Economics* (1964).

thought to be the case at the time by the participants in a debate, and what has subsequently been shown to be true with the benefit of hindsight and additional information. This is particularly true of debates on economic policy. The participants in such debates are mainly concerned with the advisability of one course of action rather than another; they are usually arguing about specific measures, and may believe—or use rhetorical licence to show—that a great deal turns on the adoption of that measure. They are rarely in the same position as the economic historian who arrives on the scene later. Nor would it necessarily be in their power or interest to attempt to anticipate his viewpoint. The economic historian is frequently interested in long-term structural change and progress in an economy. In telling this kind of story many policy issues and actions which seemed highly significant to those actually involved, may, in the longer perspective, seem less important than the ordinary, everyday changes that were going on without benefit of policy in any well-defined sense. Trends which seem obvious to an observer concerned with a decade or half-century may, of course, have been imperceptible and unimportant to contemporaries. It is not always easy for the historian of ideas to keep the two levels of discourse separate. Ideas based on "false" appearances may have as potent an effect as those based on "reality". In this study the emphasis is on ideas; but since economics is ultimately concerned with explaining reality, an effort has been made to show where and how the two have sometimes parted company.

.        .        .

The book is divided into three unequal parts, each corresponding to a particular phase of economic thought and policy. The dividing lines are provided by the two world wars. In each case, however, we find that the ideas and expectations of the previous period exercised an influence on later dispositions.

The chapters in the first part deal with the period before the outbreak of the First World War. After the war it was difficult for economists who had been brought up in the pre-1914 world to realise that this world had finally and irrevocably passed, and that many of the assumptions and a good deal of the intellectual apparatus which they had inherited from it would either have to be discarded or thoroughly transformed. The nature of the transformation which gradually took place in the inter-war period can best be appreciated by considering some of the leading features of professional economic thinking on policy questions in Britain as it existed at the turn of the century and persisted up to the outbreak of war. Since it is not possible to consider in detail the host of major and minor questions of policy and practice with which economists were concerned in this period, three representative groups of issues have been selected in order to portray the general orientation of economists towards the larger political and economic questions of the day: these are in turn, the "social question" and the economics of welfare; unemployment; and tariff reform.[1]

By the turn of the century British economists were able to look to the future with greater confidence in their métier than had been possible thirty years before. A prolonged period of crisis and methodological dissension, which threatened to undermine the authority of of its practitioners and hold back economic studies, had been successfully surmounted. A theoretical revolution, beginning in the 'seventies, had been brought to a satisfactory conclusion, leaving the subject more rigorous and unified. Disputes over the nature and scope of economics, and as to the appropriate methods of study, were either resolved or dormant. From this relatively secure base, economists felt able once more to contribute to contemporary political and economic debate, unencumbered by an earlier reputation for dismal dogmatism. Once established, the renewed feeling of confidence and consensus was able to survive largely—though as we shall see, by no means completely—unruffled until the First World War.

Although many writers and influences in the last quarter of the nineteenth century contributed to the task of placing economics on a new and firmer footing, in Britain at least, the figure of Alfred Marshall stands out among the rest. Marshall's *Principles of Economics*, first published in 1890, remained throughout successive editions the bible of British economics. It was simultaneously an original contribution to knowledge, pointing the way for future research, and a broad exposition of the problems that were, and to some extent still are, of interest to economists. Moreover, from his Chair at Cambridge Marshall was able to assume the role of father to British economics as a professionally-organised discipline, symbolised by the foundation of the British Economic Association (later the Royal Economic Society) and its organ, *The Economic Journal*, in 1890.

Nor was it simply as an economist in the pure sense that Marshall impressed his stamp on British economics before 1914. As a representative figure, sharing many of the strengths, weaknesses, prejudices and beliefs of other late Victorian students of society, he imparted a brand of middle-class moral earnestness and helped to restore a feeling of public respectability and relevance to the subject. In this respect, Marshall's contribution was to bring economics into closer

[1] For a more detailed account of the contribution made by economists to policy questions in this period, see N. Jha, *The Age of Marshall* (1968).

contact with the major social questions of the day, and the progressive intellectual tendencies of his age—just as John Stuart Mill had done before him and Keynes was to do later. For these reasons, it is mainly around Marshall's work that the introductory portrait of economics before the war, given in the next two chapters, will be organised.

The second part of the book covers the years between the two world wars. The critical nature of this period explains why so much space has been devoted to it here. It was a period during which optimism, based on the pre-1914 experience of relative stability, progress, and European economic hegemony, was forced to give way in the face of mass unemployment, stagnation, industrial and international unrest, to more pessimistic views on the recuperative powers of the capitalist system. The period can be divided into two parts centring on the world financial crisis of 1931—which marks the end of largely unsuccessful attempts to reconstruct the world economy on pre-1914 lines, and the beginning of a decade of experimentation with new ways of dealing with the economic problem.

Just as Marshall was the leading academic economist in the pre-1914 world, so Keynes became the dominant figure of the inter-war years, both as a commentator on the policy questions of the day and later as the architect of a system of analysis which laid the foundations for "economic management" as we understand it today. Marshallian economics was incapable of dealing with many of the problems of the inter-war world; it had been designed for less turbulent conditions. Keynes did not abolish Marshallian economics, but by building a large new wing on to an old house he succeeded in changing its whole appearance.

The third phase opened with the Second World War and has continued roughly to the present day. It was during this period that the Keynesian revolution in thought was carried into the realm of policy. The chapters dealing with this phase show how the revolution was carried through in Britain and, more recently, in the United States; they also discuss some aspects of post-Keynesian economics.

. . .

I have approached my subject very much as a historian rather than as one concerned with contemporary issues. Similarly, I leave to others the task of speculating on the shape of things to come in the remaining years of the century. But it would be disingenuous on my part to pretend that events and ideas of so recent a vintage are without contemporary significance or incapable of arousing strong feelings. Echoes of the inter-war period are all around us at present.

In Britain, elaborate—and in my view misguided—parallels have been drawn with the events and personalities of the 1931 crisis. The apparently interminable debate on reform of the world's monetary system frequently takes as its point of reference the period between the British return to gold in 1925 and the American devaluation of 1933. In the United States, the New Deal and "Keynesianism" have lost little of their power to arouse strong partisan feelings in some circles.

I have been conscious of the need at several points for more detailed research and documentary evidence from memoirs and official files not yet, or only recently, released. Since I am mainly concerned with public debate, I have confined myself chiefly to published material. I realise also that many of my elders and betters who lived through or took part in the discussions of the inter-war period are still very much alive to tell the tale. It is to be hoped that more of them will do so when they get over the unpleasant shock of realising that their youth is now "history".

For the record, I was born in 1935—a year before the publication of Keynes's *General Theory*. My formal education in economics, in Britain and in the United States, was completed by the end of the 'fifties. It is clear then that I belong to a post-Keynesian generation, and have no personal, as opposed to intellectual, loyalties in the issues discussed. I mention this not as a qualification: in many ways it would have been an advantage to have had direct experience of pre-Keynesian economics. Nor is it any guarantee of impartiality or sound judgment. Although I am aware of the irresponsibility that can come from not having had to take up a position at the time, verdicts must be passed on those who did. It is also impossible to escape entirely from the viewpoint and standards of the present. But I have tried to avoid writing as though all previous decisions and positions were simply blind or brilliant stumblings toward the present light. Current failures are proof against this.

# PART ONE

# Before the War

# CHAPTER TWO

# The "Social Question" and Welfare Economics

Most British economists in the decade or so before the First World War shared a general belief in the stability and capacity for progress of the British economic system. Whereas in the first half of the nineteenth century and beyond economists were still greatly preoccupied with the problems posed by population growth and diminishing returns in domestic agriculture, by the end of the century Marshall could announce that the law of diminishing returns was "almost inoperative in Britain just now".

> "Cheap transport by land and sea, combined with the opening up of a large part of the surface of the world during the last thirty years, has caused the purchasing power of wages in terms of goods to rise throughout the Western world, and especially in Britain, at a rate which has no parallel in the past, and will probably have none in the future."[1]

Free trade and Britain's enormous overseas investments ensured the maximum potential gains from this source. By the same token, cheaper food and interest payments made it unnecessary to worry unduly about the balance of payments or the future of London as the world's financial centre. Britain's earlier population difficulties had been surmounted; and with the law of increasing return at work in manufacturing, the growth of population was now likely to lead to a more than proportionate increase in aggregate production. New wants, new techniques, and new knowledge were constantly opening up opportunities for profitable investment, from which in turn further accumulation was possible. Marshall could see no reason to believe that the stationary state, at which no further new investment would take place, was in sight.[2]

This does not mean, of course, that Marshall and other economists were unaware of, or indifferent to, the problems facing the British

---

[1] A. C. Pigou (ed.), *Memorials of Alfred Marshall*, (1925) p. 326.
[2] *Principles of Economics* (1920 edn.), pp. 321-2; 692.

economy at this time.[1] Marshall's optimism was qualified: it might not always be thus. The law of diminishing returns would reassert itself in the countries supplying British needs. Trade regulations on British exports by other countries, a great war, or heavy military expenditure to ward off such a possibility, could also break the virtuous circle. Nor was optimism incompatible with the observation that relative to America or Germany, Britain had suffered a modest decline—a subject which commanded a good deal of attention during the "great depression" of the 'eighties and 'nineties. Marshall expressed concern about the growth of restrictive practices and apathy on the part of British trade unions and businessmen. Nevertheless, he also considered the causes of Britain's relative decline to be "partly natural, inevitable and from a cosmopolitan point of view, matters for satisfaction".[2]

Pride in the solid achievements of the British economy and qualified optimism about its future performance should not be confused with complacency on social and political questions. The last quarter of the nineteenth century saw a remarkable flowering in the social conscience of the English middle classes which expressed itself in a variety of ways: in the poverty studies of Charles Booth and Seebohm Rowntree; in the Christian socialist movement; in London's East End settlements; and later, in the welfare legislation of the Liberal governments after 1906. The increasing concern with the problems of urban poverty in the midst of plenty—the "social question" as it was known to contemporaries—exercised a major influence on the thinking of all serious students of society, not least the economists.

The continued existence of extensive poverty posed an acute problem to the middle classes. Beatrice Webb described this problem vividly as a "class-consciousness of sin".[3] The soothing notion that poverty was the result of lack of prudence on the part of the poor, and could not be cured by forms of philanthropy which undermined individual responsibility, began to lose its powers of absolution. Whereas in the first half of the nineteenth century it had been possible to believe that poverty was due to the presence of systematic Malthusian pressures, global hypotheses of this kind were no longer quite so tenable in the complex industrial society of the latter part of the century. More detailed enquiry into specific localities, industries,

---

[1] For the views of recent economic historians on this matter, see E. H. Phelps Brown and S. J. Handfield-Jones, "The Climacteric of the 1890s: A Study in the Expanding Economy", *Oxford Economic Papers*, Oct. 1952. D. J. Coppock, "The Climacteric of the 1890's: A Critical Note", *The Manchester School*, Jan. 1956. A. E. Musson, "The Great Depression in Britain, 1873-1888", *Journal of Economic History*, June 1959. D. J. Coppock, "The Causes of the First Depression, 1873-99", *The Manchester School*, Sept. 1961. See also, A. L. Levine, *Industrial Retardation in Britain, 1880-1914*, (1967).

[2] *Memorials*, pp. 399-401; *Industry and Trade* (1919), pp. 86-106; 650-5; 663-5.

[3] *My Apprenticeship* (1938, Penguin edn.), pp. 206-9.

trades, and occupations was required and undertaken by a large number of philanthropic and economic statisticians. Behind these inquiries lay the larger question: How was it that an economic system, which had generated economic progress and enhanced the comfort and security of the middle classes, had failed so conspicuously to improve the lot of many, perhaps even the majority?

Intimately connected with the "social question" was another broad phenomenon, usually summarised under the general heading of "the rise of collectivism". Most contemporaries, whether sympathetic or not, agreed that the legislative tide in the second half of the nineteenth century was running strongly in favour of increased state intervention. It was not simply, or even mainly, a question of the state adopting a more positive regulatory role: the spread of municipal ownership and management of public utilities, as well as the co-operative, trade union, and friendly societies' movements, were all seen as part of the trend towards corporate or collective action. Politically, of course, the movement was linked with the extension of the franchise to working-class males, and with the rise of various groups explicitly dedicated to the erection of a socialist alternative to the existing system.

For those who took the trouble to read the works of the earlier economists, ample warrant could be found for the kinds of state intervention and initiative being undertaken in this period. John Stuart Mill in particular had shown himself to be markedly sympathetic towards socialist ideas and ideals. But many of those who opposed the collectivist trend did so on the fundamentalist grounds that it ran counter to the "laws of political economy". Thus even as enlightened a writer as Arnold Toynbee could depict socialism as the antithesis of economic science.[1] Those anxious to protect the reputation of the economists were keenly aware of the damage done to their subject by amateurs and popularisers. They dissociated themselves from the cruder forms of *laissez-faire* doctrine, and attempted, where possible, to reduce the conflict between collectivist ideals and economic reasoning.

Later generations of economists are apt to regard this period as one in which there was little questioning of the basic economic and social order. Contemporaries saw it in a different light. They felt themselves to be at a parting of the ways—one which required taking a stand, for or against, the trend towards collectivism. This explains why economists in the 'eighties and 'nineties, and beyond, were preoccupied with such fundamental issues as competition, individualism, and the economics of socialism, to an extent which is inconceivable today.

[1] *Lectures on the Industrial Revolution* (1923 reprint), p. 64.

## Marshall and the "Social Question"

In this respect Marshall was typical of his generation. He had been drawn into the study of economics by an interest in practical ethics: How could the lives of the majority of mankind be improved and ennobled? What were the material limitations to human progress? It was possible for him to claim that his life had been devoted to the study of poverty, "and that very little of my work has been devoted to any inquiry which does not bear on that".[1] He was fully aware of the importance of making a distinction between the "positive" issues which concern economic science and "normative" matters of economic policy. But he did not feel that economics should be confined to questions which were amenable to scientific treatment.[2]

In the early chapters of his *Principles* he drew up a list of problems "which, though lying for the greater part outside the range of economic science, yet supply the chief motive in the background for the economist". The questions were: How should the benefits of economic freedom be increased, and the costs reduced? How should the costs and benefits be redistributed among the population? Was it possible to achieve a more equal distribution of income without impairing the capacity of the economic system to grow? Was it possible to educate workers to undertake work of a more "elevating character", and to take part in management? What were the proper roles of individual and collective action? How should the new private and public monopolies be controlled and managed?[3]

In their general approach to the problems of state intervention in economic affairs, the English economists of Marshall's generation retained many of the characteristics of their classical predecessors. They were not, for example, attracted to *harmonielehre*: the doctrine that social order, justice, harmony, and progress follow naturally from individual self-seeking under competitive conditions. Nor were they keen to spend much time on Continental formulations of the conditions likely to lead to maximum consumer satisfaction and the optimal allocation of resources for the community as a whole. Although the onus of proof was placed on those advocating state intervention, they approached such questions on a pragmatic, case-by-case, basis. And with this went a willingness to entertain the notion that in specific cases there could be conflict between the

---

[1] *Official Papers by Alfred Marshall* (1926), p. 205.

[2] *Memorials*, p. 165.

[3] *Principles*, pp. 41-2. A similar agenda can be found in the writings of all the leading English economists in this period. See e.g. the addresses to Section F of the British Association by Sidgwick and Foxwell, as well as that by Marshall, in R. L. Smyth, (ed.), *Essays in the Economics of Socialism and Capitalism, 1885-1932* (1964); W. S. Jevons, *The State in Relation to Labour* (1882); H. Sidgwick, *Principles of Political Economy* (1886), Bk. III.

economic interests of the individual and those of society—conflict
which could only be overcome by state intervention. It would also
seem that on questions involving the *distribution* of income and wealth,
the main tradition of British economic thought has always been more
consistently radical than on questions that concern state ownership,
management, and regulation of the *production* of wealth. Another
recurrent element in the tradition was an ascetic disdain for personal
ostentation and riches, which expressed itself in the low priority, or
purely instrumental value, attached to the pursuit of material gain.

More than any other economist of his generation Marshall's work
reflects the influence of theories of social evolution that were associated in his day with the names of Darwin and Spencer. As a young
man he had also been attracted to the views of the German historical
writers, notably Hegel, Roscher and the German socialists, Marx and
Lassalle. Their ideas combined to impress upon him the need to
recognise the progressive qualities of human nature and society, and
the relativity of policies and institutions to the particular state and
stage of development of each society. He confessed that the older
generation of economists had been guilty of treating man as a "constant quality". As a result of the rise to ascendency of the biological
sciences, and of the influence of ethico-historical writers, the new
generation of economists were more cognisant of the pliability of
human nature, and of the complexity and diversity of social institutions. They were also aware that "the laws of the science must have a
development corresponding to that of the things of which they treat".[1]

Marshall laid particular emphasis on the importance of human
activities in helping to shape individual and national character, and
in determining the capacity of a society to survive and progress. He
also had what many would regard as an exaggerated regard for the
"captain of industry" as a character-type. The modern businessman,
according to Marshall, was the refined product of a competitive
evolutionary process which gave scope and reward for such vital
qualities as leadership, initiative, prudence, rationality and forethought.[2] Marshall's anxiety to maintain these virtues, rather than
any specific economic doctrine, was the chief factor underlying his
attitude to questions of individualism and socialism. In so far as he
favoured free enterprise, it was not because of any supposed benefits
of the system as a means of distributing incomes or allocating goods
and services, but rather for its proved success in harnessing and
reinforcing those individual talents and energies which he regarded
as essential to economic and cultural progress.

[1] *Principles*, pp. 763-9; *Memorials*, pp. 154-9: 165-9.
[2] The seminal articles on this aspect of Marshall's work are by Talcott Parsons, "Wants
and Activities in Marshall", and "Economics and Sociology: Marshall in Relation to the
Thought of his Time", *Quarterly Journal of Economics*, Nov. 1931 and Feb. 1932.

It would not be easy, he felt, to reproduce these qualities in the bureaucratically organised public sector; and this belief made him sceptical, even hostile towards the end of his life, towards schemes involving state ownership and management of productive enterprises.

> ". . . no socialistic scheme, yet advanced, seems to make adequate provision for the maintenance of high enterprise, and individual strength of character; nor to promise a sufficiently rapid increase in the business plant and other material implements of production to enable the real incomes of the manual labour classes to continue to increase as fast as they have done in the recent past, even if the total income of the country be shared equally by all".[1]

Marshall kept up a dialogue with socialists throughout his life. His attitude is usually portrayed as one of benevolent respect for their ideals, coupled with scepticism about their understanding of the realities of economic life. There is a kind of sympathy, however, that is far more damning than overt hostility. It is true that socialist writings found a place in Marshall's expansive system. Even Marx— rather misleadingly—could be congratulated on his "daring speculations as to the conflict between individual and society, and as to their ultimate economic causes and their possible socialistic remedies".[2] But Marshall seems to have regarded socialist writings as valuable mainly in kindling human sympathies, as a harmless kind of Utopian poetry rather than as food for rational thought. The best kind of socialist writing, he once said, was typified by William Morris's *News from Nowhere*—it made no claim to be practical.[3]

Marshall did not always succeed in hiding the contempt he felt for the Utopian mentality, especially when he compared it with the virility, imagination, and dedication of the practical businessman.[4] Even with as down to earth a manifestation of socialism as the co-operative movement Marshall was apt to be patronising. In his Presidential Address to the Co-operative Congress in 1889, after praising various successes, particularly in the retail and wholesale field, he warned against entering into the field of production on the following grounds:

> "I have already laid stress on the fact that the success of the distributive societies is no proof of the efficiency of working men as undertakers of business enterprises. . . . Their success gives no ground for anticipating that a productive society would succeed when it had to run the gauntlet of competition with private firms

[1] *Industry and Trade*, p. viii.
[2] *Principles*, p. 753.
[3] *Memorials*, p. 329.
[4] *Memorials*, p. 50n and 332n.

managed by businessmen quick of thought and quick of action, full of resource and of inventive power, specially picked for their work and carefully trained."[1]

In their general attitude to state intervention and socialism, the economists of Marshall's generation shared the viewpoint of other enlightened members of the English middle classes. While they professed to dislike most forms of paternalist legislation,[2] they were not free from paternalism in their attitude to those beneath them in the social and educational scale. Like many other liberal reformers in this period, they were ambivalent towards the working-class movement in politics and on the shop-floor. How far should it be welcomed? What were its dangers? How could the movement be diverted from what they regarded as the more disruptive types of political and social reorganisation? In other words, they took the trend towards socialism sufficiently seriously to be concerned about its forms, and the pace at which it was likely to proceed. It was essential, they felt, to understand the working-class movement in order to find ways of channelling the energies and resentments which it represented towards constructive (middle-class) ends.

These views were very much to the fore in Marshall, both in his role as economist and educator. He was anxious to impart to others his own standards of concern for those less fortunate in society. He saw his task as an educator as one of raising an army of missionaries equipped with "cool heads but warm hearts, willing to give some at least of their best powers to grappling with the social suffering around them".[3] By increasing the number of "sympathetic students, who have studied working-class problems in a scientific spirit", it would be possible to prevent "unscrupulous and ambitious men" from taking hold of the leadership of the working-class movement.[4] Middle-class radicals earlier in the century had expressed fear that the extension of the suffrage might result in an attack on property, especially if the working classes were left under the control of "indigenous" leaders. To Marshall's generation a similar fear attached to the trade union movement. Might it not be tempted to

[1] *Memorials*, p. 244. In the *Principles* (pp. 305-11) the point was made more emphatic-ally, and generalised to cover all managers of co-operative enterprises; they "seldom have the alertness, the inventiveness and the ready versatility of the ablest men who have been selected by the struggle for survival".

[2] This was defined by Henry Sidgwick as legislation that was aimed "at regulating the business arrangements of any industrial class, not on account of any apprehended conflict between private interests, properly understood, of the persons concerned, and the public interests, properly understood, but on account of their supposed incapacity to take due care of their business interests." See his "The Scope and Method of Economic Science" (1885), reprinted in R. L. Smyth (ed.), *Essays in Economic Method*, pp. 73-97.

[3] *Memorials*, p. 174.

[4] See his "Economic Teaching at the University in Relation to Public Well-Being", *Charity Organisation Review*, 1903, pp. 37-8.

use its new-found strength " for the promotion of the interest of particular groups of workers, at the expense of wider interests"?[1]
Marshall did not find it incongruous to speak of the duties of the
young men leaving Cambridge in terms of shepherds leading sheep.[2]

It was not only from the ranks of university students that Marshall
hoped to recruit missionaries. He also professed to see, and tried to
encourage, the spread of what he called "economic chivalry" among
the nation's business élite. He did not believe that the motives underlying competition in business were necessarily sordid. As in war,
business rivalry could give rise to a form of chivalry, according to
which there would be "a delight in doing noble and difficult things
because they are noble and difficult". Money-making would be
incidental to the satisfaction gained from performing difficult tasks
well: the talents produced in business could be turned to public ends.[3]

Marshall was not alone in holding such views. Moreover, it is
possible to exaggerate the differences between economists and contemporary middle-class socialists on these matters. The early Fabians
did not differ from Marshall in their desire to gain control and divert
working-class energies towards constructive alternatives to the
existing system. Much later, Sidney and Beatrice Webb were still
paying tribute to businessmen and competitive capitalism in terms
which are similar to those of Marshall.

> "Profit-making was, in fact, at the opening of the nineteenth
> century, the world's substitute for qualities which did not at the
> time exist, for self-discipline, for professional technique, for
> scientific knowledge, for public service, for the spirit of free
> association, for common honesty itself."[4]

There was also very little difference between socialist critics and
liberal economists on the question of whether competitive capitalism
was merely a passing phase in the development of the economic
system on the road towards socialism. Marshall was too much under
the influence of evolutionary ideas to commit the elementary mistake
of believing that capitalism, as it then was, constituted the highest
and last stage in the development of society. He conceded that conditions, human and material, might become more favourable to
state enterprise in the future. And what was unsuitable to the enterprising Anglo-Saxon races might be acceptable to "other races who
were more patient and more easily contented, more submissive and

---

[1] *Official Papers*, p. 396.
[2] *Memorials*, p. 311. The same attitude prevailed under his successor, A. C. Pigou.
H. Dalton recalls that Pigou reminded university students of their responsibilities as
"trustees of the poor"; see *Call Back Yesterday, 1887-1931*, (1953), p. 59.
[3] *Memorials*, pp. 323-46.
[4] *The Decay of Capitalist Civilisation* (1924), p. 84.

less full of initiative".[1] He was always prepared to speculate on the emergence of a new social order which would "greatly surpass the present in justice and generosity; in the sub-ordination of material possessions to human well-being; and even in the promptness of its adjustment to changing technical and social conditions".[2] Britain had grown sufficiently "in wealth, health, in education and in morality" to be able to afford policies which placed restraints on free enterprise. It was no longer necessary for her "to subordinate almost every other consideration to the need of increasing the total produce of industry". It was possible to make a gradual transition towards a society "in which common good overrules individual caprice".[3]

Any differences, therefore, between socialists and liberal economists at this time were not so much conceptual as practical; they concerned the extensiveness and seriousness of contemporary abuses, and the pace at which society could be made to move towards new forms of social organisation without attendant loss of benefit from the old. It was only in the context of a debate of this kind that Marshall must be accounted a conservative.

On questions involving the redistribution of income and wealth there were already several important links between the orthodox tradition in economics and the views of English radicals and socialists.[4] Among the economists there seems to have been complete agreement that the gap between rich and poor was excessive, and that its existence could not be justified on economic grounds. They recognised that there were elements of rent or pure scarcity income present in the wages and salaries of the more highly paid professions and skilled trades, which could only be reduced by equalising educational opportunities. Compulsory education at the general taxpayers' expense, together with municipal provision of libraries, museums and other means of "individual improvement", fitted easily into the readily acceptable collective-help-for-self-help category. More direct methods of redistributing income inevitably provoked more disagreement. The practical issue, as they saw it, was how to reduce existing inequalities by means that would not undermine those factors which had been essential to Britain's growth in

---

[1] *Memorials*, p. 275.

[2] *Memorials*, p. 367.

[3] *Principles*, pp. 751-2.

[4] Apart from the close parallels between the Fabians and utilitarian reformers in the first half of the nineteenth century, there is also the fact that a large part of the Fabian programme was derived from a generalisation of the Ricardian interpretation of rent as a monopoly return. On this, see A. M. McBriar, *Fabian Socialism and English Politics, 1884-1918*, (1966). At one time such leading Fabian theorists as G. B. Shaw and Sidney Webb seem to have been anxious to maintain the lines of communication between themselves and academic economics; see, for example, their addresses to Section F of the British Association reprinted in R. L. Smyth (ed.), *Essays in the Economics of Socialism and Capitalism* and S. Webb's, *Socialism in England* (1893), espec. p. 84.

the past, namely the middle-class virtues of thrift, enterprise and initiative.

Again, Marshall's views on this question are fairly representative of academic opinion at this time. He drew attention to the evidence of improvement, to the increased opportunities for the working man to rise through education and higher wages, but did not feel that existing inequalities could be justified; they represented "a serious flaw in our economic organisation". For this reason he was unwilling to oppose very strongly redistributive, or what he called "financial", socialism.

> "For poverty crushes character: and though the earning of great wealth generally strengthens character, the spending of it by those who have not earned it . . . is not nearly an unmixed good. A cautious movement towards enriching the poor at the expense of the rich seems to me not to cease to be beneficial, merely because socialists say it is a step in their direction."[1]

We see in this statement evidence of the ascetic, puritanical strain mentioned earlier. Beyond a certain point, when the "comforts and decencies" appropriate to a man's station have been acquired, riches confer little extra "real" enjoyment to the individuals concerned, and cannot be justified on wider social grounds. Indeed, ostentation or "socially wasteful" expenditure by the rich was to be deplored as a bad example to the poor and a source of social envy. Large inequalities of income and wealth were no longer essential to the supply of savings. And bearing in mind the importance to a country of Britain's stage of development of investment in the improvement of human capital, Marshall believed that "any change in the distribution of wealth which gives more to the wage receivers and less to the capitalists is likely, other things being equal, to hasten the increase of material production, and that it will not perceptibly retard the storing-up of material wealth."[2]

### Marshall's Economics of Welfare[3]

It would be wrong to suggest that Marshall's contribution to the debate on socialism and state intervention was confined to somewhat pious generalities about "character". He not only contributed to the discussion of detailed questions of policy and institutional reform, but was, together with Henry Sidgwick, one of the founders of a branch of economics designed to furnish guiding principles for state inter-

---

[1] *Memorials*, pp. 462-3; see also pp. 324-5; and *Principles*, pp. 713-4.
[2] *Principles*, pp. 229-30; *Memorials*, p. 463.
[3] This section is a little more technical than the others in this chapter; the general conclusions to which it leads begin on p. 44.

vention in economic affairs. After further work by his successor to
the Cambridge Chair, Arthur Pigou, this branch of economics
became known as the economics of welfare.[1]

The object of theoretical welfare economics is to provide criteria
for deciding whether a particular economic regime or policy constitutes an improvement over its alternatives in terms of some
relevant measure of economic well-being. Traditionally, this branch
of economics has been cultivated by those who, while accepting the
positive/normative distinction, believe that it is possible for the
economist *qua* economist rather than interested citizen, to make a
scientific contribution to the assessment of policies by isolating and
measuring the purely economic ingredients of changes in total well-
being.[2] Since theoretical welfare economics confines itself to the
identification of the categories and directions of the gains and losses
to be expected from policies, it is possible to establish a *prima facie* case
only for intervention or non-intervention. In order to provide clear
policy guidance a more ambitious set of empirical estimates of the
precise gains and losses entailed would be required to enable the
*net* costs and benefits to be calculated.

Marshall's performance over this notoriously treacherous stretch
of country is a difficult one to assess; it consists of a mixture of bold
claims and high hopes accompanied by hesitancy and caution.
Economics, according to Marshall, was no less than "the study of
mankind in the ordinary business of life"; he opposed the narrow
view that it dealt only with an abstract or "economic man". At the
same time, he felt that it was chiefly concerned with those aspects of
life in which motives were more deliberate and regular in their
operation, and more easily measured, indirectly at least, by a money
yardstick.[3] It was this which made economics the most advanced
of the social sciences. The next stage in scientific progress would
come when the "qualitative" analysis of economic theory was transformed into "quantitative" analysis.[4] Marshall's "restless quest for
realism" has frequently been noted: many of the "handy tools"
which he introduced into the economists' tool-kit—notably the
demand curve and price elasticity—were designed with the possibility of empirical specification in mind.[5]

---

[1] Most of what is said here concerns Marshall, though Pigou's contribution was in many
ways more extensive and systematic. The differences between the Marshallian and
Pigovian approaches to the subject have been ignored here.

[2] For a general history of this subject see H. Myint, *Theories of Welfare Economics* (1948)
and T. W. Hutchison, *'Positive' Economics and Policy Objectives* (1967) pp. 37-41; 140-44.
For the reasons given in the text, I would not exclude Marshall, as Hutchison tentatively
does, from the founders of modern welfare analysis.

[3] *Principles*, pp. 15; 26-7.

[4] *Memorials*, pp. 301-305.

[5] See on this, G. F. Shove, "The Place of Marshall's 'Principles' in the Development of
Economic Theory", *Economic Journal*, Dec. 1942.

In its early days welfare economics was bound up with utilitarianism, or with the idea that it is possible and desirable for governments to maximise some quantity known as utility or happiness. Marshall was less of a thorough-going utilitarian than other English economists such as Jevons, Sidgwick or Edgeworth. He was too much under the influence of doctrines of social evolution to accept the view, commonly associated with some forms of utilitarianism and taken over into welfare economics, that wants are given and do not alter as a result of changes in the pattern of activities. Nevertheless, he certainly adopted a commonsense version of utilitarianism which encouraged him to use a money measure of "satisfaction" for limited practical purposes.

The basic idea behind the Marshallian demand schedule is the law of diminished marginal utility; it carries with it the notion that the price which the consumer is just willing to pay for an extra unit measures the extra satisfaction or marginal utility of that unit to him. Marshall was not content to remain at this fairly humble level of measurability; he also put forward the concept of "consumer's surplus" as a means of illustrating the total utility which an individual derives from his purchases of a particular commodity, where that commodity forms a small part of his total expenditure. Consumer's surplus arises because we are able to buy many things for less than their total worth to us; it is the difference between what we actually spend on a particular good and what we might be willing to spend rather than go without it entirely. But the consumer does not have to be placed in this hypothetical all-or-nothing position in order to reveal the total satisfaction which he derives from a good: every time that the price of a good is raised or lowered, even over small intervals, there is an extra gain or loss in consumer's surplus which is not fully taken account of in the resulting change in expenditure. It was in just such cases that Marshall wished to employ the idea, namely where the rise or fall in price was due to the imposition of taxes or the granting of subsidies, or where the prices charged were those of a monopolist compared with those of a competitive concern.

In order to use the idea in these circumstances, however, it was necessary to make the difficult transition from an individual consumer's surplus to a collective consumers' surplus, where the latter concept was intended as a measure of the gain or loss of satisfaction to a whole group of purchasers when prices change. It raises the problem of inter-personal comparisons of utility or satisfaction—an admittedly subjective magnitude varying in scale and intensity from person to person.

The law of diminishing marginal utility can be applied to indi-

vidual incomes as well as to individual purchases. It suggests that an
extra pound of income, prices unchanged, will yield less and less
additional satisfaction as the individual grows richer. It is easy to see
the temptation in this case to move from the individual level of
analysis to the inter-personal idea that the redistribution of income
from the rich to the poor will add more to the satisfaction of the
poor than it subtracts from that of the rich. The bias of Marshall's
thinking was egalitarian, but he resisted taking the idea to the logical
conclusion that a policy of equalising incomes would result in
maximum social satisfaction. He contented himself mainly with a
negative use of the argument, namely to counter those who maintained that an extra pound of income represented equal satisfaction
to all regardless of their incomes.[1] It was consistent with this position
that he should hold that a given tax levied on those with similar
incomes would represent a roughly equal sacrifice of enjoyment to
all. But what can be said of price changes (due to taxes or subsidies) which affect goods purchased by consumers from different
income groups? This is the crucial case from the point of view of
*consumers'* surplus. And it was here that Marshall, in his anxiety to
make use of the money measure for wider purposes, pressed his
point to an inconsistent and unwarranted conclusion by employing
the following argument:

> "By far the greater number of the events with which economics
> deals affect in about equal proportions all the different classes of
> society; so that if the money measures of the happiness caused by
> two events are equal, it is reasonable and in accordance with
> common usage to regard the amounts of the happiness in the two
> cases as equivalent."[2]

Having justified the use of consumers' surplus, to his own satisfaction at least, Marshall proceeded to apply it to other distinctions
which he was responsible for introducing into economics: between
industries operating under the laws of increasing, constant, or
decreasing returns. In cases where increasing returns operated, a shift
of demand upwards would lead to increased output at lower prices,
whereas prices would rise in the case of decreasing return industries.
The same results could be achieved by a shift downward in the
supply schedule due, say, to technological improvements in production. But Marshall was not interested simply in filling out a system
of classification, important though this might be to a fully-articulated
theory of price. When used in conjunction with the doctrine of

[1] *Principles*, pp. 17-20, 130-1, 471, 474, 851-2.
[2] *Ibid.*, p. 20, and repeated p. 131.

consumers' surplus the analysis suggested certain principles of taxation. It suggested that a tax should be imposed on decreasing return industries, and a bounty should be given to increasing return industries. In the former case the price would be shifted upward by less than the amount of the tax (in most cases where decreasing returns operated sharply), so that the increase in revenue would be greater than the loss of consumers' surplus. In the bounty case, the loss in terms of outlay by the state would be less than the gain in surplus to consumers.[1]

At the very least this analysis was sufficient to refute the view that maximum social satisfaction would be achieved in all cases where normal demand and supply were in equilibrium; an increase or decrease in supply on either side of ordinary market equilibrium might lead to greater aggregate satisfaction measured in terms of revenue (or outlay) and consumers' surplus.[2] It demonstrates the point made earlier about English welfare thinking, namely that English economists had little regard for Continental theories of optimal allocation and maximum satisfaction as applied to the community as a whole; they were willing, even eager, to point out cases of divergence between private and social interests.[3]

Enough has been said to illustrate the general line of Marshall's thought on these matters. What significance should be attached to it? Here opinions will differ, depending partly on the interpretation of the importance which Marshall himself placed on the doctrine of consumers' surplus, and partly on the assessment of the validity of welfare economics as a branch of economics. On the first point it is possible to argue that the whole thing was simply an intriguing intellectual toy to Marshall, which he employed chiefly to destroy the debating position occupied by the maximum satisfaction school of thought. The real meat of Marshall's welfare economics, it is argued, can be found in his detailed empirical studies of the social consequences of the trend towards larger business units in his *Industry and Trade*.[4]

Support for this interpretation can be found in Marshall's abundant qualifications to the stricter forms of welfare analysis which he had put forward. He went to great lengths to point out that his conclusions "do not by themselves afford a valid ground for government interference". Many other factors would have to be

---

[1] For the details, see *Principles*, Bk. V., Ch. XIII.

[2] *Principles*, pp. 470-3.

[3] A similar, and perhaps more practical, issue arises in relation to Marshall's discussion of monopoly price. Here the question concerned whether a private or state-regulated monopoly should charge prices which maximise monopoly revenue or consumers' surplus; see *Principles*, Bk. V, Ch. XIV.

[4] This would appear to be Hutchison's position; see his *Review of Economic Doctrines* (1953) pp. 90-92.

taken into account by those wishing to apply the tax-bounty system
in practice.

> "They would have to reckon up the direct and indirect costs of
> collecting a tax and administering a bounty; the difficulty of
> securing that the burdens of the tax and the benefits of the bounty
> were equitably distributed; the openings for fraud and corruption;
> and the danger that a trade which got a bounty and in other
> trades which hoped to get one, people would divert their energies
> from managing their own businesses to managing those persons
> who control the bounties."[1]

Having said this, and bearing in mind Marshall's fear of appearing
to be unrealistic, the tenacity with which he stuck to this type of
approach is remarkable. Whatever the difficulties and dangers, his
hopes of turning consumers' surplus into a fully effective, empirically-
specified, tool for the guidance of public policy remained undaunted.
His motives are fairly clear. The whole tax-bounty analysis exhibits
a strong bias in favour of the unorganised, majority, consumer-
interest as against the well-organised, minority, producer-interest.
He believed that the lack of suitable statistical devices for measuring
the costs and benefits of policy actions was responsible for much of
the failure of economic intervention by the state. Important decisions
were taken on the basis of information derived from especially
interested parties alone. An impartial assessment of all the interests
was needed; and the importance of marshalling (so to speak) the
relevant evidence was increased by "the rapid growth of collective
interests, and the increasing tendency towards collective action in
economic affairs". Only by doing this could the decisions of public
officials approach the precision of those of the private businessman
when weighing the advantages and disadvantages of alternative
courses of action.

> "It is perhaps not too much to hope that, as time goes on, the
> statistics of consumption will be so organised as to afford demand
> schedules, sufficiently trustworthy, to show, in diagrams that will
> appeal to the eye, the quantities of consumers' surplus that will
> result from different courses of public and private action. By the
> study of these pictures the mind may be gradually trained to get
> juster notions of the relative magnitudes of the interests which the
> community has in various schemes of public and private enter-
> prise. . . ."[2]

[1] *Principles*, pp. 473, 475, 488.
[2] *Principles*, pp. 492-3.

Marshall's faith in "diagrams that appeal to the eye" seems not to have declined with age, even though he became more wary of hasty intervention and any type of mathematical argument.[1] The idea that diagrams alone could convey the necessary information reduces the credibility of his statement about statistical evidence; but it emphasises the importance he attached to this type of approach. Thus even in his final work on the subject we find him maintaining that:

> "The function of economic analysis is to render a service within its sphere similar to, though less thorough than, that which the service of navigation renders within its sphere: *the value of such services is seldom very much diminished by a little uncertainty as to some of the data.*"[2]

This amply demonstrates Marshall's concern with the problem of social well-being, and his desire to find a practical way of articulating community interests; it shows also his anxiety to dissociate economics from crude *laissez-faire* ideas, and his willingness to provide discriminating support for limited state intervention to improve the workings of the price-system. Pigou's massive enumeration of cases of divergence between private and social marginal products—the terminology he introduced to replace Marshall's surplus analysis—in his *Wealth and Welfare* (1912) suggests that those close to Marshall certainly took his approach seriously. But those who are sceptical about this whole branch of economics might still be unconvinced that any permanent interest attaches to the Marshall-Pigou line of thought.

Although subsequent generations of economists have continued to work on the problems of welfare economics, both in its Continental and Marshallian form, opinions differ widely as to whether the enterprise was worth beginning, or can even be regarded as a noble failure. Its opponents consider the attempt to measure economic welfare as a separate entity within "Welfare" to be based on highly questionable philosophical premises. At best, it is a harmless game; at worst, an attempt to smuggle political preferences into economic analysis under a smoke-screen of pseudo-science. It would be more honest, the critics say, to introduce value-judgments explicitly.[3] Those who have been willing to jump the philosophical hurdle have frequently been brought down by the empirical difficulties of identifying and measuring the costs and benefits of intervention. The

---

[1] On industries enjoying increasing returns, for example, he seems to have been willing to allow the passage of time to bring its benefits rather than subsidies; see *Memorials*, p. 449.

[2] *Industry and Trade*, p. 676n. Italics supplied.

[3] For a sample of the modern opposition see J. R. Hicks, *Essays in World Economics* (1959) Preface, and T. W. Hutchison, *Positive Economics and Policy Objectives* (1964), Ch. IV.

famous debate aroused later by J. H. Clapham's charge that the
concepts of increasing and decreasing return industries were "empty
boxes" was only the first of many damaging attacks.[1] Later efforts to
construct a "new welfare economics", avoiding some of the more
obvious pitfalls in the Marshall-Pigou approach, have also come to
grief. In spite of the attention paid to the subject, little or no practical
guidance for policy can be derived from it—or so the argument runs.

This is not the place to rehearse the many errors of omission and
commission with which welfare economics has been charged.
But there are some grounds today for taking a more tolerant historical
view of the Marshall-Pigou enterprise, sterile and misguided though
it may have been both at that time and later. The economists of the
pre-1914 generation were living through a period in which prosperity
and a sharper social conscience were making it possible and necessary
to curb some of the excesses of competitive individualism associated
with the rise of an urban industrial civilisation in Britain. They saw
all around them a trend towards collectivism and larger size of
business units, accompanied by various schemes for state regulation,
removal of abuses, and wholesale social reorganisation. Britain was,
perhaps, the first nation to have to face the problems of poverty in
the midst of what would now be called affluence; the first to deal
with the social costs of urban life, and with the conflicts between
individual and social interests which arise in a crowded industrial
setting. As serious students of society in an age that was becoming
welfare-conscious, the economists tried to play their part in guiding
others through this unfamiliar territory.

Once the issue is put in this way certain obvious parallels with our
own age become apparent. We too are showing renewed concern
about the social costs of urban life and industrial growth. Noise, dirt,
over-crowding, and traffic congestion pose the same kind of problems
to us as their equivalents did to the Victorians. The economics of
social policy, education, urban transport, and town planning are
not dissimilar from the discussions about primary education, public
baths, recreation spaces, municipal tramways, and railway regulation which took place before 1914. What is even more telling, however, is the fact that the intellectual tools which we use to clarify and
make decisions about these problems are the lineal descendants of
those forged by Marshall and Pigou. It is not simply a question of employing the Pigovian terminology of private and social products in
our analysis of market failure.The cost/benefit techniques now being
used to appraise the outcomes of public investment projects can be
thought of as attempts to supply the kind of statistical information

---

[1] The debate can be seen in the American Economic Association's *Readings in Price
Theory* (1952), Section II.

which Marshall called for when speaking of the need to protect "collective interests". Imputing values to the benefits accruing from particular courses of action can—without straining the interpretation—be thought of as a way of estimating consumers' surplus. We are attempting to give an appropriate money value to benefits which, though received, may not have an ordinary market value. In Marshallian language this can be seen as an attempt to estimate how much something is worth by imagining (and sometimes knowing) what it would be (is) like to be without it. The problems of measurement are still severe; they cannot be solved without making certain value-judgments. The modern approach is to admit this from the start and then to proceed by settling on various explicit measurement conventions.[1] Modern exponents of these techniques would give much the same answer to their critics as Marshall did when he said:

"No doubt statistics can be easily misinterpreted; and are often very misleading when first applied to new problems. But many of the worst fallacies involved in the misapplications of statistics are definite and can be definitely exposed, till at last no-one ventures to repeat them even when addressing an uninstructed audience."[2]

The growth of the public sector in recent decades, and the recognition that governments have important regulatory functions in relation to mergers, monopolistic and other restrictive practices, has made the kind of piece-meal social engineering pioneered by Marshall and Pigou increasingly relevant to our own times.

### Conclusion

The keynote then of the economists' debate on socialism and the role of the state before 1914 is not complacency or even excessive attachment to individualism. It is to be found in the view that, provided nothing disastrous happened, and provided everybody could be brought to think and work along the lines that were already well-established without being rigid, there was little need for concern about the direction or timetable of social change. The ultimate destination might be socialism of a non-revolutionary kind, or a "chivalrous", regulated capitalism. The economists, like other liberal-minded members of the middle class, wanted to correct some of the grosser forms of injustice thrown up by the advancing economic system; they aimed at removing certain abuses in the normal operation of the capitalist system without altering the primary base of

[1] The use of cost benefit techniques to-day is discussed briefly again later; see pp. 325-9 below.
[2] *Principles*, p. 492.

private property. In other words, they set out to modify certain features *within* the production and distribution mechanism without changing the direction of the system as a whole. Those who drew attention to more basic flaws in its operation—the Marxists or radicals like J. A. Hobson—were unable to command much of an audience.

Unfortunately, however, something disastrous *did* happen in the shape of the First World War. The British economic system emerged so thoroughly shaken that the pre-war timetable and agenda of economic debate had to be discarded. If the parallels suggested above have any merit, it is only in recent years that we have been able to afford the luxury of reinstating them. In the inter-war period there was less room for optimism, gradualism, and the long view. Far more revolutionary speculations were entertained, and in some cases implemented. Problems which were treated less urgently, or remained in the background before 1914, suddenly occupied everybody's attention. Chief among these was unemployment; it became the outstanding defect in the capitalist system. Out of the unhappy experience in dealing with this defect came the revolution in economic theory and policy that we associate with the name of Keynes. It is hardly surprising that by post-Keynesian standards the efforts of economists and would-be legislators to understand and cope with unemployment in the pre-1914 period seem inadequate. But it is worth noting some of the characteristics of these efforts, if only because it was in this period that many of the assumptions and expectations of the post-1914 generation were formed.

# CHAPTER THREE

# Unemployment and Tariff Reform

It was during the depression of the 'eighties that the problem of "unemployment", or rather of "the unemployed", began to figure prominently in public discussion. But it took some time for these terms to shed their inverted commas; other popular synonyms were, inconstancy, irregularity, and variability of employment, or discontinuity of labour.[1] The problem was dramatised by socialist agitation and notably by demonstrations in Trafalgar Square in 1886 and 1889. In the wake of this came Charles Booth's study of the *Life and Labour of the London Poor*, the first volume appearing in 1889, and the Reports of the Select Committee on Distress from Want of Employment in 1895-6, both of which documented the extent of the problem and its social ramifications. Seasonal and cyclical fluctuations in employment together with unemployment due to technological change, were soon revealed by the empirical investigators as prime causes of poverty. As J. A. Hobson complained, however, these factual inquiries fragmented the problem and neglected unifying principles. He regarded this as "a grave intellectual danger which induces a paralysis of all work of practical reform", and advocated its replacement by "a unified organic treatment".[2] Unemployment was mainly thought of as a "social" problem arising out of the normal workings of the economic system, rather than as a defect in the functioning of the economic mechanism itself. As a "social" problem it was often linked with questions of charity and Poor Law relief, with the main emphasis being placed on the "character" deficiencies of the unemployed worker.

Charles Booth provides an interesting and not untypical example of the limitations of contemporary liberal thinking in this respect. His researches had clearly demonstrated the close connection between poverty and "questions of employment". Over half the cases of "great poverty" could be attributed to this category. While maintaining that "industry will not work without some unemployed margin", he considered this margin to be excessive in many trades, notably among the London dockers, where the system of casual labour was in operation. In spite of this, however, he refused to draw

[1] See T. W. Hutchison, *Review of Economic Doctrines* (1953), Ch. XXIV.
[2] *The Problem of the Unemployed* (1896), p. viii.

conclusions or support remedies which would, in his view, cast an unfavourable light on, or impede the workings of, the capitalist system.

Booth accepted the dominant middle-class view of the Poor Law, namely that provision by the state of minimum security on an indiscriminate basis could only undermine the character of those receiving relief. Ideally, he thought the Poor Law system should be an island of collectivism within a sea of individualism. By separating paupers from the more virtuous and prudent members of the working class, contamination would be avoided. It was only with great difficulty that he brought himself to accept old-age pensions as a case where across-the-board payment was justifiable. He consistently opposed "socialistic" remedies for dealing with unemployment, believing that the discipline of competition, however harsh, should be maintained; there could be no tampering with private industry or the market process. The unemployed, as a class, were the unfit—even though the evidence of his own studies showed clearly that unemployment itself, rather than defects of character, was a prime cause of poverty. Where, as was the case with unemployment, the facts might lead to conclusions adverse to the capitalist system, this proponent of letting-the-facts-speak-for-themselves allowed his prejudices to speak more loudly. His proclaimed antagonism to the a priori theorising of the economists, his unfamiliarity with their modes of thought, left him in the end more at the mercy of his own unexamined beliefs and popular dogma than those whom he attacked.[1]

But even those who might have been expected to take a more serious view of the problem did not get much further than Booth. In 1889 the first set of *Fabian Essays* appeared; the solution to the unemployment problem offered there by Annie Besant—the creation of labour colonies for the unemployed—was, as Sidney Webb later acknowledged, highly unrealistic.

> "Through lack of adequate investigation of the phenomena, we erred, in common not only with other Socialists, but also with the ordinary Economists and Politicians, in assuming that recurrent periods of widespread unemployment could not in practice be prevented under any system short of completely organized collectivism; and, like so many other well-meaning people, of diverse opinions, we were in 1889 still speculating as to the possibility of organizing 'the unemployed' as such, so that their several efforts at production might mutually supply their common needs."[2]

---

[1] See T. S. and M. B. Simey, *Charles Booth, Social Scientist*, (1960), pp. 131-4, 193-6, 306-13.

[2] Introduction to the 1920 reprint of *Fabian Essays*, reprinted in 1962 edn, p. 275.

The academic economists can hardly be said to have formulated a separate theory of unemployment before 1914, or indeed for some time after. In company with the empirical investigators they treated unemployment chiefly as a concomitant of other problems. It was, for example, one of the inevitable accompaniments to the trade cycle or monetary disorder—a view which left plenty of room for differences of opinion as to the seriousness of the problem, its long or short-term character, and the appropriate remedies. Alternatively, its existence could be taken for granted and discussed as one influence among others affecting wage differentials, choice of career, attitudes to work, and average living standards.

### Marshall and Unemployment

Marshall's treatment of inconstancy of employment is scattered throughout the *Principles*. The reason for this is that he originally intended to write a two-volume work. In the first volume he would deal with "real" problems under "normal conditions", assuming for the most part full employment and a stable monetary environment. The second volume would concentrate on the trade cycle and unemployment considered as part of the theory of short-term variations in credit and confidence. This project was never completed. The volume entitled *Money, Credit and Commerce*, which appeared in 1923 when he was over eighty, was little more than a gathering together of pieces written on these subjects over the previous forty or fifty years.

In his evidence before the Royal Commission on Gold and Silver, 1886-7, Marshall took the long view with respect to the decline of profits and prices which had occurred in the previous ten years or so; he did not consider these trends to be incompatible with increasing prosperity. At the same time he was sceptical about evidence derived from trade union returns which seemed to indicate that irregularity of employment was on the increase. His statement that "there have not been a larger number of people unemployed during the last ten years than during any other consecutive ten years" cannot have been very comforting to those actually unemployed.[1] This was still his view when he published the *Principles* a few years later. The extent of unemployment under modern business conditions, though a "great evil", could be exaggerated. In spite of the "rapidity of invention, the fickleness of fashion, and above all the instability of credit . . . there seems to be no good reason for thinking that inconstancy of employment is increasing on the whole".[2]

Marshall touched on the question at another point in relation to

[1] *Official Papers*, pp. 92-7, 99-100.
[2] *Principles*, pp. 687-8.

movements in money wages. The sympathetic movement, encouraged
by trade unions, of money wages and prices during the up-swing
of the credit cycle, and the failure of wages to fall sufficiently
or rapidly enough in the down-swing, was one of the major causes
of unemployment, particularly among "substandard" workers.[1] As a
long-term rule Marshall believed that growth and stability of business
conditions would be favoured by a stable price level. The trade cycle
was a short-term phenomenon arising out of rapid price level movements caused by fluctuations in credit conditions. The up-swing
was caused by credit inflation, leading to rising demand, profits,
prices and wages. When credit was withdrawn, the speculative
structure collapsed, producing, via a cumulative process, a crisis of
confidence and unemployment. Recovery came with the restoration
of confidence. As with all cyclical explanations, the remedy for the
"down" was to prevent or moderate the "up". This could be accomplished by checking the expansion of credit through sensible
discount policies, by preventing unhealthy speculation, and by
increasing the flow of accurate information about business conditions.
Apart from monetary remedies Marshall also favoured a more rapid
downward adjustment of money wages to bring them into line with
reductions in the general price level. He was rather vague as to how
this was to be achieved, but seems once more to have placed great
faith in "a more general and clear appreciation of the fact that high
wages, gained by means that hinder production in any branch of
industry, necessarily increase unemployment in other branches".[2]

Marshall's emphasis on long-run normal conditions, and his
treatment of unemployment as a branch of the theory of short-term
monetary disorder, is fairly representative of orthodox English
thinking at the turn of the century; the real pioneers of business cycle
theory in this period were to be found on the Continent.[3] By actual
emphasis, if not by intention and understanding, Marshall, following
classical precedent, helped to encourage the view that real and
monetary variables could be separated without great loss. On credit
cycles, on the impossibility of general over-production, and on the
treatment of unemployment as an exceptional state of affairs to be
considered outside the "normal" framework, Marshall added little
to what had been written on these subjects by Ricardo, Mill and
Bagehot. In the inter-war period, after nearly two decades of unemployment on a scale and of a duration unknown to economists
writing before 1914, these features of orthodox economic thinking
were eventually abandoned. In retrospect, the fact that these changes

[1] *Principles*, pp. 709-10.
[2] *Ibid.*, p. 710.
[3] See T. W. Hutchison, *Review of Economic Doctrines*, Chs. XII & XIII.

in economic thought were carried through by one of Marshall's most brilliant pupils makes Marshall's position all the more interesting.

Like Mill and most orthodox writers Marshall considered it necessary to underline the view known as Say's Law, according to which general over-production was impossible. In one form this law was expressed by Marshall as follows:

"Under ordinary conditions of industry, production and consumption move together: there is no consumption except that for which the way has been prepared by appropriate production: and all production is followed by the consumption for which it was designed. There may indeed be some miscalculation in particular branches of production; and a collapse of commercial credit may fill nearly all warehouses for a time with unsold goods. But such conditions are exceptional . . ."[1]

This position set the limits within which further enquiry into the problem of unemployment could be conducted. The answer was not to be sought, as some "hasty writers" believed, in terms of the failure of consumption or aggregate demand to maintain a full employment level of aggregate production. There could be unemployment in *particular* trades that were unwilling or unable to adjust to changes in fashion or demand. Marshall opposed short-term remedies to deal with unemployment, such as direct government intervention to guarantee industries against risk, and indirect intervention in the form of tariff protection; these remedies would impair the long-term ability of the system to grow and adjust. The proper remedy was to establish a general monetary framework favourable to stability of the price level. Its absence was "the chief cause of the survival of the monstrous fallacy that there can be too much produced of everything".[2]

## J. A. Hobson

One of the "hasty writers" Marshall had in mind was J. A. Hobson. With the benefit of Keynesian hindsight it is now possible to see that it was Hobson, rather than any of the orthodox academic economists, who was on the "right" track. In a series of publications beginning with *The Physiology of Industry* (1889), Hobson kept alive a tradition of dissent on these matters which goes back to Lauderdale and Malthus at the beginning of the nineteenth century, but which was only to be made academically respectable by Keynes in the nineteen-thirties.

Hobson refused to accept the impossibility of general overpro-

[1] *Principles*, p. 524.
[2] *Memorials*, p. 192; *Official Papers*, p. 91.

duction. Its existence could be explained by "a general excess of producing-power in the form of capital and labour beyond what is economically required to supply the current or prospective rate of consumption of the community".[1] In his opinion, the free play of individual interests did not always serve the interests of the community by ensuring the correct balance between consumption and those savings which went to increase production. The reason for this state of affairs lay in the mechanism by which incomes were distributed in a capitalist society. It was here that Hobson's analysis of the capitalist mechanism became confused with certain moral and political doctrines taken over from Ruskin and the Fabians. "The reason why attempts are made by individuals to establish more forms of capital than are socially required, is that they possess certain elements of income which are not earned by effort, and which are therefore not required to satisfy any present legitimate wants".[2] A good deal of the saving of the community is "idle" in the sense that it is derived from land-rents, monopoly returns, and rentier gains, rather than genuine abstinence. The main problem facing society was to find ways of transferring the "surplus" accruing to a small minority of "idle" savers to the wage-earning or consuming class. The progressive redistribution of income, taxation of "unearned" incomes, elimination of monopoly return, and trade union pressure for higher wages, were all considered by Hobson to be legitimate solutions to the chronic problem of under-consumption.

The propagation of views such as these effectively debarred Hobson from holding any academic post, even at the supposedly heterodox London School of Economics. Outside academic circles the reception given to Hobson's ideas was equally lukewarm. The Fabians, for example, were unwilling to commit themselves to Hobson's theory of general over-production on the grounds that: "We cannot pretend to sit in judgment on this explanation of the depressions of trade. It is unquestionably an attractive one, and we see no flaw in the author's argument. But we cannot yet venture on the mental revolution which its acceptance would require."[3] After the First World War Hobson did acquire a meagre following in the Labour movement, but as far as his theory of under-consumption was concerned, its attractions to socialists as the basis for a political programme did little more than confirm old ideas in favour of the redistribution of income. Hobson's best market for his ideas proved to be the United States.[4]

---

[1] *The Problem of the Unemployed* (1896), p. 61.
[2] *Ibid.* p. 88.
[3] Quoted from *Fabian News*, May 1895 by A. M. MacBriar, *Fabian Socialism and English Politics, 1884-1918* (1962),
[4] See p. 232 below.

*Relief Works and the Minority Report on the Poor Law*

On the level of practical politics, however, some definite progress was made before the First World War towards alleviating the distress caused by unemployment. The lead in these matters came more from social reformers than from economic theorists. In 1909 two important documents appeared which pointed the way to more advanced administrative methods for dealing with unemployment: the Minority Report of the Royal Commission on the Poor Laws and William Beveridge's *Unemployment; A Problem of Industry.* To appreciate the sense in which these documents and the remedies they proposed marked a step forward, it is necessary to look briefly at the type of policies which they were designed to replace.

During the nineteenth century the unemployed were catered for by a combination of provision under the Poor Law and special relief work. At a later stage these public measures were supplemented by private schemes of unemployment insurance financed by trade unions and friendly societies. Relief work has a long history. In its archetypal form it provided assistance in the form of employment on projects under the conrol of local authorities. The projects undertaken were usually of a labour-intensive kind requiring minimal, chiefly manual, skills. In order to make it less attractive than ordinary commercial employment, the wages paid for this type of work were kept below the normal market rate for unskilled labour. Relief work implied no new commitment on the part of the state beyond that already contained in the provisions of the Poor Law. It was simply a different means—open to divergent interpretation by local authorities, and liable to break down under heavy pressure—of furnishing assistance to the unemployed along semi-charitable lines.

In the depression of 1886 an attempt was made, in a circular sent to all authorities by Joseph Chamberlain, Chairman of the Local Government Board, to distinguish between charitable pauper relief and work relief for the unemployed. The Board recommended that localities suffering from heavy distress should set on foot work of an unskilled kind, but avoiding "the stigma of pauperism". This policy was renewed in 1892, and the principle was embodied in legislation by the Unemployed Workman's Act of 1905. This act obliged every local authority with more than 50,000 inhabitants to appoint Distress Committees with the responsibility of providing assistance to the unemployed on a discriminatory basis. Even before the 1905 Act, however, relief works had become widely discredited in the eyes of serious students of the problem. They were held to be both expensive and demoralising; they did little to help the worker to retrain or to find regular employment; and they suffered from the weakness that

they could only be used *after* the problem of unemployment had
become acute. Moreover, it was difficult to find work that was both
"useful" and yet met the commonly-applied principle that it would
not otherwise have been undertaken at the expense of the rates by
the local authority or by private firms. The rules also encouraged the
spreading of work among many hands and the use of costly, make-
work, methods. These criticisms of relief work are worth noting
because they tended to be extended to cover all forms of public works
proposal.[1]

This was the state of public thinking and provision in 1909 when
the two works mentioned above appeared. The chief innovation of
the Minority Report was its endorsement of a scheme for the
"regularisation of the national demand for labour", the details of
which had been worked out by the economic statistician, A. L.
Bowley. The idea was for the government to set aside part of its
normal capital appropriation for use in financing public works on a
contra-cyclical basis when unemployment rose above the "normal"
level. Bowley was anxious to distinguish his proposals from the earlier
type of relief work endorsed by the Majority Report. The scheme
would be put into operation as soon as the unemployment rose above
4%, the level then thought of as normal for frictional, seasonal, and
casual unemployment, i.e. *before* the problem became acute. It would
not constitute an "artificial" demand for labour, merely a readjustment in the timing of ordinary demand; it would not cater for the
unemployed in general on special terms, but only for those with the
requisite skills and at normal commercial rates.

On the basis of these proposals the Minority Report felt justified in
announcing that:

> "At present, it is not too much to say that the average citizen of
> middle or upper class takes for granted the constantly recurring
> destitution among wage-earning families due to unemployment,
> as part of the natural order of things, and as no more to be com-
> batted than the east wind. . . . Fifty years hence we shall be looking
> back with amazement at the helpless and ignorant acquiescence
> of the governing classes of the United Kingdom, at the opening
> of the twentieth century. . . . *We have to report that, in our judgement, it
> is now administratively possible, if it is sincerely wished to do so, to remedy
> most of the evils of unemployment.*"[2]

The announcement was, as we shall see, highly premature. Most
of the work on the Minority Report was done by Beatrice Webb, with

[1] For accounts of earlier experience in these matters, see W. Beveridge, *Unemployment; A
Problem of Industry* (1909), Ch. VIII; R. C. Davison, *The Unemployed* (1929), Ch. II.
[2] *Minority Report of the Royal Commission on the Poor Laws* (1909), Part II, pp. 323-4. Italics
in original.

Sidney Webb's assistance. A few years later the Webbs were once more confessing that: "There is at present no technique, either in treatment or prevention [for unemployment]. This has to be invented and we shall not invent it."[1] By 1938 their views underwent a further revolution. Under the pressure of continuous unemployment they were forced to conclude that the only solution was communism.[2] But all this lay in the future. By the standards of the day the proposals of the Minority Report marked an advance on the fatalism-tempered-by-charity, and the emphasis on character defects, of earlier thinking. The scheme achieved legislative recognition in the Development and Road Fund Act of 1909, which made Britain the first country to make nominal provision at least for forward planning of contra-cyclical public expenditure.

The limitations of these proposals should be made clear, especially as they were probably responsible for their early acceptance in principle. The great virtue of the scheme to contemporaries was that it called for no important change in the economic and social order, no new encroachment by the state in economic life; the timing of *existing* expenditure plans was to be modified, that was all. Furthermore, it was basically a method of compensating for swings in private economic activity; it was not based on any new insight into the root causes of such swings. The Webbs' great strength lay in organisation and administration. They saw, quite rightly, that Bowley's scheme would enable them to take a step forward which would bring realisable gains to the unemployed. With the benefit of hindsight we can now see that what was needed—if not then, certainly in the inter-war period—was a new theoretical explanation which would lay bare the causal mechanisms underlying cycles and general unemployment.

### William Beveridge, Unemployment: A Problem of Industry

In spite of the effort made to examine the economic causes of unemployment, a similar verdict must be passed on Beveridge's *Unemployment; A Problem of Industry*. At the very outset Beveridge rejected the idea that unemployment could be explained in terms of the failure of aggregate demand to grow sufficiently to absorb the aggregate supply of labour. A long-term decline in the demand for labour was conceivable, but even with a rising demand the problem of unemployment would remain. The reasons for this were "specific imperfections of adjustment" between the demand and supply of labour, cyclical fluctuations, and the existence of reserves of unemployed

---

[1] B. Webb, *Diaries, 1924-32,* (1956), p. 150.
[2] B. Webb, *Our Partnership,* (1948), pp. 484-491.

labour attached to particular trades. He accepted the inevitability of fluctuations; they were "obviously and directly the means by which the standard of production and comfort is driven upwards". "They must spring from one or more of the fundamental facts of modern life. They probably cannot be eliminated without an entire reconstruction of the industrial order. . . . Within the range of practical politics no cure for industrial fluctuations can be hoped for; the aim must be palliation."[1]

Beveridge did not presume to know the fundamental causes of fluctuations; but he knew enough to reject the explanation in terms of general over-production put forward by J. A. Hobson. According to Beveridge, under-consumption was the result, not the cause of stagnation during depressions. Beveridge's real difficulty— and it was shared by most economists until after the publication of Keynes's—*General Theory* in 1936—was in envisaging a general glut. Was it not simply a case of "misdirection of productive energy"? He was anxious not to offend economic doctrine on the impossibility of general over-production, though he admitted that monetary hoarding could account for temporary general glut. In such a case the best solution was a general agreement to lower prices.[2]

While it was not possible, in Beveridge's opinion, to prevent cyclical disturbances, it was still feasible to reduce unemployment to an unavoidable minimum by an improvement in the organisation of the labour market. Unlike the Minority Report, Beveridge did not place much trust in public works measures, except as a stop-gap. The solutions he favoured were, an increase in labour mobility through a nation-wide system of labour exchanges; the abolition of the system of casual labour; and an improved system of career guidance and industrial training. For cyclical unemployment the palliative he preferred was greater elasticity of working hours and wages, together with unemployment insurance to tide workers over the unavoidable intervals between jobs. The establishment of the labour exchange system in 1901, and the first steps taken towards a national system of unemployment insurance by the Liberal Government in 1911, were a victory for this line of thought.

Between them the Minority Report and Beveridge's *Unemployment, A Problem of Industry* contain most of the standard remedies which were to remain at the heart of the discussion on unemployment for much of the period up to and beyond the First World War.[3] There were, it is true, signs of greater interest by professional economists in the practical problems posed by unemployment just before the war.

[1] *Unemployment; A Problem of Industry* (1930 ed.), pp. 51, 64, 67.
[2] *Ibid.*, pp. 58-63.
[3] See N. Jha, *The Age of Marshall* (1968), pp. 144-257.

Pigou's *Wealth and Welfare* was a product of this interest. But it now seems significant that when he revised this work later, and transformed it into the *Economics of Welfare*, the sections on unemployment were set aside for separate treatment. The popular work which Pigou wrote on *Unemployment* in 1913 was mainly concerned with "plasticity of wages", the absence of which, apart from trade fluctuations, he considered to be the sole cause of unemployment. With varying degrees of enthusiasm, he endorsed most of the remedies and palliatives put forward by the Minority Report and Beveridge. Pigou also repeated an argument, used earlier in his inaugural lecture given in 1908, to counter what later became known as the "Treasury View"—an argument against public works remedies based on the idea that the effect of an increase in public spending on employment would be exactly offset by the decrease in private spending caused by increased taxes.[1] In the nineteen twenties the "Treasury View" was to occupy a central position in economic policy debates; and Keynes's efforts to demolish this view were to play an important part in the development of modern thought on the question of unemployment.[2] Pigou's position at this time constituted an effective defence of contra-cyclical public works spending, and a valid anticipation of later ideas on the subject. In spite of this, however, what now seems more important about Pigou's argument is is that he should endorse the notion that: "It is indeed, true that the State is unable, by action of kind contemplated [i.e. public works], to increase the demand for labour on the whole on the average of good and bad times together."[3] This apparently innocuous remark conveniently marks the boundary between the understanding achieved by economists before the First World War, and that which they were able to command on the eve of the Second World War as a result of Keynes's writings.

So far the emphasis has been largely on consensus within the academic community. But it would be wrong to close this brief and selective account of economic thinking before 1914 without mentioning one of the more important divisions of opinion.

By virtue of his moderation and eclecticism on methodological questions, Marshall did a great deal to pacify those who had criticised economics as an excessively abstract and deductive science. Schumpeter has said of Marshall that his impressive command of history and

---

[1] See *op. cit.*, pp. 171-174. In the history of economic theory Pigou's argument can be regarded as an anticipation of what later became known as the "balanced budget multiplier"; see M. Blaug, *Economic Theory in Retrospect* (2nd. edn. 1968), p. 655.

[2] See pp. 109-113 below.

[3] *Unemployment* (1913), p. 172.

detailed knowledge of the facts of contemporary industrial life was "one of the reasons why no institutionalist opposition rose against him in England".[1] But Marshall was never entirely successful in overcoming the doubts of other students of society concerning the narrowness and *laissez-faire* bias of economics. By intention, if not achievement, the foundation of the London School of Economics by Sidney and Beatrice Webb in 1895 constitutes an emphatic contradiction of Schumpeter's view. The founding of the London School was also bound up with another important contemporary division of opinion: the rejection by tariff reformers of the optimistic Marshallian "long view" with respect to the capacity for continued progress in Britain according to the tried and trusted principles of free trade.

One of the aims of the Webbs in founding the London School was to create an alternative to Marshall's Cambridge as a centre for social and economic enquiry. They evidently felt that economics, even with the historical and ethical disquisitions supplied by Marshall, was still too strongly wedded to individualism and the *status quo*. Implicit in the foundation of the School was the belief that any impartial study of society would ultimately support the cause of socialism. In the short run, however, and certainly in some of the early appointments, the Webbs took a more active line in pursuance of their aim to "break up economics, replacing analysis of concepts by collection and examination of facts".[2] The main reason for appointing W. A. S. Hewins as the School's first Director, for example, was that he shared the Webbs' dislike for orthodox economics.[3] As a leading spirit in Chamberlain's tariff reform movement, Hewins provides the first of many points of contact between the School and the anti-free trade position in this period. By favouring economic historians, and those who took an unorthodox stance, the Webbs found it difficult to avoid appointing tariff-reformers.[4] As we shall see later, the anti-Cambridge position of the London School was carried over into the inter-war period. In a curious way,

[1] See J. Schumpeter, *Ten Great Economists* (Galaxy edn. 1965) p. 94. The same view is given in Schumpeter's *History of Economic Analysis* (1950), p. 822, and only partially modified by the note on pp. 823-4. For a definition of "institutionalism" see pp. 229-32 below.

[2] The words are Beveridge's; see his *The London School of Economics and Its Problems, 1919-1937* (1960), pp. 109, 50, 57. For Beatrice Webb's views on economics, and her relations with Marshall in particular, see *My Apprenticeship* (Penguin edn. 1938), pp. 398-400, 421, 458, 482-7.

[3] See B. Webb, *Our Partnership* (1948), pp. 86-9.

[4] When Hewins resigned the Directorship to become secretary to Chamberlain's Tariff Commission in 1903, he was succeeded by Halford J. Mackinder, and later by W. Pember Reeves, both of whom were sympathetic to tariff reform. Other tariff reformers who were appointed at this time were W. M. Acworth and W. Cunningham. It was only with reluctance that the Webbs decided not to appoint W. J. Ashley, yet another tariff-reforming economic historian, on the grounds that the School was becoming too firmly wedded to the cause. See F.A. Hayek, "The London School of Economics, 1895-1945", *Economica*, Feb. 1946.

however, the roles of the two institutions were later reversed so far as the defence of orthodoxy was concerned.[1]

## Tariff Reform

The tariff reform movement launched by Joseph Chamberlain in 1903 constituted a serious challenge to one of the cardinal tenets of British economic policy. The movement offered an alternative scheme for organising Britain's trade according to "imperial" rather than cosmopolitan principles—a scheme which entailed making a sharp break with established fiscal practice. The economic circumstances which enabled tariff reform, and its predecessor in the 'eighties, the fair trade movement, to gain a public hearing are to be in the secular fall of profits and prices after 1873, and in the growing evidence of a decline in Britain's industrial position relative to Germany and the United States in the last quarter of the nineteenth century.[2] Although there was general agreement that free trade had served British interests well in the first three decades after the repeal of the Corn Laws, the advantages claimed for Britain as an island of free trade in a sea of protection no longer seemed so obvious towards the end of the century. Now that she was facing stiffer competition both at home and abroad from countries whose industries were organised in large units behind tariff barriers, many believed that the losses outweighed the gains. At the very least, some argued, unilateral free trade should be replaced by a tariff system based on reciprocity of treatment by other countries.

As advocated by Chamberlain, however, tariff reform went far beyond mere reciprocity and even protection. Chamberlain's proposals promised solution to a wide variety of social and political, as well as economic, problems. The Boer war had shown that the decline in British authority and efficiency was not confined to economic matters. Chamberlain also capitalised on the fact that during the war Britain had been able to call on the support of her colonies at a time when world opinion was hostile. Imperial solidarity, defensive strength, domestic social reform paid for by the foreign competitor rather than out of higher indirect and direct taxation, steadier employment at home based on expanding empire markets—all of these could be achieved by adopting imperial preference. A rise in the cost of imported food and raw materials could be made to seem a small price to pay for this attractive package.

Tariff reform and imperial preference put the cat among the "isms", dividing old alliances and making possible some strange new

[1] See pp. 148–51 and 189–97 below.
[2] See references cited on p. 29n.

ones. The effect on economists was to re-open one of the divisions
which Marshall had been anxious to cover over: that between economic historians and economic theorists. With few exceptions, those
committed to a historical approach to economic questions supported
tariff reform, while the theorists, with their closer links with the
English classical tradition, either joined the opposition or remained
sceptical as to the net gains to be achieved from a departure from
existing trade policies.[1]

It was inevitable that those proposing a change in the *status quo*
should feel it necessary to attack the intellectual dogmas on which
free trade was based. Within both the Liberal and Conservative
parties, and certainly within the Treasury, there were dogmatic
exponents of free trade. *Laissez-faire* and free trade were different
facets of the same liberal ideology; and both were associated in the
public mind with political economy. Those who favoured tariff
reform did so on grounds that were similar to those used to justify
other forms of state intervention. Britain had reached a stage in her
economic history in which it was necessary to embark on conscious
manipulation of the course of development in order to achieve
balanced growth and self-sufficiency within the empire. Methodological issues which had lain dormant for some years were revived,
and the old charges against economics were resuscitated: the subject
was static, un-historical, barren, unrealistic, and lacking in appreciation of ethical concerns and for the higher forms of national and
imperial aspiration.

Just as with the question of *laissez-faire*, however, it is misleading
to view the economic debate on tariff reform simply as an ideological
and methodological clash between nationalistic and imperialist-
minded historians on the one side, and liberal, orthodox economists on the other. Academic economists were not attached to
the doctrine of free trade in an unqualified form. The Anti-Corn
Law League and the writings of the Manchester School were
distorted reflections of the best economic thinking on this question.
Free trade was never a religion among economists as it was to
some Liberals and civil servants. The novelties in the case for tariff
reform were almost exclusively political or strategic in character.
All of the economic arguments employed had been familiar to
economists for some time. Indeed, it is a strange fact that the most
telling economic arguments in favour of tariffs have been advanced
by economists who have favoured free trade as a general rule.

The idea that it was possible for an individual nation to gain more

[1] For a thorough study of the relations between politicians and academic advisers on
this issue, see A. W. Coats, "Political Economy and the Tariff Reform Campaign",
*Journal of Law and Economics*, April, 1968.

from trade through tariffs was accepted by Ricardo and John Stuart Mill. The terms of trade, "reciprocity", or "making the foreigner pay", type of argument for tariffs formed the basis for the empire *zollverein* advocated by a classical economist, Robert Torrens, as early as 1832.[1] The validity of the argument for protecting infant industries had been endorsed by Mill in 1848, and by all subsequent economic theorists. As far as the argument for tariffs as a cure for unemployment was concerned, the tariff reformers confined themselves to attacks on the assumptions of labour mobility made by orthodox economic theory. The economists had no difficulty in admitting that if their assumptions were not fulfilled, their conclusions would have to be modified. They could also point out that an alternative answer was to devise ways of increasing the flexibility and adaptability of the British economy.

While the case for tariff reform contained no theoretical innovations, no statements of new economic categories and relationships, it certainly raised difficult issues involving the interpretation of empirical evidence. Here there was room for considerable disagreement on the conclusions to be drawn from the historical and statistical evidence adduced by both sides, especially in view of the obvious need to make the transition from conclusions about the past, and other countries' experience, to predictions about the future course of events. Faced with conflicting evidence on this level the best course open to an impartial observer, anxious to make up his mind one way or the other, was to consult his political preferences.

The economic theorists were not convinced by the tariff reformers' case on economic grounds, but they made no effort to claim that the political arguments were negligible, or that in order to achieve greater imperial solidarity some economic sacrifice might not be called for. They did not, therefore, attempt to settle the issue by reference to narrow economic considerations of a dogmatic kind. Nor did they flinch from making explicit their own political preferences where this seemed necessary.

On all these matters Marshall is representative of the moderate anti-tariff reform position. It was with characteristic reluctance that Marshall allowed himself to be drawn into public controversy.[2] He had always been willing to admit that free trade was not a universally applicable policy, and that its success in Britain was no guarantee of

---

[1] See L. Robbins, *Robert Torrens and the Evolution of Classical Economics* (1958). Moreover, in Torrens' case the argument was fortified by a *theory* of economic stagnation which was conspicuously lacking in the later tariff reform discussions.

[2] The main sources for Marshall's views are his *Memorandum on the Fiscal Policy of International Trade* in *Official Papers*, and H. W. Macready, "Alfred Marshall and Tariff Reform, 1903; Some Unpublished Letters," *Journal of Political Economy*, June, 1955. Pigou took a more active part in the opposition; see his *The Riddle of the Tariff* (1903) and *Protective and Preferential Duties* (1903).

its suitability for other nations at different stages of development and with different political systems. More than most English economic theorists, Marshall was familiar with and sympathetic towards the conclusions reached by German historical writers on this question. He had visited the United States in 1875 in order to study the effect of tariffs on American industry from a sympathetic point of view. He returned convinced that the infant industry argument had been misapplied; that it afforded excessive protection to "industries which were already strong enough to do without it".[1] Neither in the case of the United States nor of Germany did he believe that industrial progress could be attributed to the tariff; and with regard to Germany, he thought that real wages were lower and rising more slowly than in Britain due to the higher cost of food.

Marshall's estimate of the elasticities of demand for British exports and the supply of British imports led him to believe that Britain could not expect to pass much of the burden of higher duties onto the foreigner rather than onto the domestic consumer, certainly not in the long run and only to a small extent in a limited number of cases in the short run. He obviously felt that the morality of such tariffs was questionable, and that there was room for considerable doubt as to whether tariffs settled by a political bargaining process could ever be as discriminating as would be required in order to qualify under the terms of trade argument.

As the last point makes clear, Marshall's objections were mainly political in character. On grounds of equity alone he considered that a system which shifted the tax burden onto commodities mainly purchased by the poorer income groups should be resisted. As on other issues involving state intervention, he leaned towards the consumer interest and was fearful of the unscrupulous use of government protection by producers' interest groups, whether represented by groups of employers or by trade unions. In spite of improved moral standards and efficiency in government in recent years, he still believed that the value of free trade lay in the fact that it was "*not* a device, but the absence of a device".

> "A device contrived to deal with any set of conditions must become obsolete when they change. The simplicity and naturalness of Free Trade ... may continue to outweigh the series of small gains which could be obtained by any manipulation of tariffs, however scientific and astute."[2]

Marshall certainly felt there were genuine grounds for anxiety about Britain's future industrial position. Other nations were catching

---

[1] *Official Papers*, p. 394.
[2] loc. cit.

up quickly in the technological race, and there was evidence that British prosperity in the third quarter of the nineteenth century had led to laziness in pioneering new methods and markets. Britain needed to be flexible. But he considered protection more likely to frustrate than achieve this: "She has no industries which need protection on the ground of youth. But she has a few which have needed a stimulus because they have been sleepy."[1] Nor was Marshall willing to register alarm on the basis of export or other balance of payments statistics. It is true that British exports per head of population were not rising as quickly as those of Germany or the United States. This was not entirely the result of relative weakness in the industrial field. It was partly due to the desirable fact that a larger proportion of the working population was now employed in industries, like the service industries, producing non-exportable items. While invisible earnings from shipping and the interest on capital invested abroad were able to cover British import needs, there was no reason to worry about expanding exports or curtailing imports.

As for the "imperial" side of the case, Marshall could see no overriding reason why the poorer class of British consumer should be asked to make concessions to the richer colonies. If self-sacrifice was needed to achieve imperial solidarity, it should be acknowledged and shared fairly. On this lofty plane of speculation it is clear, however, that Marshall ranked "federated Anglo-Saxondom" above imperial unity. In this respect he belongs with such Liberals as John Morley and Charles Dilke, who were anxious not to allow imperial ties to impede closer relations between Britain and the United States.

In the election campaign of 1906 the Conservatives were still only pledged to the milder version of tariff reform enunciated by Balfour, namely reciprocity. Nevertheless, the activity of the Chamberlainites succeeded in making tariff reform in the full sense of the term a major election issue. When, therefore, the Conservatives were decisively rejected by the electorate, so too was tariff reform. Chamberlain himself was incapacitated by a stroke in the same year, leaving the field to Balfour; but he left behind him a core of dedicated followers, headed by his sons, who sought, and later found, an opportunity to implement some of their father's ideas. Having been placed firmly on the agenda of British politics in 1903, the questions raised by the tariff reform movement could not be removed. It is generally agreed that one of the reasons for the failure of the initial campaign was the return of prosperity and the revival of British exports in the period between 1900 and 1914. Chamberlain believed that his advocacy of imperial preference during a period of pros-

[1] *Official Papers*, p. 418.

perity showed that he did so in good faith and not merely as an electioneering trick.[1] But it was the unemployment of the 'twenties and finally the world depression of 1929–31, that revived the question of protection as a means of combating unemployment, thereby providing Neville Chamberlain with the opportunity to introduce imperial preference in 1932.

The verdict on the tariff reform debate to be derived from hindsight is by no means cut and dried. It depends very largely on the vantage point in time chosen. Looking back from 1930 Keynes was inclined to rank Balfour's *Economic Notes on Insular Free Trade* higher for insight than Marshall's critical remarks on the book.[2] Keynes's own reasons for abandoning free trade will be considered later. It is not clear, however, that protection or imperial preference were the answers to Britain's long-term industrial problems in the pre-war or the inter-war period. Marshall's arguments were more cogent while the British balance of payments remained in a healthy condition—as it did until 1914. The problems experienced in the 'twenties, it could be argued, were as much due to international and domestic monetary conditions as to long-term industrial decline. Neither party to the earlier dispute gave adequate treatment to the connection between foreign trade and unemployment. This was to be the one really new argument for tariffs contributed by Keynes; but it was one that required an entirely different way of looking at the determinants of the level of employment. Even in the 'thirties, imperial preference did not serve the purpose for which it was designed; and it has certainly not provided an adequate long term basis for British trading policy. Now that Britain is seeking an alternative in Europe, while trying to retain links with "Anglo-Saxondom", we are perhaps in an especially good position to appreciate the difficulties of those who faced the problem in 1903 of assessing a proposal for a major change in Britain's economic relations with the outside world.

---

[1] P. Fraser, *Joseph Chamberlain* (1966), p. 238.
[2] In his obituary of Balfour in the *Economic Journal*, June 1930, p. 337.

PART TWO

# Between the Wars

# CHAPTER FOUR

# The Inter-war Period: Introduction

There seems little need to emphasise the importance of the inter-war period as one in which a transformation in economic attitudes and policies occurred in most capitalist countries. It was over this particularly difficult terrain that the painful transition was made from the basically nineteenth-century world of pre-1914 to the modern world of post-1945. It is only within recent years that the experience of this era has faded as an active influence on our economic dispositions; and even now it is close enough to arouse passions.

The period between the end of the First World War and the 1931 crisis was one of the most confused, frustrating, and unsuccessful periods in the history of economic policy-making in Britain. At the same time, since failure led to reappraisal, it was also a formative period in the history of economic opinion and analysis. Like other European belligerents, Britain emerged from the war with a badly dislocated economy. No other country had so much at stake in the pre-war system of economic and financial interdependence. As the world's largest trader, shipper, financier, and investor, her industrial structure and institutions were geared to a healthy, expanding, international economy. The disruption of normal trading and financial channels by currency tangles, reparations, and unsettled political conditions in Europe, could all be considered as transitional problems. But superimposed on them in the British case were a number of longer-term problems postponed from the pre-war period, which reflected more fundamental changes in the pattern of international trade and the balance of economic power: the decline of her staple export industries; the permanent loss of overseas markets and earnings, and the weakening of the balance of payments position; industrialisation and the rise of economic nationalism in countries that were either her competitors or customers; the need for drastic redeployment of resources to adapt to new technologies and the changing pattern of international specialisation; the instability of the reconstructed international monetary system within which Britain still occupied a pivotal but more precarious position.

At this point an important divergence between appearance and reality must be noted. To those concerned officially or otherwise with economic policy in the 'twenties, the performance of the British economy presented a dismal picture. Failure to solve the difficulties mentioned above seemed to be responsible for the different course which Britain's economic fortunes took in the latter half of this period when compared with most other developed capitalist economies. After sharing in the immediate post-war boom and slump, Britain appeared to stagnate, while others—and notably the United States—enjoyed boom conditions between 1925 and 1929. In the words of Schumpeter, Britain had become an "arteriosclerotic economy". Whether judged by export performance or financial dominance, Britain's relative importance in the international economy was declining. Production in many key industries failed to regain pre-war levels, adaptation proceeded slowly, prices fell, and above all, unemployment persistently remained above and around 10 per cent for the whole period. The world-wide collapse of 1929–1931 seemed to confirm rather than alter the course which Britain had already been following for some time.

Recent research on the 'twenties and on the inter-war period taken as a whole has shown that this picture is not so much wrong as incomplete. It has been pointed out that the British record of growth in the inter-war period was considerably better than in the decade before the war, and compares favourably with that achieved after the Second World War.[1] For the 'twenties alone the picture is less clear, but attention has been drawn to rapid economic progress in the expansion of "new" industries.[2]

Redeeming features of the period's economic history went unnoticed in the heat of contemporary policy debate. But it is hardly surprising that they were overlooked when—to exaggerate a little—intricate statistical calculations are needed forty years later to bring them to light. Policy-making was, inevitably, more concerned with the solution of the pressing problems of the moment than with the measurement of success judged in terms of decades. It would not have been considered very helpful to point out to those faced with the decline of Britain's staple industries in the 'twenties that decline was merely the other side of "progress". It is certainly arguable that the high unemployment of the period was a far more important mark of failure than the achievement of a

---

[1] The key article here is by R. C. O. Matthews (and C. H. Feinstein), "Some Aspects of Post-War Growth in the British Economy in Relation to Historical Experience", *Manchester Statistical Society Paper* (1964); see also D. H. Aldcroft, "Economic Growth in Britain in the Inter-War Years: A Reassessment", *Economic History Review*, Aug. 1967 and J. A. Dowie, "Growth in the Inter-War Period: Some More Arithmetic", *Economic History Review*, April 1968, and further references cited therein.

[2] See D. H. Aldcroft, "Economic Progress in Britain in the 'Twenties", *Scottish Journal of Political Economy*, Nov. 1966, and the subsequent dispute with N. K. Buxton in same journal in 1967.

higher growth rate was of success. Things may not have been quite as bad in all respects as many felt at the time, but they were both disappointing and distressing when judged by the relative standards and reasonable expectations of those actually affected.

Under the circumstances, therefore, it is not surprising that British economic debate was more far-reaching than in most capitalist countries at this time. The overriding issue was the proper role of the state in the face of problems that were slowly and unevenly recognised to be quite different in magnitude and kind from those with which British economic institutions and traditional policies were designed to cope. What could or should the government do to deal with unemployment and the unemployed? How could it hasten the process of industrial transition? By what canons ought the state to conduct its finances so as best to contribute to recovery and stability? Did the situation require new initiatives to be taken, or simply a firmer application of tried and trusted methods? How were the external claims and pressures on Britain to be reconciled with domestic growth and stability? Such questions have been put with monotonous regularity since then, but it was during this period that they were first put with any regular insistence. The central question for contemporaries was, and is now for historians, whether governments, through lack of vision and understanding, by unwise action or inaction, actually impeded the solution of Britain's novel difficulties.

Britain's problems were not only perplexing to policy-makers. They also taxed the understanding of their official and self-appointed economic advisers. The persistently poor performance of the British economy, as they saw it, encouraged a spirit of self-examination among economists. The existing corpus of economic knowledge had been built up during a period of comparative calm and stability; its main strengths lay in the analysis of long-run, "normal" conditions. Was it capable of dealing with the radically altered situation? If not, was it capable of being modified to bring it to bear on contemporary problems? As in any scientific community, the first response was to modify as little as possible; the view of most was that the problems, while acute, presented no fundamental challenge to the existing apparatus of thought.

If was during this period that John Maynard Keynes emerged as an economic prophet and made his reputation for unorthodox views. For much of the period, however, he did not dissent from many of his academic colleagues on the basic tenets of economic theory. It was only after extending the accepted body of doctrine to its limits that he saw the need for a revolutionary change of direction and emphasis. If one is to understand the work of reconstruction which

Keynes accomplished in his *General Theory of Employment, Interest and Money* in 1936, it is first necessary to examine his apprenticeship in the policy debates of the 'twenties.

The period opens with the report of the Cunliffe Committee in 1918, which had been appointed to consider the problem of currency and foreign exchange after the war; the mid-point is marked by the report of the Macmillan Committee in 1931 on the relations between finance and industry. The former, with its recommendation in favour of restoring the automatic regulatory functions of the gold standard, was to provide the dominant aim of British economic policy for the first half of the period. The latter provided guide-lines for the conduct of policy in the 'thirties and beyond; it also summarised admirably the tone and direction of economic debate as it had developed during the latter half of the 'twenties.

". . . in the case of our financial, as in the case of our political and social, institutions we may well have reached the stage when an era of conscious and deliberate management must succeed the era of undirected natural evolution. There are . . . already signs that the necessity for such a change of outlook is coming to be realised. The foundations of our financial system are being reexamined. Dogmas hitherto regarded as canonical are being questioned. The feeling is growing that our former easy-going ways will no longer ensure our prosperity in a crowded and increasingly competitive world. We are, indeed, at the parting of the ways and our future depends on whether we choose the right way. Hence the need for a careful study of the economic map. We must now choose our path deliberately and consciously. In other words we stand in need as never before of a definite national policy in our financial dispositions."[1]

But if the 'twenties can be described as the time when the demands for a conscious system of state economic management first became insistent, it can equally well be described as a period when little or no actual progress was made to meet these demands. 1931 was also the year in which the report of the May Committee on National Expenditure was published; and there is no doubt that this atavistic document, with its recommendations in favour of orthodox economy measures to deal with the situation caused by world depression, exerted greater impact on the immediate course of events than did the report of the Macmillan Committee. It was one of the novelties of the Macmillan Report that it attempted for the first time to enunciate the range of goals at which the government might aim

---

[1] *Report of Committee on Finance and Industry* (1931), Cmd. 3897, p. 5.

through its control of the monetary system. The aims of government economic policy were never spelt out in detail in the 'twenties; there was even confusion as to where responsibility for the control of economic policy lay. Official policy-makers were unwilling to recognise responsibilities which would nowadays be considered a normal function of government.

The emergence of the idea of economic management, supported first by changes in economic thinking and later carried into practice, provides the major theme of the following chapters. Here it is necessary to revert to the distinction mentioned earlier, between conscious management based on an improvement in our economic understanding of the workings of capitalism, and other forms of state intervention or participation in economic life which are pragmatic and political in origin. It has to be borne in mind that behind the rhetoric of political contest and the intricacies of professional economic debate in the inter-war period, there was an expansion—sometimes interrupted but always resumed—in the coverage of the welfare services that had been initiated in the pre-war period. New responsibilities were undertaken by the state in this field, notably for housing. In others, for example in unemployment insurance, the changes introduced to meet altered conditions amounted to a change in principle and direction. The state also assumed wider regulatory powers in its relations with private industry, and extended its activities through direct subsidies to industry and through public corporations. But the accretion of these piece-meal efforts to improve and regulate economic conditions did not constitute recognition of the need for economic management as we understand this term today. Indeed, in some cases—and here again unemployment insurance provides a good example—it could be argued that attempts to meliorate the condition of the unemployed served as a substitute for more radical efforts to cure the disease.

The characteristics of economic thought in Britain during the 'twenties can best be illustrated by an examination of the debate aroused by the decision to return to gold at the pre-war parity in 1925, and by the sequence of events which led up to the "decision" to abandon gold in 1931. Both of these decisions carry us to the heart of the dilemma then facing British policy-makers.

At the end of the war most people accepted the necessity for a return to gold, with all that this implied for domestic policies. By 1925, and increasingly afterwards, the wisdom of this course of action came under heavy fire, notably from Keynes. He held that the decision had saddled Britain with an over-valued currency which acted as an impediment to her progress until she was mercifully released from the tyranny of gold in 1931. This view, unorthodox at the time, has become the accepted interpretation—though not every detail of Keynes's case would be upheld today.[1]

These are still difficult issues on which to pass judgment; there is plenty of scope for differences of opinion about what the actual situation was at the time, or could have been expected to be by those holding positions of responsibility. New evidence and hindsight do not always enable us to reconstruct what would have happened if different things had been done. Like all important questions of economic policy the choices ultimately entailed making political or moral judgments: the question of what *was* cannot easily be separated from what *should* have been.

The 1931 crisis marks the beginning of a new era of economic policy-making not only in Britain but in most capitalist countries. Nations whose economic fortunes had been linked by the gold standard and by international lending were now freer, and more anxious, to seek independent solutions to the domestic problems which all shared in differing degrees as a result of world depression. The new expedients varied from country to country according to the nature of the economic problem and the political setting. A division can be made between totalitarian experiments in Russia, Germany and Italy, where state power was used as ruthlessly in the economic as in the political field, and those which took place in the democratic capitalist countries. Within the latter group there was a wide range of choice between the bold pragmatism of Roosevelt's New Deal in the United States, the experimental approach of the Social Democratic Government in Sweden, and the muddling-through, mainly along orthodox lines, of the Conservative Government in Britain. In none of them, however, can policy be said to have exerted the decisive influence on whatever recovery took place.

The 'thirties was an era of international comparisons. Indeed, it might even be said that the study of other countries' experience and practices acted as a substitute for the international co-operation which was so seriously lacking in this period after the breakdown of the World Economic Conference in 1933. Economists, journalists and politicians visited each others' countries to find lessons that could be used at home. Europeans went to see the Tennessee Valley Authority schemes in the United States; Americans, Swedes and others came to Britain to study unemployment insurance at work; English and American observers went to Sweden to study contra-cyclical public spending schemes; the Webbs and many others looked to Soviet Communism for a solution to the ills of capitalism.

---

[1] More recently, however, there are signs that the pendulum is swinging in the opposite direction. Some intricate reasoning has been adduced to justify the choices made, and to mitigate the harshness of what might be called the Keynesian interpretation of history.

Certain broad features were common to all countries. Domestically, the new departures involved greater intervention by the state in the workings of the economy. The apparent successes of the totalitarian regimes provided a threat and a challenge to the democratic countries to pioneer new forms of partnership between the state and private industry. Internationally, the 'thirties saw a further retreat from the multilateral interdependence of the pre-1914 period towards more purely nationalist, bilateral, or regional solutions. Recovery from depression was the first order of the day, and with it went the demand for reform. Here, it seemed, was an opportunity to make a second effort to build a viable and more just economic system—the first having failed. In most countries recovery and reform went hand in hand. In some, notably the United States, full recovery proved elusive, and was frequently hampered by reformist intentions.

Everywhere, the idea of the market as a sensitive, self-regulating mechanism for allocating resources suffered a setback, not only on the familiar grounds of equity but also of efficiency. Whatever the achievements of capitalism may have been in the past, it had signally failed to provide a tolerable degree of security in the present. Features of the system which were acceptable while healthy expansion was taking place—business fluctuations and the rigours of competition—were no longer so under conditions of unemployment and sluggish recovery from depression. With the rise of larger productive units capable of dominating markets, the case for an unregulated market system lost much of its force. Given the higher priority accorded to economic security, and national as opposed to international recovery, the arguments for increased state sponsorship of larger units, and for state regulation to supply the function left vacant by the erosion of competition, were strengthened. Planning of one type or another acquired a vogue status.

Strange as it may seem from our present vantage point, when so much discussion turns once more on the question of economic growth, the economic problem of the 'thirties was frequently seen as one of coming to terms with the embarrassments caused by potential abundance. Technical advance and the growth of productive capacity were proceeding at a faster rate than could be absorbed by the increase in demand. Or as Keynes put it: "The increase of technical efficiency has been taking place faster than we can deal with the problem of labour absorption; the improvement in the standard of life has been a little too quick."[1] New types of social and economic policy were required to tailor conditions of supply to the slower rate of expansion in demand to be expected in "mature"

[1] "Economic Possibilities for Our Grandchildren" in *Essays in Persuasion* (1931), p. 358.

economies. Alternatively, private demand would have to be supplemented by an increase in collective consumption by the state. It was felt that the world economic frontier would not expand as rapidly in the future as it had in the nineteenth century. Population in the richer countries was growing more slowly. Rising standards of living were accompanied by a relative decline in the proportion of income devoted to food and the basic necessities of life. More was being spent on comforts and luxuries, the demand for which was inherently less stable, more difficult to predict.[1] The consequences of mistaken investment decisions were compounded by the larger size and bureaucratic nature of the typical business corporation and productive unit.

All of this posed a threat to international trade. Technical advances in the production of primary products, coming at a time when world demand was no longer expanding so rapidly, and when new synthetic substitutes were being pioneered, had brought about an adverse movement in the terms of trade of the primary producing countries; it had also encouraged the spread of protected manufacturing industries in such countries. With the spread of the manufacturing arts the comparative advantages to be gained from specialisation had narrowed. And while many of the difficulties of international trade in this period—protection, the drying-up of foreign investment, bilateralism, currency blocs—were clearly political in origin, there was also growing support for the idea that a secular law was at work making trade between nations less important.[2]

These, in brief, were some of the trends and developments that formed the background to economic debate in the period between the wars. We can now turn to a more detailed examination of the issues as they presented themselves to British, and later to American, policy-makers.

[1] See e.g. A. Loveday, "Problems of Economic Insecurity" in *The World's Economic Crisis* (Halley Stewart Lectures 1931), and essays by H. D. Henderson and others in G. Hutton (ed.), *The Burden of Plenty*, (1935).

[2] For a moderate statement of this view see D. H. Robertson, "The Future of International Trade", *Economic Journal*, March 1938.

# CHAPTER FIVE

# £1 = $4.86

Winston Churchill's decision in 1925, as Chancellor of the Exchequer, to return to the gold standard at the pre-war parity has been described as "the most important single act of economic policy in the decade of the 'twenties".[1] This is not an exaggeration. Preparations for the return dominated monetary policy and discussion in the first half of the 'twenties; and the political and economic consequences for Britain of the decision provided the focal point of economic debate right up to the moment when gold was abandoned in 1931. Post-mortems continue. Churchill himself came to believe that it was the greatest mistake of his life. Many agree with him, while others support his earlier view, or are inclined to believe that the mistake was unavoidable. The duty to regulate and protect the currency is the earliest example of acceptance by the state of the responsibilities of overall economic management. The debate aroused by the decision to return to gold was concerned, above all, with the way in which the state and the monetary authorities should exercise these responsibilities in the face of Britain's post-war difficulties.

## The Cunliffe Committee's Recommendation

When the Cunliffe Committee recommended that the overriding aim of British economic policy in the post-war period should be to return to the gold standard at the pre-war parity, they commanded the overwhelming support of informed opinion and sentiment of the day. The issue was settled as soon as it was raised; there was no mention of any alternative. In their interim report published in 1918 the Committee gave the following reasons for their recommendation.

"Unless the machinery which long experience has shown to be the only effective remedy for an adverse balance of trade and undue growth of credit is once more brought into play, there will be very grave danger of a credit expansion in this country and a foreign drain of gold which might jeopardise the convertibility of our note issue and the international trade position of the country.

---

[1] D. Williams, "Montagu Norman and Banking Policy in the Nineteen Twenties", *Yorkshire Bulletin of Economic and Social Research*, July, 1959, p. 46.

The uncertainty of the monetary situation will handicap our industry, our position as an international financial centre will suffer and our general commercial status in the eyes of the world will be lowered. We are glad to find that there was no difference of opinion among the witnesses who appeared before us as to the vital importance of these matters."[1]

The gold standard appeared to be the keystone of that pre-war system of economic interdependence which had provided the foundation for Britain's progress. It was also the system to which most of her financial institutions were geared, and from which she had obtained substantial invisible earnings in the past. The virtues of the gold standard were underlined by the Committee in an idealised picture of its operation. According to this picture the gold standard had two functions; "to correct unfavourable exchanges and check undue expansion of credit." When the balance of trade was unfavourable the exchange rate fell to the point at which it became profitable to export gold. The resulting loss of reserves provided a signal to the Bank of England to raise Bank Rate as a means of retaining and attracting foreign funds, and thereby, gold. As a longer term mechanism of adjustment the raising of Bank Rate could be reinforced by a tightening of domestic credit conditions; this in turn would lead to a decline in investment activity, a release of stocks of finished goods and raw materials, and a fall in the domestic price level. Furthermore, it would stimulate exports and curtail imports, thereby adjusting the balance of trade.

The adjustments required by the gold standard were made to appear relatively painless, involving simply an upward or downward adjustment of interest rates and prices. No mention was made of frictions or rigidities. No mention was made of foreign repercussions or influences. Only the briefest mention was made of the possible effects of monetary deflation on levels of employment and incomes. The automatism of the system, the elimination of scope for discretionary policies, was proclaimed as its greatest virtue.

Even as an account of how the gold standard worked under nineteenth-century conditions the Cunliffe Committee's model had considerable weaknesses. It is fair to add, however, that little research had been done at that time on this matter. It may be that the British economy was more flexible in the nineteenth century. It is certainly true that Britain's unique position at the centre of the system, the unrivalled facilities of the London capital market, and the healthy balance of payments enjoyed by Britain for much of this period,

---

[1] *First Interim Report of the Committee on Currency* as reprinted in T. E. Gregory (ed), *Select Statutes, Documents & Reports Relating to British Banking, 1832-1928*, (1929).

enabled changes in Bank Rate to act quickly on the flow of international funds, thereby reducing the need for drastic internal adjustments. But as later studies have shown, the gold standard did not guarantee price stability even during the nineteenth century. Gold movements did not provoke automatic responses; they were more the shadow than the substance of the adjustment mechanism. It is also clear now that many of the strains were borne by countries on the periphery of the system, rather than by those, like Britain, at its centre.[1]

*Preparations for Return*

The Cunliffe Committee recognised that as a result of trade dislocation and the war-time growth of the money supply and of short-term government debt, conditions no longer existed for the maintenance of an effective gold standard. But these were merely temporary obstacles; they saw no fundamental reasons for doubting that Britain could resume her place at the centre of the world's financial system.

Immediately after the war Britain formally abandoned the gold standard by placing an embargo on the export of gold. Without this embargo it was felt that the Bank of England would be forced to restrict credit sharply to protect its gold reserves at a time when demobilisation and reconstruction required monetary support. Formal abandonment of gold implied no change in long-term aims. For a time though a post-war boom, fed by credit expansion, was allowed to develop. Prices rose steeply above the already high war-time level until April 1921, when the authorities took a firm hold on the situation and began the slow and uneven process of paving the way for a return to gold.[2]

Very little was required to overtopple the unstable boom conditions which prevailed in most countries at this time. Following the American slump, throughout 1921 and 1922, prices, production and employment fell alarmingly everywhere. British prices fell further than American prices, and as a result, the sterling exchange rate with the dollar began to improve. The appreciation of the pound was also supported by temporary improvements in British coal exports due to unsettled conditions in the Ruhr. The revival of

---

[1] See e.g. P. B. Whale, "The Working of the Pre-War Gold Standard", reprinted in T. S. Ashton and R. S. Sayers (eds), *Papers in English Monetary History* (1953); A. G. Ford, "Notes on the Working of the Gold Standard before 1914", *Oxford Economic Papers*, Feb. 1960.

[2] The return to gold was, of course, an international movement in which Britain and America played leading roles. The account given here concentrates on the problem from the point of view of British policy-makers only. For the full international background, see W. A. Brown, *The International Gold Standard Reinterpreted, 1914-1934* (1940), Vol. I Book II.

sterling was to prove shortlived; the exchange rate fell from a peak of $4.30 at the end of the year.

It was not until July 1924 that the British monetary authorities made a determined effort to force up the exchange rate again by maintaining higher short-term rates in London than prevailed in New York. According to Pigou, however, who was a member of the Cunliffe Committee, the avowed aim of returning to the pre-war parity "dominated the outlook of the Treasury and the Bank of England" throughout this period. The effort to place the pound in a position where it could look the dollar in the face, he said, "meant that the state of the American exchange, rather than the industrial situation at home, was their principal preoccupation".[1] In retrospect, the movement towards restoration may appear more purposive than it probably was to those concerned with day-to-day management. But in the absence of any agreed alternative aim of policy there was a sense in which everybody acted as though impelled by forces beyond their control. This attitude of mind was summed up by D. H. Robertson when he said that: "It may have been silly to bother so much about the exchanges; but it was simpler than trying to bother about everything at once, and wiser than bothering about nothing at all."[2]

It was during this period of preparation for a return to gold that a number of doubts were expressed concerning the wisdom of the Cunliffe recommendation. These came from within the banking community and from the Federation of British Industries; they were chiefly directed against the policy of credit restriction and deflation.[3] The most important critic of the Cunliffe policy, however, was Keynes.

### Keynes's Position

Throughout the 'twenties Keynes found himself increasingly at odds with the official current of economic thought in Britain. From the outset, in his *Economic Consequences of the Peace* (1919), he stood outside the popular nostalgia for the pre-war economic arrangements. Whereas for most people the pre-war period represented sanity, "normal" conditions, and stability, Keynes went out of his way to stress the "intensely unusual, unstable, complicated, unreliable, temporary nature of the economic organisation by which Western Europe has lived for the last half century".[4] He emphasised the

---

[1] A. C. Pigou, *Aspects of British Economic History 1918-1925* (1947), p. 148.
[2] *Essays in Monetary Theory* (1940), p. 123.
[3] See L. J. Hume, "The Gold Standard and Deflation; Issues and Attitudes in the Nineteen-Twenties", *Economica*, Aug. 1963.
[4] *Economic Consequences of the Peace* (1919), p. 1.

precarious nature of the balance achieved between European population growth and world resources through international trade and
investment; and the instability of arrangements whereby rapid
accumulation was based on inequalities of wealth. Like those who
went to the trenches during the war, his experience of the peace-
making and of the chaos in Europe after the war left him out of
sympathy with the optimism of opinion at home. War had irrevocably changed the economic balance of power; it would not be
easy to reconstruct the pre-war system, even if that was thought
desirable; the future would require new expedients and not simply
a return to old ones. It was this position, as yet not fully articulated,
that provides the vital clue to an understanding of the development
of Keynes's views in this period.

In the immediate post-war period Keynes was chiefly concerned
with the issue of German reparations: by 1920 he felt free to turn
his attention to the problem of stabilising European currencies and
finance. At first he favoured a return to the gold standard. Although
for some countries this might entail devaluation, he felt that Britain
could return to the pre-war parity. There was, however, one
important *caveat*: if the return to pre-war values could not be attained
by Britain within a year, "arguments to the contrary may obtain a
hearing".[1]

Keynes's first major contribution to monetary discussion in this
period, *A Tract on Monetary Reform*, came in 1923, after the dramatic
deflation of the previous year. In this book he posed the choice before
British policy-makers in the years ahead; between deflation and
devaluation; between giving priority to stabilisation of the internal
price level and concentration on maintenance of the external value
of the pound. After considering the relative advantages and disadvantages of inflation and deflation from the point of view of the
investor, the business man, and the wage-earner, Keynes came down
distinctly on the side of moderate inflation, while at the same time
paying lip-service to the need to avoid either extreme. His arguments
were based partly on economic, and partly on distributive or moral
grounds. Inflation was injurious to the investor but beneficial to the
"active", risk-taking, business man; the interests of the wage-earner
lay somewhere between the two. Deflation had the opposite effect,
with the additional disadvantage that it increased the dead-weight
of accumulated debt on productive enterprise, and had an adverse
effect on business expectations, and thereby on production and
employment. At this point he entered a fundamental value-judgment:
"Thus Inflation is unjust and Deflation is inexpedient. Of the two
perhaps Deflation is, if we rule out exaggerated inflations such as

[1] See R. F. Harrod, *The Life of John Maynard Keynes* (1951), pp. 313-14.

that of Germany, the worse; because it is worse, in an impoverished world, to provoke unemployment than to disappoint the *rentier*."[1]

All of this was preparatory to Keynes's answer to the topical question: should countries which have suffered from inflation stabilise their currencies at the existing higher level of prices (i.e. devalue from the old parity), or deflate in order to return to pre-war values? Apart from the fact that he thought deflation would be politically unacceptable, he favoured devaluation, or fixing the value of currencies "at that figure in the neighbourhood of the existing value to which commerce and wages are adjusted."[2]

It should be noted that at this stage Keynes was not suggesting that Britain should return to gold at a lower parity. His main heresy was confined to giving an unorthodox answer to the question: should the aim of monetary policy be the stabilisation of the domestic price level or the stability of the exchange rate? This question merged with another: should an attempt be made to restore the gold standard or should some alternative system be found? While recognising the importance of stable exchanges to a nation reliant on foreign trade, he came down firmly on the side of stabilising the internal purchasing power of currencies where the two aims were in conflict. His final reason for rejecting the policy of a return to the gold standard was that under post-war conditions it would be difficult to achieve domestic stability. His chief contention was that the value of gold itself was no longer the impersonal outcome of a number of independent factors; rather it was subject to the policy decisions of a small number of Central Banks, and to the views of the largest gold-holder, the United States, in particular. There was no question, therefore, of a return to the supposed automatism of the pre-war gold standard. The only question at issue was whether there would be sufficient co-operation between Central Banks, and wisdom on the part of the American Federal Reserve Board, to make the workings of the new "managed" gold standard tolerable.

Since Keynes was sceptical on both counts he went on to suggest an alternative to gold. He proposed that the Bank of England should use its control of the monetary mechanism to maintain stability of the domestic price level and employment rather than fix its attention on the sterling-dollar exchange. If the Federal Reserve Board did likewise a firm basis for future co-operation could be established.

"We may have reached a stage in the evolution of money when a 'managed' currency is inevitable, but we have not yet reached the point when the management can be entrusted to a single authority.

[1] *Tract on Monetary Reform* (1923), p. 40.
[2] *Tract on Monetary Reform*, p. 151.

The best we can do, therefore, is to have two managed currencies, sterling and dollars, with as close a collaboration as possible between the aims and methods of the managements."[1]

How realistic was this alternative? A recent defender of the decision to return to gold, A. J. Youngson, has said that the contrast posed by Keynes was between "the weaknesses of such a gold standard regime as the next few years *might* see with the perfection of a theoretical, ideal, managed system."[2] It is matter for conjecture as to whether or not by 1923, and certainly by 1925, the signs of weakness both in the British economy and in the world financial order were as dimly visible as this statement implies. The argument which held sway at the time was that the basis for international co-operation could only be established *after* Britain had shown the way back to gold. As it is, in Youngson's own words, Keynes proved "abundantly right" in his view that it was a "pious hope" to expect the degree of co-operation required to work the post-war gold standard to be achieved. But was Keynes offering a "theoretical, ideal, managed system" as an alternative? In the *Tract on Monetary Reform* he advised building on "the actual system which has grown up, half haphazard, since the war". Keynes was arguing for the management skills used by the Bank of England to keep Britain on the gold standard between 1925 and 1931 to be applied to different ends. The real issue was whether the possible, foreseeable benefits of stable exchanges outweighed the possible, foreseeable drawbacks which Keynes predicted, namely deflation and increased unemployment. Ultimately, of course, the decision entailed a moral or political judgment. Keynes, at least, never tried to avoid making this judgment.

### The Decision to Return to Gold: Last Stages

The embargo on the export of gold passed by Parliament in 1919 was due for renewal or removal at the end of 1925. As the day for decision approached Keynes became even more convinced of the folly of linking Britain to gold, or, as he saw it, to the vicissitudes of the American economy. In February 1925 his criticisms were still concerned mainly with the question of whether a return to the gold standard at any parity should be attempted. With the faster rise of American than British prices during 1924, the signs were beginning to look more favourable for a return at the old parity. But Keynes drew attention to the weaknesses of the British situation. In contrast to the pre-war position London was more heavily indebted on short-

---

[1] *Ibid.*, p. 204.
[2] A. J. Youngson, *Britains Economic Growth, 1920-1966* (1967), p. 274.

term. He warned against relying on the temporary flow of speculative funds which was then exerting an upward pressure on the sterling-dollar exchange. He felt that the rise of American prices was not likely to be permanent: if it collapsed after the tie with the dollar had been effected then Britain would be forced to bear the full strains of deflation. He continued to favour a managed currency, but advised that if a return to gold was to be attempted, it should be *after* sterling had achieved parity and only if it looked likely that she would be able to maintain it.[1]

In the same month a report of an official advisory committee under Lord Bradbury's chairmanship was published; the committee had been set up to review the Cunliffe Committee's recommendations in the light of recent developments. At the outset they dismissed in summary fashion any suggestion of returning at a lower parity: "It was never, in our opinion, a policy which the United Kingdom could accept."[2] They also rejected the idea of a managed currency without bothering to hear evidence on the subject. Though Keynes's statement that the report was "indolent and jejune" is a little strong, it was undoubtedly a rather vague and confused document.[3] When they first began their deliberations in September 1924, the committee found a 10 to 12% difference between American and British prices. Even so, it was their opinion that there would be no difficulty in maintaining the pre-war parity "at any time it might be thought prudent to do so". They viewed the necessary deflation with reasonable equanimity: "an effective gold standard could thus be restored without further danger or inconvenience than that which is inevitable in any period of credit restriction and falling prices."

Having thus closed the issue in paragraph 14, they immediately re-opened it in paragraphs 16 and 17. Would the "undoubted advantages of an immediate return to parity" be an adequate compensation for the temporary "inconveniences" of deflation? Perhaps a waiting policy would be better? Given their earlier statements, it is difficult to believe that they considered this dilemma to be a real one. Fortunately, however, they were comforted by the subsequent rise of American prices and the further approach of the sterling-dollar rate towards parity. They calculated the existing discrepancy between American and British prices to be about $1\frac{1}{2}\%$—"a significant, though not very large, amount"—and felt that this degree of deflation was a price well worth paying to achieve exchange stability. They considered that British gold reserves were quite

---

[1] *The Nation and Athenaeum*, Feb. 21st, 1925, reprinted in *Essays in Persuasion* (1931), pp. 225-236.
[2] *Report of the Committee on the Currency and Bank of England Note Issues*, 1925, reprinted in T. E. Gregory, *op. cit.*, Vol. II.
[3] See Keynes's review of the report in the *Economic Journal*, June 1925.

sufficient to meet any gold loss due to the repatriation of speculative balances. They also took comfort from the balm of distant history; the restoration of the gold standard after the Napoleonic Wars showed that "a courageous policy in currency matters surmounts apparently formidable obstacles with surprising ease".

Further debate on the decision continued right up to the last moment. An eleventh-hour dinner party was organised by Churchill to which Sir Otto Niemeyer and Lord Bradbury, for the pros, and Keynes and R. T. McKenna, Chairman of the Midland Bank, for the cons, were invited to discuss the matter. This dinner party is usually cited as evidence that, contrary to Keynes's later charge that the decision was ill-considered, Churchill was fully aware of all points of view, and of the possible sacrifices that would be required. It is not surprising that Keynes, single-handed— McKenna having given way to the opposition by the end of the meeting—failed to sway Churchill. It is to be doubted if this was due, as has been suggested, to the fact that Keynes had an "off-day".[1] We have only the testimony of P. J. Grigg, Churchill's Private Secretary, from which to judge how the meeting went. Grigg, to say the least, was not exactly sympathetic to Keynes. Indeed, it is difficult to see how in the eyes of someone who believed that "our departure from the Gold Standard in [1931] heralded the beginning of our repellent modern world," Keynes could ever have had an "on-day".[2]

Surely the result of the meeting was a foregone conclusion? It had been the stated aim of the Bank of England and the Treasury since 1919 to return to gold at pre-war parity. The most that Keynes could have done at that late date was to delay the momentum of the official machine; and even this required special action to renew the embargo on the export of gold, with the risk of suffering the consequences of disappointing the expectations of speculators. Restoration of the gold standard at the old parity, on the other hand, was simply a matter of doing what everybody expected anyway. Economics was never Churchill's forte, and it is clear from Grigg's account of the meeting that the outcome was settled finally in Churchill's mind by moral considerations. An undertaking had been made in 1918; it was now a question of whether Britain was going to uphold this undertaking in 1925. When Churchill announced his decision not to renew the embargo on April 29th, 1925, he claimed that in returning to gold Britain was shackling herself to reality. He shed further light on his process of thought when he said that he had been convinced that it was the right decision by the experts at the Bank

[1] See R. S. Sayers, "The Return to Gold, 1925, in L. S. Pressnell (ed), *Studies in the Industrial Revolution*, (1960).
[2] P. J. Grigg, *Prejudice and Judgment* (1948), p. 257.

of England and the Treasury, whose opinions "count more than the clever arguments of academic theorists".[1]

Keynes immediately launched a final and bitter attack on Churchill and his advisers in a pamphlet entitled *The Economic Consequences of Mr. Churchill*. His main contention was that the decision entailed an overvaluation of sterling by 10%, which therefore required an equivalent reduction in wages and prices in the export industries. This step could be justified only if there were some means of reducing all wages and prices by the same amount; otherwise it constituted an unjustifiable attack on the wages of those employed in the export trades, and notably in the coal industry. He wanted to force the government to face up to the deflationary consequences of its decision: "He who wills the ends, wills the means."

## The Rationale of the Decision

What were the "undoubted advantages of an immediate return to parity" of which the Bradbury Committee spoke? The chief one was that a decisive move would be made towards the reconstruction of the international economy. It would restore London to the centre of the international financial network, and, it was hoped, create conditions favourable to a revival of multilateral trade. The advantages to the City and to British invisible earnings of the old parity were obvious. It has also been argued subsequently that far from sacrificing industry, and the export trades in particular, on the altar of high finance, the decision was essentially a policy designed to alleviate unemployment. British unemployment was heavily concentrated in the export industries; some of the difficulties of these industries could be accounted for by the decline in world trade; and one reason for this decline was the uncertainty created by currency instability. Once this uncertainty had been removed by a concerted effort to re-establish the gold standard, British exports and employment could be expected to revive.[2]

This interpretation of the effects of returning to gold rests on the view that British unemployment at this time was either due to postwar currency dislocation, or was exclusively "structural" in character. To the extent that unemployment was the result of structural changes in the economy, and required a re-deployment of resources from old to growing industries, it could not be dealt with by general reflation. No credence is given in this view to the contention of Keynes and others that some of the difficulties of British industry

---

[1] *House of Commons Debates*, May 4th 1925, c. 670.
[2] See e.g. R. S. Sayers, *op. cit.*, pp. 317-19; A. J. Youngson, *op. cit.*, pp. 231 ff; and Sir Henry Clay, *Lord Norman* (1957), Ch. IV.

could be laid at the door of the deflationary policies adopted to achieve and maintain the pre-war parity under changed conditions. For reasons given in the *Tract on Monetary Reform*, Keynes concentrated on the problem of domestic stability, while the defenders of the gold standard policy were more interested in stability of the exchange rate. At the same time they refused, or were unwilling to acknowledge, that these two aims of policy were in conflict; and they were not as frank as Keynes in recognising the implicit value judgments involved in choosing to stress one aim rather than the other.

This can be seen clearly in the evidence given by Montagu Norman, Governor of the Bank of England, and the chief architect of the return to gold, when he appeared before the Macmillan Committee on Finance and Industry in 1930.[1] The two chief opponents on the Committee of the return to gold, Keynes and Bevin, asked Norman if he considered the domestic impact of restrictive actions taken to deal with the international credit markets and to protect the exchange rate. At first Norman argued that the internal effect of changes in Bank Rate was "greatly exaggerated", that its effects were "more psychological than real", and were exhausted in the short-term money market. The problems of British industry were not due to the return to gold and the monetary policy which this necessitated, but to "ill luck". The salvation of industry lay in rationalisation—though he admitted that the effects of rationalisation on employment would take a very long time to work themselves out. Apart from this, he had nothing to offer by way of diagnosis or short-term remedy for the problem of unemployment; he clearly felt that this was not part of his responsibilities. Under pressure from Keynes, however, Norman was forced to admit that a restrictive credit policy initiated for international reasons was bound to have some effect on domestic industry and employment, and that such an effect was actually required as part of the mechanism of the gold standard.

It is unfortunate that one of the leading supporters of the return to gold should have been so inarticulate as an economic thinker.[2] Norman was quite incapable of taking an enlarged view of the monetary policy which he controlled; his difficulties in explaining his position were apt to be confused with evasiveness, passivity, and fatalism. His testimony confirms the worst fears of those critics who maintained that British monetary policy was conducted almost in spite of its effect on the domestic situation. Norman's skills were best seen in his work as an international banker; they were the

---

[1] *Committee on Finance and Industry*; *Minutes of Evidence* (1931), March 26th 1930.
[2] A sympathetic exposition of Norman's position can be found in D. Williams, "Montagu Norman and Banking Policy in the Nineteen Twenties", *Yorkshire Bulletin of Economic and Social Research*, July, 1959.

semi-instinctive skills of a craftsman. It is ironic that he should have
spent most of the latter half of the 'twenties using these accomplish-
ments to insulate and protect the domestic economy from the full
impact of the earlier decision to return to gold.

In the minds of supporters of the gold standard there was an
indissoluble link between going back to gold and going back at the
old rate. According to Pigou, the only question which the Cunliffe
Committee considered it necessary to ask was *when* shall we go back
to gold at the pre-war parity?[1] The question of a lower parity was
ruled out at an early stage of the Bradbury Committee's deliberations; and we are told by Norman's biographer that he never considered any alternative to the pre-war parity.[2] Although Norman was
more aware than the Cunliffe Committee had been of the changes
in world monetary conditions which made return difficult for
Britain, he was completely unaffected by any of the doubts expressed
by Keynes and others.

It is easy to see that a good deal of pride and prestige attached to
the pre-war parity. Most people, including the policy-makers of the
day, were hypnotised by the only parity which had any reality for
them. It may not have been entirely irrational to act on such beliefs.
When dealing with matters of high finance, involving uncertainty
and foreign confidence, what has been called the Oedipus effect in
explaining social behaviour must be taken into account. Even
prestige has a market value if enough people act as though it has.

But apart from such considerations, what reasons could be given
for being so attached to the pre-war parity that, in Norman's case
for example, no return was preferable to return at a lower rate?
This now seems an extraordinarily intransigent position. Would
not a return at a lower parity have served the cause of international
stability just as well without some of the unfortunate effects on the
domestic economy? Most people, supporters and opponents alike,
agree that the pre-war parity entailed overvaluation of sterling and
constant strain on the balance of payments throughout the latter
half of the 'twenties. The disagreement centres on whether this overvaluation could have been foreseen and whether it was due to the
choice of the pre-war parity. Some highly intricate arguments have
been put forward to show that far more than prestige was at stake
in this choice.

Undoubtedly, one source of strain on the British balance of payments and exchange rate was the relatively low rates at which France
and Belgium stabilised their currencies. Norman considered these

---

[1] *Committee on Finance and Industry; Minutes of Evidence*, May 28th 1930, Q.6074; see also
pp. 154-5 below.
[2] H. Clay, *op. cit.*, pp. 156, 164.

rates to be chosen fortuitously; other defenders of the British decision have claimed that the rates chosen were deliberately competitive with that of Britain, and that, in consequence, the benefits of a lower rate for the pound would have been offset by even lower French and Belgian rates.[1] Could this have been foreseen? Keynes at least had cast considerable doubt on the possibility of achieving effective international co-operation to make the gold standard work properly. He was not open to any charge of false optimism on this score. Sayers, speaking of another source of difficulty for British exporters in this period, the resurgence of German competition, has said that: "A thoughtful and discriminating view of 'back to 1913' should have allowed for the possibility that Germany would win back something of her former trading strength. The superficialities of economic thought in high quarters passed over all such possibilities."[2] In any event, the competitive rates chosen by other countries cannot be cited in defence of Norman. When offered a chance to say that he would not have favoured a return if he had known the rates other nations would choose, he refused.[3]

Keynes based his case against return at the pre-war parity partly on the 10% discrepancy between American and British prices, which he claimed had been underestimated by the Bradbury Committee. Even though his prediction proved more or less correct, he may have attached too much significance to a precise figure based on the questionable theory of purchasing power parity and crude statistics. All that was needed to make his case was to indicate the unfavourable changes which had taken place in Britain's international position since 1914.[4] He was on firmer ground when he accused Churchill's advisers of gambling on a rise in American prices to offset the discrepancy. This has been disputed by Sayers, who points out that the Bradbury Committee assumed no more than stability in American prices.[5] The passage in question, like a good deal of the report, is open to divergent interpretation. A leading question put by Bradbury to Norman before the Macmillan Committee suggests, however, that the expectation of a rise in American prices did form part of his thinking at the time.[6]

In so far as the discrepancy between British and American prices was not made good by a rise in American prices, it would have to be

[1] R. S. Sayers, op. cit., pp. 321-2; H. Clay, op. cit., p. 159.
[2] Ibid., pp. 322-3.
[3] Committee on Finance and Industry; Minutes of Evidence, March 26th, 1930, Q. 3358.
[4] On this see, Keith Hancock, "Unemployment and the Economists in the 1920's", Economica, Nov. 1960, p. 317.
[5] Op. cit., p. 320.
[6] Minutes of Evidence, March 26th, 1930, Q.3373: "Is it not true also that American prices were rather on the up-grade at that time, and the difference of something like 10% between British and American prices was likely to narrow?"

achieved by means of deflationary adjustments in Britain. Here again Keynes was right to suggest that Churchill's advisers either failed to point out that this was what was involved, or underestimated the difficulties of making the adjustment by speaking of it as a "temporary inconvenience". This was brought out in the testimony of supporters of the return when they appeared before the Macmillan Committee. On this occasion they admitted that it had proved far more difficult than they supposed to reduce wages and costs. They were more frank about the deflationary consequences of the decision when these did not materialise than they were before it was made.[1]

But if return at the pre-war parity did entail deflation, they were open to Keynes's further criticism that they had failed to show how monetary policy would achieve the adjustment without leading to industrial conflict. The extent to which the industrial unrest which followed the return can be attributed to the decision cannot be estimated with any precision. At the very least, the rise in export prices, which put the already hard-pressed industries under further competitive pressure, can hardly have weakened the resolve of employers to obtain some downward adjustment of wages. Ernest Bevin certainly maintained that the discrete upward movement of the exchange rate had thrown negotiations between unions and employers out of gear just at the point when they were becoming adjusted to the previous period of deflation.[2] And the adverse effect of the decision on the coal industry which Keynes predicted was upheld by Josiah Stamp in his addendum to the Report of the Court of Inquiry on the Coal Dispute.[3]

This is not to say that there were no good reasons for favouring return at the pre-war parity, though most of these have only been argued and fully explained after the event. One reason for favouring a high rate was Britain's net surplus of international payments on invisible account, much of which was owed in terms of sterling. The positive gains to the balance of payments on this score may have been important. But were they sufficiently important to offset the negative effects of a higher rate on exports? The absence of any precise calculation of these benefits at the time makes it all too likely that this item, close to City interests, was given undue weight in the calculation. Clay also tells us that Norman was anxious to keep the cost of Britain's import bill down; a high rate would lower the cost of living. He believed that this was more important than giving the exporters a temporary competitive advantage.[4] This again

---

[1] See e.g. Norman's reply to Q. 3392 in the *Minutes of Evidence*.
[2] See Qq. 3347-51 in *Minutes of Evidence*.
[3] *Parliamentary Papers*, 1924-5, XIII, pp. 21-3.
   H. Clay, *op. cit.*, pp. 169-70.

was an admirable argument, though with a favourable movement in the British terms of trade already under way in this period, and given the distress in the export trades, this effort to cheapen imports at the expense of the exporters might be considered a case of being unduly influenced by nineteenth century precedent.

One important influence on the supporters of return at the old parity has not been mentioned so far: fear of inflation. This had clearly been uppermost in the minds of the Cunliffe Committee in 1919, and the experience of the post-war boom which followed on the abandonment of gold helped to confirm this fear. Even without this, what had happened on the Continent as a result of currency mis-management provided a much-cited object lesson. It is worth stressing this influence because it helps to explain one aspect of contemporary thinking which is puzzling to a post-Keynesian generation. Why is it that so many people, especially those in authority, considered the gold standard to be the only effective way of protecting the *internal* stability and integrity of the currency? Given the existence throughout this period of over a million un-employed workers, and excess capacity in many key industries, how is it that there could be so much concern with the problem of inflation in a country with a highly sophisticated and powerful set of monetary institutions? Thus we find Churchill, in a speech made during the debate on the return to gold, taking comfort from the fact that by making this decision the nation had been saved from "hectic inflation", and arguing, somewhat ironically in the light of the General Strike in the following year, that the real potential cause of industrial unrest was inflation.[1] The same attitude can be seen later in 1931, when we find Snowden, having carried through a ruthless economy campaign while there were over two million unemployed, arguing that by so doing he had saved the country from "having to print money, which leads to uncontrolled inflation".[2]

Given the state of economic knowledge at the time it is not difficult to see how this view could take hold. Before the publication of Keynes' *General Theory* it was common to separate "real" variables, such as the level of employment and output, from monetary variables, such as the volume of credit and the price level. This separation can be seen in Norman's approach to monetary questions. On the one hand there were those "real" problems connected with the pattern of production and the long run growth of output; on the other there were those purely monetary phenomena connected with the gold standard and the money market. His operations were confined to the latter, and he had difficulty in conceiving how they might be

[1] *House of Commons Debates*, May 4th 1925, cc. 669-672.
[2] See pp. 205-6 below.

connected with the "real" issues. His interpretation of the effect of
monetary policy was extraordinarily rigid, and at the same time,
passive; his attention was so closely focused on the international and
short-term money markets that he claimed he had little influence
on domestic credit conditions, the price level, and employment. For
most people, however, there was a tendency to associate any plans
for cheaper credit with inflation. This applied also, as we shall see
later, to any increase in government spending which was not offset
by increased taxation.

It is rather more difficult to see how later commentators, with
benefit of hindsight and after the publication of the *General Theory*,
can argue similarly about the fear of inflation, not just to explain
the state of mind of policy-makers at the time, but actually to justify
the decision made. Thus we find Youngson arguing exactly as
Churchill had in 1925, that "to go back at a lower parity, or not to
go back at all, carried as much risk of industrial troubles (through
inflation instead of deflation) as did the policy actually adopted".
And it is not very reassuring or convincing to be told that the policy
"was well understood by those who made it their duty to advocate
it".[1] If we turn to Norman's biographer, Henry Clay, we find the
opinion expressed that the choice of a lower parity would, by raising
import prices, have resulted in "fresh inflation".[2] With British prices
falling almost continuously from 1921 to 1933, inflation would
now appear to have been a remote risk. Inflation is a process
and not simply a question of a once-for-all rise in some, albeit
key, prices. We cannot conclude, therefore, that the choice of a
lower parity would have been attended with the dire consequences
predicted.

### Consequences of the Decision

Whether or not the consequences of the return to gold could or
should have been foreseen or avoided, its actual ramifications were
wide and deep. Apart from its immediate impact on the export
industries, the most important consequence of the decision was that
it set the limits within which policy was framed and discussed in the
latter half of the 'twenties. Primacy was given to one aim of policy—
stability of the exchanges—over all others. It delayed acceptance by
the government of responsibility for the domestic level of employment. In the history of the idea of "conscious and deliberate management" of the economy, the return to gold in 1925 was a backward
step. This is not to say that British governments did not make efforts

[1] *Op. cit.*, pp. 271-8.
[2] *Op. cit.*, pp. 170-171.

to alleviate unemployment during this period; but fears, real and imaginary, for the external stability of the pound meant that efforts in this direction were severely hampered.

At the same time, the results of the return to gold were not in accordance with the expectations of its supporters. The weaknesses of the British balance of payments, and of London as a financial centre within the gold exchange standard as it emerged after 1925, meant that there was constant pressure on the exchange rate. The orthodox logic under these circumstances required a policy of reducing wages and prices. The inability and unwillingness of governments to risk unpopularity and industrial warfare by putting further pressure on wages meant that other methods of protecting sterling had to be employed. Domestic monetary policy in the 'twenties was not actively deflationary, but interest rates had to be maintained at a high level throughout the period in order to attract or keep short-term foreign deposits in London.[1] These short-term funds were to prove a grave embarrassment later, while the maintenance of high interest rates had a restrictive influence on domestic investment. As we shall see in subsequent chapters, the return to gold also tended to strengthen orthodox positions with regard to the contribution which the government could make to the relief of unemployment through its expenditure on public works. Instead of restoring sanity and automatism to economic policy then, the system required a good deal of discretionary management, which left neither the supporters of monetary orthodoxy nor their expansionist opponents satisfied. Since no consistent policy was pursued, both camps could claim that if their approach had been adopted things would have turned out differently.

The return to gold not only settled the basic objectives of economic policy, it also determined where initiative and control of that policy lay, namely with the Bank of England. The following statement by P. F. Drucker aptly summarises the position of those who were critical of this arrangement: "The gold standard was a constitutional barrier to the power and sphere of the political government. What was important was not only that it made the market supreme over the industrial system, but that it also prevented encroachment of the political government on the industrial system."[2] Among supporters of the return to gold, there were many who did so precisely because it provided a "constitutional barrier". The Cunliffe Committee certainly thought it was desirable that "the management of banking should be left as free as possible from State interference". And in 1924 a group of Liberals declined to follow Keynes in advocating a

[1] See R. S. Sayers, *Central Banking After Bagehot* (1937), espec. p. 79.
[2] *The Future of Industrial Man* (1943), p. 14.

managed currency because they believed that the gold standard commanded the assent of the majority of bankers, investors and businessmen; and, more significantly, because "violent changes" were to be avoided when there was "a likelihood of many changes of Government . . . and of the contingency that the Governments in power may not possess the whole-hearted confidence of a majority of the nation".[1] This line of thought is perhaps best summed up by the phrase used by Lord Bradbury when he said that the great virtue of the gold standard was that it was "knave-proof".[2] The implications of this view were that democratically elected governments in a highly-developed political system should not be trusted with matters involving the currency; these were best left to a small, dedicated élite, working outside the political arena. With it went a tendency towards anti-intellectualism, which expressed itself in conflict between the "sound" views of the practical financier and the "academic" opinions of the monetary theorist.

There was close co-operation between the Bank of England and the Treasury in this period, but Montagu Norman was allowed a large degree of autonomy and influence by virtue of the fact that the Treasury was completely in sympathy with the aims of monetary policy as dictated by the gold standard. As a result of the experience of this period, and particularly of the events which preceded the 1931 crisis, sharp criticisms were later directed at Norman from within the Labour movement; and demands were made for stricter political surveillance of what was still a semi-private institution. Yet as Keynes pointed out in 1932, in a review of the Labour Party's proposals for a state control of the banking system, Norman held sway not as an autocrat, but because he was entrusted with power by the politicians of the day. "With the personalities the same and knowledge no greater, it might not have made much difference if the machinery which the Labour Party desires had been in operation during the last ten years."[3]

This judgment is borne out by the case of Snowden, the Labour Shadow Chancellor of the Exchequer. In the debate on the return to gold in 1925, the official Labour motion merely criticised the "undue precipitancy" of the decision; and even this mild criticism was weakened by the fact that Snowden had written an article for *The Observer* a few weeks prior to the debate favouring return. As Chancellor, Snowden fully accepted the views of Norman and his Treasury advisers on monetary questions; he considered that these matters were best left to an inner circle:

[1] W. Layton et. al., *Is Unemployment Inevitable?* (1924).
[2] As reported by P. J. Grigg, *op. cit.*, p. 183.
[3] *New Statesman*, Sept. 17th, 1932.

". . . in the control of credit and currency, the administration of the control must be kept free from political influences. I will tell you why. In the first place Parliament is not a competent body to deal with the administration of such highly delicate and intricate matters. The second argument is this, that I have seen and I know something of the danger of the control of credit and the means of starting an inflation policy, and it might be highly dangerous in the hands of a Government that wanted to use this means in order to serve some purpose, or to gain popular support."[1]

It became his custom to deliver rather patronising homilies at the Labour Party's Annual Conferences on the "necessities" imposed by higher monetary considerations. There is a good deal of truth in the view that, like any nationalised industry, the day-to-day operations of the Bank of England must be kept free from political interference; but there is little doubt that acceptance of the aims imposed by the gold standard led to an evasion of responsibility for overall direction as well. Thus we find Norman before the Macmillan Committee claiming that the domestic consequences of monetary policy were not part of his responsibilities, and Snowden denying at much the same time that he had any responsibility for changes in Bank Rate. This is typical of the kind of fatalism and confusion of responsibility and purpose that infected every aspect of British economic policy in the 'twenties.

---

[1] *Report of the 29th Annual Conference of the Labour Party* (1929), pp. 227-8.

# CHAPTER SIX

# Unemployment and Public Spending in Britain During the 'Twenties

As a result of the return to gold, the monetary weapons at the dis-posal of British governments in the 'twenties were mainly committed in support of a single policy aim, namely external stability. Leaving aside the difficult question of whether an intelligent use of monetary policy along the lines suggested by Keynes would have prevented unemployment from being as severe as it was, there remains the problem of assessing the rationale and merits of the policies actually adopted to deal with unemployment in this period. What light do they shed on the characteristics of official economic thinking, and what alternatives were proposed? More especially, why was public spending and the power of the budget not used more purposefully to influence the domestic level of output and employment? The answer, of course, is that general fiscal policy—effecting changes in the level of economic activity by manipulating the relationship between government expenditures and revenues—is largely a post-Keynesian construction. It was in this period that Keynes began the work of construction. By examining the debates of this period it is possible to see how the modern concept of fiscal policy developed in its early stages, and what intellectual and political obstacles it had to overcome.

One of the main obstacles to the use of the budget as a tool of management in the inter-war period was the orthodox attachment, on economic, political and moral grounds, to the idea of achieving an annual balance between government revenue and expenditure, regardless of the state of the economy. We now recognise that conscious variation in the relationship of expenditures and revenues provides one of the most effective weapons in the armoury of the modern state for dealing with the kind of problems which existed in the inter-war period. Moreover, we understand that changes in any item of expenditure on current or capital account, every tax, subsidy, loan, pension or benefit paid out or received by the government, can be made to serve the cause of economic management. The recog-nition that these fiscal powers exist, and the understanding required to make proper economic use of them, has come slowly and sometimes painfully. Although several generations of economists had devoted attention to the problems of public finance, before the First World War very little progress had been made towards the kind of understanding required to operate fiscal policy. In the nineteenth century this can partly be explained by the relatively small share of the national product which passed through the government's hands. Nevertheless, the practice of paying little attention to the effects of budgetary changes on the state of the economy was continued far beyond the point at which the budget had become quantitatively significant as an influence. This was less true on the taxation and revenue side of the account, but even here the problem was seen mainly as one involving the incidence of taxes and their equitable distribution among citizens.

Mass unemployment in the inter-war period provided the necessary spur for this work to be undertaken. Increasingly the question was asked: What can the government do by way of public expenditure to alleviate or cure unemployment? The early stages of post-war debate on this question turned on various public works proposals of a relief or contra-cyclical kind derived from the pre-war discussions and experience of unemployment. But side by side with these older types of proposal there developed a more radical view that the state should not merely alleviate distress or offset fluctuatings in private economic activity, but should eliminate fluctuations and the causes of stagnation at their source by using its expenditure and taxation powers to control the level of investment and employment. By the end of the 'twenties some of the first steps towards this new interpretation of the economic responsibilities of the state had been taken.

Although this chapter is entirely taken up, as was the last, with British discussions, it is not without significance for other countries. In the matter of unemployment insurance, for example, Britain was the envy of many other countries, including those, like Sweden, which later became "model" welfare states themselves. And since many British problems were similar to those experienced later by other countries, notably the United States in the 'thirties, the British discussions of the 'twenties anticipated those which took place elsewhere. The advocates of public spending policies, for example, faced similar opposition from orthodoxy everywhere; and it was from the British literature on this subject that many abroad took their answers.

### Budgetary Policy in the 'Twenties: Precepts and Problems

The years between the wars comprise a difficult transitional period in the history of government finances. For British governments the period of greatest difficulty came in the period before 1931. Inherited precept became more difficult to follow, but new guide lines for the conduct of policy had either not been fully worked out or proved unacceptable to politicians. As a result, stated intention and deed frequently diverged from one another. And though a retreat from established principle was made under pressure of circumstances, it was often covered up by elaborate and sometimes damaging concessions to old forms and ideas.

The overriding aim of nineteenth century Chancellors of the Exchequer, following in the footsteps of Peel and Gladstone, was to achieve an annually balanced budget, with some preference, where possible, in favour of a surplus for purposes of debt-retirement or tax-reduction. As a further constraint it was argued that the overall size of the budget should be kept at a minimum. Under nineteenth-century conditions, particularly during periods of rapid economic growth, these precepts could be justified on technical and economic grounds. Annual balance, together with some allowance for a surplus, served a useful purpose at a time when methods of accountability control and budget estimation were in their infancy.[1] At the same time, preference in favour of a surplus for use in reducing taxes or outstanding debt did little harm, and possibly some good, while the economy was expanding rapidly. Towards the end of the nineteenth century, as a result of the experience of trade cycles, there was some recognition of the dangers of making a rigid annual commitment to debt-retirement, and of raising taxes during depressions. There was also a distinct weakening in the doctrine of retrenchment for retrench-ment's sake as the revenue possibilities of the progressive income tax were realised, expenditure on defence increased, and new social and redistributive responsibilities were undertaken by the central government.

During the First World War total government expenditure as a percentage of gross national product leapt from its pre-war figure of just over 12% to 51% in 1918. After the war it fell rapidly, but remained well above the pre-war figure for the whole of the inter-war period, fluctuating between 24% and 29%.[2] Post-war governments exercised a far greater claim on community resources than before the war; they possessed, therefore, greater potential powers of leverage on national income and output.

To appreciate the problems faced by Chancellors in the 'twenties, it is necessary to examine the composition of the central government's budget in this period. The most striking feature, undoubtedly, was

---

[1] See U. K. Hicks, *British Public Finances, 1880-1952* (1958), Ch. V.
[2] A.T. Peacock and J. Wiseman, *The Growth of Public Expenditure in the U.K.* (1961). Most of the figures cited here are taken from this book unless otherwise stated.

the growth in the proportion of the budget devoted to interest payments on the National Debt. The First World War was financed by government borrowing to a much greater extent than the second. Annual interest payments on the National Debt rose from under £20 million in 1913 to £325 million in 1920; they remained around £300 million until the conversion operations of 1932. As a percentage of central government expenditure at current prices, interest payments rose from 11% in 1913 to 24% in 1920, rising steadily to over 40% by the latter half of the 'twenties. After the Second World War the equivalent figure was around 14%. As a percentage of gross national product at current prices, they rose from under 1% in 1913 to 5.4% in 1920, reaching a peak of over 7% by 1930. After the Second World War, despite the vast increase in the size of the debt, the equivalent figure settled around 4%. This was largely due to wiser methods of war-financing, to cheap money policies, and to post-war inflation. Throughout the 'twenties, however, high interest rates and the downward trend of prices tended to increase the real burden of the national debt on the budget and on taxpayers.

In the absence of accurate figures relating to the ownership of the National Debt and the incidence of the tax system on different classes of taxpayer, it is difficult to say anything precise about the redistributive effects of interest payments.[1] They were widely regarded as acting in an "adverse" direction, redistributing income from the "productive" members of the community towards the *rentier* classes, and thereby exerting a depressing influence on the level of economic activity. On this matter critics from the left and right tended to converge. Those on the left saw nothing wrong with higher taxes in themselves—so long as they hit the rich hardest—but they felt that the revenue taken up by interest payments could be better, and more justly, directed towards the social services. Those on the right saw the burden of the National Debt in terms of the higher taxes which interest payments necessitated.

The most serious depressing effect of the National Debt in this period, however, lay in the Treasury's response to its existence. A premium was placed on annual provision for debt retirement. It encouraged Treasury opposition to further government borrowing, which would, they believed, raise interest rates and make debt conversion more difficult. By the same token, of course, it strengthened the case for economy in current expenditure.

Interest on the National Debt was not the only new or enlarged charge on the budget of the central government. After the war there was an increase in expenditure on such social services as education, housing subsidies, old age and widows' pensions, health and unem-

---

[1] See, however, E. Nevin, *The Problem of National Debt* (1954), esp. pp. 53-5.

D

ployment benefits. The tendency for expenditure on unemployment
to grow will be considered in the next section of this chapter; it was
to be the source of many of the most troublesome political and
budgetary problems in this period. The same applies in lesser
degree to the whole category of expenditure on the social services.
What bothered contemporary observers most about this category
was the fact that it represented a quasi-permanent or continuing
charge on the Exchequer which was particularly difficult to control
or liquidate. Fears on this score were heightened by a tendency to
regard such expenditure not as a form of investment in human
capital, but as largely uncompensated current outgoing, justifiable
perhaps on political and humanitarian grounds, but constituting a
dangerously open-ended commitment on the part of the state,
especially during conditions of financial stringency. This negative
attitude to the social services carried more weight at a time when
the state's finances were thought of as being analogous with those
of an individual or private firm. The classic expression of this
feature of contemporary thinking can be found in the Report of the
Committee of National Expenditure (the May Committee) in 1931:

> "So heavily loaded are the dice in favour of expenditure that no
> representation we can make is more important than to emphasise
> the need for caution in undertaking any commitments of a con-
> tinuing character. . . . The cause is not far to seek. After the heavy
> sacrifices of the war large sections of the nation looked to the
> post-war period with the natural expectation of a general improve-
> ment in the old conditions of life. . . . Had we still been living in
> the pre-war period of growing prosperity and rising revenue, with
> national taxation absorbing but a comparatively small part of
> the annual income of the people, such a development in the
> working of our political machinery, though undesirable at any
> time, might not have had serious reactions. . . . Far different has
> been the post-war position with its unprecedented trade stagna-
> tion, heavy unemployment, falling price level, and declining
> incomes under a system of taxation which appropriates year by
> year an unduly large proportion of national income."[1]

Chancellors in the 'twenties found themselves in a peculiarly difficult position. A large proportion of their revenue resources was firmly
committed to interest payments on the National Debt. Added to
this was the strain imposed by the extended social services, which
exhibited an alarming tendency to grow when ordinary sources of
revenue were less fruitful. In addition to the technical problems
associated with the management of the Debt, Chancellors in this

[1] *Report of the Committee on National Expenditure* (1931), Cmd. 3920, pp. 12-13.

period became obsessed with two main problems: the need to make provision for debt-retirement, and the need to find ways of reducing the level of total expenditure. They were not entirely successful on either front, but the attempt, together with the requirement of presenting in April of each year an account which was supposedly balanced out of current revenue, explains why many of the activities of the government in its efforts to deal with unemployment were timid and at cross-purposes with one another.

On the surface at least considerable progress was made. Central government expenditure fell from its war-time peak of over £2,287 million to £1,029 million in 1921; it continued to fall slowly and irregularly throughout the 'twenties, only rising again during the years of world depression.[1] After a succession of war and immediate post-war years in which large budget deficits were incurred, a heroic effort was made to get back to pre-war practice: a deficit of over £300 million in 1920 was turned into a surplus of over £200 million in 1921. Nominal budget surpluses for the purposes of debt-retirement were declared in every year between 1921 and 1929.[2] It was possible for the Excess Profits Duty to be abolished in 1921, and for income tax to be reduced in 1922–3 and 1925. The arbitrary nature of the expedients employed by Churchill in presenting the accounts in years between 1925 and 1929 makes it virtually impossible to reach any firm conclusion as to the impact of budgetary policy on the economy in this period. The accepted interpretation seems to be that in the years prior to the return to gold, fiscal policy acted as a deflationary influence. This was the period in which the most drastic cuts were made in government expenditure, acting largely on the advice of the Geddes Committee appointed in 1921. After 1925 the emphasis was reversed.[3] One expert has said of this period that "an unequalled ingenuity was displayed in producing a balanced budget out of what was on any reasonable reckoning a deficit".[4]

It may be worth noting some of the difficulties involved in reaching any definite conclusions as to the final outcome, reflationary or deflationary, of budgetary policy in this period. Even if the figures showing a balanced budget represented "true" items of current expenditure and revenue, it would be impossible to answer this question without detailed information as to how the balance was arrived at. A balance achieved, for example, by reducing expenditure

[1] See A. T. Peacock and J. Wiseman, *op. cit.* Table A.20. The trend is the same in real and monetary terms.
[2] See figures compiled by K. J. Hancock, "The Reduction of Unemployment as a Problem of Public Policy, 1920-29", *Economic History Review*, Dec. 1962, pp. 328-343.
[3] See U.K. Hicks, *The Finance of British Government 1920-1936* (1938), pp. 4-7; S. Pollard, *The Development of the British Economy, 1914-1950* (1962), pp. 210-12.
[4] U.K. Hicks, *British Public Finances*, p. 151.

and increasing taxes would tend to be deflationary, whereas an increase in expenditure together with a reduction of taxes could be reflationary. In any event, a priori reasoning would merely indicate the possible *direction* of influence; it would not tell us anything about the quantitative result.[1] A further complication is that in order to gauge the results of fiscal action by the central government, it would be necessary to consider the state of various extra-budgetary accounts like the Road Fund and the Unemployment Insurance Fund, and the extent to which increases in central government expenditure were offset by reductions in local authority spending. Neither of these factors can be dismissed at a time when the need to keep up the appearance of "sound finance" gave Chancellors the incentive to "juggle" with the extra-budgetary accounts. There is also good evidence to suggest that the central government thrust extra burdens on local authorities in order to relieve the Exchequer.[2] As one group of reformers pointed out at the time: "We should consider a private enterprise which showed its accounts in this shape as unbusinesslike and unsound."[3] The point of all this is that if it is only possible to reach conclusions on this vital question by means of econometric techniques which have only recently been applied to public finance, it is hardly surprising that by modern standards fiscal policy was confused and contradictory. The unfortunate aspect of this was that to a large extent these contradictions were visited upon the unemployed.

### Unemployment Insurance

As in the case of monetary policy, the public attitude towards the state's responsibilities in dealing with unemployment in the immediate post-war period was shaped by pre-war experience. The basic machinery—labour exchanges, unemployment insurance, and public works—was inherited from the pre-war Liberal legislation. The labour exchanges had proved valuable as a means of mobilising labour for the war effort and had therefore emerged greatly strengthened. The modest system of unemployment insurance of the pre-war period was improved and made more comprehensive by the Unemployment Insurance Act of 1920 which extended coverage to nearly 12 million workers.

The contributory insurance principle was designed to cope with seasonal and cyclical unemployment; good times alternating with bad. The actuarial basis of the post-war scheme was provided by

---

[1] Thus it would seem that apparently simple assertions like that made by W. Ashworth (*Economic History of England 1870-1939* (1960), p. 389) that "fiscal policy [under Churchill] was *slightly* inflationary" conceal powerful, and unsupported, quantitative judgments.
[2] See U.K. Hicks, *The Finance of British Government*, pp. 153-5.
[3] *Britain's Industrial Future*, Report of the Liberal Enquiry (1928), pp. 418-25.

pre-war figures which appeared to suggest that the average or "normal" level of unemployment was around 4 to 5 per cent of the working population. As one of its champions said:

> "The 1920 scheme was an endeavour to carry on and apply to all industrial workers the scientific theory of unemployment insurance which prevailed in the years 1909–14. The theory was that a certain minimum of unavoidable unemployment would always be created by the fluctuations and transitions of industry. Spells of worklessness might be short, but they were to be expected by all workers. Thus the risks would, on the whole, be fairly evenly spread."[1]

By present-day standards of welfare provision and social justice, the unemployment insurance schemes of the 'twenties might be regarded as rather conservative. Their underlying rationale was one of state-help-for-self-help, with the government acting as promoter, umpire, and, as it turned out, long-stop, in a system whereby employed workers and their employers (at least those who were unable to pass the increase in their costs onto the consumer) contributed to a revolving fund for the support of the unemployed. By the standards of the day a scheme which covered such a large proportion of the work-force, and extended benefits as of right rather than according to need, placed Britain in the van of progress in this field. The scheme was a peculiarly English mixture of paternalism, individualism, and "fair play", all interpreted within the given class context of English society.[2] At the end of the war this mixture was given all-party support. Cracks in the façade appeared later.

The economic circumstances of the 'twenties prevented the scheme from working as intended by its founders. Before the insurance fund had a chance to accumulate reserves the post-war boom collapsed; unemployment rose to the unprecedented height of 17% of the insured population in 1921, and during the coal strike of that year actually reached 23%. No respite was given in the following years when aggregate unemployment fluctuated around 10%. In the depressed staple industries, and in the regions where these were concentrated, unemployment was much higher and lasted for longer periods; in 1921, for example, 36% of the workers in shipbuilding and iron and steel, and 27% in engineering, were unemployed. As a result, the actuarial basis of the scheme was undermined, and numerous expedients were required—the chief one being massive Treasury support—to prop the system up.

[1] R. C. Davison, *The Unemployed* (1929), p. 99.
[2] For comment on these features of the scheme, see W. G. Runciman, *Relative Deprivation and Social Justice* (1966), pp. 69-71.

The present-day approach to increased expenditure on unemployment benefit in time of depression would recognise it as a stabilising
device, preventing incomes and spending from falling as drastically
as they would in its absence. Some contemporary commentators
noticed this feature of expenditure on unemployment, but they were
few and far between.[1] They were certainly not influential enough
to prevent governments from becoming worried by the increase in
their outlay under this heading as depression deepened. Most
contemporary discussion of unemployment insurance turned on the
question of the various incidental effects on the nation's finances,
and on the unemployed themselves of the Treasury contributions
to the hard-pressed unemployment fund; and of the changes in
contributions, benefits, and conditions of eligibility, necessitated by
the situation.

There were those, like Professor Edwin Cannan of the London
School of Economics, who felt that the insurance principle was
totally inapplicable to unemployment: "Wherever an evil can be
increased by human slackness or carelessness, insurance against that
evil tends to increase it."[2] On these harsh grounds, reminiscent of
those used in the nineteenth century to support the 1834 Poor Law,
he proposed a reduction in the eligibility rules. While this may
have been an extreme view, there were many who supported the
related position that the existence of unemployment insurance
benefits, claimable as of right, hindered the mobility of labour, and
tended to stiffen the resistance of organised labour to the wage-cuts
which many considered essential to the structural readjustment of
the British economy.[3] There is little doubt that unemployment
benefits frequently encouraged employers to organise the available
work in such a way that it was spread over a large number of workers;
short work was made more acceptable to the individual worker
because he received unemployment benefit in the off-period.[4] The
trade union movement was aware of many of these anomalies, but,
in the absence of any alternative, preferred to keep the existing
system rather than accept the kind of changes proposed by some
Conservatives and Liberals, which entailed placing the insurance
scheme on a fully self-supporting basis and reducing the contribution
made by the general taxpayer.[5]

The anomalies arose out of the difficulties of operating a scheme

---

[1] See *Royal Commission on Unemployment Insurance, Final Report* (1932), Cmd. 418, p. 103;
see also Keynes's remarks quoted p. 130 below.
[2] "The Problem of Unemployment", *Economic Journal*, March 1930, pp. 45-55.
[3] See e.g. H. Clay *The Post-War Unemployment Problem* (1929), pp. 117-8; and A. C. Pigou's
evidence before the Macmillan Committee, *Minutes of Evidence*, Qq. 5976 and 6070.
[4] See the *Final Report of the Royal Commission on Unemployment Insurance* (1932), pp. 98-105
for an analysis of "reactions on employment of state provisions for unemployment".
[5] See A. Bullock, *The Life and Times of Ernest Bevin* (1960), Vol. I, p. 463.

designed to deal with occasional or cyclical unemployment under conditions of chronic unemployment. Until a proper remedy could be found for persistent unemployment, much of the discussion of whether and how to preserve the insurance façade was bound to be futile. The expedients employed could not conceal the fact that to all intents and purposes the state was no longer in the insurance business but was acting as a relief agency.

One of the side-effects of the insurance scheme was that it yielded a great deal of regular information about unemployment. This may not have been as useful to the cause of the unemployed as might at first appear. Cannan advised a former pupil who became a member of the Labour Government in 1929 to stop publication of the figures.[1] Whatever Cannan's motives may have been, there is some truth in the view that the stream of monthly figures, always monotonously high, may have encouraged a helpless attitude rather than a sense of urgency: the unemployed, like the poor, are always with us. Over and above this conjecture, however, there is evidence to show that unemployment insurance encouraged complacency and fatalism by acting as a substitute for more active remedies: the good was enemy of the best.

The limitations of William Beveridge's views on insurance and the trade cycle have been mentioned earlier.[2] Similar attitudes persisted in the 'twenties. Thus we find one of the interpreters of the "new venture in scientific social legislation" arguing that: "Maintenance for all may be a right and a duty, but there are times and places when work for all cannot be provided without flying in the face of economics and sound statesmanship."[3] With such views went a tendency to believe that unemployment could only be *cured* by a drastic replacement of capitalism by wholesale nationalisation of the means of production. For those to whom such a solution was anathema, unemployment insurance became a kind of compensation paid to the working classes in return for being allowed to retain a system in which unemployment was unavoidable. There seems to have been an element of political insurance, by means of compensation for the differential impact of economic hardship, in the social legislation of this period.[4] On the left, for the opposite reasons, there was a tendency to believe that only palliatives could be implemented under the existing political and economic system. But if "work" for the unemployed was not likely to be forthcoming on a regular basis, and if socialism was still a dream, this left only "maintenance"

[1] Quoted in H. Clay, *Lord Norman* (1957), p. 168.
[2] See pp. 55-6 above.
[3] R. C. Davison, *The Unemployed* (1929), p. 60.
[4] For an explicit statement of this view, see H. Clay, "The Authoritarian Element in Distribution", *Economic Journal*, March 1927.

as the proximate goal of political and industrial action. From this point of view, it was not so much a case of the good being enemy of the best, as one of aiming so high that it was necessary to settle for much less. For a variety of reasons then, the essential middle-ground was left untilled.

## Contra-Cyclical Public Works

There were, however, those in the Labour movement who argued that more positive action should be taken by the state than was implied by insurance within the existing framework. The leading spokesmen for this group were Sydney Webb and later, with more insistence, G. D. H. Cole. Their position was based on the recommendations of the Minority Report of the Royal Commission on the Poor Laws of 1909 in favour of contra-cyclical public works. During the war Webb had said that Labour would press for the use of public works "to maintain a constant aggregate the total demand for labour" as part of its post-war reconstruction policy. This policy was endorsed later in the party's first post-war manifesto, *Labour and the New Social Order*.[1] From the trade union wing of the party, notably from Ernest Bevin, there was also some support for this approach.

The case was usually accompanied by an attack on the passive policy of the "dole". At best, maintenance should only be a stop-gap measure before work was provided. One reason why the government favoured maintenance rather than work, it was argued, arose out of a short-sighted belief in its relative cheapness. For those who believed in the effectiveness of public works policy this amounted to a charge that unemployment was the result of a deliberate decision.

Successive governments did in fact make use of public works schemes to supplement unemployment insurance and Poor Law relief, though they did so with gradually declining ardour and confidence. It is perhaps a significant omen that the inauguration of schemes to deal with the slump of 1920–1 more or less coincided with the campaign for economy in public expenditure which eventually led to the establishment of the Geddes Committee. All of the schemes entailed co-operation between the Treasury, or the separate Ministries, and local authorities. The work of co-ordination was performed by the Unemployment Grants Committee, whose job it was to give financial assistance in the form of grants, or by underwriting loans, for approved projects submitted by local authorities. The conditions attached to the assistance were: that unemployment had to be severe in the locality; that the work had to be of "real utility", and yet of a type

[1] See also *When Peace Comes: The Way of Industrial Reconstruction* (1916); and S. Webb, *Unemployment: A Labour Policy* (1921).

which would not have been undertaken without a grant; that the projects had to be of a labour-intensive kind employing genuinely unemployed labour at wage rates beneath the local market level.

These were, of course, the classic features of the relief work; and after two years the same kinds of criticisms that had been made in pre-war years were brought forward again: "They are uneconomical, suitable only for general unskilled labour, and calculated to impair rather than maintain the industrial quality of more skilled workers".[1] Moreover, the inducements to local authorities were considered not to be large enough; and since much of the expense had to be met by local authorities themselves, the authorities that were particularly hard-hit by depression were least likely to be able to take advantage of the system.

There are several reasons why recourse was had to a policy of relief works. Strangely enough, it accorded well with the economy campaign; it minimised the burden falling on the Exchequer, and required relatively little central government machinery or initiative. In the early post-war years there was also a disposition to believe that the slump was a temporary affair, conditional upon a revival of European and world trade. The maintenance of the system in the face of criticism from all sides was also attributed to political motives: "The grants became a kind of conscience money paid out by the central Government because it was properly sensitive to the reproach that it was laying impossible burdens on the shoulders of Local Government bodies."[2] A study by Keith Hancock of the contribution made by the Unemployment Grants Committee to the solution of the problem of unemployment in the period 1920 to 1928, estimates that it aided projects which supported 1% of the work force.[3]

After 1925, when it became clear that unemployment was not a temporary post-war phenomenon, the official attitude towards relief works hardened. One of the conditions for receiving a grant had been that the work should be in advance of future requirements; but as Hancock has pointed out, "stealing work from the future appeared to be less justified where there could be no confidence that the future could afford it".[4] Those who favoured contra-cyclical public works were equally vulnerable to this sort of criticism in spite of efforts to distinguish their schemes from the relief systems actually being used. They pointed out that relief schemes were hurriedly improvised; that they suffered from bad associations with task-work under the old Poor Law; that under a proper system men would be selected on grounds of suitability and skills; and that the schemes would be

[1] W. Layton et. al., *The Third Winter of Unemployment* (1921), p. 82.
[2] R. C. Davison, *The Unemployed*, p. 59.
[3] K. J. Hancock, *op. cit.*, p. 335.
[4] *Ibid.*, p. 336.

organised on a national rather than a local basis.[1] Nevertheless, all forms of public work had become associated in the public mind with simple relief measures.[2]

In the second half of the 'twenties the emphasis shifted away from cyclical interpretations and measures towards more thorough-going structuralist remedies—rationalisation, labour mobility, and wage- and cost-reduction. One sign of this shift was the Industrial Trans- ference Scheme started in 1928, the object of which was to aid the process of labour mobility from areas and trades with high unem- ployment. Apart from the inherent slowness of any such policy, there was the added drawback that many of the men moved were un- suitable for other work, which, in any case, was not easy to find in a generally stagnant environment. As we have seen in the previous chapter, the structuralist approach to unemployment in this period was generally accompanied by the view that there was limited scope for general reflationary measures by the government. The lasting solution to Britain's problems, it was claimed, would come through ordinary industrial channels. In so far as the state could make any contribution, it would be by reducing the tax burden and economis- ing in its expenditure. The Bank of England could act as sponsor to rationalisation schemes, but the state should ensure that its assistance to capital projects was confined to those likely to prove remunerative in the ordinary commercial sense.

Within the space of a few years, therefore, both relief and contra- cyclical public works had been discredited, and the Treasury was enunciating the view for which it later became infamous. In answer to a questionnaire on public work policies sent by the International Labour Office in 1927 the following reply was given:

"The decision taken by the Government at the end of 1925 to restrict grants for relief schemes was based mainly on the view that, the supply of capital in this country being limited, it was undesirable to divert any appreciable proportion of this supply from normal trade channels."[3]

This innocent statement contains a far more fundamental objection to public works policies than any of the administrative criticisms mentioned so far. It was against this view that new advocates of public spending as a remedy for unemployment were forced to contend.

[1] G. D. H. Cole, *The Next Ten Years in British Social and Economic Policy* (1929), pp. 66-7; A. L. Bowley in W. Layton, et. al. *Is Unemployment Inevitable?* (1924), p. 372.
[2] See e.g. *Final Report of the Committee on Industry and Trade* (1929), Cmd. 3282, p. 136.
[3] I.L.O., *Unemployment and Public Works* (1931), p. 30.

## Keynes and Lloyd George

In spite of the Liberal decline in the country at large in this period, the party continued to provide a forum for many intellectuals and public-spirited men who found the other parties either too doctrinaire or too dominated by sectional interest. By 1924, one group of Liberals under the chairmanship of Walter Layton had already produced important surveys of the nature and incidence of unemployment.[1] It was from another Liberal group, with some overlap in its membership but with an infusion of younger minds under the intellectual leadership of Keynes, that some of the most interesting and advanced ideas for dealing with the post-war economic situation emerged. By means of a series of Liberal Summer Schools beginning in 1923, and through the pages of their organ, *The Nation and Athenaeum*, this group attempted to alter the focus of liberalism. They formulated a "forward" but pragmatic political philosophy of state intervention in economic affairs, which attempted to steer a course between *laissez-faire* individualism and collectivism.[2]

Keynes' first important contribution to the discussion of remedies for unemployment came in May 1924, in the form of an article for *The Nation* with the rhetorical title, "Does Unemployment Need a Drastic Remedy?". In this article he came out decisively in favour of proposals made by Lloyd George for a large-scale public investment programme. Up to this point Keynes had mainly been concerned with the connection between the gold standard, monetary deflation and unemployment. He still considered deflation to be a potent cause and was to return to this theme when the gold standard was re-established in the following year; but at this juncture he considered that the worst effects of deflation had worked themselves out. The British economic machine had "stuck in a rut"; it needed a jolt. In the nineteenth century Britain had enjoyed cumulative prosperity as a result of investment in railways; in the United States, a boom was currently under way based on high investment in the motor and construction industries. Keynes had little faith in structuralist or deflationary remedies which entailed forcing workers out of depressed industries by depressing wages: "Rather we must seek to submerge the rocks in a rising sea—not forcing labour out of what is depressed, but attracting it into what is prosperous." The confidence required to bring about a revival of private investment activity was lacking; savings were "drifting abroad to destinations from which we as a society shall gain the least advantage". To provide outlets for these

---

[1] *The Third Winter of Unemployment* (1922), and *Is Unemployment Inevitable?* (1924)
[2] For fuller accounts of the activities of this group see R. F. Harrod, *Life of Keynes* (1951) pp. 331-8, 392-6; and A. Briggs, *Seebohm Rowntree* (1961), Ch. VII.

savings at home, and to restore confidence, the Treasury should use the Sinking Fund productively by promoting public investment in road-building and electricity-generation projects, which private enterprise was incapable of undertaking.

These proposals went beyond the then familiar case for contra-cyclical public works. They demanded an increase in public investment not simply to compensate for fluctuations in private investment, but to start a cumulative upward movement. Like his arguments in favour of a managed currency, Keynes's views ran counter to orthodox opinion at several points. He had offended the upholders of "responsible" finance by suggesting that the Sinking Fund should be "raided" to the tune of £10 million; and by implying that the normal market process was incapable of allocating savings between home and foreign investment in accordance with national advantage.[1] He had cast doubt not only on the beneficence of free market forces and the capacity of private enterprise to respond to them, but also on the traditional linkage between British exports and her foreign investments. He charged that British institutions and legislation favoured the export of capital at the expense of worth-while domestic projects.[2]

The political implications of these new economic priorities were spelled out in more detail by Keynes in lectures entitled *The End of Laissez-Faire* given in the same year. Marshall's "captain of industry" had become a "tarnished idol"; the significant developments in the industrial field lay in the growth of large joint-stock corporations, with their divorce of control from ownership and semi-public character. Keynes rejected state socialism as "little better than a dusty survival of a plan to meet the problem of fifty years ago", in favour of experimenting with the semi-autonomous public corporation. In addition to drawing attention to these new types of industrial organisation, he proposed that the state should undertake the co-ordination and direction of the community's saving and investment decisions.[3]

The position outlined by Keynes in these lectures was to provide the theme for the Liberal Industrial Inquiry undertaken in the latter half of the 'twenties. This eventually resulted in the publication of *Britain's Industrial Future* (1928), better known as the Liberal "Yellow Book". The "Yellow Book" contained proposals covering the whole field of industrial and economic policy; but at the heart of what has been described as a blueprint for a British "New Deal" lay the

[1] A selection of criticisms together with Keynes's reply appeared in *The Nation*, May 31st and June 7th, 1924.
[2] See *The Nation*, Aug. 9th, 1924.
[3] The economic rationale of these proposals will be considered in a later chapter, see pp. 155-6 below.

recommendations for a "vigorous policy of national reconstruction and development", the financing of which was to be made the responsibility of a National Investment Board. A policy of greatly increased public investment in roads, housing, electricity, waterways, telephones and agriculture was to be directed towards removing the "abnormal unemployment of a quasi-permanent character" that had developed since the war.

This programme, with its emphasis on the mobilisation of national rather than local resources to deal with exceptional rather than cyclical or frictional unemployment, marked a clear step forward on earlier relief and contra-cyclical public works proposals. It was from this part of the "Yellow Book" that Lloyd George mainly drew his election manifesto *We Can Conquer Unemployment* in 1929. For the first time a major political party was proposing to treat unemployment on a scale and in a manner comparable to war. An Economic General Staff was to be created "to mobilise for prosperity". Each year, for three years, £100 million was to be spent on capital expenditure, which, it was claimed, would eventually provide employment for one and a half million workers. The budget was to be divided between capital and revenue accounts in order to prevent temporary embarrassments on revenue account from standing in the way of capital expenditure. Unemployment was to be looked upon not as a misfortune to be tempered by piece-meal expedients, but as an opportunity to modernise Britain.

### The Treasury View

The official Treasury position on public works as a solution to unemployment in the latter half of the 'twenties was one of growing coolness. By 1929 coolness had hardened into the dogma known as the "Treasury View". The classic statement of this view was given by Churchill in his budget speech of the same year.

> "It is orthodox Treasury dogma, steadfastly held, that whatever might be the political or social advantages, very little additional employment can, in fact, and as a general rule, be created by State borrowing and expenditure."[1]

The Treasury view can be shown to have roots going back as far as Ricardo and possibly earlier. But the important point to note is that in the 'twenties there was very little opposition from professional economists to public works policies, certainly none as fundamentalist

[1] *House of Commons Debates*, April 15th, 1929, 54.

as the Churchill statement implies.[1] As first enunciated, the official view was hardly a model of clarity or consistency. Hancock has pointed out, for example, that official spokesmen apparently found no difficulty in combining the view that *no* net increase in employment could be achieved, with the contradictory position that public works merely increase employment now at the expense of the future.[2] When so much ingenuity is used to support inaction, it is to be suspected that the true grounds for opposition lie hidden deeper.

The "Treasury View" was given its most extensive airing during the election campaign of 1929, and before the Macmillan Committee in the following year. At Baldwin's request, a White Paper criticising the Liberal programme was published in which several Ministers defended their records with regard to capital expenditure on the services for which they were responsible.[3] The heart of the White Paper lay in Memorandum prepared by the Treasury on the effects of a development loan programme. The document comprises a rag-bag of objections to public works which give the impression of proving too much. An expansion of public works, it was claimed, would "disturb" the general industrial situation by drawing off labour from "normal industry", by hindering transference from depressed areas, and by discouraging private enterprise. Increased government borrowing would either be inflationary or lead to a rise of interest rates, thereby diverting savings from home enterprise or foreign ventures. The real remedy for unemployment was to be found in the reduction of wages and costs, greater industrial efficiency, and rationalisation. Public works would hinder such remedies, and lead to a deterioration in the balance of payments. The ultimate test of schemes for increasing government expenditure financed by borrowing was whether they would "yield an economic return on capital outlay".

These arguments had been anticipated by Keynes and H. D. Henderson in a pamphlet entitled "Can Lloyd George Do It?" The argument that there was a fixed and fully employed lump of capital in existence at any given time, such that increases in any direction implied diversion from "normal" channels, went too far: if true, it was a valid objection to any "new business enterprise entailing capital expenditure" as well as government spending.[4]

---

[1] The theoretical merits and financial soundness of public works proposals had been discussed before the war; see p. 57 above and the references to Pigou, Hawtrey and Robertson in T. W. Hutchison, *Review of Economic Doctrines, 1870-1929* (1953), pp. 416-7. The discussion was taken up again after the war with Hawtrey once more emerging as the only leading sceptic on the subject; see his "Public Expenditure and the Demand for Labour", *Economica*, March 1925.

[2] *Op. cit.*, pp. 336-7.

[3] *Memoranda on Certain Proposals Relating to Unemployment* (1929), Cmd. 3331.

[4] *Op. cit.*, as reprinted in *Essays in Persuasion*, p. 121.

They insisted that instead of diversion from alternative uses a number of additional "savings" would be made, the most obvious of which was that on unemployment pay. In his review of the Treasury memorandum, Keynes repeated some of these arguments and embellished others. Not only would there be a saving on the dole, but the Exchequer would recoup about an eighth of its outlay through the resulting increase in national income and tax yields; a proportion of the original capital expenditure would go to business profits, and would therefore be saved. A large part of the wages of those directly employed on public works would provide indirect employment to others in the consumption-goods industries; these secondary repercussions "though not precisely calculable, are substantial". There might also be some reduction of foreign lending, but Keynes did not believe that this would materially affect British exports.

The appearance of Sir Richard Hopkins, Controller of the Finance and Supply Department at the Treasury, before the Macmillan Committee in 1930 gave Keynes another opportunity to criticise the Treasury position on capital expenditure. Hopkins began by saying that the official view had been misunderstood; they were not opposed to public works in principle but merely to the Liberal schemes in practice. After detailing some of the difficulties involved in planning and carrying out large schemes of capital expenditure, he added that there was likely to be an adverse public reaction to the additional bureaucracy created by the increase in state intervention. This argument clearly indicates the bias in favour of the political and economic *status quo* which lurks behind the Treasury position.[1] Hopkins also argued that public works schemes would raise rates of interest and lead to "despondency on the part of general business"; that they would raise prices in Britain in relation to foreign competitors, thereby damaging the export trades; that, by raising the demand for resources engaged in particular capital goods industries like road-building, they would lead to "a singularly lop-sided form of prosperity, and one which could not possibly be permanent".

Hopkins succeeded in convincing the Committee that the Treasury was not implacably opposed to all schemes of capital development as a means of reducing unemployment. The real problem, as he saw it, was to find worthwhile projects to support. The differences between the Treasury and Keynes on this matter derived from the narrowness of the criteria used by the Treasury in calculating the costs and benefits of capital expenditure. Keynes was able to exploit Hopkins' inconsistencies to the full and to obtain damaging

[1] Ernest Bevin thought that such considerations did not fall properly within the province of the official adviser; See *Minutes of Evidence*, Vol. II, Qq. 5574-6.

admissions of what amounts to fatalism. What constitutes a worth-while scheme? It would have to be "economically justifiable" and not seem "silly to public opinion". How was this to be proved when both "good" and "bad" schemes helped to relieve unemploy-ment? At this point Hopkins sought refuge in the view which he had just repudiated: the capital has got to come from somewhere and "it does make a hole in the capital which is available for the pur-poses of the community". Do bad schemes make a bigger hole than good schemes? What in fact is a good scheme? Hopkins felt that a 4% return provided a bench-mark. Were 3% schemes incapable of reducing unemployment? At this point Hopkins asked for the Chairman's protection, but he eventually agreed that even schemes with zero % return in the ordinary commercial sense could reduce unemployment. In calculating the rate of return Hopkins accepted the view that the savings on the dole should be taken into account, but felt that the saving from the increased tax revenue produced by an expansionist policy would be "small and speculative".

The timidity of official thinking comes out most clearly in an exchange on the connection between capital investment and rising prices.

"Keynes: 'You take objection to the cure of unemployment on the grounds that it might have some effect on the raising of prices. . . .'

"Hopkins: 'I am sorry but my diagnosis is different. I should have thought that what we want is some tendency which will create a rise of prices throughout the world to begin with, excepting here, so that we may follow in its wake.'

"Keynes: 'You want all other countries to adopt plans which you wish to reject for your own?'

"Hopkins: 'Yes, that might serve.' "[1]

Hopkins succeeded in getting the Treasury out of a tight spot. Keynes admitted afterwards that the Treasury view had been "gravely misjudged". They had only themselves to blame for allow-ing this to happen. As it was, Hopkins left no doubt that the Treasury was totally unsympathetic to the kind of schemes being proposed by Keynes, and would take no initiative in furthering them. Hopkins was in a difficult position because the professional civil service had been dragged into the political fray by Baldwin and Churchill. But this should not have prevented him from putting up as good a case before the Macmillan Committee as he would have done within the Treasury. The real difficulty arose on an intellectual level. Keynes's case was novel; it required the use of theoretical arguments and terminology which were unfamiliar. But it is difficult to see how

[1] *Op. cit.*, Qq. 5637-40.

anyone reading the Keynes-Hopkins exchange today could agree with the Chairman's description of it as "a drawn battle".[1] It was certainly an inconclusive one.

In terms of economic analysis the difference between Keynes's position and the Treasury view was not easy to locate. An air of "ad hoc-ness" hung over both positions. Given the weakness of the British balance of payments, a fixed and overvalued exchange rate, and the monetary climate which these two conditions required, the Treasury view contained an element of truth. It was the familiar vicious circle of policy-making in the 'twenties: external pressures dictated a policy of monetary caution, which in turn restricted freedom to use "active" fiscal measures for fear of adding to external difficulties. The argument would have been less confused if the Treasury had been more frank in relying exclusively on this type of reasoning rather than on its forced position with regard to the effect of public works expenditure on the domestic situation. As Keynes pointed out, this argument would be sound only if full employment existed already.

As was true of the thinking which led to the restoration of the gold standard at pre-war parity, the difference between expansionists and contractionists was ultimately one of political priorities rather than economic analysis. The Treasury position gave lower priority to short-term solutions to the unemployment problem than to external stability and "sound finance". The deflationary bias of gold standard policies, and the exclusive reliance on palliatives like unemployment insurance, while waiting for long-term structural readjustments to take place, encouraged passivity towards acceptance of the level of employment as a responsibility of the state. The objections raised against additional state capital expenditure could be made against *all* active remedies for unemployment except wage-cuts. That logic alone did not determine the Treasury position is borne out by the fact that long after these objections had been met by argument and by altered circumstance, orthodoxy in matters of government expenditure remained the rule in Britain.

The last two chapters have been somewhat in the nature of a review of the troops; the personalities and issues reappear later in different combinations and circumstances. But the crucial test of the ideas so far mentioned came in the world depression which closed the decade. Britain's local difficulties were made more obdurate as she and other nations found themselves swept up in a tide of financial events which originated in the stock market crash that took place in the United States in September 1929.

[1] See, however, R. F. Harrod, *op. cit.*, p. 422.

# CHAPTER SEVEN

# The Political Economy of Crisis, 1929-1931

## The Nature of the Crisis

For the latter half of the 'twenties the United States, in common with most European countries, enjoyed boom conditions. Like most booms it can be seen in restrospect to have been a lop-sided affair. It was based to a considerable extent on an upsurge in investment activity in construction and manufacturing industry, financed by a peculiar combination of high profits together with stable prices and wages. The prosperity of the manufacturing sector was not shared by agriculture, which suffered a steady erosion of its relative position in terms of prices and incomes. The boom was accompanied by a marked increase in speculation which raised the paper value of financial assets to unprecedented heights. By mid-1929 there were signs of a falling-off in investment, but speculation on the New York Stock Exchange continued at a hectic rate for a few months longer. The collapse came in September, and within a matter of weeks the market value of most assets had either been liquidated or drastically reduced. This was to be the prelude to the longest and deepest slump in the history of the United States.[1] It brought with it the collapse of the system of international finance which had been so laboriously reconstructed since 1925.

The United States emerged at the end of the First World War as the leading creditor country. During the 'twenties there was a large outflow of funds from America directed chiefly towards European countries and Latin America. The main debtor countries were Germany and the primary producers, who had come to rely on regular dollar injections, frequently in the form of short-term credits, to maintain balance of payments equilibrium and to pay interest on previous borrowings. The first effect of the American speculative boom, and of the collapse which followed, was the repatriation and subsequent cessation of foreign investment. The American depression also rapidly accelerated the downward trend of world commodity prices. The initial impact of both these developments was felt on the periphery of the world financial and trading system by the primary producing countries; but the effects were soon communicated to Europe.

[1] See J. K. Galbraith, *The Great Crash* (1954).

The world depression affected Britain in her twin capacity as international trader and banker. The fall in world commodity prices, and the decline of international trade with increasing protection and the cessation of American foreign investment, reduced British exports and invisible receipts from shipping, interest, and dividends. The effect of this on the balance of payments was compensated to a large extent by the fall in the price of imports, and by a cut-back in British long-term foreign investment. As far as one can tell from the crude balance of payments statistics of the period, it was not until the first half of 1931 that a small net deficit on current account developed. A more rapid deterioration in the balance of trade took place in the latter half of the year as imports rose steeply in anticipation of possible future import restrictions. Yet Britain fared much better on this front than other countries. It was not so much from the normal trading and investment accounts, as from short-term financial movements, that international pressure was to come.[1]

The initial effect of the collapse of the American boom on London as a financial centre was not entirely unfavourable; it relieved some of the pressure which had built up during the latter stages of the speculative movement. Interest rates, which had risen sharply towards the end of 1929, were brought down to the lowest point achieved in the whole previous decade. Bank Rate reached $2\frac{1}{2}\%$ early in 1931 before rising sharply when the European scramble for liquidity finally reached London.

The earliest serious effects of world depression on Britain manifested themselves in the steady rise in the unemployment figures to over $2\frac{1}{2}$ million by 1931. It was cold comfort that conditions were much worse elsewhere. In the United States, for example, national income was halved; and the numbers unemployed remained between 6 and 10 million from 1930 to 1933, none of whom were supported, as in Britain, by unemployment insurance. In Germany too, unemployment was much more severe than in Britain. As the Macmillan Report pointed out in 1931, for those in employment the fall in the price of imported goods meant that "the general standard of consumption remained substantially unaffected, notwithstanding the economic depression".[2]

The depression was also reflected in a growing budget deficit caused by the tendency for revenues to fall faster than government outlay, and by the increase in borrowings from the Treasury to meet the deficit on the Unemployment Insurance Fund. Here again though, the budgetary situation was much worse in other countries.[3]

---

[1] See H. V. Hodgson, *Slump and Recovery, 1929-1937* (1938), pp. 80-1.
[2] *Op. cit.*, p. 7.
[3] Hodgson, *op. cit.*, p. 32.

It was the convergence and interaction of the domestic problems posed by the budgetary situation with the world liquidity crisis which led to the political upheaval in Britain in August 1931.

In May the Credit-Anstalt, a large Austrian bank with important domestic and foreign interests, ran into severe difficulties. A hurried support operation was mounted by the Austrian government and by the Bank of International Settlements aided by the Bank of England. The apparent success of this operation could not allay widespread fears for the safety of foreign assets. Efforts to liquidate such assets soon placed pressure on the German banking system. Once more an international rescue operation was required, which included central bank credits and an agreement on a year's moratorium on inter-governmental war debts and reparations. Internal political and economic difficulties in Germany arising out of the success of the National Socialist party at the elections, and the failure of an important industrial concern, the Nordwolle, led to domestic as well as external withdrawals. Drastic restrictive measures, including exchange control by the Reichsbank, were needed to stave off total collapse. By mid-July international pressure was switched to London, encouraged possibly by the revelation of the extent of Britain's short-term indebtedness in the Macmillan Report, published on July 14th. For two weeks the Bank of England suffered heavy gold losses, chiefly to Paris. To deal with the situation, credits were negotiated with the Bank of France and the Federal Reserve Board of New York.

At this juncture the report of the May Committee on the state of the nation's internal finances appeared. Its gloomy findings were given considerable prominence in the foreign and domestic press. By mid-August, with the previous line of credit practically exhausted, and many British assets immobilised in Central Europe, it was necessary for new foreign credits to be obtained to support the pound. The Labour Government was informed by foreign bankers that further assistance would only be forthcoming if a determined effort was made to balance the budget by cuts in expenditure along the lines suggested by the May Committee. Failure to agree on a definite course of action led to the breakup of the Labour Government and the formation of a National Government under MacDonald on August 24th. The tide was stemmed for a time; foreign credits were obtained and an emergency budget incorporating substantial cuts in government expenditure was introduced by Snowden on September 10th. But neither of these measures was able to prevent the further run on the pound which eventually forced Britain off the gold standard on September 21st.

## Preliminary Dispositions and Personalities

The British election fought in the spring of 1929, before the world depression had begun, was dominated by the unemployment question. All hope that it might prove to be a temporary phenomenon, attributable to post-war maladjustments, had evaporated long ago. America and Europe were enjoying boom conditions; the gold standard had restored exchange stability; world trade had revived. But Britain still seemed unable to take advantage of these improved conditions. Labour emerged from the election as the largest single party, but without an overall majority. When Ramsay MacDonald formed his second minority government in June, unemployment remained stubbornly around the million mark. Attention was focused on what by then was clearly recognised to be a problem peculiar to Britain. By the end of the year, however, the situation was radically transformed by the onset of world-wide depression.

It was ironic that the one party whose ultimate goal was the abolition of capitalism by parliamentary means should be in office during capitalism's greatest economic crisis. It is more ironic that the Labour Government should break up as a result of internal dissension over the appropriate methods of saving capitalism. The circumstances surrounding the fall of this government, the defection of the leaders, the atmosphere of conspiracy and betrayal, have given this episode a peculiar and haunting significance in Labour history and mythology. A Labour Government, with its claim to represent those hardest hit by the economic stagnation of the 'twenties, and later by the world depression, embodied hopes that did not attach to the other parties. The apparent inability to break away from the orthodox policies of its predecessors led to bitter disillusionment. But the misfortunes of the government should not be looked at entirely in Labour terms; their failures were also the outcome of the general state of economic understanding and opinion at the time.

The economic and financial causes of the depression and of the liquidity crisis have been examined exhaustively on many occasions. So, too, have the political events leading up to the fall of the Labour Government.[1] Here we shall mainly be concerned with the economic arguments employed by the decision-makers and their advisers. One very obvious point must be made at the outset: the Labour Government was extremely unfortunate to be overtaken by world depression. It would have been difficult for any government to emerge with credit from this unprecedented predicament. But if

---

[1] See especially R. Bassett, *Nineteen-Thirty-One; Political Crisis* (1950); and R. Milliband, *Parliamentary Socialism* (1961). More recently, a complete study has been made of the Labour Government's response to depression by R. Skidelsky, *Politicians and the Slump* (1967).

they were victims, they were certainly not helpless victims. Choices were forced upon them at every turn. Were these choices the right ones in the light of the situation as they saw it then, and as we now see it? Was an alternative course open to them at any stage—one which would have been both economically credible and politically feasible? Or is it a case of *tout comprendre, tout pardonner*?

The political economy of the crisis can only be understood against the background of the failure of successive governments to make any real impression on the unemployment problem *before* the world depression made its presence felt. One of the most interesting features of contemporary economic debate was the fact that policy alignments no longer corresponded in any simple way with the party divisions. Economic debate, and possibly policy, might have been clearer and more decisive if they had. Within each of the three major parties there was a minority in favour of new solutions of a much more activist kind than had hitherto been tried, but they did not succeed either in gaining access to power or in influencing their leaders. As remains true today, when in office the opposing parties accepted similar priorities and similar limitations.

The Conservative Party was not the sole or even the main repository of monetary and fiscal orthodoxy. Within the Conservative ranks there was a small but vocal group of critics of the general trend of policy. In the debates on the return to gold in 1925, Sir Alfred Mond (who claimed to speak for the Federation of British Industries) and Robert Boothby voiced doubts as to the wisdom of this course of action.[1] Dissatisfaction with their party's handling of economic affairs appears to have grown among the younger Tory back-benchers during the years of office between 1925 and 1929. Much of this centred on Baldwin's unwillingness to commit the party to a thorough-going programme of tariff protection and imperial preference. There was nothing particularly unorthodox in the ordinary Conservative businessman's advocacy of this solution. Quite the contrary. But there were others, like L. S. Amery for example, who not only criticised the deflationary policies associated with the gold standard, but argued for a general system of protection and imperial preference as a natural complement to an expansionary domestic policy.[2] A book produced by Boothby, Harold Macmillan and Oliver Stanley, *Industry and Trade* (1927), was notably cool towards *laissez-faire*, and urged a more *dirigiste* approach towards industry and employment.[3] It was probably with this group in mind

[1] Boothby remained an advocate of expansionist policies throughout the 'thirties; see *The New Economy* (1943).

[2] See L. S. Amery, *My Political Life* (1953), vol. II, pp. 480 ff.; Vol. III, pp. 30 ff., 48 ff.

[3] See H. Macmillan, *Winds of Change*, 1914-1939 (1966), pp. 222-4. Macmillan's dissent from his own party on economic questions is one of the themes of the whole book.

that Keynes said: "It is often no more than an accident of temperament or of past associations, and not a real difference of policy or of
ideals, which now separates the progressive young Conservative
from the average Liberal."[1]

As we have seen though, it was the Liberals who emerged in 1929
as the leading exponents of expansionist remedies in their election
manifesto, *We Can Conquer Unemployment*. The "new" Liberals produced a series of documents which together constituted a remarkable
blueprint for novel forms of partnership between the state and
industry. But they had temporarily captured the party, not converted
it; there were still many "old" Liberals in the party committed to
free trade and Gladstonian finance as if to a religion. In Parliament,
after an election result which finally put paid to their hopes of
forming a government again, they showed themselves to be totally
disunited, and, in the end, inclined towards orthodoxy.[2]

Lloyd George, however, continued to press for bolder schemes of
public works expenditure. In response to MacDonald's invitation to
a three-party conference on unemployment and the economic situation in 1930, the Liberals produced a rehash of their election
programme under the title, *How to Tackle Unemployment*. Significantly,
however, this pamphlet also contained some warning comments on the
growing strain of the social services on the budget, and called for the
setting-up of a new committee on national expenditure along
Geddes lines to explore ways in which current expenditure could be
cut.[3] It is illustrative of the confusion of economic thought on this
matter at the time, that one of the documents sometimes thought
of as being most progressive in its advocacy of public works should
also have suggested the setting up of the May Committee, whose
report became the symbol of orthodox finance in 1931.

In their manifesto, *Labour and the Nation*, the Labour Party made
an "unqualified pledge to deal immediately and practically" with
unemployment. This document, largely the work of R. H. Tawney,
was strong on moral rhetoric, but weaker on practical remedies than
the Liberal manifesto. The Labour manifesto stood firmly against
the extension of the "dole", but insisted that "as long as the nation
chooses to maintain an economic system by which unemployment is
produced, the weight must not be allowed to fall with crushing
severity either upon its helpless victims or upon the over-burdened
ratepayers."[4] Since it was generally believed in the Labour Party that
unemployment was the inevitable outcome of capitalism, apart from

[1] *Essays in Persuasion*, p. 326.
[2] See A. J. P. Taylor, *English History, 1914-1945* (1965), pp. 266-9, 280.
[3] *How to Tackle Unemployment, The Liberal Plans as laid before the Government and the Nation*
(1930), pp. 13, 28-9.
[4] *Op. cit.*, p. 15.

such short-term solutions as more generous unemployment benefits and shifting the burden of maintenance from the ratepayer to the taxpayer, less attention was paid than in the Liberal literature to expedients which fell short of transformation of the whole system.[1]

The disagreement between left and right within the Labour movement focused mainly on how quickly the abolition of private ownership in industry could be achieved. The influence of Marxist ideas in favour of the view that capitalism would inevitably collapse as a result of increasingly severe crises was not very great within the British Labour movement at this time. There were some though who argued that a Labour Government should not lift a hand to prevent the system from committing suicide. Hobson's underconsumptionist ideas had some supporters on the left, notably John Wheatley.[2] But apart from various slogans like "Britain is Britain's best market", arguments derived from Hobson merely tended to strengthen the case for old-fashioned redistributive measures and the abolition of private ownership of the means of production.

### Labour in Office

When the Labour Government took office a special team was appointed to deal with unemployment. It consisted of J. H. Thomas, acting with the assistance of George Lansbury, Oswald Mosley and Tom Johnston. The first effects of the world depression did not make themselves felt until the end of 1929. It is important to note that before this it was evident, even to well-wishers, that the Labour Government was just as unlikely to come to grips with unemployment as its predecessors.

Thomas brought to his job a deep respect for businessmen and the "normal channels of employment". At the party's Annual Conference in Brighton in 1929, his proudest claim was to have reached an agreement whereby Canada would import more British coal and steel. For as Thomas said: "It is far better . . . to get permanent trade than to resort to any artificial means by the mere spending of money." He later piloted through a Colonial Development Bill which he claimed would raise employment in the export trades. It was easier, it would seem, to get support for measures which involved the export of capital than for spending equivalent sums on providing employment directly at home. A more determined effort was made, however,

[1] Even Labour sympathisers with the Liberal plans, like Beatrice Webb, were sceptical as to whether they would really do the trick. "The worst of it is that Lloyd George's schemes, though brilliantly conceived and advocated, are always unsound and turn out terribly expensive. And I doubt whether Great Britain can afford any more expensive remedies—like insurance for health and unemployment—which neither alter the environment nor cure the patient." B. Webb, *Diaries, 1924-1932*, (1948), pp. 191-2.
[2] See e.g. J. Wheatley, *Starving in the Midst of Plenty* (1923).

to increase public works spending by increasing the capital grants made to local authorities. As in the past though, it proved difficult to initiate large schemes at short notice. Thomas showed little desire to move far from the beaten track, and if he had, he would have soon realised the truth of L. S. Amery's warning that by not obtaining assurances of Treasury support before accepting the job, he had started with a noose round his neck, the other end of which was in the hands of the Chancellor of the Exchequer.[1]

This would not have been quite so dangerous if the hands had not belonged to Philip Snowden, who was thoroughly in sympathy with the Treasury position on public works spending. Churchill paid lip-service to budgetary orthodoxy, Snowden believed. When asked how the Civil Service felt about the change-over from Churchill to Snowden, a Treasury official replied that it was like being moved from the pantry to the drawing-room. More than any other person Snowden was responsible for keeping the Labour Government within the narrow limits set by conventional finance. Indeed, he seems to have regarded this as his chief political mission. When he took office in 1929 his main task, as he saw it, was to repair the damage done to the nation's finances by his predecessor.[2] Instead of a projected surplus, he found himself with a deficit of £14½ million. Under these circumstances, his natural inclinations in favour of economy were strengthened. He resisted strenuously, but largely unsuccessfully, left-wing demands for higher unemployment benefits, and applied the strictest criteria to all public works schemes. He opposed Lloyd George's demands for a £250 million loan to be used for "undefined purposes", for as he said: "I was quite prepared to raise the money if necessary to carry through well-thought-out schemes of public works of a useful and remunerative nature. But I set my face against a shovelling out of money to be worse than wasted to provide work of no public utility."[3] The position is precisely that of Sir Richard Hopkins mentioned earlier. Snowden showed no sign of having noticed or understood Keynes's crude calculations of the multiplier effects of public spending in his contributions to the Liberal election literature. The only criterion for public investment which Snowden recognised was the ordinary market rate of return.

The Labour Party's traditional suspicion of the banking and financial community was heartily reciprocated. In their election manifesto they promised to "institute a searching inquiry into financial methods and credit policy, with a view to the removal of practices which are injurious or obsolete, and to the more effective

---

[1] *My Political Life*, Vol. II, p. 502.
[2] *An Autobiography* (1939), vol. II, p. 758 and p. 853.
[3] *Ibid.*, pp. 874-5.

control of banking and finance in the national interests." The debate on monetary policy, never really silent since the return to gold, was revived again in the first months of the Labour Government when Bank Rate was raised in order to counteract the outflow of funds from London resulting from the boom on the New York Stock Exchange. At the Labour Party Conference in Brighton at the beginning of October, Ernest Bevin asked Thomas whether or not the recent rises in Bank Rate would nullify his efforts to provide employment. Thomas was unable to give an adequate answer; but on the following day Snowden assured the conference that "the Treasury have no influence in this matter, and they have no responsibility for it"; he considered that it would have "practically no effect whatever upon long-term loans and investments". Montagu Norman, with whom Snowden had discussed his speech beforehand, congratulated him on his defence of the gold standard, "indigestible and unattractive" though it must have seemed to the Conference. On one important point, however, Snowden did not follow Norman's advice: he promised a full inquiry into relations between industry and finance. The Macmillan Committee was set up a few weeks later. Norman believed that even this promise might endanger the gold standard.[1] He may have been closer to the truth than he realised.

The frustration felt by Labour's supporters in the face of the government's incapacity was given focus by Mosley's resignation in 1930. Mosley, Lansbury and Johnston were becoming impatient with Thomas's unwillingness to consult with them or take action on their proposals. In February 1930, Mosley, with Lansbury's support, submitted a lengthy memorandum to the Cabinet over the head of Thomas. When the memorandum was rejected he resigned his post and placed the proposals before a special meeting of the Parliamentary Labour Party, where, largely as a result of unwillingness to embarrass the government, and distrust of Mosley's character and motives, they were once more rejected. When the same thing happened at the party's Annual Conference at Llandudno—though by a comparatively small margin—Mosley left the Labour Party to form one of his own.

Mosley's recommendations were bold and iconoclastic. Unemployment should be tackled on the same lines that war had been waged. A revolution in the machinery of government was required to take initiative in policy-making out of the hands of the professional civil service. As a short-term measure, domestic purchasing power should be increased by loan-financed public works and increased expenditure on retirement pensions. The latter, together with a rise in the school-leaving age, would reduce the numbers seeking

[1] See H. Clay, *Lord Norman*, p. 363.

employment. As a long-term remedy, he proposed a complete reorganisation of the banking system along the lines of the German industrial banks to enable constructive credit expansion for the purposes of rationalisation to be undertaken. The state was to assume direct responsibility for the direction and planning of industry; and foreign trade was to be planned by means of import controls and state bargaining with foreign suppliers.[1]

The whole scheme was an amalgam of ideas picked up from Keynes, Hobson, Germany, and Mussolini's Italy. Ignoring the details and the fact that Mosley himself did not inspire trust, the instinct behind Mosley's memorandum was sound. It offered a chance to deal with unemployment on a scale and along the only lines likely to have any impact on the problem. Keynes himself believed that it provided a useful "starting point for thought and action", and could not see "how anyone professing and calling himself a Socialist can keep away from the Manifesto".[2]

One incidental result of the furore aroused by Mosley's memorandum was the translation of Thomas from his post as "Minister of Unemployment" to the office of Dominions Secretary. From this point on MacDonald took personal charge of unemployment. At this juncture, therefore, MacDonald's views on economic questions must be taken into account.

In his foreword to *Labour and the Nation* MacDonald claimed that the Labour Party, unlike the others, was "not concerned with patching up the rents in a bad system, but with transforming Capitalism into Socialism". Even after tasting the bitter fruits of office MacDonald continued to maintain, to his followers at least, that the government was laying the foundations for socialism. The depression itself had demonstrated and confirmed the wisdom of the founding fathers of the movement in seeking an alternative to the present system.

> "It is not the Labour Government that is on trial, it is Capitalism that is being tried. . . . It has broken down in Europe, in Asia, in America; it has broken down everywhere, as it was bound to break down. And the cure, the new path, the new idea is organisation—organisation which will protect life, not property. . . . That is the policy that we are going to pursue slowly, steadily, persistently, with knowledge, and with our minds working upon a plan. . . . I appeal to you to go back on to your Socialist faith."[3]

[1] See Mosley's speech, *House of Commons Debates*, May 28th 1930, cc. 1348-1372; and *Report of the 30th Annual Conference of the Labour Party*, (1930), pp. 200-204.
[2] *Nation and Athenaeum*, December 13th, 1930.
[3] *Report of the Annual Conference*, (1930), p. 185.

MacDonald freely confessed to being mystified by the problems of finance. Many disparate ideas and solutions could enter this mental vacuum, but only orthodoxy could survive. He liked to think of himself as consulting all shades of opinion. Already by January 1930 he had created an Economic Advisory Council to keep him informed as to the economic situation and of possible remedies.[1] The economists were represented by Keynes, Cole, Tawney, and Hubert Henderson; the trade unions by Bevin and Citrine; and business by Sir Andrew Duncan, Sir Arthur Balfour, Sir John Cadman and Sir Josiah Stamp (also an economist). The Council met infrequently and failed to agree on any of the important policy questions, with the businessmen, particularly Cadman and Balfour, opposing any departure from the orthodoxy.[2] Even if they had been more united in their advice, there is little evidence to show that MacDonald would have accepted and argued the case where it conflicted with the views of the Treasury, the Bank of England, and Snowden. MacDonald's vague intellectualism was no match for Snowden's rigid faith.

There is in fact nothing to suggest that MacDonald ever entertained any serious doubts about the wisdom of conventional finance. It is perhaps typical of his political and economic stance that on the very first occasion on which he faced Parliament as the first Labour Prime Minister in 1924, he should go out of his way to give the following reassurance:

> "I want to make it perfectly clear that the Government have no intention of drawing off from the normal channels of trade large sums for extemporised measures which can only be palliatives. This is the old, sound Socialist doctrine, and the necessity of expenditure for subsidised schemes in direct relief of unemployment will be judged in relation to the great necessity for maintaining undisturbed the ordinary financial facilities and the reserves of trade and industry.[3]

In the stirring speech which he made to the Annual Conference at Llandudno in 1930, his statements on unemployment policy would have done credit to the average Treasury official or City banker. "You cannot put up a successful settlement of the unemployment problem

---

[1] This was a revival of a proposal for a Committee of Economic Inquiry, probably originating from the Haldane *Committee on the Machinery of Government*, 1918, which had been endorsed by MacDonald in 1924. No action could be taken before the first Labour Government fell, though a Committee of Civil Research, incorporating some of the original idea, was appointed in 1925. In its turn this body was absorbed in the Economic Advisory Council. On this see, J. Anderson, *The Organization of Economic Studies in Relation to the Problems of Government*, Stamp Memorial Lecture, 1947.

[2] For further comments on this body see pp. 265-6 below.

[3] *House of Commons Debates*, Feb. 12th 1924, c. 760.

unless you work to remove the international causes of it." The government was negotiating at Geneva for lower tariffs and for a means of improving the distribution of gold. On public works: "It is not money so much we are short of; it is work." It takes time to organise co-operation with the local authorities: "And then, do remember that much of what we call relief work is, first of all, only drawing on future normal demands. . . . Secondly, it is not as a matter of fact contributing to the solution of the unemployment problem. It is a provision of temporary work, very often at high cost, for men who do not want it, but want to get into permanent occupation." The only novel element in the whole speech was the suggestion that, for the moral and economic health of the nation, the best thing any government could do would be to encourage a movement back to the land. That MacDonald could seriously make this plea for a return to rough rural delights in a speech dealing with unemployment as it existed in 1930, while at the same time being content to rehearse Treasury conventions, illustrates how little grasp he had of the problem.

### The May Committee and Retrenchment

By the end of 1930, as a result of the world depression, unemployment had risen to 2½ million. The first signs of the domestic budgetary difficulties which were to play such a large part in the latter days of the crisis and in the breakup of the Labour Government also made their appearance at this time. In January 1930 the government redeemed its pledge to provide more adequate standards of maintenance. The Insurance Acts were modified to give slightly increased rates of benefit, and the condition that the unemployed worker should be "genuinely seeking work" was dropped. The cost of the "transitional benefits" payable to those whose rights under the contributory principle had been exhausted was transferred to the Treasury. This attempt to protect the insurance element in the original scheme did not prevent the Insurance Fund from having to increase its borrowings from the Treasury. On both counts, therefore, the rising tide of unemployment placed a strain on the nation's finances.

By the end of 1930 the debt on the Insurance Fund had reached around £100 million and borrowing was increasing at the rate of £40 million per annum. A Royal Commission was appointed to look into the situation. At an early stage of its proceedings the Commission heard gloomy evidence from the Treasury in the person of Sir Richard Hopkins. In his memorandum Hopkins maintained that "continued State borrowing on the present vast scale without adequate provision for repayment by the fund would quickly call in question the stability of the British financial system." This memorandum sparked off demands for an economy campaign. Snowden had seen the document in advance, and although he later denied responsibility for it welcomed the agitation in favour of economy because, as he said, "no Government could embark upon a drastic reduction unless it were supported by a strong public opinion".[1]

In February 1931 the Conservatives censured the government "for its policy of continuous additions to the public expenditure at a time when the avoidance of all new charges and strict economy of the existing services are necessary to restore confidence and to promote employment." The government accepted a Liberal amendment calling for an independent inquiry to suggest means of reducing public expenditure on current account. The Committee later set up under Sir George May's Chairmanship was composed of five members (including the Chairman) representing business interests, four of whom were nominated by the Liberals and Conservatives, and two Labour nominees.

It was in this censure debate that Snowden made one of the classic statements of the orthodox position.

"I say with all the seriousness I can command that the national position is so grave that drastic and disagreeable measures will have to be taken if Budget equilibrium is to be maintained and if industrial progress is to be made. An expenditure which may be easy and tolerable in prosperous times becomes intolerable in a time of grave industrial depression. . . . I believe . . . that an increase of taxation in present conditions which fell on industry would be the last straw. Schemes involving heavy expenditure, however desirable they may be, will have to wait until prosperity returns. This is necessary . . . to uphold the present standard of living, and no class will ultimately benefit more by present economy than the wage-earners."[2]

In April, however, Snowden surprised most people by introducing a mild budget. For this he gave two incompatible reasons: that the situation was not as bad as he had led everybody to expect in February; and that it was only a stop-gap budget while waiting for the weighty authority of the May Committee report to carry through drastic economy measures. Political expediency and economic diagnosis were in conflict. By the criteria of his own logic there was something economically dishonest about the April budget in 1931. It was in fact true that the budgetary situation was not serious at this stage; a small nominal deficit of £23 million, even after adding to

[1] *An Autobiography*, Vol. II, p. 892.
[2] *House of Commons Debates*, Feb. 11th 1931, cc. 447-9.

this the current borrowing on the Unemployment Fund, was more than offset by the £60 million paid into the Sinking Fund. He was able to cover the deficit without additional direct taxation by resort to minor expedients of a type which he had condemned when used by Churchill. The discussion proceeded on two levels: on the one hand the budget was balanced in accommodation with the economic situation but without great sacrifice of orthodox principles, while on the other hand alarmist views were encouraged in order to provide backing for a more active policy of retrenchment.

The extent of gold loss at this time was small enough to be handled by existing reserves or a cut-back in long-term foreign investment. It must be admitted though that the machinery for extensive control over foreign investment was rudimentary. The problem of foreign confidence was mentioned by domestic commentators to gain support for the economy campaign, but in the early part of 1931 it does not seem to have been a major factor in the situation; it became so later partly as a result of the vigour, bordering on masochism, with which the supporters of budgetary orthodoxy beat their chests. By the time the May Report was presented on July 31st, the European liquidity crisis, together with rumours of the contents of the report, had made foreign confidence a prime factor in the situation.

The doctrine of balanced budgeting had acquired a rather elastic meaning during the 'twenties. With a more flexible Chancellor it might have been possible to continue in the same vein, making use of short-term expedients, raising taxes a little, trimming the Sinking Fund, putting on a brave front, muddling through. It would not have been an adventurous policy, but it would have stopped short of conscious contraction in the scale of government expenditure. Instead, there was a deliberate lurch towards orthodoxy. Foreign confidence, the liquidity crisis, and the advice of those extending foreign credits to the government, merely confirmed and hastened a course already decided on.

In view of the purposiveness with which retrenchment was pursued, it is important to understand its rationale. The May Committee did the job it was appointed to do with considerable thoroughness. They were solely concerned with the narrow task of suggesting cuts in expenditure in order to balance the budget at a lower level. Both with respect to reasoning and recommendations the May Report was an atavistic document. The Committee estimated that in the course of 1931–2 there would be a budgetary deficit of £120 million.[1] In arriving at this figure they included an estimate of the borrowings of the Unemployment and Road Funds, and "the usual provision for the redemption of debt" of £50 million. This amounts to saying that

[1] *Report of Committee on National Expenditure* (1931), Cmd. 3920, p. 15.

in the depths of a most severe depression, all expenditure on unemployment and road construction should be met out of current
revenue, while provision for debt repayment was maintained
at a level which would have been appropriate only under conditions
of high prosperity. It is difficult to conceive of a more complete
inversion, not only of modern thinking on the subject, but also of the
well-established budgetary practice of soft-pedalling during depression years. Even supporters of economy found this an excess of
virtue. "No doubt it was prudent, in order to convince the owners
of the large foreign deposits in London, to proceed on the basis of
the strictest Gladstonian orthodoxy, but this was to apply a standard
which no other country in the world was willing or able to accept."[1]

To meet an exaggerated deficit the May Committee reluctantly
proposed an increase of taxation, and cuts in expenditure totalling
£96 million, two-thirds (£66½ million) of which was to be met by
cuts in unemployment insurance, £13½ million from education, £8
million from cuts in the road programme, and the rest from cuts in
the pay of the services.

The arbitrary nature of the assumptions, both with regard to
financial expediency and social justice, upon which the Committee's
conclusions were based deserve to be underlined. There was nothing
"usual" or sacrosanct about the annual provision for debt retirement. It is true that expenditure on unemployment was the most
rapidly growing item of expenditure, but there was no special reason
why, if a balanced budget was to be achieved, the cuts, amounting
to 20 per cent of the average benefit, should have been so heavily
concentrated on the unemployed. Nevertheless, it must be noted that
to the orthodox mind there was something particularly egregious
about borrowing to meet what was regarded simply as current outlay
on unemployment. On grounds of social justice, as opposed to con-
venience and docility, the singling out of teachers and the armed
services for pay cuts had little to be said for it unless it was hoped that
this would be a preliminary to a general reduction of wages and other
forms of income. The Committee was aware of this problem: if there
was little chance of an all-round reduction of incomes, public servants
and pensioners could not be singled out for special sacrifice. For this
reason alone they were willing to consider additional taxation, as
long as it did not impose "any further burden on productive
industry".[2] Yet, of course, the increase in the contributions under
the unemployment insurance scheme amounted to just this.

In justifying cuts in pay and benefits they said that "the rise in the

---

[1] P. J. Grigg, *Prejudice and Judgement* (1948), p. 255; see also H. D. Henderson, *The Inter-
war Years* (1955), pp. 71-7.
[2] *Op. cit.*, pp. 221-222.

value of money in recent years provides a strong prima facie case for the revision of money obligations fixed under other conditions".[1] On similar grounds a case could be made for scaling down the heavy burden of interest payments on the National Debt; but this was excluded from the Committee's terms of reference. In a Minority Report, however, the two Labour representatives on the Committee pointed out that interest charges represented about one-third of the total budget. Owing to the fall of prices the real burden of these payments had risen by 73 per cent;[2] they believed that there was "ample scope for securing such additional revenue as would enable budgetary stability to be maintained by the adjustment of taxation in relation to the uncovenanted benefits now being received by the holders of fixed incomes".[3] The practical difficulties involved in implementing this suggestion would have been great. Nevertheless, it is perhaps worth pointing out that in Australia a "voluntary" funding operation, which reduced interest payments in step with other incomes, was carried through quickly and successfully.

The attitude of the majority of the committee to the social services has been cited earlier.[4] To the Minority Report must go the credit for pointing out the narrowness of the majority point of view under modern industrial conditions. In addition to the powerful redistributive arguments in favour of the social services, they noted also the long-term economic benefits.

"The growth of the social services is a natural corollary to the development of industry and commerce and it cannot be denied that these have profited materially from services often narrowly regarded as amenities, and it is not an overstatement of the case to say that improved health and sanitation, better education, wide and clean roads, quicker communications and even open spaces and playing fields are essential to modern large scale industry."[5]

They struck another modern note when they pointed out that the drift of new industries to the South of England was attributable to "the fact that these social services are more generally available at less cost than in older industrial districts still handicapped by the neglect of the past". In view of the increase in the burden of interest payments mentioned earlier, the minority did not feel that the budgetary difficulties could be attributed exclusively to the rising level of social expenditure.

[1] *Ibid.*, p. 220.
[2] *Ibid.*, pp. 237-8.
[3] *Ibid.*, p. 271.
[4] See p. 98 above.
[5] *Report of Committee on National Expenditure*, p. 229.

E

A related difference between the Majority and Minority Reports can be observed in the case of capital expenditure. The majority reflected the Treasury view in its narrowest form. Economic benefit should be kept clearly in mind: "It is to be expected that the more nearly a scheme approaches ordinary commercial activity of the kind to which [the unemployed] are accustomed, both in the nature of the work and in the manner in which it is being executed, the more the employment approximates in its effect to normal employment."[1] On these grounds they proposed to abolish the Road Fund and to cut down spending by the Unemployment Grants Committee. The minority demurred.[2] In spite of the fact that it was signed by the two Labour representatives, the Minority Report was completely ignored by the Labour Government.

The May Committee, and the bulk of the political discussion to which it gave rise, was solely concerned with the immediate budgetary results of cuts in expenditure; the effect of cuts on the economic situation of the country taken as a whole was completely ignored. The case for retrenchment was fully in line with the deflationist case which had been argued by some throughout the 'twenties. Most of the supporters of retrenchment lacked the courage of their convictions; they refused to admit the logical economic consequence of the policy of balancing budgets by cuts in expenditure. For this reason, it is necessary to distinguish between the confessed aim of balancing the budget, and its natural but unacknowledged consequence, namely deflation.

Keynes, as usual, was not content to allow the underlying assumptions of this position to be obscured. He claimed that "it invites us to decide whether it is our intention to make the Deflation effective by transmitting the reduction of international prices to British salaries and wages". He charged the May Committee with not "having given a moment's thought to the possible repercussions of their programme, either on the volume of unemployment or on the receipts of taxation". The reduction in purchasing power which the cuts entailed would reduce income and employment and thereby decrease the yield of taxation by a multiple of the original cuts. He was unable to give an accurate estimate of the quantitative impact of attempting to eliminate the budget deficit, but he saw clearly that such deficits, financed by borrowing, were "nature's remedy" for reducing the cumulative consequences of the slump: "For this is a case, fortunately perhaps, where the weakness of human nature . . . comes to the rescue of human wrong-headedness."[3]

---

[1] *Ibid.*, pp. 98-99.
[2] *Ibid.*, pp. 242-4, 251.
[3] *New Statesman*, Aug. 15th, 1931.

If most politicians were unwilling or unable to spell out the expected consequences of deflation, there were others who were willing to do so. To those who believed in deflation the problem was simple: Britain had been living beyond her means and sustaining a level of costs which made industry uncompetitive; lavish expenditure by the state on unproductive services, which included the maintenance of the unemployed as well as the payment of interest on National Debt, had necessitated a scale of taxation which was crippling to industry; prices had fallen but wages had not fallen in step; profits and saving were being squeezed. In the absence of effective international co-operation to raise the world price level, Britain's salvation lay in stimulating the export trade by reducing the domestic level of prices and costs. It was irresponsible to advocate credit expansion and capital expenditure by the government under the existing circumstances; this could only be inflationary if unmatched by increased savings. An expansionist policy, therefore, would raise wages and prices, increase imports, and diminish exports.

The moral of this, so far as the government was concerned, was summed up by Lord Bradbury in a memorandum of almost total dissent from the findings of the Macmillan Committee:

> "The best contribution which the State can make to assist industry and promote employment is strict economy in public expenditure and lightening the burden of debt by prudent financial administration. Attempts to give positive assistance by diverting international trade from its natural channels, the State-financing of enterprises other than the ordinary public services, or the artificial cheapening by State guarantee of the supply of capital to particular undertakings are more likely to retard than to accelerate the restoration of a healthy and progressive national economy."[1]

Recent sterling crises have prompted many to draw parallels with 1931. The temptations are obvious: a Labour Government, loss of foreign confidence, flight from sterling, devaluation, negotiations for support from foreign bankers, deflationary monetary and fiscal policies, cuts in expenditure, wage freezes. But as far as domestic policy is concerned, parallels with 1931 are totally misleading. Crudely speaking, the post-war problem has been one of inflation and over-full employment, not deflation and mass unemployment. Internal deflationary measures to overcome a loss of foreign confidence may be short-sighted and expensive in terms of the loss of

---

[1] *Report of Committee on Finance and Industry*, p. 201. For a forthright statement of the deflationist position by a professional economist see F. Benham, *British Monetary Policy* (1932), espec. pp. 30-31, 45.

potential growth, but they undoubtedly operate in the right direction in helping to reduce inflation and improve the balance of trade. In 1931 it was not a simple case of pressure on a single financial centre, but of worldwide collapse in the international monetary and trading system brought about by simultaneous depression in all countries. Deflationary measures today are directed towards a reduction of the level of domestic expenditure on home and foreign goods and services. In 1931 the problem was still largely seen as one of balancing the budget in order to restore foreign confidence. It seems worth stressing this in view of the tendency, particularly in the apologetic literature, to speak as though policy-makers in 1931 argued their position in sophisticated modern terms, and should be judged accordingly. Thus we find Youngson making out a case for what was actually done on the grounds that, for example, new borrowing by the government to create employment "would have made matters worse by keeping up money incomes and hence the demand for imports".[1] Even if the actions of the British government in 1931 are regarded as appropriate or unavoidable, given the circumstances and the state of knowledge at the time, this should not blind us to the fact that their reasoning was faulty or incomplete by present-day standards.

## The Climax

The publication of the report of the May Committee came at a time when the liquidity crisis made it necessary to negotiate with foreign banks for new lines of credit. When it met in August to consider the report, the Cabinet Economy Committee was informed by the British banking community that "the cause of the trouble was not financial but political, and lay in the complete want of confidence in H.M.G. existing among foreigners."[2] They were further informed that the only way confidence could be restored was by balancing the budget and by making cuts in expenditure, particularly on unemployment benefits. It is typical of the one-sidedness of the response to the financial crisis of the representatives of "sound" financial opinion that no advice was given concerning the possibility of direct controls over the exchanges. This lent credence later to the idea of a "banker's ramp"; it encouraged the view that the banking community was

---

[1] *British Economic Growth, 1920-1966* (1967), p. 83. It has also been said in mitigation of the enormous attention paid to balanced budgets in 1931 that " the Government lacked the more extensive means . . . open to modern governments of reducing demand". This statement implies not only that in 1931 those in power were concerned with level of demand (a post-Keynesian concept), but also that the reduction of demand was a desirable aim under the circumstances. See R. Skidelsky, "The Summer We Went Off Gold", *The Guardian*, July 26th, 1966.

[2] K. Feiling, *Neville Chamberlain* (1946), p. 191.

calling on the government to exact sacrifices from the unemployed in order to save them from difficulties which were partly of their own creation. Despite the fact that there was no evidence to suggest that increased internal "indebtedness", even if it had been as large as the May Committee estimated, impaired the ability or reduced the willingness of the government to protect the existing parity and meet its foreign obligations, the attention of international bankers had certainly been drawn to a weakness. Quite understandably, therefore, they were unwilling to extend more credit unless assurances were given that an effort would be made to put this right.

The government was also under considerable pressure from the press and the Opposition to implement drastic economies. Despite public protestation by Conservative leaders of the need for economy measures on "national" grounds, in private they confessed to less disinterested motives. As Neville Chamberlain wrote at the time, "the only way in which the economy figures could be raised was by cutting the dole and if we once could fasten that on the Labour Party they would be irrevocably split".[1] At a later stage, when the National Government was being formed, one of the reasons why retention of MacDonald as Prime Minister was favoured by leaders of the other parties was that this would help to make the cuts in the dole more acceptable to working-class opinion.

There is no need to reconstruct in detail the tortuous course of the weeks of Cabinet discussion which preceded the downfall of the Labour Government.[2] The estimate for the budget deficit had been raised from the May Committee's figure of £120 million to £170 million. Cuts amounting to £56 million were agreed on by the Cabinet, but a minority of nine or ten members refused to swallow the 10 per cent cut in unemployment benefits which would have brought the figure up to the £78 million considered essential to restore foreign confidence and to obtain international credits. The important point to note is that it was on matters of social justice that the Cabinet failed to reach agreement on a course of action which would have been acceptable to the leaders of the other parties, to foreign bankers, and to the General Council of the TUC. Those who were unwilling to countenance a cut in the dole did not dispute the need to achieve a balanced budget—though there was a good deal of disagreement later as to how far they had been willing to go in this direction.

The possibility of reducing payments to the Sinking Fund and a revenue tariff proposal were among the alternatives discussed; but both of these were resisted strongly by Snowden. The Labour Party,

[1] I. Macleod, *Neville Chamberlain* (1961), p. 151.
[2] For this see R. Basset, *op. cit.*

in common with the Liberals, was traditionally opposed to any protective measures which might raise the cost of living of the working classes. Nevertheless, when a 10% tariff on manufactured goods was proposed as an alternative to cuts in unemployment pay, a majority in the Cabinet supported the tariff. MacDonald and J. H. Thomas were with the majority, but Snowden was implacably opposed. If the majority had pressed their advantage, the government would have broken up on this issue, and, in addition, would not have received Liberal support. The majority allowed the proposal to drop in the hope of finding other alternatives.

Another crucial point in the discussions came when the General Council of the TUC was called in to give its opinion on the economies which had been agreed to, or were being considered. The TUC rejected the assumptions which lay behind the whole exercise; they were bitterly opposed to cuts in the dole, which they believed would merely be a preliminary to wholesale wage-reduction.[1] In place of the government's deflationary programme they suggested suspension of the Sinking Fund, new taxation on fixed-interest-bearing securities, a revenue tariff, and a scheme whereby the unemployed were to be supported not by insurance but by a graduated levy on the whole community. They were firmly of the opinion that the crisis had its origin in the financial mismanagement of the banking community, and in the alarmist picture of the nation's finances given currency by the May Committee and a hostile press. As representatives of the organised working class they refused to be stampeded into accepting a programme which they felt was irrelevant and blatantly unequal in the sacrifices called for from different sections of the community. Their intervention undoubtedly played an important part in stiffening the resistance of Henderson and other dissidents within the Cabinet to cuts in the dole. Failure to agree on this issue led to the breakup of the Labour Government on August 24th.

The stated aim of the "National" Government formed by MacDonald was to deal with the emergency. Among the first measures introduced was a second budget and an Economy Bill. In the budget Snowden increased taxation to a greater extent than had been proposed by the May Committee, and reduced the provision for the Sinking Fund by £20 million—a device which the Labour Cabinet had not been "allowed" to consider (by Snowden). The Economy Bill proposed cuts in expenditure of £70 million, to be achieved by reductions in the pay of ministers, civil servants, teachers, the police and the armed services. Borrowing for the Unemployment and Road Funds was to cease. Unemployment benefits were

[1] See A. Bullock, *The Life and Times of Ernest Bevin* (1950), pp. 470-73, 480-491.

cut by 10%, contributions were increased, and a means test was introduced for those applying for "transitional benefits".

These measures succeeded in stopping the gold drain and enabled new foreign credits to be obtained. The success lasted for twelve days. A minor mutiny among naval ratings at Invergordon in protest against the pay cuts led to a panic withdrawal of funds. At the moment of its greatest triumph orthodoxy failed in its object. On September 21st the government was forced to suspend the gold standard.

### The Alternatives: The Expansionist Case

Was there any alternative to the policy of retrenchment actually pursued? Chronology is obviously important here. At any stage in the life of the Labour Government, from its formation right up to July 15th 1931, two weeks before the report of the May Committee was made public, the alternatives advocated by the opponents of orthodoxy as a solution to Britain's difficulties could have been tried. After this date, with the beginnings of the flight from the pound, the problem for most people, including the expansionists, was how to restore confidence and save the gold standard. There was still a good deal of room for differences of opinion as to the most effective and least harmful methods of doing this. With the benefit of hindsight we can see that in the absence of some heroic international effort the gold standard was doomed; the causes of its collapse were deeply embedded in the fabric of international economic relations as they had developed since 1925. This means that whatever the mistakes of the past may have been, most of the remedies so feverishly canvassed in the last months of the crisis, whether contractionist or expansionist, were fundamentally irrelevant—although not without serious domestic consequences. The fact that contractionist remedies were tried and found wanting, while those put forward by opponents of orthodoxy were rejected, proves little. We can only speculate about what might have happened if bolder action of the type suggested by Keynes and others had been adopted, and it would still be possible to argue against this that the orthodox medicine would have worked if it had been tried earlier. However attractive, one must ignore such speculations and concentrate on the issues as they appeared to decision-makers at the time.

The expansionist alternative was put before the government on numerous occasions and by varying groups. But perhaps the most potent source of pressure for this policy in the penultimate stages of the crisis came from Keynes and Bevin acting through the media of the Macmillan Committee, the Economic Advisory Council, and the General Council of the TUC.

In an addendum to the Macmillan Report, six members of the Committee, led by Keynes, emphasised that the proposals of the report for improving British monetary institutions and policy could not, of themselves, improve the employment situation without some direct action to increase the general level of output. The main problem was not "a limitation on the amount of available credit, but the reluctance of acceptable borrowers to come forward". Among the alternatives which they examined as stimulants to employment were (a) reduction of salaries and wages (b) control of imports and aids to exports, and (c) state action to increase domestic investment.

While they did not regard the existing level of wages as sacrosanct, they criticised the first alternative on several grounds. A wage-reduction in one industry might benefit employment in that industry; but a general wage-reduction would reduce incomes, and therefore demand, as well as costs. The advantages of such a policy to the export trades could be offset by competitive reductions on the part of other countries. In order to achieve any result, a large general reduction would have to be attempted, and this might produce "social chaos". A more enlightened course of action would be to accept the present level of costs and implement measures to raise home and foreign demand. They also drew attention to the socially divisive effects of deflation, especially in view of the "uncovenanted blessings which accrued to the holders of the National Debt"and other forms of fixed income. They agreed, however, that it was "theoretically conceivable" for a national treaty to be negotiated, by which all forms of income would be reduced simultaneously.

They looked more favourably upon controls over imports and aids to exports as a solution. An improved balance of trade could help employment; it need not have disastrous repercussions on British exports if accompanied by increased domestic investment and foreign lending. Rebates could be used to eliminate the adverse effects of higher import prices on export costs; similarly with the effect of higher food prices on working-class standards of living. As an additional benefit, the revenue from import duties would relieve some of the burden on the budget.

Measures designed to improve the balance of trade could be used in harness with the third type of stimulant, namely state schemes of capital development. Point by point they refuted the negative official position on this matter as it had been argued before them by Sir Richard Hopkins.[1] They refused to accept the idea that there was a fixed loan fund; increases in government investment would not necessarily entail diversion from other outlets, nor would state schemes compete with private enterprise and reduce the level of

---

[1] See pp. 111-13 above.

private investment. Given the existing level of unused productive capacity in the country, they thought it unlikely that an increase in government demand would raise prices and hamper exports. Nor did they feel that the increase in imports likely to come with expansion should stand in the way of an attempt to increase employment. This objection could be applied to any remedy which raised employment. The state of the budget need not act as a restraint on such schemes if the decrease in government expenditure on unemployment, and the increase in the yield of taxation, were taken into account. They did not accept the view that government borrowing would materially damage the chances of debt-conversion by raising interest rates. They felt that in the long run the rate of interest "must tend to fall as the accumulated wealth and prosperity of the country in the shape of capital assets increases". A nation, as distinct from an individual firm, could not increase its liquid savings by refraining from investment. Since they believed that the problem of mobilising current savings would be present for some time to come, nothing could be lost by setting up the proper machinery for preparing schemes for long-term national investment well in advance.[1]

## Abandonment of Gold

Only a few bold spirits like Bevin were willing to countenance abandonment of the gold standard before it became inevitable. Although devaluation had been ruled out by Snowden from the beginning, in the private hearings of the Macmillan Committee Bevin continued to argue that maintenance of the present parity was incompatible with any policy likely to have any real impact on the unemployment question.[2] Bevin deserves credit for being the only expansionist to put forward the kind of consistent and radical case which we now recognise as being an effective solution to the unemployment problem at that time. He failed to convince Keynes and the majority of the Committee on this matter and had to be content with a cryptic reservation to the expansionist addendum to the report.[3]

While being fully aware that since 1925 the gold standard had operated in an unsatisfactory way, particularly as far as domestic stability was concerned, the Committee as a whole refused to recommend its abandonment in 1931. Its reasons for endorsing the system,

[1] *Report of the Committee on Finance and Industry*, Addendum I.
[2] See A. Bullock, *op. cit.*, Vol. I, pp. 430-432.
[3] "We should have preferred the course of devaluation because of its effect upon the whole of the dead-weight debt and other fixed charges, but we agree that great weight must be attached to the consideration that to endorse a de facto devaluation is easier than to devalue after a return to pre-war parity." *Op. cit.*, pp. 209-10. Signed also by Thomas Allen.

E*

however, were more heavily qualified than those given by their predecessors on the Cunliffe and Bradbury Committees. The arguments they used were much more akin to those used today, namely that the earnings of the City depended on international monetary stability; and that the export trade was likely to be damaged by fluctuating exchanges. For these reasons they refused to consider devaluation as a positive course of action for a major creditor nation. Nevertheless, they admitted that it was unlikely that the earnings of the City "have gone even a fraction of the way towards compensating the losses of wealth through unemployment in recent years". They believed that "the next phase of monetary policy must consist of a wholehearted attempt to make the existing international standard work more satisfactorily". The best solution to the world's monetary problems, which had not by then become acute, would be for Britain to take the lead in an international effort to raise prices.[1]

Like so much else in the report, this was Keynes's position. It is interesting to note that the leading opponent of the return to gold in 1925 was unwilling to recommend its abandonment in 1931, even though he welcomed it when it happened. This apparent inconsistency can partly be explained by Keynes's fundamental realism: he did not think that the advice would be followed, and he did not wish the discussion of the alternatives which he proposed to be obscured by raising a red herring. He also had more positive grounds for wishing Britain to remain on the gold standard at a time when it was not simply a matter of Britain being out of step with the world, but with the whole world being subjected to pressures which he felt could only be lessened by international action. The key to finding an international cure, he became convinced, lay in maintaining foreign confidence in London as a financial centre.

"[I] believe that our exchange position should be relentlessly defended today, in order . . . that we may resume the vacant financial leadership of the world, which no-one has the experience or the public spirit to occupy, speaking out of acknowledged strength and not out of weakness."[2]

### The Revenue Tariff

The other remedy favoured by some expansionists, and one which gathered increasing support as the crisis deepened, was a revenue tariff. The tariff had been an essential part of Conservative policy for some time. Control over imports was also an element in Mosley's

[1] *Op. cit.*, pp. 109-118.
[2] *New Statesman*, Mar. 7th, 1931.

memorandum. But the case was to receive powerful and unsuspected support from Keynes at private hearings of the Macmillan Committee. Keynes completely reversed his earlier position on this question. In 1923 he had argued the traditional case for free trade on grounds of efficient allocation of resources, and had maintained that any restriction on imports would either lead to a reduction of exports or act as a stimulus to the export of capital. This, he argued, would be folly at a time when the problem was to keep capital at home to make good the deficiency between "our diminished savings and our increasing needs". He had been emphatic on one point, namely that "if there is one thing that protection *cannot* do, it is to cure unemployment"; it could only contract the volume of trade in an effort to improve the *terms* on which Britain traded.[1]

By 1930, Keynes no longer thought in conventional terms of a simultaneous deficiency in savings *and* investment as the root of British difficulties; he now spoke of a tendency for voluntary savings to exceed investment.[2] The issue was one of finding ways of increasing investment, foreign and domestic, to offset this deficiency. Protection, by improving the balance of trade, would either increase foreign investment or provide greater leeway for an increase in domestic investment. He also felt that the traditional free trade case was of secondary importance when the resources to be allocated were not already fully employed.

But one cannot understand Keynes's volte-face on this question without regard to the alternatives which a revenue tariff would replace. As we have seen, he was not in favour of devaluation at this stage; it could only weaken Britain's capacity to take the lead in a fight against world deflationary pressures. For similar reasons, in the months immediately prior to the last stages of the crisis, he believed that the direct effect of expansionary policies on the balance of trade and on the budget would undermine the confidence of businessmen and foreign holders of sterling. Given the need to retain initiative in British hands by remaining on the gold standard, other measures were required to neutralise the effect of expansionary policies on confidence. He was prepared to see some reform in the unemployment insurance acts to remove abuses, and to postpone new social service charges on the budget; but he felt that the most effective neutralising agency would be a large revenue tariff. This would relieve the budgetary situation and help to revive business confidence. As in the addendum to the Macmillan Report, he argued that the effect on the cost of living and exports could be minimised by rebates and by a lower scale of duties on foodstuffs and raw materials. He

[1] *The New Republic*, Dec. 19th, 1923.
[2] See pp. 158-9 below.

hoped that the revenue tariff would increase employment at home without having a harmful effect on other countries. It would give Britain a breathing-space which would allow her to be bolder in her loans to debtor countries, and to implement expansionary policies which would ultimately improve her capacity to purchase foreign goods. It was to be an emergency solution only and could be removed when world prices recovered. The main point of the exercise was to strengthen London without recourse to the negative and socially unjust contractionist policies being contemplated, which, in Keynes' view, were not likely to do the trick anyway.[1]

Keynes also raised the issue in the economists' sub-committee of the Economic Advisory Council, where he was able to carry Henderson, Stamp, and to a lesser extent, Pigou, with him, but not Robbins, who submitted a minority report in favour of free trade. The report which they produced, therefore, like the Macmillan Report which appeared just before, showed the experts to be divided.[2]

## Cogency of the Expansionists' Case

The question naturally arises as to how cogent the expansionist case was at this time. It would certainly be unfair, as Mowat has pointed out in the case of the advice given by the banking community, "to blame them for lacking a belief in economic theories which only became fashionable later".[3] It has been said that "the Keynes of 1931 was not yet the Keynes of the *General Theory*";[4] and that the general public had not yet learned to hum the tunes of Keynesian economics. There is some truth in these statements. It has also been suggested that it would have been difficult "to frame a policy on the somewhat fluctuating views of J. M. Keynes".[5] This was certainly a view held by others both then and later. It was possibly in relation to the proceedings of the Economic Advisory Council, for example, that the well-known jibe that "where five economists are gathered together there will be six conflicting opinions and two of them will be held by Keynes" first gained currency.[6] Keynes was certainly fertile in putting forward new expedients at each stage of the crisis. Perhaps too fertile for the sake of his reputation, and for him to have influence in the slow-moving circles of a civil service weighed down by

[1] See the citation by Harrod from the minutes of the private hearing of the Macmillan Committee, *op. cit.*, pp. 425-6.
[2] See R. Skidelsky, *op. cit.*, pp. 208-15.
[3] C. L. Mowat, *Britain Between the Wars, 1918-1940* (1955), p. 383.
[4] W. G. Runciman, *Relative Deprivation and Social Justice* (1966), p. 62n.
[5] R. Bassett, *op. cit.*, p. 339. But Bassett merely demonstrates his anxiety to whitewash MacDonald when he says that "the new theories, in so far as they have been tested, have not proved unqualifiedly useful". Nor is it very reassuring to find this statement supported by a quotation from a work written in 1934 commenting on the situation in 1925.
[6] T. Jones, *A Diary with Letters, 1931-1950* (1954), p. 19.

precedent and having to operate the cumbrous machinery of the Parliamentary system.

This raises the whole question of the role of the economic expert at this time. The Economic Advisory Council was a new innovation; not only were the experts divided, but their views carried none of the weight attached to advice coming from Treasury and Bank of England sources.[1] The attitude of the permanent civil service to the "expert" at this time is perhaps best summarised by P. J. Grigg, private secretary to most of the Chancellors of the Exchequer in the 'twenties: "Let me say plainly . . . that I do not like 'experts' and technicians who have never occupied or alternatively have failed in executive positions of responsibility, and yet write books to prove how wise they are and how foolish is everybody else."[2] Keynes felt that there was an antipathy to new and constructive ideas in the Treasury right up to the eve of the Second World War.[3]

The charge that Keynes's views were "somewhat fluctuating" cannot really be substantiated. Behind all the different remedies he favoured in turn, was a consistent desire to avoid deflationary solutions. Although a good deal of work still had to be done before he could present to the academic community a satisfactory theory of output and employment, from the point of view of policy, the essence of the position later occupied by Keynes can be found in the 1929 election literature.[4] The real difficulty with expansionary ideas in 1931 was that they were still the property of a small band of followers scattered among the major parties, with none of the backing of professional consensus which they were later to acquire.

One criticism that might be levelled at Keynes himself in this period is of excessive optimism. He was too anxious to make the most of the narrow limitations set by circumstances and the official mentality. This was due partly to an admirable desire to be relevant at all times, but it led him to expect and claim more than was justified for such stop-gap measures as the revenue tariff. With the benefit of hindsight we can see that Bevin was correct in believing that an effective expansionist policy to deal with unemployment would require the abandonment of gold. This Keynes was unwilling to contemplate until the final stages of the crisis. By August, he had come to the conclusion that Britain had lost the international initiative which she had possessed earlier, and that "when doubts as to the prosperity of

---

[1] For further comment on the Economic Advisory Council see pp. 265-6 below.

[2] *Prejudice and Judgement*, pp. 7-8. For further evidence of Grigg's antipathy to Keynes see also pp. 183-4, 257-61.

[3] See p. 255 below.

[4] This matter will be taken up more fully in the next chapter.

a currency such as now exist about sterling, have come into existence, the game's up".[1]

The only point at which Keynes could be accused of faltering in his advice was for a brief period in the early days of the National Government.[2] By the time that Snowden was ready to present his emergency budget and the Economy Bill, however, Keynes had regained his nerve. He was convinced that "the moral energies of the nation are being directed into the wrong channels", and that Snowden's measures were "replete with folly and injustice". He was now in favour of devaluation, or, since this would not be accepted, import controls. The most constructive proposal he had to make at this, the eleventh hour, was for Britain to convene an international gold conference and "announce to the world that it cannot and will not work the international gold standard if the other creditor countries do not play the 'rules of the game'." Pending the outcome of this threat to leave the gold standard, there should be restrictions on foreign exchange dealings and an embargo on capital exports.[3]

## Political Postscript

MacDonald's conduct and motives in forming the National Government have been the subject of considerable debate. One way of looking at this question is to start from the simple proposition that MacDonald's behaviour can be seen as the outcome of his conviction that the crisis could only be overcome by a strict application of the orthodox medicine recommended by "responsible" opinion. From the rejection of any alternative everything else follows. "Conviction" may be too strong a wrong word to describe Mac-Donald's position, but he was sufficiently wedded to the orthodox view to risk the odium of his life-long political associates by calling upon the support of his political enemies. The formation of the National Government was the logical result of the economic priorities accepted by the Labour leaders, not simply in the last stages of the crisis, but throughout their whole term of office. While the Labour Government was willing to move within orthodox boundaries, they continued in office; when this was no longer acceptable to some members of the Cabinet, those who believed in such measures were forced to seek support elsewhere.

It has been claimed that the minority status of the government

[1] Letter to R. MacDonald, Aug. 5th, 1931, as cited in R. Skidelsky, "The Summer We Went Off Gold", *The Guardian*, July 26th, 1966.
[2] On Aug. 29th 1931, he wrote an unusually confused article for the *New Statesman*, from which it would be impossible to derive any clear idea as to the best course of action.
[3] *Evening Standard*, Sept. 10th, 1931, as reprinted in *Essays in Persuasion*, p. 281; see also his *New Statesman* articles on Sept. 12th and 19th, 1931.

prevented them from doing anything else.[1] There is no evidence to suggest, however, that MacDonald and Snowden would have acted differently with a majority to command. They considered that the measures for which they fought in the Labour Cabinet were the correct ones. If they had really believed in alternative policies, they could have resigned in support of them. Snowden certainly found no difficulty in doing this later over protection, and would have done so earlier if the revenue tariff had been pressed in the Cabinet. For the same reason, the weaknesses in the arguments put by Keynes and others, real or imagined, provide little comfort for the defenders of Snowden and MacDonald. There is not the slightest evidence that Snowden was ever open to any but the most orthodox advice. MacDonald may have listened but it seems unlikely that he understood. The experts on the Macmillan Committee and the Economic Advisory Council may have been divided, but it is still relevant to ask why such exclusive credence was given to "sound finance" by a Labour Government, especially when one remembers the volume of criticism coming not only from "irresponsible" left-wing circles, but also from the General Council of the TUC, a body that was neither divided nor inconsistent in its opposition to deflation, and which could fairly claim to be in close touch with working-class opinion.

Largely as a result of the work done by Bassett, some of the worst charges of duplicity made against MacDonald at the time have been rebutted. There is little reason to doubt MacDonald's sincerity. Whatever his personal tastes and ambitions may have become, his faith in socialism was genuine. But his socialist belief was of a moral and millennialist kind, quite unsuited to the problems which he faced. It furnished a guide to the next hundred years, but not for the next hundred days. He quite rightly rejected as irrelevant left-wing demands for public ownership. He was anxious to demonstrate Labour's ability to rule responsibly. The crisis provided an ideal opportunity to do this. Once the crisis was over it would be possible for a future Labour government to embark on the slow path to the socialist millennium with its reputation enhanced.

The charges against the defendant's honour having been refuted, his monomania and political naïveté stand out all the more clearly. How could he expect the Labour Party to forgive the way in which he had treated them once the crisis was past? He had consistently favoured the opinion of the Opposition and the banking community over that of his own followers. The May Committee Report was clearly a bludgeon to be used against his own party; the Minority Report was passed over. When the bankers offered advice (which it

[1] See R. Bassett, *op. cit.*, pp. 338-357.

was), it was called simply advice; when the TUC offered advice (which it was), it was called dictation. It is not difficult to understand what an impossible strain MacDonald's behaviour placed on the credulity of his perplexed and frustrated followers.

# CHAPTER EIGHT

# Keynes and the Academic Community, 1919-1936

In the economic debates of the 'twenties Keynes emerged as the leading critic of official policies and financial orthodoxy. By 1931 he had made a good deal of progress towards the policy position which we associate with his name today. But it would be difficult to point to any case where Keynes's intervention served to alter or even modify policy. He described his contribution to the debates of this period as "the croakings of a Cassandra who could never influence the course of events in time".[1] It was largely as a result of this failure that he recognised the need for a complete reconstruction of the accepted body of economic doctrine. He also realised that if he was to influence policy in the future he would first have to gain academic acceptance for his ideas. As he said in the preface to the *General Theory of Employment, Interest and Money*:

"... if my explanations are right, it is my fellow economists, not the general public, whom I must first convince. At this stage of the argument the general public, though welcome at the debate, are only eavesdroppers at an attempt by an economist to bring to an issue the deep divergences of opinion between fellow economists which have for the time being almost destroyed the practical influence of economic theory, and will, until they are resolved, continue to do so."

Keynes's main achievement as an economist was that he carried through a palace—or perhaps more appropriately—an ivory tower revolution within the academic community. This remains true in spite of the profound influence his work had later on economic policy-making and on political thinking. In the next two chapters, therefore, we shall consider Keynes's relations with his fellow economists in Britain and America, both before and after the publication of the *General Theory*.

---

[1] *Essays in Persuasion*, p. v.

### Keynes and his Fellow Cambridge Economists

In spite of the heterodoxy of Keynes's views on policy, it is important to realise that for most of the 'twenties he was not at odds with his fellow Cambridge economists on fundamental issues of economic theory. Differences of opinion on such questions as exchange rates, monetary policy, wage-cuts, and public works did not turn so much on matters of economic analysis as on alternative interpretations of the political and practical weights to be attached to various possible outcomes.[1] With the *General Theory* before us it is possible to detect hints of Keynes's later position in the earlier writings, but he was only at the beginning of what he later described as the long "struggle of escape from habitual modes of thought and expression". By 1930, when he published the *Treatise on Money*, the hints were much stronger; but his instinctual grasp of policy priorities was still ahead of his capacity to furnish an acceptable supporting theoretical framework.

In 1936 Keynes was able to pose a choice between his own theory and something which he called, rather loosely, the "classical" theory. But in 1925 he spoke of two views of economic society which were differentiated not so much in theoretical as in political or moral terms.

> "The one theory maintains that wages should be fixed by reference to what is 'fair' and 'reasonable' as between classes. The other theory—the theory of the economic Juggernaut—is that wages should be settled by economic pressure, otherwise called 'hard facts', and that our vast machine should crash along with regard only to its equilibrium as a whole, and without attention to the chance consequences of the journey to individual groups."[2]

There is, of course, a connection between this and the later choice offered by Keynes. Those who consider that it is difficult, perhaps even dishonest, to make sharp distinctions between positive and normative questions in economics would argue that Keynes's contribution as a theorist lay precisely in his re-introduction of "the moral problem that *laissez-faire* theory had abolished".[3] But while the moral dimension should never be obscured, the distinction between Keynes of the 'twenties and Keynes of the mid-'thirties must also be kept in view if we are to understand the purely intellectual steps that had to be taken to reach the *General Theory*. It was only

[1] For further detail on the cohesion of the Cambridge school of monetary thought at this time see E. Eshag, *From Marshall to Keynes* (1963).
[2] *Economic Consequences of Mr Churchill* (1925), p. 23.
[3] J. Robinson, *Economic Philosophy* (1962), p. 74.

after extending to its limits the apparatus of thought which he had inherited from Marshall that he saw the need for a change of direction.

As an academic economist Keynes's chief interest was in monetary theory and practice; all of his scholarly writings, *Indian Currency and Finance* (1913), the *Tract on Monetary Reform* (1923), and the *Treatise on Money* (1930), were contributions to this field. The first two of these works were based squarely on the quantity theory of money as it had been developed in Cambridge by Marshall and his immediate followers with an emphasis on the quasi-psychological motives for holding money.[1] Some refinements in the allied doctrine of the purchasing-power-parity theory of exchange rates were introduced in the *Tract*, and the influence of Irving Fisher can be detected in the importance given to monetary management; but in all other respects, as Keynes admitted, the book was well within the broad framework laid down by Marshall.[2] In common with other pupils of Marshall writing at this time, D. H. Robertson, R. G. Hawtrey and, to a lesser extent, A. C. Pigou, and in response to post-war conditions of mal-adjustment and instability, the focus of the *Tract* was consciously shifted from long- to short-run questions. It is from this work that the famous remark comes: "In the long run we are all dead. Econo-mists set themselves too easy a task if in tempestuous seasons they can only tell us that when the storm is long past the ocean is flat again."[3]

It is true that Keynes argued that "it has long been recognised, by the business world and by economists alike, that a period of rising prices acts as a stimulus to enterprise and is beneficial to business men",[4] whereas Marshall's mature view on this subject was that: "One wants very much stronger statistical evidence than we yet have, to prove that a fall of price diminishes perceptibly and in the long run, the total productiveness of industry."[5] But even here there is a strain within the orthodox monetary tradition supporting Keynes's view, though it must be admitted that it featured more strongly in the heterodox literature. Marshall himself at one time had inclined to the mildly pro-inflationist position.[6] It is perhaps symptomatic of Keynes's views at this time that he should have deplored the fact that what was basically a sound doctrine had got into the wrong hands.[7] He was later to be much more sympathetic towards heretics.

---

[1] On this see J. Schumpeter, *History of Economic Analysis* (1954), p. 1084; E. Eshag, *op. cit.*
[2] *Tract on Monetary Reform*, p. 85.
[3] *Ibid.*, p. 80.
[4] *Ibid.*, p. 18.
[5] *Official Papers by Alfred Marshall* (1926), p. 91.
[6] See Eshag, *op. cit.*, p. 74.
[7] *The Nation and Athenaeum*, May 24th, 1924, p. 235.

On the important question of the relationship between the behaviour of banks, changes in the price level, and their effect on business expectations, a less equivocal Marshallian basis could be found for the analysis put forward by Keynes in the *Tract*. In the first half of the decade after the First World War, Keynes's explanation of unemployment was almost exclusively monetary in character. Monetary variables were treated as the main short-run determinants of the level of output and employment through their effect on price levels, business expectations, and investment behaviour. Keynes's chief argument in favour of monetary management was that trade fluctuations and unemployment "were mainly diseases of our credit and banking system, and that it will be easier to apply the remedies if we retain control of our currency in our own hands".[1] In this respect Keynes found himself in agreement with Hawtrey, the leading exponent of the monetary theory of the trade cycle at this time. This explains why, in spite of the fact that Keynes and Hawtrey took up diametrically opposed positions on the return to gold and on public works, he could still say as late as 1930 that: "There are very few writers on monetary subjects from whom one receives more stimulus and useful suggestion than Mr Hawtrey, and I think there are few writers with whom I personally feel in more fundamental sympathy and agreement."[2]

### Academic Opposition to Keynes

The main academic opposition to Keynes's views on the gold standard and monetary management came not so much from his fellow Cambridge economists as from the London School of Economics. In the 'twenties the most outspoken opposition came from Professor Edwin Cannan, whose chief qualities as an economist were of a critical rather than a constructive kind. In his frequent contributions to public debate, Cannan maintained a dogged belief in the virtues of a commonsense approach to economic problems. He was, as a result, highly sceptical towards extended theoretical work of the kind favoured in Cambridge.[3] At the end of the First World War Cannan championed the return to pre-war price levels as an aim of policy, and the restoration of monetary policy to the care of an automatic, non-political mechanism. He showed little concern for the problems of distributive justice which such a policy entailed, and confidently predicted that "the cow of deflation has been swallowed

---

[1] *Essays in Persuasion*, pp. 232-3.
[2] *Journal of the Royal Statistical Society*, Part I, 1930, p. 86.
[3] See H. Dalton's account of Cannan's point of view in *London Essays in Economics in Honour of Edwin Cannan* (1927), p. 7.

in 1920–22, and the historian of 'fifty years on' will not waste much time over the disappearance of the tail in 1925".[1]

It was this type of thinking, more common in banking circles, that Keynes attacked in his *Tract*. Contrary to all enlightened opinion on the subject Cannan believed that banks were more like cloakrooms than creators of credit; he consistently opposed the advocates of a managed currency. As Keynes complained:

"Professor Cannan is unsympathetic with nearly everything worth reading, which has been written on monetary theory in the last ten years. . . . It is natural that middle-aged bankers should feel shy. But it is not natural that Professor Cannan should write as though none of all this existed, as though his own subject were incapable of development and progress, and as though the last word had been said years ago in elementary textbooks."[2]

In 1933, at the height of the depression, Cannan published a collection of articles, significantly entitled *Economic Scares*, in which he stated that "it seems at the present time to be the urgent duty of every economist to do all he can to allay the fear of insufficiency of work which is giving rise to all sorts of crazy schemes of social reorganisation".[3] The book is chiefly of interest now as a repository of the kind of thinking which Keynes considered it necessary to attack because it acted as a barrier to effective understanding and action.[4]

Cannan, it could be argued, was a special case. No other economist at the London School was quite as philistine on matters of theory. Nevertheless, there does seem to have been an especially orthodox bias to much of the writing on monetary questions by those who held senior posts at the School. It was Professor T. E. Gregory, for example, who accused Keynes of lending respectability to those who resisted adjustment to the lower price level required by return to the gold standard. By making monetary policy a political and class issue, Keynes had done the unforgivable; for "whilst it is not desirable to increase unemployment, reduce money wages and offend working class sentiment without good reason, it is useless to allow working class sentiment to govern monetary policy".[5]

Professor Lionel Robbins, in his work on *The Great Depression* (1934), placed a good deal of the blame for the breakdown in 1931 on

---

[1] *Economic Journal*, March 1927, p. 83. See also "Limitation of Currency or Limitation of Credit", *Economic Journal*, March 1924 and *An Economist's Protest* (1927).
[2] "A Comment on Professor Cannan's Article" *Economic Journal*, March 1924, p. 65.
[3] *Op. cit.*, p. v.
[4] Thus, for example, on the subject of unemployment, Cannan's book provides an excellent dogmatic statement of the comforting notion known as Say's Law which Keynes later did so much to undermine; see *op. cit.*, pp. 25, 37-38, 104-5.
[5] *The First Year of the Gold Standard* (1926), pp. 18, 44-5, 93-4.

propaganda for a managed currency, which, he said, "encouraged the belief that the stable price-level was the be-all and end-all of monetary policy", and "created an attitude of mind on the part of the educated public which in subsequent years made it more and more difficult to work the Gold Standard successfully". By contrast, he praised the "responsible men charged with the conduct of policy, although ignorant of the profound theoretical strictures which could have been passed upon the plan for a managed currency, [who] turned a deaf ear to all this talk and resolved upon the restoration of the Gold Standard." Unfortunately, those in charge of policy later in the period refused to accept the logic of Britain's situation, which called for courageous deflation and a high Bank Rate. Without knowing it then, the monetary reformers had undermined the resolve of the Bank of England.[1]

### The Tariff Question

One of Keynes's sharpest clashes with orthodox academic opinion before 1936 was over the tariff question. In 1930–1 Keynes brought down upon himself the wrath of many of his fellow economists when he advocated the revenue tariff as an alternative to devaluation, and as a means of providing leeway for more adventurous policies at home. The issue had been discussed earlier by the Macmillan Committee and the Economic Advisory Council, but in March 1931 Keynes made his apostasy public in an article which appeared in the *New Statesman*.[2] In the debate on tariff reform which took place at the turn of the century, Cambridge, in the shape of Marshall and Pigou, had provided two of the most authoritative defenders of the free trade position, while the London School furnished a base for the heretics.[3] In 1931 the roles of the two institutions were to a large extent reversed. In the Economic Advisory Council Keynes received somewhat reluctant support for a revenue tariff even from Pigou; it was Robbins who opposed the measure fervently. Most of the replies to Keynes's *New Statesman* article came from economists associated with the London School.[4] Much of the correspondence was taken up with technical questions concerning the likely effect of tariffs on British imports, exports, and foreign investment, but the underlying tone of outrage can be gauged from Robbins' remark that it was "a tragedy that he who shattered the moral foundations

[1] *Op. cit.*, pp. 77-8, 85, 97. For a similar, though much sharper, attack by another L. S. E. economist on British monetary policy in the period leading up to the 1931 crisis, see F. Benham, *British Monetary Policy* (1932).
[2] March 7th, 1931.
[3] See pp. 58-9 above.
[4] See e.g. the letters by L. Robbins, W. Beveridge, T. E. Gregory, A. Plant, G. L. Schwarz and E. M. F. Durbin in the *New Statesman*, March 14, 1931.

of the Treaty of Versailles should now turn his magnificent gifts to the service of the mean and petty devices of economic nationalism".

In the same year a group of economists, mainly connected with the London School, and under the chairmanship of Beveridge, produced an extensive refutation of the arguments currently being used to support tariffs.[1] Among these arguments, of course, were those recently associated with the name of Keynes. The authors were able to make full use of citations from Keynes's earlier writings to make their case.[2] They acknowledged that the deterioration in Britain's economic position as compared with the turn of the century made it necessary to re-examine the tariff question, but their conclusions, both on economic and moral grounds, were not significantly different from those of Marshall a quarter of a century earlier. Modernisation and flexibility were the proper solution to Britain's difficulties, not the application of short-term expedients likely to exacerbate the regrettable trend towards economic nationalism.

The differences between Keynes and the orthodox defenders of free trade at this time did not turn on matters of economic theory. As Keynes complained, his opponents had forced him "to chew over again a lot of stale mutton, dragging me along a route I have known all about as long as I have known anything, which cannot, as I have discovered by many attempts, lead me to a solution of our present difficulties—a peregrination of the catacombs with a guttering candle".[3] He was the first to admit the irrelevance of the revenue tariff after the abandonment of the gold standard, and in this at least he was at one with his opponents. The differences between Keynes and other economists on this matter were mainly ones of timing, urgency and priorities. Keynes was driven out of the free trade camp by his responsiveness to the pressure of immediate policy circumstances. A temporary revenue tariff might buy some valuable time for Britain's policy-makers, but above all it provided a way of avoiding the negative, contractionist solutions to Britain's problems espoused by more orthodox academic economists.

### Fundamental Maladjustments

Although in his attacks on the return to gold Keynes continued to argue that the deflationary monetary policy that would be required to support this decision was a potent source of unemployment, he also believed that other, more fundamental, causes of maladjustment

---

[1] *Tariffs: The Case Examined* (1931). The members of the group were F. C. Buchan, W. H. Beveridge, A. L. Bowley, T. E. Gregory, J. R. Hicks, W. T. Layton, A. Plant, L. Robbins, and G. L. Schwarz.

[2] See e.g. *ibid.*, pp. 52, 62, 242.

[3] *New Statesman*, April 11th, 1931.

were at work. One of these, he felt, was the growth of population. In the *Economic Consequences of the Peace* he had expressed some concern about the possibility of a resurgence of the Malthusian devil that had been successfully kept at bay during the expansive phase of European capitalism in the second half of the nineteenth century. Was this devil about to manifest itself now, when, for a variety of reasons, Europe's capacity to command, and the New World's ability to supply, foodstuffs was likely to diminish?[1] These remarks drew a rebuttal from Beveridge and led to a further statement by Keynes in which he claimed that the growth of population could not be ruled out as a possible cause of unemployment; it could be responsible for the "attempt on the part of organised labour, of the community as a whole, to maintain real wages at a higher level than the underlying economic conditions are able to support".[2]

In the light of later concern about declining rates of population growth in the developed countries, and the evidence of surplus capacity in many primary-producing countries, these views must be accounted among Keynes's less successful *obiter dicta*. By 1930 he had reversed his position on this subject, bringing him closer to the one that he later expounded in the *General Theory*, which was to form the basis for what became known as stagnationism. Nevertheless, the 1923 position on population is interesting as evidence of Keynes's willingness to entertain explanations of Britain's unemployment problem which were couched in terms of *maladjustments*, rather than systematic defects in the *normal* operation of the economy.

An instructive contrast can be made at this point with the views of Pigou. It bears out an earlier statement concerning the underlying theoretical consensus among Cambridge economists in spite of differences over policy conclusions. Unlike Keynes and Hawtrey, Pigou placed less emphasis on the monetary causes of unemployment; he chose to stress failure in the level of money wages to fall as prices fell (i.e. maladjustment in the level of real wages), and lack of labour mobility, for both of which there was some warrant in the works of Marshall.[3] As a member of both the Cunliffe and Bradbury Committees, Pigou had come under the lash of Keynes's criticism. In the *General Theory*, Keynes, somewhat unfairly, selected Pigou's *Theory of Unemployment* out for special criticism as a typical example of the shortcomings of the "classical" wage-reduction approach to unemployment. Not unnaturally, Pigou's review of the *General Theory* was

[1] *Op. cit.*, Chapter II. Here again the influence of Marshall can perhaps be seen. It was from this quarter that Marshall anticipated the threat to British progress; see pp. 28–9 above.

[2] See W. Beveridge, "Population and Unemployment", *Economic Journal*, Dec. 1923; J. M. Keynes "A Reply to Sir William Beveridge", *ibid.*, and "Population and Unemployment", *Nation and Athenaeum*, Oct. 6th, 1923.

[3] See pp. 49-50 above.

among the least sympathetic, largely because he believed that Keynes had been unfair in his treatment of Marshall.

But these differences of opinion, both in the 'twenties and later, should not be exaggerated.[1] In the first half of the 'twenties Keynes did not rule out the possibility that "excessive" real wages might be a cause of unemployment. He did not oppose cuts in money wages as a solution on *theoretical* grounds until much later, probably when he was on the point of finishing the *Treatise*. His objections to this type of remedy were chiefly on grounds of social justice and political feasibility.[2] Moreover, Pigou's position was more flexible than Keynes later gave him credit for in the *General Theory*. While Pigou in his evidence before the Macmillan Committee spoke of unemployment largely as a structural phenomenon, he refused to commit himself to wage-cuts as a definite policy, and suggested public works as an alternative.[3]

The differences between Pigou and Keynes can be explained in terms of temperament and personality as much as anything else. Hugh Dalton reported that whereas Pigou was regarded by Cambridge undergraduates in his day as the "Man of the Temple of Truth", Keynes was looked upon as the "Man of the World".[4] It is certainly true that Keynes was more often in the public limelight in the inter-war period, while Pigou was much closer to—perhaps even a caricature of—the conventional picture of the "Professor". Pigou himself once said that most of his life had been "that of a crab sitting in its shell, emitting from time to time streams of ink, but not coming out itself into the bad black world".[5] This was not always the case: as a young man he had certainly taken a more active role, even to the extent of appearing on public platforms in the campaign against tariff reform in 1903. A number of economists entered the lists on this occasion and the professional propriety of this incursion was questioned. Pigou's later cynicism about politics and his anxiety to remain aloof may have its origins in this period.[6] Whatever the reason, Pigou was certainly more inclined to caution, less willing than Keynes to try to impress his will on politics and politicians.

This is brought out by their respective attitudes to the gold standard. Pigou had no permanent allegiance to gold as the basis for the monetary system, but unlike Keynes felt that:

[1] For a more extensive treatment of the relationship between Keynes and Pigou on this matter, reaching a similar conclusion, see T. W. Hutchison, *Economics and Economic Policy in Britain, 1946-1966*, (1968), Appendix.
[2] See e.g. his conditional support for the *economic* principle of a national treaty to effect a uniform wage reduction in *Economic Consequences of Mr Churchill* (1925), pp. 28-30.
[3] *Minutes of Evidence*, May 28th and 29th, 1930.
[4] *Memoirs: Call Back Yesterday*, (1953), p. 60.
[5] *Economic Essays* (1952), p. 29.
[6] See *ibid.*, pp. 82-4. See also A. W. Coats, " The Role of Authority in the Development of British Economics", *Journal of Law and Economics*, April 1968.

"In practical affairs, to introduce large changes, the meaning of which most people cannot understand, is dangerous. So far as the United Kingdom is concerned, until the gold standard is re-established, more elaborate improvements in our monetary system are not practical politics."[1]

The same difference can be observed in the exchange which took place between Keynes and Pigou before the Macmillan Committee; it reveals a complete divergence in their interpretation of the proper role of the official adviser in economic affairs and may, for this reason, be worth quoting at length as an illustration of two possible views of this difficult, but now more widespread, art. Pigou was asked (and was anxious) to explain the attitude of the Cunliffe Committee towards currency management and devaluation; he said that the only question they felt it necessary to address themselves to was: "Shall we go back to the pre-war gold now or later?"

"Mr. Keynes: Did the Terms of Reference of the Committee rule out one or other of the alternatives? No, I do not mean that. Perhaps I should put my view. Prior to that it had been the decided policy of all Governments to go back to gold, and as a matter of practice, it was felt that nothing else could be done. No politician at the time advocated not going back to the gold system; of course, since then it has been attacked, but certainly my view as a member of the Committee was not, 'Shall we have some other system', though personally I was a stabiliser long before; it rather seemed to me that the practical issue was, 'Are we to go back to gold now, or are we to go back to gold later?'

"You ruled out the question, 'ought we to go back to gold, say at 10 per cent below the pre-war parity'? Yes. I thought it was not a practical policy.

"Was it not for the expert economic advisers to say what should be done and leave it to the politicians to say whether they would do it? The real practical alternative in my view was, to go back now or later. It may have been wrong. Of course one might be apt to say now that it was wrong because gold is not so sacred as it was, but this was very soon after an inflation, and my impression of the general atmosphere was that it was quite impossible then to have done anything else.

"You mean you recommended it, not because you thought it wise, but because you thought nothing else would be accepted? No, that was not the point. The alternative was not, 'Shall we have a stabilised system or shall we go back to gold?' The question

[1] *Is Unemployment Inevitable?* p. 121.

was, 'Shall we go back to gold now or shall we go back later?' and I answered that."[1]

### The Economic Rationale of Public Works

While Keynes believed that much of the unemployment of the 'twenties was attributable to deflationary monetary policies, his attention was not confined to monetary remedies. Even before the decision to return to gold had been taken, he had come out in favour of a public investment programme. After the decision, feeling that the path to a monetary solution had been blocked, the public works remedy acquired a new urgency. With the benefit of hindsight it is possible to see that pursuit of this line of thought was crucial to the position later adopted in the *General Theory*. It is interesting, there-fore, to trace the changes in the rationale put forward by Keynes to support his case for loan-financed public investment in this period.

In the earlier writings the case was connected with his scepticism about the benefits to be derived from foreign investment. In 1923, for example, he spoke of the importance of retaining more capital at home to preserve "our diminished savings", and to meet the increased need for housing, social overhead capital, and more efficient factories.[2] In the following year the same plea was sup-ported by the argument that, "current savings are already available on a sufficient scale—savings which, from lack of an outlet at home, are now drifting abroad to destinations from which we as a society shall gain the least possible advantage."[3]

Keynes had diagnosed that Britain was suffering from an inade-quate volume of domestic investment, but his explanation for this state of affairs was based on confidence factors connected with the fall in the price level, the inability of private enterprise to undertake certain types of large-scale project without state assistance, and the presence of institutional biases and frictions which tended to shunt British savings abroad rather than into domestic investment. One of his arguments to counter the traditional claim that foreign invest-ment was necessary to support British exports was as follows:

> "With home investment, even if it be ill-advised or extravagantly carried out, at least the country has the improvement for what it is worth. The worst conceived and most extravagant housing scheme imaginable leaves us with some houses. A bad foreign investment is wholly engulfed. . . . Investment abroad stimulates employment by expanding exports. Certainly. But it does not

---

[1] *Minutes of Evidence*, May 28th, 1930, Qq. 6075-6078.
[2] *New Republic*, Dec. 19th, 1923.
[3] *Nation and Athenaeum*, May 24th, 1924.

stimulate employment a scrap more than would an equal investment at home."[1]

In the lectures which he gave in 1924, under the title *The End of
Laissez-Faire*, he advocated state intervention in this field for reasons
which, though they sound familiar in the light of the *General Theory*,
were in fact based on quite different considerations.

"I believe that some coordinating act of intelligent judgment is
required as to the scale on which it is desirable that the community
as a whole should save, the scale on which these savings should go
abroad in the form of foreign investments, and whether the present
organisation of the investment market distributes savings along the
most nationally productive channels. I do not think that these
matters should be left entirely to the chances of private judgment
and private profits, as they are at present."[2]

We can see now that he had hit upon a theoretical issue, the importance of which went far beyond the immediate question to which
he was addressing himself. But there was still a good deal of confusion in his reasoning which was to remain until he was forced to
defend his position against the Treasury view, and was not finally
resolved until Richard Kahn worked out the theory of the "multiplier" in 1931. In the above quotations the brunt of his case for
increased participation by the state is directed against the existing
system of organising and distributing the flow of aggregate savings;
it is not an argument in favour of using fiscal methods to control the
volume of savings in relation to the flow of investment. As Harrod
has shown, the weakness in Keynes's case at this time is that he
assumes, as did the proponents of the Treasury view later, that there
is a fixed lump of savings; he was merely drawing attention to the
fact that existing institutions favoured foreign over domestic use of
that lump. He had distinguished between the employment-generating
effects of different forms of investment and their ordinary commercial rates of return, but was unable to provide a full theoretical
basis for the distinction.[3] The irony of it is that this was precisely
the kind of distinction with which he was able to confuse Sir Richard
Hopkins when Hopkins tried to defend the Treasury position.[4]

### Treatise on Money

By 1929, or thereabouts, Keynes's views on these and other matters
had undergone considerable refinement. The time was ripe for a

[1] *Nation and Athenaeum*, Aug. 9th, 1924.
[2] *Op. cit.*, pp. 48-9.
[3] See R. F. Harrod, *op. cit.*, pp. 350-2.
[4] See pp. 111-13 above.

major statement of the new theoretical conclusions which he had reached; this was certainly his intention when he began work on his *Treatise on Money* in 1926–7. In some respects the *Treatise* is a more conventional academic work than the *General Theory*; its scope is ambitious, attempting to cover both pure and applied topics, containing lengthy descriptions of banking systems and disquisitions on index numbers, as well as "a novel means of approach to the fundamentals of monetary theory". There are a few polemical passages, but on the whole it is a dry book aiming consciously at being authoritative rather than topical in its chosen field.

By the time it was published in September 1930, it no longer accurately reflected his state of mind; he immediately began work on its demolition. Instead of being an authoritative statement, therefore, it turned out to be more in the nature of a clearing of the decks, a record of what he had thought at a previous stage. It is an interesting side-commentary on Keynes's personality and his position in the British academic world that he could afford to be frank in admitting all this in the preface.

> "There are many skins which I have sloughed still littering the pages. It follows that I could do it better and much shorter if I were to start over again. . . . Nevertheless, I expect I shall do well to offer my book to the world for what it is worth at the stage it has now reached, even if it represents a collection of material rather than a finished work."[1]

In previous chapters we have mentioned the existence of what is now known as the classical dichotomy between the "real" variables connecting investment, output, employment and relative prices, and the "monetary" variables that determine the general price level.[2] Related to this was the lacuna noted by the Macmillan Committee when they complained that "there are no general principles universally accepted as to the mode in which monetary institutions and activities affect the economic situation, still less as to the precise degree of their importance as compared with other causes".[3] The *Treatise* marks an important step towards meeting this need, and it was as such that Keynes presented the reasoning on which the book was based to his fellow members of the Macmillan Committee.[4] Keynes did not abandon the basically monetary interpretation of the

---

[1] Keynes was always anxious to force the pace and move on to the next stage. This was partly a matter of temperament, and partly a reflection of the urgency of the sort of problems which he was tackling. Ironically enough though, the two-volume treatise now seems rather old-fashioned.

[2] See pp. 89-90 above.

[3] *Op. cit.*, p. 8.

[4] For accounts of Keynes's exposition before private sessions of the Committee, see Harrod, *op. cit.*, pp. 415-418; and A. Bullock, *The Life and Times of Ernest Bevin*, (1960).

trade cycle which is implied in his earlier writings; he was still chiefly interested in the monetary causes of boom and slump, inflation and deflation. But his analysis of these situations was considerably improved in the *Treatise* by the introduction of the distinction between aggregate savings and investment.

In earlier theoretical writings he had discussed the process of change from one price level to another in terms of changes in the quantity of money and its velocity of circulation. He now defined inflation and deflation in terms of the divergence between savings and investment. Accepting the view that in modern industrial societies with developed banking systems, savings and investment decisions are carried out by different people and institutions at different times and for different motives, the problem becomes one of analysing the consequences of divergences between the voluntary savings and investment of the community. Attention was shifted away from the monetary variables associated with the quantity theory of money towards the flow of money incomes, and towards the way in which these are received and then divided between the purchase of consumption and investment goods. Deflation, or the tendency for the price level to fall, was now defined as the outcome of an excess of savings, whether in the form of hoards, bank deposits, or purchases of securities, over net investment; and conversely for inflation. When subtractions from the income flow in the form of savings exceeded injections back into that flow in the form of purchases of new producers' goods, there was a tendency for the prices of consumers' goods to fall and for business losses to be incurred. The demonstration that "thrift" unaccompanied by "enterprise" could set on foot a cumulative downward process was clearly a step in the direction of a *General Theory*, even though in the later work savings and investment were defined in a different way. Investment was also identified as the volatile factor in causing trade cycles, while saving was spoken of as "essentially a steady process".

The policy conclusions of the model were that in order to maintain price stability the banking system should so regulate the terms of borrowing as to maintain equality between savings and investment. In the terminology which Keynes borrowed from the Swedish economist, Knut Wicksell, the market rate of interest should be equated with the "natural rate of interest", where the natural rate was defined as that which kept savings and investment in balance.[1] The problem of the slump was to reduce market rates sufficiently in order to stimulate investment. To a large degree

[1] For Keynes's acknowledgments to Wicksell see *Treatise*, Vol. 1, pp. 186, 196-8. There is no evidence of direct influence, and Keynes considered his product to be differentiated from Wicksell's at crucial points.

Britain's post-war difficulties could be attributed to the fact that, for a variety of reasons chiefly connected with the gold standard, the market rate had been kept too high in relation to the natural rate. Keynes also believed that there was a secular tendency in developed countries for the natural rate to fall, a situation which would dictate a policy of much lower interest rates over the long haul. The model also allowed him to show why policies for increasing savings, economy campaigns, and wage cuts were inappropriate and harmful during a period in which the real problem was one of finding ways of preventing excess savings running to waste in the form of unemployment.

## D. H. Robertson

The credit for first introducing the savings and investment terminology into the English discussion of banking policy must go to D. H. Robertson, whose book on *Banking Policy and the Price Level* appeared in 1926.[1] In this book Robertson clearly distinguished between the decisions to save and to invest, and explored a variety of circumstances in which decisions to save would not, without appropriate action on the part of the banking system, eventuate in any equivalent addition to productive capacity but rather would tend to lower the general price level.

At this time Robertson and Keynes were working along parallel lines, and although they ended up at different destinations, there is little doubt that they influenced each other considerably.[2] To some extent it is helpful to think of Robertson and Keynes as reversing roles in the 'twenties and 'thirties. In the period before 1931 it was Robertson who strayed furthest from the Marshallian path; afterwards, it was Keynes who did this, while Robertson, if he did not actually fully return to the fold, certainly became more cautious. Robertson's first book, *A Study of Industrial Fluctuations* (1915), although a work of synthesis, was conspicuous in the English literature for its emphasis on the effect of real factors—harvest failures, innovations, the "lumpiness" of capital goods, and the possibilities of investment booms overshooting the mark—on the level of economic activity. In this respect his work has strong affinities with Continental investment theories of the business cycle.[3]

[1] Almost all statements in the history of economic analysis containing the word "first' can be refuted: there is an extensive nineteenth century literature on "forced saving', which can be related to the points made in the 1920's; see F. A. Hayek, "Note on the' Development of the Doctrine of Forced Saving", *Quarterly Journal of Economics*, Nov. 1932.

[2] See e.g. Robertson's remark in *Banking Policy*, p. 5. that they had discussed the subject so much together that "neither of us now know how much of the ideas ... is his and how much is mine". For Keynes's acknowledgement of Robertson's influence see *Treatise*, Vol. I, p. vii and pp. 171-2.

[3] For an analysis and classification of the vast literature on this subject see G. Haberler, *Prosperity and Depression* (1937).

So far as policy was concerned Robertson had taken a fairly advanced line as early as 1915 when he supported "a more central-ised investment policy", and welcomed Bowley's public works proposals.[1] He continued to maintain this position in the post-war period, joining with Keynes in putting forward the Liberal case for increased state intervention to offset unemployment.[2] At this time, and notably in his evidence before the Macmillan Committee, Robertson subscribed to the view that depression could be explained as a temporary saturation of wants arising out of disequilibrating factors in the process of real investment. The drying-up of invest-ment opportunities to which this led could be aggravated by the failure of the banks to channel the savings of the community into productive enterprises. Unlike Keynes of the *Treatise*, he was pessi-mistic about the remedial effects on investment of lower interest rates. Under these circumstances, therefore, he placed great emphasis on direct action by the state to revive investment activity.[3]

After the *Treatise on Money* was published Robertson found him-self increasingly out of sympathy with the direction in which Keynes and his zealous band of Cambridge followers was moving. He preferred to retain his own interpretative scheme and terminology, and kept up a rear-guard action on their behalf. As the Keynesians moved on to more radical diagnoses and remedies, he became more and more convinced of the drawbacks and difficulties involved in the state commitment to full employment.[4]

## The Treatise and the General Theory

Judged by the highest standards, the *Treatise* was not as successful as might have been expected from a man of Keynes's stature at the time. Monetary and real factors had been brought closer together; he had moved beyond the quantity theory of money which had so far been the stock-in-trade of Cambridge monetary theorists; and there was a valuable discussion of "bullishness" and "bearishness" which was to stand Keynes in good stead when he put forward his liquidity preference theory of interest later. But the book could be said to be a brilliant performance along largely conventional lines. Even the

[1] *Industrial Fluctuations*, pp. 249-54.
[2] See e.g. *Nation and Athenaeum*, Aug. 11, 1923 and *Money*, first published 1922 (1948 edition), pp. 178-9.
[3] See *Report of the Committee on Finance and Industry, Minutes of Evidence*, May 8th and 9th, 1930.
[4] The above account by no means constitutes a full appraisal of Robertson's contribu-tion. For a short but balanced account see Sir John Hick's "Memoir" prefaced to a collec-tion of Robertson's *Essays on Money and Interest* (1966). For Robertsonian interpretations of the Keynesian revolution see W. Fellner, "The Robertsonian Evolution", *American Economic Review*, June 1952; "What is Surviving?" *ibid.*, May 1957; and A. J. Youngson, *Britain's Economic Growth, 1920-66* (1967), Appendix.

novelties, where they were correct, were only novel to those not acquainted with Continental thinking on these matters.

Looking back from the *General Theory* Keynes described the *Treatise* as part of a process of "natural evolution", though he admitted that this fact might be clearer to himself than to others. There are reasons for believing, however, that this interpretation of the relationship between the two works gives a misleading picture of the development of Keynes's thought. If the policy writings which are roughly contemporaneous with the *Treatise* are taken into account, it would seem that the *Treatise* does not fully represent the position which Keynes had reached by 1931. In these *ad hoc* writings he was freed from the constraints of an academic work, and the requirement of putting forward a totally consistent and determinate model. As a result, some of the weaknesses which he later noticed in the *Treatise* are not nearly so clearly marked in these policy writings. In this respect it seems more accurate to regard the *Treatise* as a retrograde step. This does not, of course, rule out the possibility that it was a case of *reculer pour mieux sauter*, or that judged by different criteria the *Treatise* is not the superior work.[1]

One of the main weaknesses of the *Treatise*, in Keynes's own words, was that he was "still moving along traditional lines in regarding the influence of money as something so to speak separate from the general theory of supply and demand" for output. He had "failed to deal thoroughly with effects of *changes* in the level of output as a whole". The "fundamental equations" which he had put forward required the assumption of a *given* level of output, and this prevented him from considering one of the issues which clearly arose from his savings-investment analysis, namely the possible existence of a number of situations in which savings and investment were equated at *different* levels of output. He had not entirely neglected output and employment changes in the *Treatise*, but he was primarily interested in explaining changes in price levels; variations in the level of output, where they were taken into account, were treated as a by-product of price level changes. In the *General Theory* this emphasis was reversed. At the same time he abandoned the Wicksellian notion that there was something which could be called unequivocally *the* natural rate of interest at which savings and investment were equated. Continental writers who continued to adhere to the

---

[1] The *Treatise* has recently acquired an impressive array of devotees, many of whom feel that it speaks more clearly to present conditions than does the *General Theory*. See R. F. Harrod in R. Lekachman (ed.) *Keynes' General Theory: Reports of Three Decades*, (1964), pp. 140-151; J. R. Hicks, *Critical Essays in Monetary Theory*, (1967), pp. 189-202: G. L. Shackle's reasons for favouring the *Treatise* are different; they relate to his belief that the *Treatise* contains a more genuine insight into dynamic processes; see his *The Years of High Theory* (1967), p. 148.

F

Wicksellian framework arrived at conclusions which were at variance with the *General Theory*.[1]

Another major difference between the *Treatise* and the *General Theory* was that in the former work he placed great emphasis on lower interest rates and easier credit conditions as the means of raising investment. He even went as far as to claim that investment could be influenced "to any required extent" by the appropriate monetary policy. He completely ignored fiscal measures on the grounds, presumably, that they had no place in a work devoted to the theory and practice of money. Once more, in the *General Theory* this emphasis was reversed.

Nevertheless, in the policy of writings of the *Treatise* period Keynes came closer to, without actually reaching, the position adopted in the *General Theory*. Thus, for example, in his defence of Lloyd George's public spending proposals against the Treasury attack in 1929, Keynes made full use of the savings-investment analysis, and revealed very clearly that the critics' case rested on the inappropriate assumption of full employment (i.e. a given level of output). His own position was based on the view that during a depression the excess savings merely ran to waste in the form of foreign investment, reduced incomes, and unemployment. Prior to the introduction of an explicit relationship between income and savings he was unable to explain precisely how a new equilibrium between savings and investment would be established. Even so, in lectures given in 1931 on the causes of the world depression, we find him using the terminology of the *Treatise*, but speaking of "an equilibrium point of decline" being reached—though he also described it as "a kind of spurious equilibrium".

This "spurious" equilibrium position was the outcome of two simultaneous processes: the fall of investment in working capital induced by declining output; and the eventual decline in savings, overcoming an initial tendency for them to rise as falling security prices eroded past savings. Both of these processes would operate to eliminate the tendency to excess savings and stop the cumulative process of decline. The desire on the part of the unemployed to protect their standard of life would lead them not only to cease saving but actually to dissave (i.e. borrow). More important than this was "the emergence of negative saving on the part of the govern-

---

[1] For Keynes's recantation on this point see the *General Theory*, pp. 242-3. For a detailed study of relations between Keynesian and Swedish modes of analysis see Karl-Gustav Landgren, *Den 'Nya Ekonomien' i Sverige* (1960); see also L. Klein, *The Keynesian Revolution* (1961) pp. 49-54. Sir John Hicks has explored this problem recently in relation to F. A. Hayek: see his essay on "The Hayek Story" in his *Critical Essays in Monetary Theory*. Keynes himself said that the Austrian School combined Wicksell with their own ideas in a way that obscured Wicksell's essential unorthodoxy and brought him back within the classical fold; see Keynes's preface to the German edition of the *General Theory*.

ment, whether by diminished payments to sinking funds or by actual borrowing", chiefly to finance relief or dole payments. These acts of negative saving placed a floor under the process of decline just as effectively—though with less visible benefit—as an increase in public capital expenditure.[1]

But this was not the only question on which Keynes in the policy writings, while still using the terminology of the *Treatise*, was moving beyond the confines of that work. As we have noted, in the *Treatise* his attention was confined to monetary anti-depression remedies, about which he entertained rather optimistic views. Nevertheless, in his defence of Lloyd George's proposals and in the addendum to the Macmillan Committee Report, he emphasised that a co-ordination of monetary and fiscal policies would be required. The Treasury was arguing that public expenditure on capital projects would either be diversionary or inflationary. An easing of credit conditions, leading to a fall in interest rates, undertaken without any attempt being made to increase the home demand for credit, Keynes argued, would merely lead to the export of capital and gold loss. A public works programme undertaken without a supporting credit policy would be ineffective and diversionary. Public works expenditure then, far from being inflationary, would create "a necessary condition for the expansion of credit to be safe". Only simultaneous action on both fronts would be effective.[2] This was the rationale also for the expansionist addendum to the Macmillan Report, where it was argued that the proposals of the main report for improving British monetary institutions and policy could not, of themselves, improve the employment situation without direct action by the government to prime the pump and increase the demand for credit. Despite the optimism about lower interest rates expressed in the *Treatise*, and his continued advocacy of this solution, in 1931 he did not believe that small changes in long-term interest rates would suffice to overcome the dramatic loss of confidence resulting from the world depression.[3]

Instead of regarding the *Treatise* as part of a process of natural evolution towards the *General Theory*, therefore, it is possible to regard the *Treatise* as the culmination of a separate line of monetary enquiry. Side by side with this, and gradually replacing it, there was another line of investigation which had begun with Keynes' interest in the economics of public works spending as a direct method of raising employment. When completed by Kahn's theory of the multiplier this

---

[1] See *Unemployment as a World Problem*, Harris Foundation Lectures, 1931, pp. 20-7.
[2] See *Essays in Persuasion*, pp. 124-6.
[3] See the *World's Economic Crisis*, Halley Stewart Lectures, 1931, p. 71, and *Unemployment as a World Problem*, pp. 38-9.

line of thought led more directly to the propositions of the aggregate demand theory which lie at the heart of the *General Theory*.

## Last Steps Towards the General Theory

The final stages in Keynes's intellectual journey towards the *General Theory* in the years between 1930 and 1935 were undertaken, to some extent, as part of a collective enterprise. By this time Keynes had secured the interest and allegiance of a brilliant group of young economists at Cambridge, the substance of whose discussions and criticisms of the *Treatise* were conveyed to Keynes by R. F. Kahn.[1] The first point which this group brought out was the dependence of Keynes's "fundamental equations" on the assumption that variations in the relationship of investment and savings would affect prices directly, and output and employment only indirectly. The extreme case, where prices changed with no alteration in output, depended on the implicit assumption that total employment was given; an increase in the demand for consumption goods (a reduction in savings) would have to be accompanied by a reduction in the demand for investment goods. This they christened the "buckets-in-the-well" theory. It was plainly not a very useful one for conditions of less than full employment, and had, indeed, been attacked by Keynes himself when dealing with the Treasury view. But if changes in the relationship of investment to savings were permitted to alter the level of output, employment, and income directly, a further question arises as to the retroactive effects of this on the original investment-savings relationship. The key to the solution of this knotty problem was provided by work by Kahn and James Meade on the cumulative or multiplier processes set on foot by changes in investment and saving.

Ostensibly, the main purpose of Kahn's article, "The Relation of Home Investment to Unemployment",[2] was to provide a precise means of calculating the stream of benefits to be derived from public works expenditure. In this respect it was a pioneer effort in a field now known as cost-benefit analysis. Other writers, including Keynes himself, had noted that additional secondary employment would be generated by the direct primary employment on public works, but had been unable to state precisely what determined the relationship.[3] By filling this gap Kahn strengthened the case for public

[1] Professor E. A. G. Robinson lists the following names as being part of the "circus" at Cambridge at the time: R. F. Kahn, J. E. Meade, P. Sraffa, C. H. P. Gifford, A. E. W. Plumptre and Joan Robinson; see his memoir reprinted in R. Lekachman (ed.) *Keynes's General Theory*, p. 55 and pp. 89-90. See also R. Harrod, *op. cit.*, p. 432.

[1] *Economic Journal*, June 1931.

[2] See A. L. Wright. "The Genesis of the Multiplier Theory", *Oxford Economic Papers*, June 1956.

works. But this was not the most significant part of his contribution. In order to make his calculations he had first to relate an increase in public investment directly to the employment that it would generate. To do this required consideration of the elasticity of supply of output for the economy taken as a whole. If the supply of output was inelastic an increase in demand in the form of a rise in primary employment on public works would raise both output and prices. If supply was perfectly elastic, as was likely when men and equipment lay idle, then only output would rise. In contrast with Keynes's *Treatise*, therefore, the rise in prices, if it took place at all, was not considered to be a direct result of divergences between investment and saving, but a by-product of changes in the demand and supply of output, and thereby employment. Any rise in prices resulting from increased public investment was important now only in determining the extent of the secondary benefits: in so far as prices rose rather than employment the secondary benefits would be restricted.

A further important feature of Kahn's article was that by making use of work by Meade he was able to show the equality between the stream of savings brought into existence by the increase in secondary employment, and the original increase in investment. By so doing he pointed the way to the new theory of savings and investment used by Keynes later, whereby these were brought into equilibrium, not by changes in the rate of interest, but by changes in the level of output, employment and income. Kahn and Meade, therefore, helped to carry the discussion beyond the theory of money and prices of the *Treatise* towards the "theory of output as a whole" of the *General Theory*.[1]

By 1933 then, many of the essential ingredients of the *General Theory* were assembled. Armed with Kahn's theory of the multiplier, Keynes renewed his campaign to get the British government to abandon the restrictions placed on local authority capital spending in 1931, and to embark on a programme of loan-financed public expenditure on roads, housing, telephones, and public utilities. The idea was the same as in 1924 and 1929, but the case was strengthened by being made part of a consistent theory of incomes and expenditure flows. The size of the multiplier effect on any genuinely new item of expenditure would depend on the proportion of additional income "leaked" away in the form of savings, repayment of old debt, unspent

---

[1] It is impossible to agree with Klein's patronising judgment that Kahn "obviously did not see the great theoretical implications of his work"; see L. Klein. *The Keynesian Revolution*. p.36. See section IX of Kahn's article, where the implications of the argument for Keynes's *Treatise* are clearly spelled out. Kahn also generalised the multiplier principle to cover foreign trade, budget deficits and the burden of the debt; see *Economic Journal*, June 1931, pp. 181-7.

profits, taxes, imported, goods, and higher prices; the greater the
leakages the smaller the multiplier effect. Keynes's own conservative
estimate was that for every two men employed directly, an additional
man would be brought into employment. In answer to those who
objected to such schemes on simple budgetary grounds, he used the
same calculations to show that one half of every £3 million spent
on public works would return to the Treasury in the form of reduced
dole payments and increased yield from income taxes. His conclusion
was that "it is a complete mistake to believe that there is a dilemma
between schemes for increasing employment and schemes for
balancing the Budget. . . . Quite the contrary. There is no possibility
of balancing the Budget except by increasing the national income,
which is much the same as increasing employment".[1] The same effect
could be achieved by reducing taxation, thereby directly increasing
purchasing power in the hands of the consumer. In order to give
leeway for this he suggested suspension of the Sinking Fund—and
this, strangely enough, was the nearest he came at this time to
demanding deliberate unbalanced budgeting and deficit finance.[2]

---

[1] See *The Means to Prosperity* (1933), and articles in the *New Statesman*, Feb. 4th and April
1st, 1933.
[2] See R. F. Harrod. op. cit., p. 441. Keynes's motive for holding back from deliberate
advocacy of unbalanced budgets was probably that he did not wish to give the public too
much to swallow at one gulp. Kahn certainly considered that advocacy of budget deficits
at this juncture "must be regarded as a hopeless cause"; see his "Public Works and Inflat-
tion", *Journal of the American Statistical Association* (1933).

# CHAPTER NINE

# The Keynesian Revolution and the Academic Community

## The General Theory of Employment, Interest and Money

A year before the publication of the *General Theory* Keynes wrote a famous and characteristically immodest letter to Bernard Shaw in which he announced that he was engaged on a work which would "largely revolutionise the way in which the world thinks about economic problems".[1] There are few today who do not share Keynes's confident verdict in some degree, though some do so with more enthusiasm than others. The book posed a new problem and proceeded to solve it by creating a new branch of economics. The new problem was to explain short-term variations in the level of national income and employment; the new branch of economics we now call macro-economics.

Unemployment itself was not a new problem, but economists had either not tackled it frontally, or had worked with assumptions which minimised its importance; it was either treated as a pathological rather than a physiological condition, or as the inevitable by-product of other, and possibly desirable, features of the capitalist system. Similarly with the concepts of national income and output: these were not unfamiliar to economists, but the chief emphasis had been on long-term growth rather than short-term variation.

Keynes's first task was to remove certain intellectual obstacles which he felt had prevented serious consideration of this problem in the past and had led to misdirected effort. He had to show that involuntary, as opposed to frictional or voluntary, unemployment actually existed, and could not be attributed solely to the intransigence of workers in refusing to accept lower real wages. Wage-cuts might be a feasible remedy for unemployment in particular trades taken singly, just as improved labour mobility could help to remove frictional unemployment; but neither of these remedies could be regarded as an effective weapon against involuntary unemployment on an economy-wide basis, certainly not in the manner suggested by ordinary price theory. More powerful and systematic forces were at work on the level of employment and wages than could be discerned

[1] Quoted in R.F. Harrod, *Life of Keynes*, p. 462.

by an examination of the frictions and maladjustments of the labour market alone. In presenting the main outline of his theory Keynes preferred to operate with the assumption, which he believed to be a realistic one, that money wages are rigid so far as downward movements are concerned; in other words, that organised groups of workers would resist cuts in money wages. It was in this context too that Keynes set out to show that Say's Law—the notion that since aggregate supply creates (is identical with) aggregate demand there need be no concern about the level of demand—was an erroneous attempt to abolish the problem of general unemployment in a money economy.

All of this was by way of setting the stage for his own theory of income and employment. In the short run—the period with which Keynes was primarily concerned—the aggregate supply of output and its relationship to total employment is not subject to large shifts. It follows under these circumstances that at any given moment of time the quantity of employment offered depends on the level of the aggregate effective demand for output. In a simplified version of the economy, with no government and no foreign trade sector, the two main components of effective demand are consumption and new investment goods. According to Keynes the aggregate level of consumption demand could best be treated as a stable function of current income, varying in the same direction but to a lesser extent than income. Savings were defined as the passive residual between income and consumption. By contrast the decision to purchase new investment goods was treated as a highly volatile element in the system, dependent partly on the rate of interest but mainly on the shifting and uncertain expectations about the future prevalent among businessmen. The decisions to save and invest, though taken largely independently, were linked with one another through the level of income. For an equilibrium level of income to be established and maintained the decisions of consumers as to the amount of current income which they planned to save would have to be exactly counterbalanced by the plans of investors to purchase new capital equipment. An increase in planned saving unmatched by an equivalent increase in planned investment would result in a cumulative fall in incomes until a new equilibrium was established at which planned savings and investment were once more equated. In the absence of any direct mechanism for reconciling the intentions of savers and investors there was no guarantee that equilibrium would be established at a level of income sufficiently high to eliminate involuntary unemployment. The multiplier doctrine fitted within this framework as the device relating changes in investment and saving to the resulting cumulative change in incomes at less than full employment.

As given so far the system concentrated on "real" factors and implicitly assumed that money enters only as a unit of account. It was also indeterminate in that it takes the rate of interest as given. In the "classical" scheme of things the rate of interest was treated as a "real" phenomenon mutually determined by the basic forces of thrift on the one side, and the opportunities for productive employment of capital on the other.[1] Keynes dethroned the rate of interest as the mechanism for reconciling savings and investment decisions; it reappeared in his system largely as a monetary phenomenon—as a reward for parting with cash, the most liquid of all assets. The monetary side of the Keynesian system consisted of a set of equations relating the supply of money to demand through the level of income and the rate of interest. Changes in the level of income that were not counterbalanced by increases in the quantity of money would shift the demand for money upwards, thereby raising the rate of interest. A policy designed to increase the quantity of money would operate on the system initially by lowering the rate of interest, and possibly by raising investment, rather than, as in some "classical" versions, by stimulating spending on consumption and investment directly. By being integrated with a theory of output, monetary theory changed its character. Instead of being concerned with changes in the general price level considered largely as a separate issue, it became a subsidiary element in a broader system determining the level of output as well as prices.

Although the *General Theory* was chiefly addressed to the short-term problems of income determination, it also contained observations on the possible long-term fate of mature capitalist economies. Keynes, it seems, like Adam Smith, Ricardo, John Stuart Mill, and Marshall before him, could not resist the temptation to speculate broadly on such matters. In the *Treatise on Money* he had remarked, more or less in passing, on the possibility in an old country like Britain of a permanent excess of savings over opportunities for their profitable domestic employment.[2] By 1936 these hints of long-term inadequacy in investment opportunities were more fully developed. When expanded and applied to the United States economy in the late 'thirties by Keynes's followers they provided the basis for a theory of secular stagnation.[3]

"During the 19th century, the growth of population and of invention, the opening-up of new lands, the state of confidence and the frequency of war over the average of (say) each decade seems to have been sufficient, taken in conjunction with the propensity

[1] The special meaning of the word "classical" here is discussed further below.
[2] *Op. cit.*, Vol. II, pp. 188-9.
[3] See pp. 246-51 below.

F*

to consume, to establish a schedule of the marginal efficiency of capital which allowed a reasonably satisfactory average level of employment to be compatible with a rate of interest high enough to be psychologically acceptable to wealth-owners. . . . Today and presumably for the future the schedule of the marginal efficiency of capital is, for a variety of reasons, much lower than it was in the nineteenth century. The acuteness and the peculiarity of our contemporary problem arises, therefore, out of the possibility that the average rate of interest which will allow a reasonable average level of employment is one so unacceptable to wealth owners that it cannot be readily established merely by manipulating the quantity of money."[1]

The significance to be attached to these remarks is problematical. They can be looked upon simply as an historical extrapolation of Keynes's short-term theory of employment. Like Ricardo's vision of the stationary state they served to dramatise what might happen if Keynes's policy conclusions were not heeded.[2] But Keynes could not preserve the pessimistic stance for long. He professed to see great social advantages in the gradual "euthanasia of the *rentier*", provided that rates of interest were kept low and the state acted as a balancing factor. In this respect his position has more in common with that of John Stuart Mill than Ricardo. Mill, too, welcomed the imminent arrival of a condition in which economic striving would be a less prominent feature of society. For Keynes, the advantages of the situation lay in the elimination of certain objectionable features associated with capital-scarcity. By reducing the need for abstinence an important argument for inequalities of wealth would be removed. Marshall dreamt of such a state but worried more about the need to preserve the virtues of economic individualism. Keynes, at this stage at least, considered that the dream might be realised within a generation, and was less concerned about—though still not oblivious to—the diminished scope for individual enterprise.

The shift of focus in economic theory brought about by Keynes was complex and pervasive. After over thirty years of debate there is still disagreement among economists as to the precise nature of Keynes's contribution.[3] Some of the problems entailed in inter-

---

[1] *General Theory*, pp. 307-9; see also pp. 218-221; 373-7.

[2] "This disturbing conclusion depends, of course, on the assumption that the propensity to consume and the rate of investment are not deliberately controlled in the social interest but are mainly left to the influences of *laissez-faire*." *Ibid.*, p. 219.

[3] Two useful collections of articles on this question can be recommended: S. Harris (ed.) *The New Economics*, (1949); R. Lekachman (ed.) *Keynes' General Theory; Reports of Three Decades* (1964). To these should be added H. G. Johnson, "The General Theory after Twenty-Five Years", reprinted in his *Money, Trade and Economic Growth* (1961).

preting the revolution, and in deciding in what sense the word can be justified, will be discussed in later sections of this chapter. A few of the leading questions can be mentioned here. Did Keynes's contribution consist in the proof of "under-employment equilibrium", the abolition of Say's Law, or in the overthrow of the quantity theory of money? Was the chief novelty to be found in his theory of consumption and saving behaviour, or in the concept of liquidity preference and the emphasis on uncertainty and expectations in the theory of investment? Can it be found in the integration of money and real variables, and in the shift from price to output levels as the object of analysis? Or is it to be seen in the shift away from micro- to macro-economics?

All of these positions have their spokesmen, and all must in some measure be taken into account. But the most straightforward way of interpreting the *General Theory* is in terms of the policies to which it lends support; and that is the special theme of this book. In this respect it represents the end of a purposive journey begun in the 'twenties with the rejection of deflationary monetary policies as a solution to Britain's problems, and largely completed with the publication of an expansionist programme in *The Means to Prosperity* in 1933. Keynes's instinctive understanding of policy questions was always more highly developed than his powers of consistent exposition of the underlying theoretical system.

From a policy point of view the importance of Keynes's book derives from its theory of income determination and effective demand, the crux of which lies in the relationship of savings and investment behaviour. Without this theory the connection between output, employment, and prices was unclear. It enabled Keynes to cut through the confusion of debate in the inter-war period, much of which centred on the conflict between expansion and contraction, reflation and deflation, increased spending and economy. The contractionist case had all the strength which comes from being in accord with ordinary household prudence. If business is depressed, incomes are falling, and excess capacity exists, the answer is to revive profits by cutting costs, reducing "unnecessary" expenditures, scaling down operations, and improving efficiency. There were plenty who took the opposite line, but they were only able to achieve token support until Keynes provided them with firm ground on which to stand.

It is a measure of Keynes's success that the basic ideas he was trying to get across now seem terribly simple, and far more compelling than those of his hard-headed orthodox opponents. Keynes showed that in conditions of heavy unemployment greater saving (or abstinence from spending) by the general public and by governments would not, of itself, raise employment. Indeed the reverse: every successful attempt to raise saving would merely reduce other people's incomes. He provided reasons for believing that monetary policy might be ineffective in depressions, and showed that a policy of wage-cutting could be disastrous as well as unjust as a means of increasing employment. He eliminated many of the cruder objections to public works spending and unbalanced budgets, and he showed why many of the fears that "uncontrollable inflation" would result from an expansionist approach were, to say the least, premature and ill-supported. By overcoming inhibitions and prejudices he provided governments with the tools needed to make them active and intelligent partners in the maintenance of acceptable levels of employment.

## Was it a Revolution?

Such in brief are the leading components of the Keynesian system as expounded in the *General Theory*. In the past thirty years or so they have been subjected to a vast amount of development and refinement as a result of theoretical debate, empirical studies, and practical experience of economic management along Keynesian lines. The Keynesian theory of income determination and employment, with all its accretions in the fields of international economics, monetary theory, and public finance, now forms an essential part of the standard undergraduate curriculum in economics. Several generations of students have learnt their macro-economics, if not without tears, then certainly free from the vituperation which the *General Theory* first aroused. The sharper distinctions between the "old" and the "new" have been eroded, or rather, they have been rendered less capable of provoking strong passions by being presented in schematic form. What was once revolutionary is now the new orthodoxy; and, as with most successful revolutions, it is sometimes difficult to remember what the world was like before. Each new generation of students finds greater difficulty in understanding the heated controversies of the past. Perhaps, they ask, "revolution" is the wrong word to describe what happened?

It may be worth asking whether the term "revolution" can ever be given anything more than "persuasive" meaning when applied to developments in a discipline like economics. It could be argued, for instance, that it is only in the mature natural sciences, with their impressive techniques for carrying out conclusive experiments, and their more highly developed sense of professional cohesion, that we can speak confidently of scientific progress—of one system of thought being discarded in favour of another and superior one. Are changes in what economists consider important anything more than changes of fashion, such that if you say the same things for long enough, like Sir Roger de Coverley and his clothes, you will find yourself in vogue some of the time.[1] We are back with some of the problems posed in the introduction to this study. Can differences of opinion concerning the ends of economic policy be distinguished from differences of opinion about the means of achieving those ends? In what sense, if at all, can economics be spoken of as a "positive" science like the natural sciences? But even if one were to accept the superior capacity for progress of the natural sciences when working "normally", there would still be room for the view that during a period of revolution similar conditions hold in all professional scientific communities.

Before this view can be considered an answer must be given to those who maintain that the term "revolution" is an inappropriate one when applied to *any* branch of scientific enquiry; that is, to those who reject the idea that the advancement of knowledge proceeds in a discreet rather than a continuous fashion. Something of this sort is implied by Gottfried Haberler when defending his refusal to regard Keynes's work as "revolutionary".

"As I see it, what is true of other sciences, among them the queen of sciences, mathematics, is also true of economics, pure and applied: the accumulated mass of knowledge is so enormous that it has become impossible for any single man, however great a genius he may be, to bring about a real revolution. It does, of course, require men of genius to increase the stock of knowledge, but the contribution of any single one is small compared with the existing stock."[2]

The idea that the growth of knowledge is cumulative is indisputable. There is good reason to believe, however, that a genuinely new piece of knowledge makes a *net* addition to the common stock, in the sense that like all innovations it also makes some of the existing body of knowledge obsolete. When looking at a successful revolution it is necessary to guard against optical illusion. After the event it is possible to round off the edges, heal the wounds caused by revolution, and redraw the line of continuity. This is what Marshall did after the marginal revolution in the eighteen-seventies. But it may be possible to do this—and it is an important task in any mature discipline —only by reformulating earlier theories in terms of the newer ones.

The idea that science advances in a smooth, unilinear fashion has

---

[1] There are those who would maintain, perhaps unfairly, that something of this sort has happened to the French economist, Jacques Rueff, an early opponent of Keynes, General de Gaulle's adviser, and one of the leading present-day advocates of a return to the gold standard.

[2] R. Lekachman (ed.), *Keynes's General Theory*, p. 296 and p. 284.

been considerably modified in recent years, partly as a result of Thomas Kuhn's important work on *The Structure of Scientific Revolutions* (1962). According to Kuhn, "normal science" requires the existence of a "paradigm" to which a particular scientific community is committed. A paradigm, such as Newtonian dynamics, consists of a set of acknowledged scientific achievements, a well-specified conception of the entities requiring explanation, together with the associated experimental procedures and standards of performance. At any given time the paradigm provides a programme of research, a method, and a promise of future positive results. Normal science proceeds by articulating, generalising, and making the existing paradigm more rigorous. Although research is geared to the existing paradigm in the sense that experiments presuppose results which are in keeping with it, anomalies will arise which cannot readily be assimilated or adequately dealt with by *ad hoc* elaborations of the paradigm. When the anomalies are thought to be serious, a state of crisis arises within the scientific community: the paradigm begins to lose its power to command allegiance; competing explanations will be advanced; there will be increasing disagreement among practitioners. It may take some time for a satisfactory alternative theory to be worked out in answer to recognised anomalies. It will take even longer for it to gain adherents in competition with the existing paradigm. The "old" may have an impressive list of achievements to its credit, the "new" will have none; an act of faith as well as of scientific judgment may be required.

The essence of Kuhn's position lies in his interpretation of the replacement of the old by the new in science as a revolutionary rather than cumulative process. Revolution is necessary because the choice between competing paradigms is a choice involving fundamental incompatibilities, which, by their nature, cannot be settled by standard criteria. Each paradigm contains its own evaluative procedures and concepts; there is no neutral court of appeal. The protagonists do not speak the same language or even see the same things; the competing paradigms embody different notions of what is significant; they do not solve exactly the same problems by the same methods. Under these circumstances the process of change must be one of creative destruction followed only later by reconstruction. Moreover, the debate on the relative merits of new and old is bound to be confused and inconclusive. And since there may be few commonly-accepted "internal" criteria, appeal may be made to extra-scientific norms and values. Conflict is not simply a product of incredulity and stubbornness in the face of unequivocal results, but it may be overlaid by personalities and a struggle for leadership and status within the professional community.

## The Crisis Within the Economics Profession

Making due allowance for differences in the attainments and circumstances of some of the natural sciences and of economics, Kuhn's perspectives can also be applied to the Keynesian revolution. The economic instability of the inter-war period, and more especially the depression and prolonged mass unemployment, provoked a state of crisis within the economics profession. The relative imprecision of the relevant research paradigms may have made it more difficult than in the natural sciences to highlight the existence of critical "internal" anomalies; but this was more than compensated by the existence of persistent pressures coming from outside the professional community for policy solutions.[1] The failure of economists to agree on diagnosis or remedies, and the ineffectiveness or political unacceptability of those remedies that were advocated or tried, helped to undermine the authority of the profession. Consciousness of this fact brought about a state of crisis.

So far as mass unemployment was concerned, the neo-classical paradigm might be said, in Kuhn's words, to have insulated the economics profession "from socially important problems that are not reducible to the puzzle form, because they cannot be stated in terms of the conceptual and instrumental tools the paradigm supplies".[2] In the period before 1914 this was not necessarily a shortcoming; it is the function of paradigms to concentrate attention on some problems rather than others. Any discipline that was at the beck and call, so to speak, of everyday events would hardly deserve the name.[3] It was not so much, perhaps, that economists had ignored unemployment as that they had concentrated on the problems of allocation within a fully employed economy. And when the problems of unemployment *had* been tackled, explanations which ran in terms of systematic break-down, over and above that caused by cycles of economic activity, had been rejected. The idea of general breakdown had been put forward on previous occasions by many writers whom we now recognise loosely as predecessors of Keynes; but what appeared to be effective answers had been given to these heretics. This may explain why it was possible for many to regard the issue as closed, and why the sense of failure was so acute when it was realised that existing answers were inadequate. It is more disappointing, as Kuhn has indicated, to find that accepted solutions

[1] Kuhn does not deal with the "external" influences acting on scientific revolutions in his book, but he recognises their existence and has indicated that they may have a significant effect on the timing of revolutions; see *op. cit.*, p. 69.

[2] *Ibid.*, p. 37.

[3] See G. J. Stigler, "The Influence of Events and Policies on Economic Theory", in his *Essays in the History of Economics* (1965), pp. 29-30.

to old problems are inadequate than to fail when faced with entirely new problems.[1]

There were, however, novel features in the inter-war situation both with respect to the extent and duration of unemployment which made it more important than ever before to re-open the issue. During the depression professional attention was concentrated on a fairly narrow range of problems; there was, as a result, less room for divergences of opinion as to the social order of research priorities. Many economists began to realise that they could not argue indefinitely that unemployment would not exist if only the world were a different place from the one in which they actually lived.

Kuhn helps us to see why we should not expect all members of a scientific community to recognise the existence of a crisis; and why it is more likely that the younger members of the community, with less at stake in the existing paradigm, should be more dissatisfied with *ad hoc* elaborations. Personal testimony as to the state of mind of some of the younger economists at this time has been furnished by Paul Samuelson, speaking as one who entered the profession before the publication of the *General Theory*.

"Events of the years following 1929 destroyed the previous economic synthesis. The economists' belief in the orthodox synthesis was not overthrown, but had simply atrophied; it was not as though one's soul had faced a showdown as to the existence of the deity and that faith was unthroned, or even that one had awakened in the morning to find that belief had flown away in the night; rather it was realised with a sense of belated recognition that one no longer had faith, that one had been living without faith for a long time, and that what, after all, was the difference?"[2]

A state of crisis merely provides the setting for revolution. In the absence of a systematic alternative to a paradigm which was being eroded by events, the only course open to those suffering from a loss of faith would be to desert or avoid economics altogether. Keynes himself had no doubts that his work would fill the vacuum, that it would "revolutionise the way in which the world thinks about economic problems". But the use of the term "revolution" at this stage, and for some time later, was still largely polemical. A revolution, after all, is a public event, requiring in this case the conversion of a significant proportion of the international academic community of the economists.[3]

[1] *Op. cit.*, p. 75.
[2] See R. Lekachman (ed.), *Keynes's General Theory*, p. 317.
[3] A contrast can be made between the marginal and Keynesian revolutions in this respect. The former took place when the idea of an economics "profession" was, to say the

Many reasons have been given for Keynes's success in carrying through the revolution. Keynes's personal standing in the profession definitely played a part; he was already an established leader. It is entirely possible that if the *General Theory* had been his first publication, it would probably have been dismissed as the work of a clever but pretentious crank. Recognition would certainly have been much slower. Advance credentials are essential in securing the serious and rapid attention of a professional audience: Keynes's credentials were impeccable. The assault on orthodoxy was all the more effective coming from one who had been brought up in its midst. Keynes certainly exploited this fact to the full, adopting a very different course of action from that of his mentor, Marshall. Most commentators agree that the extreme tactic was necessary; a more balanced work, stressing continuity, would have had less effect. By posing a stark, and in several respects over-simplified, choice between his own system and that of his contemporaries and predecessors, Keynes "helped to crystallise a compact group of followers by repelling and annoying some readers and attracting others".[1] The iconoclasm of the book was calculated to appeal to the disaffected younger members of the profession; it gave them a weapon with which to attack their elders. The fact that it also purveyed what might be called an activist philosophy sealed its success.

It is not surprising that those who lived through the episode use the language of religious conversion. Paul Samuelson has said that "the *General Theory* caught most economists under the age of thirty-five with the unexpected virulence of a disease first attacking and decimating an isolated tribe of South Sea islanders".[2] In view of the fact, however, that advance notice of the book led economists at Harvard to make special arrangements to get hold of it quickly, it would seem that some of the younger economists in the United States were only too anxious to expose themselves to the disease. It can safely be said that the low price of the book (five shillings in Britain and two dollars in the United States) had nothing to do with its success.

### Keynes and the "Classics"

While it was useful from the point of view of strategy to dramatise the differences between the old and the new, the same stance was not

---

least, embryonic; a mere handful of people was involved in the first instance. In the case of the Keynesian revolution, however, the profession was already well-established. It was, therefore, much more of a public event.

[1] The words are G. Haberler's; see R. Lekachman (ed.), *Keynes's General Theory*, p. 235; see also E. A. G. Robinson, *ibid.*, pp. 56-7 and 95.

[2] *Ibid.*, p. 315.

conducive to a sober appraisal of the relationship between the two ways of thinking. Keynes's own pronouncements on the relationship between his work and that of those he was attacking were frequently misleading and inconsistent with one another; they pointed in several different directions at once, some of which have proved less fruitful than others.

In the early chapters of the *General Theory* Keynes mounted an attack on something he called "classical economics". It was to be the first of several attempts to state the differences between his own and previous ways of thinking. In the first half of the 'thirties Keynes became convinced that some deeply-embedded inhibiting factor was at work within popular and professional economic thinking. This alone could account for his failure to make headway with the various remedies he had canvassed. The underlying cause of the log-jam had to be an intellectual one; it could not be explained simply in terms of Treasury intransigence or lack of political courage, important though these were. Most contemporary thinking was based on suppositions "which are only properly applicable to a society which is in equilibrium with all its productive resources already employed". It was no exaggeration to say that "many people are trying to solve unemployment with a theory which is based on the assumption that there is no unemployment".[1] It became essential for Keynes to track down the source of the assumption of full employment which had enthralled the academic community for so long, and had hampered his own and others' investigation of the contemporary breakdown.

Keynes now began to think of the history of economic thought along new lines. On the one side there was the dominant "classical" school of thought, who viewed the economic system basically as self-regulatory, capable of—though not always succeeding in—achieving a "normal" state of full employment. On the other side there was a long line of heretics who rejected this view and concentrated their attention, however unsuccessfully, on the inherent failures of the system to guarantee full employment. The first signs of the stance that he was to adopt towards the "classical" tradition can be found in his essay on Malthus published in 1933.[2] In this essay he championed the cause of Malthus against Ricardo, the father, as he saw it, of orthodoxy. "If only Malthus, instead of Ricardo, had been the parent from which nineteenth century economics proceeded, what a much wiser and richer place the world would be today." Presum-

---

[1] *New Statesman*, April 1st, 1933.
[2] The essay was originally given as a lecture but was modified at crucial points when it was published. It is now reprinted in *Essays in Biography*. An earlier sign of his shift of view can be found in the more kindly and tolerant remarks on J. A. Hobson made in the *Treatise*, Vol. I, p. 179.

ably, the work of reconstruction on which Keynes was then engaged would have been unnecessary.

Later scholars have shown that Malthus cannot properly be regarded as a predecessor of Keynes; the problem tackled and the tools employed by Malthus were fundamentally different.[1] But Keynes's essay remains an interesting source of hints as to his position at the time. He speaks as one who has "painfully escaped from the intellectual domination of [such] pseudo-arithmetical doctrines" as the quantity theory; and criticises Malthus for failing to recognise the need to provide a theory of interest which would show "how an excess of frugality does not bring with it a decline to zero of the rate of interest".[2]

By 1935 he was prepared to side more openly with the long line of cranks and heretics who had questioned the capacity of competitive capitalism, left to its own devices, to adjust to a level of full employment.[3] The publication of the *General Theory* in the following year marks the high-water mark of Keynes's revolt against his upbringing. It was at this stage that Keynes traced the common source of error in the "classical" tradition back to the acceptance of Say's Law; the allegiance to this Law of every economist from Ricardo up to Marshall and Pigou became the defining characteristic of orthodox economics.

There is undoubtedly a sense in which Say's Law is a unifying characteristic of orthodoxy, but in criticising a fairly crude version of the Law Keynes did little to clarify its various possible meanings, and the different role played by each in the work of earlier writers. Since he did not pinpoint the source of error sufficiently clearly, it was fairly easy for defenders of orthodoxy to show that earlier economists were not quite as primitive as Keynes supposed.[4] The task of unravelling the complex issues which underly Say's Law has been accomplished by later theorists, more conversant than Keynes with the part played by money in a general equilibrium system.[5] It is only fair to say, however, that Keynes provided the spur for this work to be undertaken. The selection of Say's Law as the source of classical error was not entirely a red herring, but it raised a number of issues which were not strictly relevant to Keynes's case; and even where they were, he did little to solve them. There is no doubt,

---

[1] See e.g. B. A. Corry, *Money, Savings and Investment in English Economics, 1800-1850* (1962), p 126; R. D. C. Black, "Parson Malthus, The General and the Captain", *Economic Journal*, March, 1967.
[2] *Essays in Biography*, p. 34.
[3] "A Self-Adjusting System", *New Republic*, February 20th, 1935.
[4] See e.g. G. Haberler in R. Lekachman (ed.), *Keynes's General Theory*, pp. 281-4.
[5] The classic summing up of this literature is to be found in G. Becker and W. J. Baumol, "The Classical Monetary Theory: The Outcome of the Discussion", *Economica*, Nov. 1952.

however, that the classification of the opposition in terms of their allegiance to Say's Law served a useful polemical purpose. It is also true that the Keynesian revolution in economic theory has made it necessary to reinterpret certain aspects of the history of economics. Although Keynes himself was a superficial and inaccurate intellectual historian, others searching with the light he provided have brought forward a genuine dissenting tradition which had been forced underground.

What has been said so far is probably not very surprising. It amounts to saying that those who carry through a revolution are not always the best people to make an impartial assessment of their achievements. Dissatisfaction with Keynes's account of his relationship to the classical tradition induced others to put forward an alternative version. One of the earliest alternatives was advanced by J. R. Hicks, and it is this version which figures in most modern text books.[1] Whatever the merits of such schematic presentations as teaching devices—and they are considerable—they are not particularly helpful as a means of understanding the Keynesian revolution as a historical phenomenon. The classical model in these accounts is a completely *a*historical fabrication compounded of elements which may appear in the writings of dozens of economists before Keynes, but which no single author, certainly none known to Keynes, can be held entirely responsible for. The classical system in this sense is a post-Keynesian construction.[2]

The process of re-interpreting the "old" in terms of the "new", so as to make it appear logically related, is one of the ways in which the unilinear view of scientific progress is perpetuated.[3] In spite of the psychological attractions of this view of history, however, it is likely to involve an optical illusion when dealing with revolutionary changes of direction. In the light of the Keynesian system it is possible to construct a coherent theory of output and employment that is capable of making *theoretical* sense of what many economists were recommending as solutions to unemployment in the inter-war period. As Samuelson has said, "the *General Theory* provided the tools of analysis for classical writers to understand and defend their own

---

[1] J. R. Hicks, "Mr Keynes of the Classics", *Econometrica*, April, 1937.

[2] In his original article Hicks made it perfectly clear that his version of "classical", theory was an intellectual rather than a historical construction. He hoped it would be more helpful in isolating Keynes's innovations than Keynes's own recontruction of "classical" theory. Naturally, he also considered that apart from being consistent in itself, his version of classical theory would be "consistent with the pronouncements of a recognisable group of economists". More recently Hicks has returned to the scene to put historical flesh on the bones of his "classical" theory. He now regards his earlier diagnosis of the revolution as unsatisfactory in its treatment of classicism; he feels it necessary to provide a historical as well as an analytical dimension to the problem. See his *Critical Essays in Monetary Theory* (1968), especially essays 8, 9 and 10.

[3] Kuhn (*op. cit.*, pp. 96–109 and 140) has shown how the reinterpretation is only made possible by grafting concepts derived from the new paradigm back on to the old.

views."[1] Similarly, we only realise the significance of the work of predecessors, or indeed call them such, when we are in possession of a new way of looking at the present.

By the same methods of assimilation it is possible to show that the Keynesian theory is not "general" in the sense that he thought it to be. Keynes himself was highly inconsistent in his use of this term. In the *General Theory* he claimed that his conclusions were "general" in the sense that the "classical" position could be subsumed under his theory as a special case. He was referring here to what has been called "fundamental-theoretic Keynesianism". According to this interpretation Keynes was emphasising the novelty of his proof that an economic system could be in equilibrium at less than full employment. It can now be shown, however, that the proof of under-employment equilibrium given by Keynes is incomplete, or that it depends on certain rigidities, inelasticities, and assumed patterns of expectation, which make the Keynesian model a special version of the fabricated "classical" one. This does not mean, of course, that Keynes's model was not the most relevant one, both economically and politically, for the problems of the inter-war period. And the plain fact is that this classical system did not exist at the time.

In the preface to the German edition of the *General Theory* written in 1936 Keynes said that by "general" he also meant to imply that his theory of aggregate output and employment was capable of being adapted to a wide range of politico-economic systems, ranging from *laissez-faire* to the more thorough-going interventionist conditions ruling in Germany at that time. But in the preface to the French edition written in 1939 the term was redefined once more to mean that the Keynesian theory dealt with aggregate or macroscopic, rather than with individual or microscopic, entities. This is the most useful way of interpreting "general", and it is noticeable that this usage emphasises differences rather than logical inclusiveness. The integration of the two ways of looking at an economic system has provided a research programme for subsequent generations of economists.

## Keynes and Contemporary Orthodoxy

The reception given to a major work like the *General Theory* is a vast subject; it might be said to comprise a large part of the subsequent history of economics. So far as the immediate reception is concerned, Kuhn's approach to scientific revolutions provides an explanation for the initial confusion. Those advocating change cannot depict with clarity all the features of the new world they wish to enter; the

[1] See R. Lekachman (ed.), *Keynes's General Theory*, p. 334.

old and the new do not face each other directly over the same terrain. This is certainly borne out by the early stages of the Keynesian revolution. Although Keynes had given plenty of notice of the general direction in which he was travelling—enough to arouse expectations and suspicions—the book itself was difficult to understand, abounding in novel and abstruse terminology, incidental excursions and obscurities. Apart from a number of brilliant passages, it was not even particularly well-written. Keynes himself did not fully appreciate what he had done until a few years later.

It is hardly surprising that the professional reception given to the *General Theory* covered a wide spectrum of views. Some were converted already, or only too willing to be converted immediately, while others met the work with stony incomprehension. In between there was a large group of sympathetic but by no means uncritical observers, who accepted some of Keynes's innovations while remaining sceptical about others. Some of those who began as sceptics later became converts; others—a dwindling band—remain convinced that the whole Keynesian system is either trivial or dangerous nonsense, or both. A striking example of the convert is Alvin Hansen, later to become the leading American Keynesian. His original review of the *General Theory*, while by no means unsympathetic, was rather aloof. He acknowledged that "we are living in an age when economics stands in danger of sterile orthodoxy", but did not consider Keynes's book to be "a landmark in the sense that it lays a foundation for a 'new economics' ". At this stage he felt it was "more a symptom of economic trends than a foundation stone upon which a science can be built".[1]

As we get further away from the event there is even less justification for apportioning credit or blame according to the closeness of the early reviewers' opinions to what we now regard as Keynesian orthodoxy.[2] Many of the early disputes were based on understandable misunderstandings on both sides, which have later been cleared up by argument and evidence. It seems more relevant now to concentrate on the broad conceptual differences between Keynes and his contemporaries rather than on points of theoretical detail. As Keynes himself said in answer to his early critics: "I am much more attached to the comparatively simple fundamental ideas which underlie my theory than to the particular forms in which I have embodied them."[3]

[1] "Mr. Keynes on Underemployment Equilibrium", *Journal of Political Economy*, Oct. 1936, p. 686. Conversion was rapid: the sentences quoted above were left out of the reprint of the review which appeared in *Full Recovery or Stagnation*, first published in 1938.
[2] For a thorough, but partisan, review of the reviews of the *General Theory*, see L. Klein, *The Keynesian Revolution*, Ch. IV.
[3] "The General Theory", reprinted in S. Harris (ed.) *The New Economics*, p. 183.

One of the leading features of what might be called advanced orthodoxy in the 'thirties was an attachment to the view that the business cycle was a "natural" and ineluctable feature of capitalism.[1] Considered as a "natural" phenomenon the downswing phase of the business cycle had a therapeutic role to play; it provided an opportunity to weed out antiquated modes of production; it killed off the "unsound" investment projects fostered by the preceding boom; and it prepared the way for healthy progress. It might be possible to smooth out or mitigate some of the consequences of violent fluctuations, but since the cyclical process was connected with essential, even beneficial, aspects of capitalism, great care had to be exercised in the choice of remedies; some remedies could worsen the patient's condition and impair his capacity to recover and carry on a "normal" existence in the future. The idea that nature has its own cures encouraged caution and scepticism concerning radical interventionist solutions of a short-term character.

Orthodox theories of the business cycle tended to lay stress on over-investment as the prime cause of economic instability; the differences within the orthodox camp mainly turned on the respective roles assigned to "real" and monetary causes of over-investment. From a Keynesian point of view, however, the similarities between these positions are more striking than the differences.

Joseph Schumpeter can be taken as a fairly representative example of the "real" interpretation. Schumpeter's model of the cycle envisaged a competitive economic system operating on a rising growth trend, but subject to random shocks arising out of the "bunching" of technological innovations; these shocks carried the system away from equilibrium, and cycles could be seen as the result of efforts on the part of the system to adjust to such disturbances. The close connection between innovatory activity and cycles implied that depression was a necessary feature of the process of adaptation involved in progress. A similar position led Alvin Hansen to conclude that it was actually dangerous to attempt to flatten out the cycle.

> "Cyclical fluctuations have the effect of giving the whole economic structure a good shake-up and keeping the system reasonably flexible and mobile. With the business cycle eliminated there would not be the periodic rubbing down, so to speak, which gives industry a fresh lease on life. Depression, like a cruel and heartless

---

[1] It is impossible to do justice in a few pages to what was a major academic industry for nearly fifty years, during which models of the business cycle were produced almost as freely as growth models are today; for a comprehensive survey see G. Haberler, *Prosperity and Depression* (1937).

tyrant, clubs down the impossible demands made by the employed agents of production, until the earnings of the factors have again reached a point at which full employment becomes profitable. With the business cycle ironed out, it can scarcely be doubted that the price and wage structures would become more rigid; the capacity to absorb labor displaced by technological innovations would therefore be reduced."[1]

Similar conclusions were arrived at via a different route by those who stressed the monetary determinants of over-investment. The leading representatives of this school of thought in Britain in the 'thirties were Hayek and Robbins.[2] They maintained that the causes of the slump were to be found in the nature of the boom, which typically began as a result of monetary expansion and a reduction in the terms on which money could be borrowed. The increase brought with it a "lengthening" of the production process. But an unstable and distorted set of relationships could exist between the investment and consumption goods' sectors, as well as between price and wage levels, if this process of "lengthening" was not the result of a genuine increase in voluntary saving. If no increase in the supply of voluntary savings was forthcoming out of the higher incomes created by the initial investment boom, the existing investment structure would collapse, bringing with it prices and incomes. It was possible, however, for the unstable structure to be supported artificially by further credit creation, by government spending, and by the "forced" savings resulting from inflation. This solution was capable only of prolonging the boom by creating further structural maladjustments, thereby increasing the length and depth of the inevitably succeeding depression. The most sensible solution for depressions was not to allow the inflationary boom to get out of hand. When depressions did occur, the remedy—if it can be called such— was to allow the restorative forces of the slump to work, purging the excesses of the boom, reducing wages and other costs, and eliminating the inefficient. Like the "real" over-investment theorists, therefore, this school of thought was largely opposed to expansionist and interventionist remedies, whether of a monetary or fiscal kind.

For the business cycle theorist the problem posed by the extent and duration of the world depression in the early 'thirties was to explain why the normal adjustment processes had failed to operate. A host of special factors could, with justification, be adduced; but a good deal of emphasis in orthodox circles was placed on the international

[1] "The Theory of Technical Progress and the Dislocation of Employment", *American Economic Review*, March 1932, p. 31.
[2] The relevant works are F. A. Hayek, *Prices and Production* (1934) and L. Robbins, *The Great Depression* (1934).

causes of depression:[1] the collapse of a weakened gold exchange standard; abnormal capital movements and reparations; stabilisation of currencies at high price levels; the failure or inability of monetary authorities to follow the "rules of the game"; and the growth of economic nationalism. According to this reading of the problem, the preconditions for recovery were a return to the virtues of free(r) trade and the automatic gold standard. The restabilisation of currencies in terms of gold was given first priority; only thus could trade, confidence, and international lending be revived. This view contrasts with Keynes's emphasis on achieving domestic stability, if possible by an international co-ordination of domestic reflationary policies.

Running through the orthodox accounts of the depression was the view that the interventionist trend of government activity in the post-war period was itself a prime reason for the failure of adjustment mechanisms to work as well as they had in the past. A good deal of attention was paid to labour immobility, wage rigidities, and militant trade union pressure in discussing unemployment in this period. Wage flexibility might not eliminate business cycles but it could certainly reduce their amplitude by helping to restore business confidence and profits. But it was not in the labour market alone that rigidity had increased; the growth of monopolies and cartels, state-sponsored producers' agreements, price-fixing arrangements, tariffs, and all manner of controls, had seriously impaired the normal operation of the system, making it respond sluggishly to changes in demand and supply conditions. Instead of permitting the forces of competition to pare down excess capacity, instead of allowing technical change to eliminate obsolescent methods and producers, the state had undertaken to protect the sectors most affected and most in need of change. Everyone from farmers to financial institutions was being sheltered from the consequences of change and their own folly; the forces of renewal could not take over while out-dated structures were being propped up instead of being allowed to crumble away. As Robbins said: "We eschew the sharp purge. We prefer the lingering disease."[2]

The assumptions shaping the orthodox position on this matter can be seen clearly in certain statements by Schumpeter. Like most economists, he believed that there was an underlying economic order with its own methods of adjustment. Separate from but superimposed on this natural economic order were a number of social and political influences. In trying to understand the inter-war situation, therefore,

---

[1] This was true even in the United States where, one would have thought, such factors would have been accorded lower priority; see e.g. Alvin Hansen, *Economic Stabilisation in an Unbalanced World* (1932).

[2] *Great Depression*, p. 73.

he warned that "we must always bear in mind that what we are faced with is never simply a depression but always a depression *moulded and made worse* by forces not inherent to the working of the economic engine as such". The distinctive feature of the world depression, in his view, was "the fact that non-economic causes play the dominant role in its drama". These causes he summarised as follows:

> ". . . impediments to the working of the gold standard, economic nationalism heaping maladjustment upon maladjustment, a fiscal policy incompatible with the smooth running of industry and trade, a mistaken wage policy, political pressure on the rate of interest, organised resistance to necessary adjustments and the like. . . . What we face is not merely the working of capitalism, but of a capitalism which nations are determined not to allow to function."[1]

With this composite picture as background the contrast with the position adopted by Keynes is easier to appreciate. In common with most economists in the 'twenties Keynes had shown interest in cyclical activity. There were, for example, chapters on the credit cycle in the *Treatise*. But in the 'thirties he began to break away from this type of approach. There were some "Notes on the Trade Cycle" in the *General Theory*, but as the title suggests, these were incidental to Keynes's main task. In the Keynesian scheme of things business cycles appeared mainly as a special combination of circumstances which could be subsumed under the general theory of employment.

Like many business cycle theorists Keynes emphasised the volatility of investment as the main cause of instability. But his policy conclusions differ from those of the majority in that he went beyond the normal type of contra-cyclical proposal, whereby the state, usually in the form of the monetary authorities acting on credit conditions and rates of interest, was advised to lean against the prevailing wind. In view of the damaging consequences attributable to the inherent waywardness of investment markets, he believed that "the duty of ordering the current volume of investment cannot safely be left in private hands".[2] Nor was he satisfied with remedies for slumps which mainly consisted of curbing the exuberance of the boom. "The right remedy for the trade cycle is not to be found in abolishing booms and thus keeping us permanently in a semi-

---

[1] See his contribution to D. Brown (ed.) *The Economics of the Recovery Program*, (1934), pp. 15-16; his views seem not to have altered later, see e.g. "The American Economy in the Interwar Period: The Decade of the Twenties", *American Economic Review*, May 1946.
[2] *General Theory*, p. 320.

slump; but in abolishing slumps and thus keeping us permanently in a quasi-boom."[1]

In these respects the approach adopted by Keynes in the *General Theory* was at odds with most of the views put forward by other economists in the inter-war period, including many who have usually been regarded, on some grounds, as allies or anticipators of Keynes. The contrast is particularly clear in the case of the monetary over-investment theorists. Keynes stood much of this type of diagnosis on its head: in his eyes the problem was to reduce voluntary saving and increase investment and consumption, not the reverse; consumption and investment were complementary rather than competitive with one another in a world of heavy unemployment.[2]

By shifting his attention from the determination of price levels to output levels, Keynes left many economists behind. He had never been particularly wedded to stable as opposed to rising prices, but his theory of aggregate output helped to confirm this disposition by suggesting that rising prices were simply the by-product of desirable increases in output and employment.[3] Those who associated rising prices exclusively with monetary mis-management or currency instability took a less favourable view of the boom. Here we have the source of an important charge against Keynes, that his system was *in*flationist rather than merely *re*flationist. Quite apart from the inevitable value-judgments involved in weighing the relative merits of stable prices and high employment as policy aims, this is one of the most fundamental analytical reasons for differences of opinion among economists on this question.

There is a world of difference between Keynes's espousal of "permanent boom" as a policy aim, and the kind of reasoning which led Robbins to conclude that "complete stability is probably un-attainable"—though a good deal of discussion could still take place on what exactly "complete" means in this context.[4] By curbing the boom in the manner suggested by most business cycle theorists, Keynes believed that the more worthwhile investment projects would be cut off, while "unsound" ones would continue. Except during wars no boom in the inter-war period had succeeded in achieving full employment; it was absurd to speak of "over-investment" in such

---

[1] Only if less courageous policy alternatives were ruled out would Keynes have agreed to use interest rates in the manner suggested by the contracyclical approach. But he considered this to be "unnecessarily defeatist" because "it recommends, or at least assumes for permanent acceptance, too much that is defective in our existing economic scheme". *Ibid.*, pp. 322, 327.

[2] On this see L. R. Klein, *The Keynesian Revolution*, Ch. II.

[3] *General Theory*, p. 328.

[4] See L. Robbins, *The Great Depression*, p. 130. See also his statement that: "No matter how resolutely we attempt to curb the boom, it is unlikely that we shall succeed in producing a state of affairs in which prosperity lasts for ever. To believe that this can be done is to live in a fool's paradise." *The Economic Basis of Class Conflict* (1939), pp. 242-3.

circumstances. There was still room even in mature countries for further capital accumulation up to the point where capital ceased to be scarce. On this question Keynes was also in conflict with unorthodox under-consumptionist writers like Hobson whom he had saluted as comrades on other matters. Only when the position of capital satiety had been reached would it be necessary to concentrate on methods of raising the average level of consumption rather than investment.[1]

Another way of depicting the contrast between Keynes and many of his contemporaries is to consider the whole question of relations between the state and the economy. The orthodox liberal tradition in economics, especially as interpreted by such writers as Hayek, Robbins and Schumpeter, tended to regard the ideal economic order as a relatively autonomous system operating according to its own laws. There is a sense, of course, in which this is true of all economic theory; but within the orthodox tradition the relevant peculiarity derives from the nature of the separation of economic and non-economic forces. Schumpeter's remarks cited earlier provide the clue; they imply that the state has a strictly limited role to play in the running of the economic machine, and that in cases where this role is exceeded, maladjustment and mal-functioning of the economy are bound to occur. Given a stable domestic and international monetary mechanism, and a flexible, competitive economy, the adjustment to internally-generated changes could be accomplished, or explained at least, relatively easily. The operations of the state should be confined to a limited and separate sphere. Hostility to the encroachment of the state on economic and other freedoms, and the belief that extension of state activity would undermine business confidence, was an important feature of the orthodox economists' point of view.

So much can be taken for granted. But there is a further issue: the presence of these attitudes had shaped the development of economic analysis in a way that inhibited consideration of a crucial range of problems. The separation of state and economy, combined with the emphasis on problems of allocating given resources, ensured that, apart from the traditional maxims of public finance and price theory, few tools had been developed to explain how the greatly-increased size of government operations affected the economic system taken as a whole. One of Keynes's chief contributions lay in integrating the concepts of state and economy, not merely by placing new items on the agenda of the state, but also by showing

---

[1] *General Theory*, pp. 324-6; 365-371. Keynes was more perceptive in his account of the relationship between his own views and those of Hobson than in other cases where he tried to establish ancestors.

how the private and governmental accounts combined to form a national income account.[1]

### Keynes versus the London School of Economics

An enumeration of the points of difference on matters of economic analysis and policy between Keynes and the majority of his contemporaries within the academic community does not provide an adequate account of the nature of the disagreement. A number of methodological and ideological issues were also at stake, as well as other questions involving the role of the economist in public life, the authority of the "profession", and the proper style of professional conduct. These points can be illustrated by developing some of the remarks made earlier about the contrast between Cambridge and the London School of Economics.[2]

One of the motives of the founders of the London School was to provide an alternative to Marshall's Cambridge; they also hoped that it would lead to what the Webbs referred to as the "break-up" of traditional economic inquiry. In its early days the School certainly succeeded in providing a base for unorthodox tariff reformers. Within thirty years of its foundation, however, the School had become the leading centre of economic orthodoxy in Britain.

One qualification to this statement must be made at the outset. As judged by the eclecticism of its recruitment of staff and students, London has always been an "open" university, certainly more so than Cambridge at this time. There has always been room for a wide variety of backgrounds and views, and there has never been a London "school" of economic thought in the same sense that it is possible to speak of Marshall's pupils as forming a Cambridge "school", owing allegiance to a single master or unifying body of ideas. There have frequently been dominant individuals, but they seem either to have been unwilling or unable to recruit an easily identifiable band of followers and disciples. It may be that a large city university lacks the necessary élitism and intimate community spirit to be found in an older university. By the same token, of course, differences of opinion can be tolerated more easily without the

---

[1] The characteristics and deficiencies of orthodox thinking on matters involving public finance in this period can be seen in the basically similar conclusions of two figures with contrasting political views, namely Robbins and Dalton. Robbins's most advanced treatment of the question of government expenditure and economic activity was published in *The Economic Basis of Class Conflict* (1939), Part II. For Dalton's views, see pp. 346-7 below. Robbins and Dalton were extremely tentative, not to say timid, in their approach to the problem; their treatment was also confined to the simpler question of public works and contra-cyclical budgeting.

[2] See pp. 58-9 and pp. 148-51 above.

vituperative partisanship that has sometimes characterised Cambridge intellectual life. Having made this point, it is still true to say that many of the staunchest defenders of the orthodox viewpoint in the inter-war period were connected with the London School. The two most prominent spokesmen for this position in the 'thirties were Professors Hayek and Robbins; and it is from their writings that one gets the clearest notion of the contrasts which lie beneath the analytical debate initiated by Keynes.[1]

One of Keynes's motives in writing the *General Theory* was "to bring to an issue the deep divergences of opinion between fellow economists which have for the time being almost destroyed the practical influence of economic theory, and will, until they are resolved, continue to do so". Hayek, in his inaugural lecture given in 1933, addressed himself to a similar problem: Why was it that in spite of the practical relevance of his subject "the economist appears to be hopelessly out of tune with his time, giving impractical advice to which the public is not disposed to listen, and having no influence upon contemporary events?"[2] Hayek's approach could not be more different from that of Keynes, or indeed that of Marshall faced with a similar crisis in the 'eighties. Intellectual isolation and unpopularity, he maintained, was the normal and proper state of affairs for the economist—it was ever thus.

> ". . . it is probably no exaggeration to say that economics developed mainly as the outcome of the investigation and refutation of successive Utopian proposals—if by 'Utopian' we mean proposals for the improvement of undesirable effects of the existing system, based on a complete disregard of those forces which actually enable it to work."[3]

According to Hayek it was the job of the economist to bring to light the hidden connections between individual actions, to reveal "unsuspected order" in economic affairs.

> ". . . to show that . . . the co-ordination of individual efforts in society is not the product of deliberate planning, but has been brought about . . . by means which nobody wanted or understood,

---

[1] It should be made clear that the contrasts dealt with here, unlike some of the policy and theory issues dealt with earlier, rarely resulted in direct confrontation between Keynes and the representatives of orthodoxy at the L.S.E. On many of the points made here it is at least as likely that economists at the L.S.E. were carrying on a domestic battle with their colleagues in other departments—notably perhaps Harold Laski and R. H. Tawney.

[2] "The Trend of Economic Thinking", *Economica*, May 1933.

[3] A similar view was put forward by W. H. Hutt in a book explicitly devoted to a defence of classical orthodoxy when he acknowledged that "the orthodox economist is deeply conscious of his impotence to influence opinion". See *Economists and the Public* (1936), p. 34. Hutt acknowledged his debt to Cannan and Robbins in the Preface.

and which in isolation might be regarded as some of the most objectionable features of the system."

The trend of such statements is clear. It is not difficult to see how this belief in the organic nature of economic life, the idea of an underlying harmonious order which is obscured from the view of the over-zealous reformer of particular abuses, could form the basis for an elaborate defence of the *status quo*. Even abuses have their place in maintaining the system if we look at them in the proper "objective" spirit. One consequence of adopting the Hayekian position—which has, of course, a venerable ancestry—is that the economist becomes an apologist for certain features of an unregulated, competitive form of capitalism. A more serious consequence for the economist who was exclusively attached to this ideal was that he became little more than a Jeremiah in the circumstances of the 'thirties. As the range of state economic intervention expanded, the upholder of the organic position found himself increasingly isolated from public opinion and action, condemning all around him by reference to an ideal state of affairs, perfect markets and the rest, which no longer and perhaps never had existed.

In addition to aloofness the other main characteristic of the orthodox stance at this time was professional defensiveness. At a time when Keynes was stressing the disagreements within the academic community, and adopting an increasingly favourable attitude to economic heretics, Robbins and Hayek were engaged in an effort to close the ranks and protect the authority of economics from attacks from within and without. Robbins's famous *Essay on the Nature and Significance of Economic Science*, first published in 1932, typifies this attitude. From the tone adopted in this work it would be difficult to tell that economics was on the brink of revolution. Robbins obviously felt that the paradigmatic form of economics had been settled, and that the time was ripe for a summary statement of the scope of the subject. For as he said, "there is no longer any ground for serious differences of opinion on these matters, once the issues are clearly stated". "The efforts of economists during the last hundred and fifty years have resulted in the establishment of a body of generalisations whose substantial accuracy and importance are open to question only by the ignorant and perverse."[1] The definition of economics as "a science which studies human behaviour as a relationship between ends and scarce means which have alternative uses" virtually confines the subject to the economic problem as conceived by the neo-classical tradition, particularly as interpreted by Vienna rather than Cambridge.

[1] *Op. cit.*, Preface and p. 1.

An important feature of Robbins's methodological position was a firm application of the means/ends distinction. The economist was qualified to speak on the former but went beyond his proper provenance as a scientist by commenting on the latter. He later denied that he "had urged that economists should play no part in shaping the conduct of affairs", but the emphasis of the work is decidedly defensive of "purism". By reiterating this position at a time when many economists were, quite understandably, anxious to contribute to the public debate on policy, he created the impression that they would be better employed in cultivating the established fields of theoretical interest.

Robbins also maintained that economics was chiefly concerned with "ends" which are those of individuals rather than collectivities, and with situations where the "means" are privately owned and exchanged. It was not so much that economics was inapplicable to communist societies, but that "where independent initiative in social relationships is permitted to the individual there economic analysis comes into its own".[1] It is surely one of the ironies of the history of the London School that an institution founded on the belief that any objective study of society would inevitably support socialism should have had in two of its chairs in the 'thirties the most outspoken advocates of the view that the laws of economics demonstrate the impossibility and/or impractability of socialist planning as a rational economic system.[2] Moreover, the intrusion of Robbins's own value-judgments concerning the desirability of a particular socio-economic framework or set of means did not chime well with his belief in the necessity for objectivity in the economists' assessment of alternative means.

In a world which saw a retreat on all fronts from liberal ideals, a world which saw the dramatic rise of economic nationalism, the spread of state intervention in industry and agriculture, not to mention Soviet Communism, and German and Italian Fascism, it is not difficult to understand the feelings of the economic liberals of the London School at this time. They deplored the encroachment of politics on economic life; they did not consider it incongruous in the circumstances of the day to couple efforts by the British government to "co-ordinate" transport with the attempt to establish a Fascist corporate state.[3] Hayek's *Road to Serfdom* (1944) represents the high-water mark of this kind of reaction.

Keynes can hardly be described as indifferent to the claims of the liberal tradition on many matters. He was no less critical than

---

[1] *Ibid.*, p. 19.
[2] See e.g. L. Robbins, *The Great Depression*, pp. 148-159; and F. A. Hayek (ed.) *Collectivist Economic Planning* (1935).
[3] See e.g. L. Robbins, *The Economic Basis of Class Conflict* (1939), p. vii.

Robbins of the restrictionist philosophy which underlay many of the policies for recovery being tried in Britain and the United States.[1] Nor was he enamoured of doctrinaire socialist ideas on state ownership and intervention.[2] After reading Hayek's *Road to Serfdom*, he wrote that "morally and philosophically I find myself in agreement with virtually the whole of it". It is quite clear, however, that Keynes was optimistic about the prospects of moderate planning in a society like Britain. "Dangerous acts can be done safely in a community which thinks and feels rightly, which would be the way to hell if they were executed by those who think and feel wrongly."[3] But there is sufficient evidence of Keynes's basic sympathy with the liberal tradition—even though he lavished none of the care, attention and understanding on it that Hayek and Robbins have done—to make it necessary to ask why he did not react in the same way to the signs of its decaying influence. The answer seems to lie in the divergent backgrounds and styles of professional conduct of Keynes and the London School liberals.

As an economic theorist Keynes was not so exclusively concerned, as Hayek and Robbins were, with monetary stability and the efficiency of the price mechanism. His whole approach to the problems of economic policy was more optimistic, more pragmatic, more insular, more opportunist, more concerned with short-term advance. He criticised restrictionist measures but did so with less emotion; he believed that his own theory of employment provided a practicable alternative. He could be placed in the position of Cassandra but did not find it necessary to become a Jeremiah. In other words, Keynes found it easier to come to terms with the rigidities and opportunities created by the rise of a mixed form of welfare capitalism.

To appreciate the contrasting position taken up by Hayek and Robbins it seems important to mention the Austrian influence on both, the one by birth and education, the other by intellectual influence.[4] In Austria and Germany the forces of anti-positivism were stronger, the attachment to liberal ideas more precarious. No clearer proof of this was needed than the rise of National Socialism in Germany. In terms of intellectual debate, however, the roots go back to the *methodenstreit* which began towards the end of the nineteenth century. This was a more virulent and long-standing Austro-

---

[1] For Keynes's views on this matter see pp. 232-5 below. His criticisms of certain aspects of the New Deal are close to those of L. Robbins, *Great Depression*, Ch. VIII.

[2] See pp. 322-3 below.

[3] See R. F. Harrod, *op. cit.*, pp. 436-7.

[4] It should be made clear that the Austrian influence on the position adopted by Hayek and Robbins is merely one strand in the liberal tradition which they represent. Few people have done more to establish the English and Scottish ancestry of "true" liberalism than Hayek; see e.g. his *Studies in Philosophy, Politics and Economics* (1967).

G

German equivalent of the English debate between economic theorists and historians. In Germany, where the historical school held sway, many of the holders of academic chairs considered it part of their duties to act as advocates for social reform along paternalist lines. It was at one and the same time a national and a nationalist school of economic thought, in the same way that the English economic historians who supported tariff reform were frequently "Big Englanders".[1] The Austrian School, the spokesmen for deductive theory, liberal rationalism, and individualism were ranged against the historians. In addition to the methodological and ideological issues which divided the two schools of thought there were questions involving the "proper" rules of academic conduct. Many theorists, for example, believed that the historians abused their academic position and forsook claims to objectivity by identifying themselves openly with particular types of policy.

The echoes of the *methodenstreit* are frequent in Robbins's *Nature and Significance*. They underlie the rigid ends/means division, the stress on objectivity, and the weight attached to the distinction made between the propositions of economic theory and statements based on historical or empirical evidence. According to Robbins, economic theory was a deductive structure erected on the basis of a few intuitively obvious postulates which are impervious to empirical tests. While paying lip-service to empirical research on grounds of "practical utility", he went out of his way to stress the conventional and arbitrary nature of all quantitative evidence. It could never aspire to the status of economic law, and therefore could never provide a firm foundation for detailed planning or prediction.

In a wider sense too there was a tendency to import categories into English discussions that had proved necessary in the Austro-German debates. There may have been an element of professional distaste for the kind of open and popular advocacy that Keynes indulged in. Keynes's behaviour was extremely "unacademic" in many ways, certainly by the standards of the day. As a result of financial speculation in the foreign exchange market he had made himself a wealthy man. He was an active journalist and broadcaster; he had City interests. He was often careless and unscholarly in his academic writings. His language was extravagant; there was a disconcerting streak of perversity in his character which manifested itself in a desire to shock his audience. At the same time, however, he was an acknowledged leader in his profession, and the editor of the *Economic Journal*.[2]

---

[1] See pp. 57-8 above.

[2] Here again W. H. Hutt's *Economist and the Public* may provide a clue to the attitude of London School liberals on this matter. In this book he formulated a number of rules of professional conduct for ensuring "disinterestedness", which he hoped would help to restore

There were in addition specific causes for complaint by those of an orthodox turn of mind. Keynes had advocated "inflationary" ideas on monetary management in the 'twenties and sided with the protectionists in 1931. In 1933 he had written a long article on "National Self-Sufficiency" in which he spoke of the changing attitude towards cosmopolitan free trade doctrines in terms of a movement away from nineteenth century methods and values. Nor is it difficult to see the offence which the following remarks could give to men like Hayek and Robbins, especially when it is remembered that the "law of diminishing importance of foreign trade" featured prominently in the works of several German historical economists.

"I sympathise . . . with those who would minimise, rather than with those who would maximise, economic entanglement between nations. Ideas, knowledge, art, hospitality, travel—these are the things which should of their nature be international. But let goods be homespun whenever it is reasonably and conveniently possible; and, above all, let finance be primarily national."

Keynes's motive in stressing the need to forsake nineteenth century ideas of individualistic capitalism, free trade, and the rest, were bound up with a vague belief that freedom from "economic entanglement" was essential "in order to make our own favourite experiments towards the ideal social republic of the future".[1] What was this ideal social republic? Those already suspicious of the trend of Keynes's thinking could only view with further alarm the statement in the preface to the German edition of the *General Theory*, written in 1936, in which he commended the work to a German audience on the following grounds:

". . . the theory of production as a whole, which is the goal of this book, can much more easily be adapted to the conditions of a total state. . . . Although I have worked out the theory mainly with Anglo-Saxon conditions in view, where *laissez-faire* remains in control over large areas, my theory can equally be applied to

---

and preserve the authority of orthodox economics. Keynes offended against most of them And while Keynes was not mentioned in this context, Hutt was certainly aware of the dangers to "authority" of Keynes's attack; see *op. cit.*, p. 245. For comment on Hutt in the light of a general treatment of the problem of "authority" see A. W. Coats, "The Role of Authority in the Development of British Economics", *Journal of Law and Economics*, Oct. 1964. The propriety of academic involvement in party politics was an active issue at the L.S.E. during the 'thirties. See e.g. H. Dalton, *Call Back Yesterday* (1953), pp. 120-4; K. Martin, *Harold Laski* (1953), pp. 43-4, 69; and W. Beveridge, *The London School of Economics and Its Problems, 1919-1937* (1960), pp. 52-8.

[1] "National Self-Sufficiency" was originally given as a lecture in Dublin. It appeared in *Quarterly*, an Irish journal, *Yale Review*, June 1933, and the *New Statesman*, July 8th and 15th, 1933. The fact that it also appeared in German in *Schmoller's Jahrbuch*, one of the leading journals of the Historical School, cannot have been comforting to liberal anxieties.

situations in which state intervention [guidance] is more extensive."[1]

Ostensibly standing outside the rival theoretical camps was what
might be called the empiricist point of view. A leading contributor
to this school of thought was the Director of the London School
himself, William Beveridge, a second edition of whose massive
empirical study, *Unemployment, a Problem of Industry*, appeared in
1930. Beveridge believed that economics should be based more
firmly—as he thought the natural sciences were—on the observation
of facts and not on the analysis of concepts. In his farewell address to
the School in 1937, he took as his theme Keynes's *General Theory* and
its reception. He criticised both Keynes and his reviewers for con-
juring with terms like "involuntary unemployment" without making
any attempt at empirical verification. "The distinguishing mark of
economic science, as illustrated by this debate, is that it is a science
in which verification of generalisations by reference to facts is
neglected as irrelevant." He regretted that "he had failed only in
converting sufficiently to the new gospel of Sidney and Beatrice the
heathen in Cambridge and other outlying places, who still cling to
theory untested by facts."[2] He might well have turned his gaze
nearer to home, where he would have found Robbins claiming
something which no Cambridge theorist ever did, namely that the
foundations of pure economic theory were self-evident, such that
conclusions derived from them required no further empirical proof.

There was some justice in Beveridge's charge. Much of the argument in this period was based on "suggestive" statistics rather than
on some of the detailed information then available; and some of the
crucial questions were ones of magnitude rather than direction of
influence. The work of re-examining the empirical record of the
inter-war period in the light of Keynesian and alternative theories
has only just begun. But there is also something naïve about
Beveridge's position. The "facts" do not speak clearly for themselves.
Nor should one expect decisive refutation or confirmation of theories
as complex as those dealing with the causes of unemployment in the
inter-war period—and certainly not one year after the publication
of such a difficult work as the *General Theory*.[3]

These points can be illustrated from Beveridge's own pronouncements on unemployment in the 'thirties. His statistics on this question
were the best available at the time, but they did not enable their

[1] For Hayek's comments on this and some of the other matters dealt with here see his
review of Harrod's *Life of Keynes* in *The Journal of Modern History*, June 1952.
[2] See his account of the lecture in his *The London School of Economics* (1960) pp. 94-5.
[3] On the methodological issue at stake here see G. C. Archibald, "Refutation or
Comparison?", *British Journal for the Philosophy of Science*, Dec. 1967.

compiler to penetrate beyond the orthodox wisdom of the day. He remained committed to the view that "some degree of unemployment, or at least some risk of unemployment for individuals, is probably an essential part of economic health for the community". His main efforts were bent on restoring the insurance scheme to its pre-1914 position as a device for offsetting cyclical unemployment.[1] Wherever he touched on the root causes of unemployment his diagnosis tended towards the liberal orthodox view: unemployment was the result of wage rigidity, immobility, the credit cycle, and defects in the insurance scheme. While Keynes was drawing attention to the problems of excess saving, Beveridge was reiterating traditional arguments against the redistribution of income: "If incomes were less unequal than they are today in Britain or the United States of America, it might well prove that voluntary savings fell short of what was required even to replace, far less extend, the capital equipment of those countries." He also seems to have remained entirely impervious to the expansionists' case against balanced budgets.[2] It was not until the Second World War that Beveridge, along with many others, became a convert to the Keynesian analysis of unemployment as a problem of inadequate aggregate demand. And even then it could be argued that Beveridge's hand was guided by the team of young Keynesians who helped to write his well-known book on *Full Employment in a Free Society*.[3]

---

[1] See *The Past and Present of Unemployment Insurance*, Sydney Ball Lectures, 1930; *Causes and Cures of Unemployment* (1931).

[2] *Planning Under Socialism* (1936), pp. 9, 113, 119.

[3] The book was published in 1944. While doing full justice to Keynes, the account given there (especially pp. 89-109) exaggerates the compatibility of Beveridge's own earlier views with those of Keynes. Beveridge claimed that he had never actually denied the possibility of overall deficiency of demand, yet such a denial is implicit throughout his writings and underlies his criticism in 1909 of J. A. Hobson; see p. 56 above.

# CHAPTER TEN

# Britain in the 'Thirties: a Managed Economy?

The 'thirties in Britain pose many difficulties for the historian, not least the historian of economic thought. For those to whom the continuing high level of unemployment in the newly-designated "special areas" was the leading feature of the period's economic history, the 'thirties were "one of the most tragic and futile periods in our history".[1] Against the dismal record of mass unemployment, however, must be set the advance in the standard of living of the employed majority, concentrated more and more in the prosperous midland and southern regions of the country. This was a period which saw the spread of car-ownership, electrical goods, and suburban housing estates, and the rise of consumer service, wireless and the cinema— all of which gave Britain some of the surface characteristics of the "affluent society" we speak of today.[2]

For many with progressive economic ideas this was a decade in which Britain was a divided, stagnant and unadventurous society led by mediocrities. Yet Neville Chamberlain, the chief architect of economic policy in this period, could, with some justification, say: "How false is the suggestion that this is a safety-first government destitute of new ideas, and how in fact it is continually introducing changes of a really revolutionary character."[3] It has been claimed recently that the radical departures made by the Conservative Government in this period from traditional policies of support for the gold standard, free trade, and *laissez-faire* in matters of industrial organisation, laid a foundation for the techniques of economic management employed after the Second World War. "In their reassertion of state power over the operation of the economic system as a whole, they not only broke with fundamentals of British policy in the previous hundred years, but also created many patterns of government action which, in spite of important modifications, have been followed since that time. In this respect, British Conservatism was an innovating force."[4] We must ask not only in what

[1] R. Boothby, *The New Economy* (1943), p. 5.
[2] More comprehensive surveys of this paradoxical period can be found in C. L. Mowat, *Britain between the Wars: 1918-1940* (1955) and H. W. Richardson, *Economic Recovery in Britain, 1932-4* (1967).
[3] K. Feiling, *Life of Neville Chamberlain* (1946), p. 229.
[4] S. H. Beer, *Modern British Politics* (1965), p. 277.

sense were the departures "revolutionary", but also in what sense it is correct to speak of them as marking an advance towards control of the system "as a whole"? Can we in fact use the term "managed economy" to describe these changes?

Leaving aside for the moment the actual achievements of policy, a related question arises concerning the development of ideology and opinion in this period. In contrast with the accepted picture of the 'thirties as one largely dominated by extremism, division, and disagreement, attention has been drawn to important elements of consensus from which "there arose the ideological structure which took Britain safely through the 'forties and brought her to rest in the 'fifties. That is to say the mixed economy, 'Butskellism' (in all but name), all-party acceptance for the welfare state, all-party rejection of the nineteenth-century vision of state planning as a horrible evil, were concepts which received their vital nurture in the nineteen-thirties."[1] It is undoubtedly true that the widespread acceptance of the need for some kind of planning was an important feature of economic opinion in the 'thirties. What was the relationship of the planning movement to Keynesian ideas? Was acceptance of the "mixed economy" necessarily synonymous or in harmony with the idea of a "managed economy"?

We have noted the tendency for cross-party affiliations to be formed on economic matters in the late 'twenties; this trend was continued under the Conservative Government in the 'thirties. Many centre-progressives felt that party divisions were irrelevant in conditions where democracy itself seemed to be in danger of succumbing to totalitarian forces; they hoped, initially at least, to bring pressure of enlightenment on what they still considered to be a "National" government.[2] Others were less hopeful of progress coming from this source, or even from the official Labour opposition. New alliances and break-away groups were formed at the extremes: Mosley's "New Party" eventually became a fascist movement; and a Workers' Front was favoured by those who saw the main battle lines as being drawn between socialism and capitalism rather than between democracy and totalitarianism.

Other signs of what might variously be described as vain optimism, desperation, or impotence, were the hunger marches of the unemployed, or, for the intellectual, the signing of manifestos and petitions. But perhaps the clearest evidence of frustration can be seen in the attention paid to the economic experiments taking place elsewhere. As Hugh Dalton said: "If the excitement of trying to be active is

---

[1] A. Marwick, "Middle Opinion in the Thirties: Planning, Progress and Politica 'Agreement'," *English Historical Review*, April 1964, p. 285.
[2] For a full discussion of these groups see *Ibid*.

forbidden to invalids by their doctors, the milder excitement of watching others try may still, perhaps, be permitted."[1] The two great experiments of the period were Soviet Communism and Roosevelt's New Deal; both, according to the taste of the observer, furnished lessons for the unadventurous. Germany and Italy provided a threat, a challenge, a laboratory, again according to taste. For those with social democratic sympathies bitter lessons could be drawn from the failures of the Bruning government in Germany and the Blum experiment in France; more hope could be found in the experience of Sweden and New Zealand.

### *Economic Policy and the Recovery*

The depression in Britain was milder, and recovery started earlier and was more sustained than in most other countries. Not having enjoyed the investment boom of the 'twenties, it proved easier to regain and surpass pre-depression levels of output; by 1934 production was higher than in 1929. In this respect a contrast can be drawn with the post-war era; between 1921 and 1929 real national income rose by just under 10%; in the shorter period between 1929 and 1937 it rose by over 17%. Unemployment reached its peak of around 3 million in January 1933, and declined slowly to about half this figure by 1937, after which it rose again before being eliminated by rearmament and war. Before 1914 foreign trade acted as a powerful support to employment. One reason for Britain's poor performance on the employment front in the 'twenties was that the domestic forces of expansion were not strong enough to take up the slack when the foreign trade engine started to misfire. British recovery in the 'thirties mainly took the form of a resurgence of domestic investment and consumption of home-produced goods and services.

The expressed purpose of the National Government was to bring about recovery. The extent to which official policy was responsible for the revival which occurred is doubtful. The verdict appears to be a neutral one: such policies as devaluation, cheap money, and protection acted in the right direction, but were not, in themselves, sufficient to bring about recovery. But if policy cannot be assigned the determining influence, still less can it be said to have been based on any conscious or comprehensive plan of action. Moreover, it is clear from the above figures that recovery was entirely compatible with failure to solve the unemployment problem. This fact alone underlines the gulf between economic thinking then and now.

---

[1] *Unbalanced Budgets* (1934), p. 10.

## Devaluation

The most important "decision" so far as recovery was concerned, the abandonment of gold, was one that was forced on an unwilling government by pressure of circumstances. After the trauma of September 1931 had passed few people were prepared to mourn the passing of the gold standard. Those who advocated a speedy restoration of the old system found themselves in a totally different position from that of the Cunliffe Committee in 1919. Opponents of the old system rejoiced in Britain's new-found freedom; here was an opportunity to begin anew unhampered by the deflationary pressures of the previous decade. According to Keynes, the devaluation of sterling which accompanied abandonment had strengthened the British economy by cheapening her exports, restricting imports, and stimulating employment—all without recourse to wage-reduction or a tariff.[1] He was heartened, too, by the array of countries that had decided to link themselves to sterling rather than suffer further deflation by remaining on gold. Britain had regained the initiative as an international centre and could now lead the march against world deflation by lowering interest rates, expanding investment at home, and lending abroad. He hoped that the deflationary pressure now concentrated on France and the United States, the two remaining creditor countries still linked to gold, would eventually force them to join the rest.[2]

Britain did benefit from leaving gold, though the competitive edge granted by devaluation was quickly dissipated when others, particularly the United States, followed suit. The Exchange Equalisation Account set up to manage the pound proved highly successful in protecting the exchange rate from short-term pressures; and there is also some evidence to show that it counteracted any tendency for the pound to appreciate in terms of other currencies.[3] The success of the EEA in managing the pound, together with the belief that many of Britain's earlier difficulties were due to overvaluation, reduced the incentive to return to an era of gold-stabilised currencies.[4] Nevertheless, Britain did not make use of the extra freedom and initiative conferred by these developments to make a move in the direction indicated by Keynes and his growing band of supporters. The best

[1] For this reason, in a letter to *The Times*, Sept. 28th 1931 (reprinted in *Essays in Persuasion*, pp. 286-7), he withdrew his support for a revenue tariff.

[2] See *New Statesman*, Sept. 12th 1931, reprinted in *Essays in Persuasion*, pp. 288-194, and his Halley Stewart Lecture reprinted in *The World's Economic Crisis* (1931).

[3] See L. Waight, *History and Mechanism of the Exchange Equalisation Account 1932-9* (1939).

[4] Harry Dexter White, who visited Britain in 1935 on behalf of the U.S. Treasury, reported that there was a complete lack of interest in British business circles in exchange problems. None of the Treasury officials and only two of the economists whom he interviewed believed that the time was ripe for stabilisation of the pound in terms of gold. White Papers, Princeton University Library, Memo. June 13th 1935.

that can be said for the government is that, unlike their predecessors in 1925, they refused to subject Britain to the "discipline" of gold in the absence of clear evidence of improved international co-operation.

The World Economic Conference held in London in 1933 proved to be the last effort to achieve recovery by international means. In spite of pious declarations in favour of exchange stability, the reduction of tariffs, and the resumption of foreign lending, it became obvious that no basis for agreement on practical measures existed. Roosevelt's decision to abandon gold just before the conference began, and his refusal to commit the United States to a policy of international stabilisation of the dollar, was regarded by many as the chief reason for the failure of the conference. But even without this bombshell it seems unlikely that the gap between the gold and non-gold countries could have been bridged.[1] Having already begun to manage sterling by means of the Exchange Equalisation Account, Britain was in a weak position to criticise the United States for taking similar action. By this time too, Britain had embarked on a policy of protection and imperial preference; it seems unlikely that she would have abandoned this new course of action even if the prospects for international co-operation had been much more favourable than they were. It was made perfectly clear by the British government that they were not willing to take part in any international campaign to raise world demand and prices by means of public works. This would have required simultaneous implementation of expansionist policies by all creditor countries, together with the creation of new forms of international liquidity of a type which were only brought into existence with the founding of the International Monetary Fund after the Second World War.[2]

According to one of the Swedish delegates to the conference, it was impossible to fathom what the British government wanted. MacDonald, who presided, and Chamberlain, who led the British delegation, conveyed an air of polite indifference to much that went on.[3] Roosevelt's action provided the British government with a convenient excuse for the failure of the conference.

### Cheap Money

The most important effect of the break with gold was internal; it insulated domestic monetary policy from external pressure. After the repayment of the foreign credits negotiated during the crisis,

---

[1] See H. V. Hodgson, *Slump and Recovery* (1938), Ch. VI.
[2] This is what Keynes was proposing at the time; see "The World Economic Conference", *New Statesman*, Dec. 24th, 1932, and *The Means to Prosperity* (1933). A comparison of these proposals with the I.M.F. is made in R. Harrod, *Life of Keynes*, pp. 442-5.
[3] See E. Wigforss, *Minnen* (1950), Vol. III, p. 56.

interest rates began to fall, providing the Treasury with an opportunity to carry through a large-scale conversion operation in June 1932. This, like the adoption of a managed "external" currency, was in line with the policy advocated by the expansionists throughout the 'twenties, and was applauded as such.[1] But the chief motive of the Treasury at the time was to ease the burden of interest payments on the budget; it was in keeping with Treasury aims frequently expressed in the 'twenties and was primarily an adjunct of the orthodox policy of economy and balanced budgets. It was only later that "cheap money" assumed the role of a policy commitment designed expressly—it was claimed—to help recovery; and even then the view taken by the authorities was one of "benevolent neutrality" rather than firm conviction.[2] Lower interest rates, which were only partially and slowly reflected in lower charges made by the Building Societies, certainly aided the boom in housing which was such a notable feature of the British recovery. But they were only one, and perhaps not the most important, factor operating on the supply side to make housing a popular form of investment. The significant factors producing the housing boom appear to have been on the demand side: the early 'thirties coincided with an upward phase of the building cycle; and rising real incomes for those in employment resulted in an upward shift in demand for housing and the "new" durable consumer goods.[3]

Even if cheap money had been the determining factor in producing the housing boom, and thereby recovery, the government would not be able to claim much credit for having seen housing investment as the key to recovery. Over two-thirds of the houses built in the 'thirties were the product of unaided private enterprise. Throughout this period there was hardly any increase in the proportion of houses built by local authorities with central government assistance. The essential enabling legislation for slum clearance was the "Greenwood" Housing Act of 1930, yet no effective action was taken during the period when the depression was at its worst. Public investment in housing, as in other fields, was not used as a contra-cyclical device; in fact, it generally operated in the opposite direction.[4]

## Protection

Another leading plank in the government's economic policy was protection. Unlike cheap money the groundwork for this had been

---

[1] See Keynes's article on the conversion operation in the *Economic Journal*, Sept. 1932
[2] See E. Nevin, *The Mechanism of Cheap Money 1931-39* (1955), p. 158.
[3] See H. W. Richardson, *op. cit.*, especially Chapters 5-8.
[4] See U. K. Hicks, *Finance of British Government* (1938), Ch. VII, and G. P. Braae, "Investment in Housing in the U.K. ,1924-1938", *Manchester School*, Jan. 1964, pp. 15-24.

laid well in advance. Within the Conservative Party the origins go back to the tariff reform movement at the turn of the century. It cannot therefore be described simply as a pragmatic adjustment to events, though the depression and the financial crisis undoubtedly helped to create a favourable climate of opinion for protection.[1]

In introducing the Import Duties Bill which enabled him to fulfil some of the dreams of his father, Chamberlain claimed that among its many virtues protection would help recovery. Viewed simply from this angle its contribution was not great. Internationally, protection went hand in hand with imperial preference and bilateral trading agreements. The net effect of the trading agreements negotiated between Commonwealth countries in Ottawa in 1932 is difficult to assess, especially if account is taken of the adverse effects on British trade of retaliatory or emulatory action by those outside the charmed imperial circle. It is generally believed that they merely diverted rather than created trade. Diverted it, moreover, into less profitable and less rapidly growing avenues. In the case of bilateral trading agreements with countries outside the empire, it is possible that Britain was able to use its bargaining position as a large importer to achieve more favourable terms. Domestically, the tariff helped to channel the increasing purchasing power attributable to improvements in productivity and the terms of trade onto domestically produced goods. It may also have helped to stimulate investment in certain industries, notably iron and steel.[2]

Keynes regarded protection, like cheap money, as a preliminary to more adventurous measures of government-induced expansion. These did not materialise. The real significance of protection for the Conservatives lay elsewhere: it provided the government with a planning lever to be used in support of its policies for industrial and agricultural reorganisation. We shall return to this later when discussing the planning movement.

### Balanced Budgets

The final element in the Conservative recovery programme was balanced budgeting. It was pursued with such deliberation that it must be considered as an explicit measure of policy on an equal footing with protection. Since this policy provides the chief reason for the frustration felt by progressives in this period it must be considered at some length.

After all the efforts to achieve a balanced budget for the purposes of protecting the gold standard had failed, some relaxation in

---

[1] On this see S. H. Beer, *op. cit.*, p. 288.
[2] On this see H. W. Richardson, *op. cit.*, Ch. 10.

budgetary orthodoxy might have been expected, especially when one remembers that unemployment continued to rise until January 1933. As D. H. Robertson said after the break with gold, "the policy of strict economy has become an advanced guard without an army".[1] The fact that the policy was maintained long after the crisis had passed shows that achieving a balanced budget had become a fetish to be worshipped in its own right regardless of circumstance. It was necessary, of course, for members of the new government to put a brave front on their failure; it would have been difficult for them to admit the irrelevance of the sacrifices which they had exacted. If anything, therefore, budgetary orthodoxy, shaken in the 'twenties, gained a new lease of life in the 'thirties. The defence of the dogma now switched from the need to maintain foreign confidence and external stability, to the need to avoid inflation at home. Having left gold we were back to the arguments used to support the return to gold in 1925. As Snowden said in a speech not long after the abandonment of gold:

"It is one thing to go off the Gold Standard with an unbalanced Budget and uncontrollable inflation, but it is far less serious to take this measure, not because of internal financial difficulties, but because of excessive withdrawals of borrowed money. We have balanced our Budget and therefore removed the danger of having to print paper, which leads to uncontrolled inflation."[2]

This was to provide one of the few themes which united supporters of the "National" Government in the general election which took place in October 1931. They may not have stopped Britain going off gold, but they had certainly saved the country from the fiscal irresponsibility of those in the Labour Government who had deserted their posts under fire. In his highly effective election broadcasts Snowden returned again and again to the virtue of the government's action in avoiding "a tremendous increase in the cost of living". The Labour Party's programme, he said, was "Bolshevism run mad".

"At a time when national retrenchment is vital ... this programme is issued ... which ... would destroy every vestige of confidence and plunge the country into irretrievable ruin. ... The Labour Party has announced that ... it will undo the work of the National Government. It promises to increase expenditure enormously. It will take the money out of industry by vast increases in taxation. ... This will result in works closing down and unemployment will go up by leaps and bounds. Such a policy would destroy our

[1] *Essays in Monetary Theory* (1940), p. 75.
[2] *An Autobiography*, Vol. II, p. 1055.

national credit, the currency would collapse and your income and wages and pensions and unemployment pay would have their purchasing power reduced enormously."[1]

Making every allowance for election fever, the repetition of such words as "uncontrollable", "irretrievable", "tremendously" and "enormously" indicate an unreasoning concern for fiscal righteousness. MacDonald was less at home in these abstruse economic matters: he contented himself with brandishing a fistful of worthless German mark notes at his election meetings.

After a massive win recorded for the government, MacDonald and Snowden were lauded in "sound" circles as saviours of the nation. It proved all too easy to convict the Labour Party and the TUC on charges of irresponsibility and the pursuit of sectional interest. The election result was seen in orthodox circles as a victory for democracy in more than the obvious sense. During the 'twenties, and especially in the crisis year, those who advocated economy and wage-cuts had begun to feel that "democracy" was fundamentally incapable of coming to terms with economic reality. Anxiety was expressed as to "whether indeed [democracy] will not always prefer immediate benefits for the wage-earners to the ultimate welfare of the nation".[2] The same view lurks behind the May Committee's gloss on the problem of curbing government expenditure on the social services; and it is present also in Henry Clay's rebuke to Keynes over the return to gold in 1925 for having paid too much attention to "working-class sentiment".[3] But in 1931 the nation had been saved, and was temporarily united behind its disparate collection of leaders. A Dunkirk spirit prevailed, and with it, complacency. It was this smugness, the government's claim to have solved—while failing to solve—a "national" problem, by methods that were blatantly unequal in the demands made on different sections of the population, which left such a bitter taste in the mouths of their opponents.

Snowden's replacement by Chamberlain as Chancellor of the Exchequer brought no change in the policy of strict economy, or of seeking an annual balance in the accounts of the central government. This policy must be seen against the changed background of the 'thirties. Arguments against an active policy that were plausible while Britain was on the gold standard had lost their force. Yet another barrier to expensive schemes of capital expenditure was removed by the conversion operation in 1932.

The case for loan-financed expenditure as a means of raising the level of home demand was put with renewed vigour in 1933, prior

[1] *Ibid.*, pp. 1063 and 1066.
[2] Sir William Dampier-Whetham in *Lloyd's Bank Review*, July 1931, p. 269.
[3] See p. 149 below.

to Chamberlain's second budget. The campaign opened in the pages of *The Times* with a series of leaders calling for a bold policy of "national reflation" by means of development expenditure and reduced taxation.[1] It was supported by a letter signed by thirty-seven academic economists proposing expansionist finance and a division of the budget into capital and current accounts.[2] Keynes contributed a series of articles under the general title of "The Means to Prosperity", and elicited support from a number of letter-writers.[3] In the same month he was given an opportunity to explain his position to the Conservative Trade and Industry Committee. Before the budget was presented in April, the theme had been taken up by a number of MP's and by the *Daily Express* and *Daily Mail*. Keynes was no longer a voice in the wilderness. By this time also his case was greatly strengthened internally by Kahn's theory of the 'employment multiplier'.[4]

Chamberlain's answer to all this in his budget speech was a resounding negative:

"Look round the world today and you see that badly unbalanced Budgets are the rule rather than the exception. Everywhere there appear Budget deficits piling up, yet they do not produce those favourable results which it is claimed would happen to us. On the contrary, I find that Budget deficits repeated year after year may be accompanied by deepening depression and by a constantly falling price level. . . . Of all countries passing through these difficult times the one that has stood the test with the greatest measure of success is the United Kingdom. . . . We owe our freedom from [the fear that things are going to get worse] to the fact that we have balanced our Budget."[5]

In his first two budgets in 1932 and 1933 Chamberlain aimed at a budget surplus, achieving it in the latter case only by suspending the Sinking Fund. In spite of the relief afforded by conversion of the National Debt, in those years when the depression was at its greatest, the budget was balanced by the particularly deflationary method of cutting back expenditure and raising taxes; a budget balanced by raising expenditure and taxes might have had some reflationary effect. It was not until 1934, after recovery had started, that Chamberlain decided to restore some of the 1931 cuts; taxation was not reduced until 1935.

[1] See e.g. *The Times*, Jan. 25th, Feb. 25th, Mar. 10th, 13th, 21st, 31st, 1933.
[2] See *The Times*, Mar. 10th, 1933. Among the signatories were G. C. Allen, E. H. Phelps-Brown, A. M. Carr-Saunders, H. Gaitskell, C. W. Guillebaud, R. Hall, R. F. Harrod, D. H. MacGregor, J. E. Meade, E. A. G. Robinson and Joan Robinson, P. Sargent-Florence, G. Walker and B. Wootton.
[3] See *The Times*, Mar. 13th, 14th, 15th and 16th, 1933.
[4] See pp. 164-6 above.
[5] *House of Commons Debates*, April 25th, 1933, cc. 60-61.

It was noted earlier that it is not easy to measure the total impact, reflationary or deflationary, of the budget.[1] By using our present knowledge of these matters we can at least indicate the possible direction of influence of particular aspects of budgetary action. It seems likely that prior to 1937—the year that rearmament began to upset the Chancellor's calculations—the pursuit of balanced budgets acted as a deflationary influence on the economy. There were, of course, countervailing reflationary factors at work arising out of the rise in domestic investment, consumption, and the improvement in the trade balance. But it does mean that recovery proceeded less strongly and rapidly than it would have done with more enlightened budgetary policies.

One defence of orthodox budgeting during the depression is that by satisfying business sentiment in favour of economy, confidence was restored; and confidence expressed itself in greater willingness to undertake new schemes of capital expenditure. The trouble with this type of psychological argument is that it can never be proved or disproved. It tends to be circular: if things go well, it must be because confidence has been restored; if things go badly, it must be because there is insufficient confidence. However, there is something suspect about arguments that can only be used to support the *status quo*. It is often simply another way of saying "Be orthodox", or "I dislike what is being done", while at the same time evading the uncomfortable business of having to say why. In the case of Chamberlain's early budgets, where taxes were raised to safeguard the Sinking Fund, the confidence argument requires us to believe that he went through something like the following tortuous thought-process: "I have decided to balance the Budget by deflating the economy. The harmful effects of this will not be as great as they would otherwise have been because businessmen want me to balance the budget, and will respond positively to my having done so in spite of its adverse effects on them and the community." It seems simpler to say that Chamberlain and his Treasury advisers concentrated on narrow budgetary considerations, and were unaware of the deflationary consequences of what they were doing.

More credence might be given to the view that balanced budgets were actually conceived of as making a positive contribution to recovery, if the notion of what constituted "balance" had been given precise formulation by its adherents. In fact though, despite the inordinate amount of attention paid to this aim of policy, no clear distinction was made between revenue and expenditure on capital and current account, between capital expenditure financed by loans or the sale of assets and that financed by taxation, between "produc-

[1] See pp. 99-100 above.

tive" and "non-productive" debt. No attempt was made to integrate information concerning central government expenditure and the plans of local authorities in this regard. Finally, there was no official recognition or discussion of the appropriate accounting period over which budgets should be balanced.

These were not abstruse matters depending on the acceptance of complicated multiplier theories. The idea of balancing the capital budget over the length of the cycle can be found, for instance, in the Liberal "Yellow Book" published in 1928. Economists had frequently pointed out how arbitrary the notion of an annual balance was: if every year, why not every month? Once recovery had started, the confidence argument lost much of its force. Nevertheless, the government persisted in its earlier policy. It seems, therefore, to have been more in the nature of customary rather than rational behaviour.

The conservatism of the British government in these matters was highlighted by what was happening elsewhere at this time. Many countries faced with falling tax revenues and rising expenditures on relief stumbled into budget deficits. Most, including the United States as we shall see in the next chapter, did so unwillingly. But few tried to climb back on to the straight and narrow path of orthodoxy with quite the zeal exhibited by British governments. Once more, as in the case of return to the gold standard in 1925, and later during the financial crisis of 1931, Britain ploughed a lonely furrow, applying to its affairs a standard of fiscal righteousness which others were no longer willing to match.[1]

Some countries embraced loan-financed capital projects with more conscious intent. Nazi Germany was one. There were also more propitious examples. The Swedish government formally abandoned the principle of annually balanced budgets in favour of a policy of achieving balance over the length of the trade cycle in 1933. Indeed, but for domestic opposition, the Social Democratic Party in Sweden would have moved on to the more ambitious aim of a full employment policy. The fact that a Swedish government produced more enlightened policies under similar conditions may not seem surprising. What makes the Swedish comparison such a telling indictment of British complacency is the fact that the policies pursued by the Social Democrats were, to a large extent, influenced by the very ideas and writings by Keynes that were being spurned by the British government.[2]

[1] For a comparative study of budgetary policies in this period see H. Dalton (ed.) *Unbalanced Budgets*, (1934).
[2] For the intellectual background to the Swedish policy revolution see Karl-Gustav Landgren, *Den 'Nya Ekonomien' i Sverige* (1960); see also Donald Winch, "The Keynesian Revolution in Sweden", *Journal of Political Economy*, April 1966.

*Unemployment Policy*

The dominant feature of British economic policy-making in the 'thirties is its fragmentation; there was no overall strategy imposed by the government. Recovery was sought in a piece-meal fashion; and unemployment was treated as an issue which could be separated from the general problem of recovery. It is hardly surprising that the government was no more enthusiastic about capital expenditure solutions for unemployment than were any of its predecessors in the 'twenties. The activities of the Unemployment Grants Committee were virtually suspended during the worst years of the depression. Runciman, President of the Board of Trade, restated the Treasury view at the World Economic Conference in July 1933, when he flatly refused to co-operate with any international scheme for a co-ordinated expansion of demand. "We have terminated our schemes for dealing with unemployment by way of capital expenditure works, and we shall not reopen these schemes, no matter what may be done elsewhere."[1] Runciman could not see beyond the old idea that public works were simply relief measures; he made no allowance for secondary repercussions.

The government's policy for dealing with unemployment was to initiate legislation to help improve amenities, and later to attract new employment to certain "special areas" of high and long-standing unemployment. The fact remains, however, that unemployment in the special areas only fell significantly when there was a general fall in unemployment throughout the country. Apart from this new departure, the government continued to place complete reliance on the traditional stand-by, unemployment insurance. In 1934 an attempt was made "to take unemployment insurance out of politics" by creating the Unemployment Insurance Statutory Committee under the Chairmanship of Sir William Beveridge. This body was to administer the finances of the unemployment fund in a semi-autonomous way. At the same time, the 1931 cuts were restored and the whole scheme was made more comprehensive. Those not covered by the scheme, or whose benefits had been exhausted, were to be catered for by a new centrally-organised Unemployment Assistance Board. The most interesting feature of the Statutory Committee's work, in the words of its Chairman, was that "we insisted on regarding cyclical fluctuation of trade as one of the risks to be taken into account in considering whether or not the fund was solvent, and on building up a reserve in good years to ensure that benefits could be maintained in bad years and contributions stabilised."[2] There

---

[1] See report in *The Times*, July 14th, 1933; and Keynes's reply, July 17th.
[2] W. H. Beveridge, *Power and Influence* (1953), pp. 226-7.

is nothing novel in this; indeed, it was bound to happen under whatever arrangements were adopted. Nevertheless, Beveridge maintained that it was not part of the intention of the government when the Bill was introduced; they actually opposed an amendment which would have made the contra-cyclical element explicit. It is interesting to note, therefore, that one of the few contra-cyclical devices at work in this period had a surreptitious existence so far as the government was concerned.

One of the intentions of the 1934 Act was to protect the Treasury. In addition to this, however, the Statutory Committee was charged with the responsibility of ensuring that future contributions repaid past debts. It is not clear why this debt should not have been added to the National Debt—as ordinary budget deficits were—and the burden assumed by the general taxpayer. It meant that the modest contra-cyclical element in the scheme was hampered by the extra burden placed on the employee and employer to meet this obligation. It is an interesting comment on prevailing attitudes to unemployment and government spending that one of Beveridge's proudest boasts was that, under the aegis of his Committee, contributors had repaid all previous borrowings from the Treasury. Even book-keeping transactions, it would seem, could be represented as policy triumphs.[1]

In January 1935 Lloyd George made yet another bid to place himself at the head of a progressive movement which drew its inspiration from Roosevelt's New Deal policies. The government gave polite consideration to his plans, but in February Chamberlain made it clear once more that there would be no experiments in this direction.

"The continually repeated cry that the Government have no policy on employment always has behind it the implication that there can be no policy which does not involve a large expenditure of public money, whether directly in public works carried out by the Government, or in subventions to other bodies doing similar things. I believe that to contain a complete fallacy. There may be circumstances when it is right and sound to follow a policy of that kind, but not for the purpose of providing employment, because the whole experience of the past shows that, for the purpose of providing employment, this policy of public works is always disappointing. In that respect the experience of this country is no different from that of other countries which have tried the same thing . . . the quickest and most effective contribution which any Government can make towards an increase of employment is to create conditions which will encourage and facilitate improvement in ordinary trade."[2]

[1] I am grateful to Professor Alan Peacock for having drawn my attention to the matter.
[2] *House of Commons Debates*, Feb. 14th, 1935. cc. 2208-9.

The last statement might well stand as an epitaph to the recovery policies of the British government.

Thus stands the record up to 1937. It might be argued in defence of this record that once recovery had got under way, whatever the merits of expansionist finance might have been during the depression, there was no longer any need to "pioneer" new methods. Towards the end of 1937, however, there were clouds on the horizon, chiefly in the form of an expected recession in the United States. Fears that another slump was on the way were widely expressed. A campaign was mounted privately in the Economic Advisory Council by Keynes, Sir Arthur Salter, H. D. Henderson and Sir Josiah Stamp, and publicly in *The Times*, to induce the government to put in hand preparations for a contra-cyclical public works policy.[1] Once more it should be borne in mind that such a policy was already in operation in countries such as Sweden. In support of the campaign a letter was written and signed by every Oxford economist of note. The response of the government in the person of Oliver Stanley, President of the Board of Trade, was a facetious one: economics, as everybody knew, was only half a science; its practitioners were not in touch with the "real" world and never agreed with one another.[2] A small incident, but one which seems to typify the attitude of the government. The American recession did not lead to a slump in Britain, partly no doubt because Britain was by then better insulated from American disturbances, but largely because mounting rearmament expenditure did what many economists had long been urging the government to do for other reasons.

### Industrial Reorganisation and Planning

Before turning to the questions raised at the beginning of this chapter we must consider briefly the part played by the government in bringing about industrial reorganisation in this period. It is on this that much of Beer's case for saying that "government decisions in these years endowed Britain with a pattern of economic policy that was comprehensive and radically different from that of previous generations" rests.[3] Protection provided the government with a bargaining weapon in its relations with industrialists which it used to induce them to undertake measures of reorganisation.

The best example of this can be seen in the case of iron and steel. The Import Duties Advisory Committee's recommendation of

---

[1] See A. Salter, *Memoirs of a Public Servant* (1961), pp. 253-4. Keynes, as usual, had started earlier; see his articles "How To Avoid a Slump", *The Times*, Jan. 12th, 13th, 14th, 1937. See also *The Economist*, Jan. 1938, and P. E. P. Broadsheet, No. 114, Jan. 11th, 1938.
[2] See *House of Commons Debates*, Nov. 2nd. 1937, cc. 785-6.
[3] S. H. Beer, *op. cit.*, p. 279.

protection for the industry was made conditional upon the formation of a quasi-cartel arrangement that would co-ordinate the activities of the various producers' associations and regulate output and prices. Similar schemes for fostering combination among producers and sellers for the purpose of abridging competition, restricting output, price-fixing, and the elimination of excess capacity, were encouraged tacitly and explicitly in every major British industry in the 'thirties.[1] The most significant break with tradition came in agriculture, where there was a complete reversal of nineteenth-century policies. In support of agricultural protection, import regulation, and subsidies to farmers, a number of government-sponsored marketing boards were established; the aim of these was to control output and set prices. As a result of its "special areas" policy the government also acquired new powers for giving aid to special or depressed areas, and for influencing the location of industry.

The fact that there were clear precedents in the 'twenties for this type of intervention makes it doubtful whether we should speak of it as being "radically different", or as "a *re*assertion of state power". Nor would it seem that only with the arrival of protection in 1932 were such attempts made possible. One example can be cited, the Coal Mines Act of 1930, introduced by a Labour government with Liberal support. This Act provided a prototype for later schemes for promoting amalgamation and eliminating "unnecessary" competition. But these are debating points. There is little doubt that the number of schemes entailing state encouragement of industrial combination increased after 1931, and that protection and the Import Duties Advisory Council were useful in support of them. For Beer's purposes it is only necessary to show that the Conservatives, partly through their links with the business community and partly for reasons which are connected with the Tory conception of state authority, were willing to further and accommodate themselves to the trend towards industrial concentration and combination. By so doing they took a significant step away from *laissez-faire* towards planning and the mixed economy as we know it today.

Most historians regard the activities of the Conservative Government in the industrial field as piece-meal and opportunist. The general direction in which the government was moving, however, was supported by a growing body of opinion in favour of closer relations between government and industry. This does not mean, of course, that policy was systematic or well thought out. The increase in the size of business corporations, the divorce of

[1] See A. F. Lucas, *Industrial Reconstruction and the Control of Competition* (1937); G. C. Allen, *British Industries and Their Organisation* (1933).

ownership and control, the rise of schemes for concerted action by producers, and the attempt to encourage and regulate this movement by governments, provide one of the dominant themes of British industrial history in the twentieth century. The same trend towards combination and monopoly can be seen at work in all industrialised countries in this period; indeed, it was well-established in some countries before the First World War. During the war itself the curtailment of competition and formation of trade associations was encouraged. The report of the Standing Committee on Trusts in 1919 gave its blessing to a movement which it thought was both inevitable and desirable in the interests of greater efficiency; they also raised the question of whether or not public regulation might be needed to ensure that the benefits of increased size were not offset by the exercise of monopoly power. The depression of the 'twenties, and the emergence of excess capacity in Britain's staple industries, encouraged the trend towards rationalisation; the trend was also supported by producers within the industries concerned and by numerous official inquiries, notably by the Balfour Committee on Industry and Trade. Keynes had noted the rise of "business collectivism" in *The End of Laissez-Faire*, and a large part of the Liberal "Yellow Book" had been devoted to the need to regulate and/or experiment with new forms of corporate intervention by the State.

For our purpose it is important to note the Topsy-like quality of the movement towards larger units and business combination. The part played by the economist was an insignificant one; the motive force came from within the business community. Economists from Marshall onwards had watched, interpreted, criticised, and appraised the movement, but they exercised no influence over its pace and direction. It was in this period that most of the important theoretical work on imperfect competition, and oligopoly was done; the result was a substantial modification of the theorems of competitive equilibrium. But while this was of great significance to the professional scientific community, its relationship to policy decisions in the industrial field, particularly in Britain during the inter-war period, was negligible.[1]

The planning movement of the 'thirties was based very largely on these developments in the industrial field. The nineteenth-century competitive ideal having broken down, it was necessary to find an alternative principle upon which to base the system of production, distribution and exchange. In this respect, the differences between

[1] This statement does not apply to the same extent in America where the writings of Berle and Means and of the Institutional School of economists seem to have influenced the climate of opinion in favour of the New Deal measures of industrial regulation. One reason for this is the fact that in its early stages the New Deal made a larger break with traditional anti-trust sentiments than was necessary in the case of Britain. See pp. 227-32 below.

Conservative and Socialist planners were mainly ones of degree, ideological overtone, and language. The similarities between nationalisation and rationalisation went beyond mere assonance; in the 'thirties at least, they drew their economic inspiration from a common experience. This accounts for the growing consensus on these matters which gave rise to such organisations as Political and Economic Planning (PEP) and the Next Five Years group, bodies which drew their support from a wide range of centre-progressive opinion.[1]

In the political and social histories of this period the demand for more comprehensive economic planning is frequently treated as though it was perfectly harmonious, even synonymous, with the type of policies associated with the name of Keynes.[2] Apart from contemporaneity and the fact that some planners were also advocates of expansionist finance *à la* Keynes, the two sets of ideas are logically and historically distinct; they sprang from different roots, and had different aims and priorities in view. While they could be combined, there were also possibilities for conflict. The logical differences are best expressed in terms of the modern distinction made by economists between macro- and micro-economics.[3] The distinction is a useful one both pedagogically and historically. Failure to observe it leads to the conflation of micro-economic planning and macro-economic stabilisation policies. This point is related to one made earlier: the historian of economic thought cannot be content to register the different forms of state intervention; he must ask what new or improved economic insight, if any, lay behind the types of intervention?

The planning movement of the 'thirties was based on an amorphous and eclectic set of ideas possessing none of the intellectual clarity of Keynesianism. This, of course, does not make it any the less significant historically. Like the rationalisation movement of the 'twenties, it made an immediate common-sense appeal. All movements calling for greater co-ordination of economic and financial activities have certain basic features in common, but the motives and the ends in

---

[1] See A. Marwick, *op. cit.*, and C. L. Mowat, *op. cit.*, pp. 462-3.

[2] See e.g. Mowat, *op. cit.*, p. 462. A. J. P. Taylor *English History, 1914-1945*, (1965) is particularly muddled on this issue, as on most matters involving Keynes. On p. 354 we are told that: "The academic economists [all of them?], who were moving towards *planning* with Keynes at their head, were discredited by their association with Lloyd George." On the next page, however, Keynes is criticised for having "rejected the alternative [to public works] course of a directed, or *planned* economy". Earlier (p. 348) we are told (wrongly) that "Keynes did not work out his ideas for overcoming cyclical unemployment until 1936", and these are equated with the New Deal and "Swedish experiments in *planned* economy (emphasis: supplied). Another example of Taylor's perversity can be seen in the statement (p. 268) that Keynes had not hit on the multiplier doctrine in 1929. This is not strictly accurate, but even if it were, Taylor's description of this doctrine as one where putting one man to work "puts half a dozen more men to work also", would either seem to indicate incredible optimism on his part, or the fact that Taylor had not yet hit upon the multiplier doctrine in 1965.

[3] For definitions of these terms see p. 20 above.

view tend to differ. Today, planning is largely discussed in relation
to the problem of achieving higher rates of growth; in the 'thirties
the motive for planning was to aid recovery from depression. Just
as today's planning is based, implicitly at least, on some theory of
growth, so in the 'thirties the planning movement required some
theory of the causes of economic breakdown. One of the features of
the capitalist system to which planners attached great importance
in the 'thirties was the growth in the size of the corporation, and the
enormous productive potential which this and modern science placed
at the disposal of society. With larger production units, however,
went enlarged consequences of miscalculation.

A good example of this point of view is provided by the writings
and speeches of Harold Macmillan, one of the key figures in the
centre-progressive movement in this period. As he freely admitted
in his first book, *Reconstruction: A Plea for a National Policy* (1933), his
views on planning did not proceed from any new theoretical insight;
they arose "out of the realities of industrial and commercial life".

> "The idea of planning . . . has found its adherents not so much
> among theorists as among those industrialists who see that it is
> in harmony with what they find it necessary to aim at in the daily
> conduct of their business. Economic planning is the attempt to
> regulate production in accordance with effective demand. It is
> not a new or strange idea. It is, in fact, what every producer must
> attempt in order to sell his products at a profit rather than a loss.
> What *is* new is the set of circumstances which requires the co-
> ordination of the efforts of private individuals and groups to
> achieve and maintain an equilibrium which in former times could
> well be preserved by an automatic reaction to the indicator of
> price fluctuation."[1]

Malfunctioning of the system was seen as a simple demand and
supply problem caused by the growth in size of the supplying units
in relation to the growth of markets; a problem involving the price
mechanism considered as a set of relative prices.

Macmillan approached the problem as one requiring an improvement in the co-ordination of a system of linked individual markets.
The solution which he advocated in this early work was for a larger
measure of "industrial self-government" to be granted to producers
so as to enable them to work out methods of regulating investment
and output which would replace the market system. Pursuing this
line of attack, he and his Conservative supporters pressed for the
setting up of a departmental committee, similar to the Balfour
Committee, to advise on methods of eliminating redundant plant,

[1] *Op. cit.*, p. 16.

and on other matters involving industrial efficiency and organisation. In 1935, for example, they introduced an Industrial Reorganisation (Enabling) Bill, which would have given statutory powers to the majority of producers in an industry to coerce any recalcitrant minority into accepting plans for reorganisation.[1]

At this stage Macmillan's views on fiscal policy were rudimentary. He hinted at the possibility of a decline in investment opportunities as a result of the closure of the world economic frontier, but this merely led him to favour protection of the home market as an adjunct to planning. He firmly closed the door on any of the radical views which might derive from the notion that capitalism was stagnating by denying that the condition was due to "general over-production".[2] He mentioned in passing the need to co-ordinate the savings and investment decisions of the community, but the footnote in which he refers the reader to Keynes, Hobson *and* Hayek does not inspire much confidence that he understood what was at stake.[3] The emphasis was on restrictive measures to regulate the supply of individual commodities rather than on Keynesian measures to raise overall effective demand. Even by 1935 Macmillan does not seem to have found a satisfactory way of reconciling the two sets of ideas.[4] Thus we find him claiming that industrial reorganisation would prevent the "artificial" slump and over-investment which would otherwise be likely to arise from the "artificial" boom created by public works policies.[5] It was not until 1938, when he wrote *The Middle Way*, that largely as a result of reading Keynes's *General Theory*, he arrived at a more satisfactory understanding of the whole question.[6]

The innovations of the Conservative Government were confined to the restrictive micro-economic planning side of Macmillan's case. Like the rationalisation movement of the 'twenties which took place under the gold standard, these measures *could* be regarded as employment policies. In so far as the British unemployment problem was thought of as being of a structural kind, improvements in industrial organisation resulting from the elimination of excess capacity might be expected to reduce unemployment in the long run; in the short run the effect on employment was likely to be adverse. An indication of just how long the long run might be was given by Chamberlain in

[1] See the PEP Broadsheet No. 40, Dec. 18th 1934 for an examination of the proposals of this group; see also H. Macmillan, *Planning for Employment* (1935).

[2] *Reconstruction* (1933), p. 23.

[3] *Ibid.*, pp. 57-9.

[4] This was the essence of Keynes's friendly criticisms in a letter to Macmillan encouraging him to emphasise reflation rather than industrial reorganisation; see H. Macmillan, *Winds of Change*, p. 363.

[5] See *House of Commons Debates*, April 3rd 1935, c. 445.

[6] See *op. cit.*, especially Ch. 11. See also H. Macmillan, *Winds of Change*, Ch. 12.

1933, when he said that the nation should be prepared to face the prospect of ten years of large-scale unemployment.[1] The dedication of the government to the view that the most effective contribution they could make towards a solution of unemployment was "to create conditions which will encourage and facilitate improvement in ordinary trade" effectively prevented any progress towards the Keynesian position.

By 1936 Keynes had moved far beyond contra-cyclical ideas; the whole weight of his advocacy lay behind his proposal for "a somewhat comprehensive socialisation of investment".[2] Despite the fact that Keynes had urged rationalisation for the cotton industry, and had anticipated much of the literature on industrial reorganisation in his writings in the 'twenties, he had rejected the structuralist solution to unemployment, and took no part in the planning movement of the 'thirties. He became increasingly concerned with macro- rather than micro-economic problems. Once armed with a theory of effective demand he became even more critical of attempts to raise prices and employment by restricting output.[3] Certainly for Keynes then, planning and "Keynesianism" were separate issues. Considered as contributions to the unemployment problem, the efforts of the planners in this period were likely to be in conflict with those of Keynes.[4] It is still true to say, therefore, that while the Conservative governments of the 'thirties may have furthered the idea of a "mixed economy", they did nothing to advance the cause of a "managed economy" as we understand the term today.

---

[1] K. Feiling, *Life of Neville Chamberlain* (1946), p. 220.
[2] *General Theory*, p. 378.
[3] See e.g. his criticisms of some New Deal policies, pp. 232-5 below.
[4] There is no inherent reason why the two sets of ideas should not be used in harness—as they are today; for further comment on this see p. 322 ff. below.

# CHAPTER ELEVEN

# Keynes and the New Deal

Of all the countries affected by the world depression the United States was the first and in many respects the hardest hit. In the seven years prior to the summer of 1929 American capitalism assumed its most triumphant and reckless form. Industrial productivity and national income both rose by over 40% in this period. Between 1929 and 1932, however, national income fell by 38%, and unemployment rose at its peak to at least 12 and possibly 15 million. The massive deflationary effect of the decline of incomes, and the curtailment of all forms of private consumption and investment expenditure, brought with it widespread bankruptcy in manufacturing and agriculture; the increase in the burden of past indebtedness was accompanied by the collapse of the financial infra-structure of the economy, typified by the failure of over five thousand banks. The depression reached its nadir in the winter of 1932–3, as the reins of office were handed over by the discredited Hoover Administration to Franklin D. Roosevelt.

No single index can be used to appraise the success or failure of the New Deal. Measures which were unsuccessful, considered simply as contributions to economic recovery, succeeded in changing permanently the fabric of American social and economic life. By what standards, short or long-term, can success even on the narrow economic front be assessed? A parcel of measures which coped successfully with an emergency situation and prevented further collapse might have had little to contribute—and may even have hampered—permanent recovery. How can policies which altered the balance of economic power and advantage among citizens be judged? There are no simple answers. Even the indices of aggregate economic activity present a complex picture. Between 1933 and 1937 net national product in real terms rose by 55%; but even this meant only a 3% increase in real incomes since 1929. The extraordinary rate of recovery was largely confined to the output of the consumer sector; private investment failed to regain its pre-1929 momentum: net investment became negative in 1931 and remained negative until 1936. In 1937 the American economy went into another steep decline: unemployment which at the peak of the boom remained around 6 million suddenly increased to over 10

million. In other countries, including Britain, recovery was more
sustained and complete. The Second World War found the United
States facing another depression. As *The Economist* said in 1939:
"The United States is the only country which, in an economic sense
has passed through this decade with a reminiscent eye, fixed over its
shoulder, on the fabulous records of the past—the only country
which is producing less wealth than a decade ago."[1] Britain was the
sick capitalist economy of the 'twenties. The United States took over
this unfortunate role in the 'thirties.

Of all the recovery programmes introduced by democratic
capitalist countries in the 'thirties the New Deal was the boldest.
It has a special significance to the historian of economic thought,
partly because, for a long time, Keynes was regarded as the main
intellectual influence behind Roosevelt's policies. There is very little
truth in this claim, but it is perhaps true that by the late 'thirties
Keynes had acquired a greater number of fervent disciples in
America than in his own country. The sombre background of the
American depression led to more far-reaching re-appraisals of
capitalism than took place elsewhere; and it was here that the
bankruptcy of traditional economic thinking was felt most keenly.
Given the attachment of powerful sections of the American public
to the private enterprise ideal, "Keynesianism" acquired an emotive
and ideological significance in the United States which it retains in
some circles to the present day. At the same time, the disillusionment
and frustration engendered among Keynes's disciples by the failure
of the New Deal to achieve full recovery led them to give the
Keynesian "revolution" a special and more revolutionary interpretation.

The idea that Keynes's influence lay behind the policies of the
New Deal began to take root fairly early. In December 1933, for
example, barely a year after the New Deal had been inaugurated, the
*New York Times* welcomed some of Keynes's criticisms of Roosevelt
with surprise because "he had been rather generally regarded as
the economic authority on which the Administration leaned". Even
today, when so much qualifying evidence has been adduced, we still
find statements like the following in the American press: "The
fundamental theory underlying the New Deal was largely that of
John Maynard Keynes and his colleagues on both sides of the
Atlantic."[2] It is a legend that has been sedulously cultivated by
friend and foe of the New Deal.

Keynes was fairly well known in America as a result of his
*Economic Consequences of the Peace*; his articles on various subjects

[1] *The Economist*, Dec. 2, 1939.
[2] *New Republic* Oct. 20th, 1962.

appeared regularly in the *New Republic* throughout the 'thirties; and he made two visits to the United States in 1931 and 1934, on the last of which he had several conversations with Roosevelt and his advisers. Keynes took a keen interest in the New Deal and became one of its chief defenders and interpreters to the British public. It was to Washington rather than London that Keynes began to look for the first practical applications of the ideas which he had developed in over a decade of advocacy directed primarily at British problems. It is not difficult to see why this should be so. In 1932 Roosevelt had spoken for the need of "bold, persistent experimentation", and had defined the word "Deal" in New Deal to mean "that the Government itself was going to use affirmative action to bring about its avowed objective, rather than stand by and hope that general economic laws would attain them"[1] Roosevelt's willingness to experiment was his most attractive quality so far as Keynes was concerned. In his own country orthodoxy and complacency prevailed. Elsewhere, in Russia and Germany, revolution and dictatorship had been the chosen course. The degree of Keynes's hopes and enthusiasm can be gauged from the opening sentence of his famous open letter to Roosevelt written in December 1933.[2]

> "You have made yourself the trustee for those in every country who seek to mend the evils of our condition by reasoned experiment, within the famework of the existing social system. If you fail, rational change will be gravely prejudiced throughout the world, leaving orthodoxy and revolution to fight it out. But if you succeed, new and bolder methods will be tried everywhere, and we may date the first chapter of a new economic era from your accession to office."

But interest and hopes are not influence on the course of events, still less a determining influence. It would be strange indeed if it were possible to ascribe to one man, and a foreigner at that, a dominant role in anything as complex and confused as the parcel of measures which comprise the New Deal. Nevertheless, the full story of the Keynesian revolution in America, when it comes to be written, will make fascinating reading.[3] It will also be a difficult one to write even

[1] *Public Papers and Addresses* (1938), vol. II, p. 5.

[2] Keynes was not alone among British economists in expressing such hopes or in offering advice to the new President. On November 20th, 1933 a long letter was sent to F. D. R. by a group of Oxford economists, pressing him to undertake a public works programme. The signatories were: D. H. Macgregor, L. M. Fraser, W. M. Alten, E. L. Hargraves, R. F. Bretherton, J. E. Meade, R. Opie, R. L. Hall and R. F. Harrod.

[3] A lively account of the episode has been given recently by R. Lekachman, *The Age of Keynes* (1967), Ch. 5. A full account would require a more detailed picture of academic and public opinion on economic policy questions in the United States in the inter-war period than is given here or in Lekachman's book. Fortunately, there is J. Dorfman's massive study *The Economic Mind in American Civilisation*, in five volumes, of which Vols. IV and V

for an American scholar with full access to the memoirs and documents of the participants.

The difficulties are interesting in themselves; they relate to the complexity of the American system of government with its bewildering array of competing departments, agencies, and pressure groupings. Compared with this, the process of policy formation and implementation in a Parliamentary system with a Cabinet advised by the professional civil service is relatively straightforward. Over and above the problem posed by the institutional structure lies the potential, and essentially personal, influence of the President of the day. In Roosevelt's case this raises numerous problems connected with his well-known penchant towards pragmatism, and his habit of attempting to weld together diametrically opposed advice coming from different sources. In the course of his presidency Roosevelt invited and received guidance from a large number of personal economic advisers. He was also subjected to a regular flow of opinion issuing from the heads of departments and agencies, each of which had its own staff of economic advisers. Needless to say, the departmental opinions were frequently in conflict with one another. Just as Roosevelt shuffled his personal advisers, giving prominence to the ideas first of one and then to another, so he also swayed in his support for the policies coming from the different departments. Without even considering the political problems involved in placating various interest groups and in dealing with Congress, therefore, the task of establishing the links between economic thought and policy is extraordinarily difficult in the case of the New Deal. Here we shall merely isolate a few strands of this tangled web for the purposes of contrast with the British situation.[1]

### Depreciation of the Dollar

The "bold persistent experimentation" of which Roosevelt had spoken was first to be seen in monetary policy. Roosevelt's inauguration coincided with a banking crisis. He dealt with this by declaring a banking holiday and imposing an embargo on domestic gold hoarding and the export of gold. The internal gold standard was thereby abolished, and the operation of the international standard made subject to regulation. These emergency measures were formalised later in the year when the gold standard was abandoned and the

---

are most relevant. The best general accounts of the New Deal are to be found in A. M. Schlesinger, *The Age of Roosevelt* in three volumes (1947-1959); W. A. Leuchtenberg, *Franklin D. Roosevelt and the New Deal, 1932-1940* (1963); and J. M. Burns *Roosevelt: The Lion and the Fox* (1956).

[1] For further comment on the relationship of economic advice and policy in the American system see pp. 331-6 below.

dollar allowed to depreciate. The policy was confirmed by Roosevelt's refusal to commit the United States to stabilisation of the dollar in terms of gold at the World Economic Conference in 1933.[1] While action was confined to making it clear that the United States was not going to allow exchange rate considerations to inhibit domestic reflationary plans, it commanded support from expansionists both at home and abroad. Keynes gave a warm welcome to Roosevelt's decision not to support a return to the gold standard.

"The President's message to the World Economic Conference is, in substance, a challenge to us to decide whether we propose to tread the old, unfortunate ways, or to explore new paths; paths new to statesmen and bankers, but not new to thought. For they lead to the managed currency of the future, the examination of which had been the prime topic of post-war economics."[2]

In October 1933 Roosevelt took the policy of allowing the dollar to find its own level one step further by initiating a positive policy of raising the dollar price of gold. In pursuing this policy of deliberate depreciation Roosevelt ignored the advice of his more conservative monetary advisers and followed the quantity theory of money ideas of George F. Warren. The economic rationale of the gold-purchase policy seems to have been as follows: by forcing the gold-dollar parity downwards, an upward leverage could be exerted on commodity prices, and more especially on agricultural and raw material prices.

Given the relative unimportance of the foreign trade sector to the American economy—the prices of internationally traded goods were the only ones directly affected by depreciation—it is difficult to see how these ideas could be entertained. In his open letter in December 1933 Keynes criticised the undue attention being paid to views based on the quantity theory of money; it had led, he believed, to a false set of priorities.

"In so far as an overvaluation of the dollar was impeding the freedom of domestic price-raising policies or disturbing the balance of payments with foreign countries, it was advisable to depreciate it. But exchange depreciation should follow the success of your domestic price-raising policy as its natural consequence, and should not be allowed to disturb the whole world by preceding its justification at an entirely arbitrary pace. This is another example of trying to put on flesh by letting out the belt.

"These criticisms do not mean that I have weakened in my

[1] See A. W. Crawford, *Monetary Management Under the New Deal* (1940); A. Schlesinger, *op. cit.*, Vol. I, Chapters 12-14.
[2] *Daily Mail*, July 1933 quoted in Harrod, *Life of Keynes*, p. 445.

advocacy of a managed currency or in preferring stable prices to stable exchanges. The currency and exchange policy of a country should be entirely subservient to the aim of raising output and employment to the right level. But the recent gyrations of the dollar have looked to me more like a gold standard on the booze than the ideal managed currency of my dreams."[1]

Keynes's own immediate suggestion was that the dollar should be pegged, but with the declared option of adjusting the peg in accordance with any possible future imbalance in the international accounts, or where the domestic price level was out of step with world prices. He welcomed, therefore, the announcement by the President in January 1934 of his intention to stabilise the purchasing power of the dollar at a provisional parity.[2]

This episode provides an excellent illustration of the strengths and weaknesses of Roosevelt's approach to economic questions, and of the cross-currents at work determining the direction of his policies. A decisive response to an emergency was perpetuated and elevated to the status of a positive recovery measure on the basis of theories which were superficially attractive from a political point of view.

As Keynes said, the possibility of achieving a managed currency had been discussed by economists since the end of the First World War. In the United States the idea that by controlling the domestic money supply it was possible to control and stabilise the price level, and thereby iron out booms and slumps, was widely canvassed by Irving Fisher in the 'twenties.[3] Since prices had fallen drastically in the depression, the policy of stabilisation was frequently linked with reflation as a means of restoring prices to the pre-depression level. The banking and liquidity aspects of the depression were more dominant in the United States than in Britain. Indeed, it has recently been argued that the failure of the monetary authorities to use their powers to prevent a contraction of the money supply, let alone expand it, in the years between 1929 and 1933, was one of the primary causes of the slump.[4] Hawtrey and Keynes were simply the leading British representatives of an Anglo-American monetary line of thought supporting monetary management and expansion. One of Roosevelt's advisers at this time, Raymond Moley, later claimed that the policy pursued by Roosevelt was fully in line with proposals for an

---

[1] *New York Times*, Dec. 31st 1933. He would have been confirmed in this view if he had known how the gold purchase price was settled each day by Roosevelt, Morgenthau and Jesse Jones over breakfast; see Schlesinger *op. cit.*, Vol. II, p. 233.

[2] *New Statesman*, Jan. 20th 1934.

[3] See e.g. I. Fisher (with H. R. L. Cohrssen), *Stabilised Money: A History of the Movement* (1935).

[4] See M. Friedman and A. Schwarz, *A Monetary History of the United States 1867-1960* (1965), Ch. 7.

international commodity standard made by Keynes in the last chapter of his *Treatise on Money*.[1] By the late 'twenties, however, Keynes had moved away from exclusive emphasis on the monetary determinants of instability and unemployment. He still believed that currencies should be managed internally and internationally, and that cheaper credit was a necessary pre-condition for expansion. But as his attention became more focused on fiscal methods of controlling the volume of savings and investment, and thereby the level of employment, the manipulation of monetary policy slipped into the background. But, bearing in mind the usual time-lag between ideas and policy, it is true to say that a tenuous link could be made between some aspects of Roosevelt's monetary policy and earlier professional quantity theory thinking. Nevertheless, very little professional support was given to the cruder Warren thesis.[2]

Another supporting influence on the gold purchase policy which deserves brief mention is the fact that other countries, notably Britain, had already shown the way towards international exchange rate management. Henry Morgenthau, who owed his later appointment as Secretary of the Treasury largely to the support which he gave to Roosevelt in his gold-buying policy, certainly showed interest in the manipulations of the British Exchange Equalisation Account.[3] The gold-purchase policy, therefore, could be looked on simply as an attempt to follow in Britain's footsteps, and as a counter-move to the sterling devaluation of 1931.

The most important motives behind the policy, however, were domestic and political. Popular economic opinion in America has always been more influenced by unorthodox monetary schemes than by unorthodox fiscal ideas. In the 1932 election campaign Roosevelt and Hoover had vied with each other in proclaiming the need for fiscal righteousness as represented by a balanced budget. The Republicans, however, had taken a strong stand on the need to maintain the gold standard at all costs. Roosevelt had been equivocal, contenting himself with a vague declaration in favour of a "sound currency". Once in office Roosevelt came under considerable pressure from the representatives of agrarian interests to do something to raise the price of farm products. The depression had activated a long-standing tradition of economic protest on the part of the agrarian debtor groups against the creditor interests of the Eastern financial community. Senator Elwes Thomas, for example, had succeeded in tacking onto the Administration's Bill to help agriculture

[1] See R. Moley, *After Seven Years* (1939), p. 225; and A. Schlesinger, *op. cit.*, Vol. II, p. 211.

[2] For a recent and rare defence by a modern quantity theorist, see M. Friedman and A. Schwartz, *op. cit.*, pp. 465-6.

[3] See J. M. Blum, *From the Morgenthau Diaries* (1959), p. 121.

a crude pro-inflationist amendment empowering the President to print money.

The debtor-creditor split has had no real counterpart in British monetary debate since the demise of the Birmingham currency school under Thomas Attwood's leadership in the first half of the nineteenth century. Apart from isolated heretics, the dominant tradition in British monetary thought has always been orthodox and élitist. By contrast, the American public has frequently supported movements based on populist views on such questions as the value of money, banking policy, and the national debt, which, in Britain, are normally considered to be the technical preserve of experts. In following the advice of George Warren (who was, incidentally, an agricultural rather than a monetary specialist), Roosevelt was attempting to placate the extreme pro-inflationists in Congress, while at the same time capitalising on the anti-banker sentiment which had grown up as a result of bank failures and the post-mortem on financial practices during the boom. The latter aspect of the gold purchase policy has been summed up by a recent biographer of Morgenthau, Roosevelt's chief ally in this venture, as follows:

> "Roosevelt and Morgenthau seized the particular tool that seemed best to them at the time, and they used it boldly. They made the manipulation of the value of the currency an open and admitted instrument of public policy. This in itself signified the intention of the New Deal to free government from the decisions of bankers, who, whatever their talents, had fallen into the habit of timorous inactivity."[1]

On the one hand, therefore, Roosevelt's gold policy can be seen as part and parcel of the early New Deal measures to protect and raise agricultural incomes, notably the Agricultural Adjustment Act and the Emergency Farm Mortgage Act, which set up machinery to enable the federal government to purchase agricultural surpluses, curtail output, and take over the burden of mortgage debt. On the other hand, it was a policy which, symbolically at least, went hand in hand with such reforms of the banking system as the establishment of the Federal Deposit Insurance Scheme, the expansion of the activities of the Reconstruction Finance Corporation, and the enlargement of the powers of the Federal Reserve System to inspect and regulate the activities of member banks. Some of Roosevelt's supporters felt that he had missed a vital opportunity in the early days of his Administration to bring the banks more firmly under government control. More recent students of the monetary history of this period regard the powers assumed as being adequate but

[1] J. M. Blum, *op. cit.*, p. 75.

poorly used. They would claim that the most solid achievements of the New Deal in this field were of an institutional rather than a policy kind; that domestic monetary policy itself was "accorded little importance in affecting the course of economic affairs and the policy actually followed was hesitant and almost entirely passive".[1] In this respect it probably played a lesser role than cheap money did in Britain at this time. There was no American equivalent of the British housing boom in the 'thirties, and while interest rates were kept fairly low, there was also a persistent problem of "excess reserves" in the American banking system throughout the period.

### The National Industrial Recovery Act

In many respects the most typical piece of early New Deal recovery and reform legislation was the National Industrial Recovery Act, approved in June 1933, and declared unconstitutional by the Supreme Court in 1935. It was a characteristic Rooseveltian hotch-potch of measures designed to satisfy a number of conflicting interests. Some idea of the multiplicity of ends which the Act was supposed to serve can be obtained from the following quotation from its first article.

> "It is hereby declared to be the policy of Congress to remove obstructions to the free flow on interstate and foreign commerce which tend to diminish the amount thereof; and to provide for the general welfare by promoting the organisation of industry for the purpose of collective action among trade groups, to induce and maintain united action by labour and management under adequate governmental sanctions and supervision, to eliminate unfair competitive practices, to promote the fullest utilisation of the present productive capacity of industries, to avoid undue restriction of production (except as may be temporarily required), to increase the consumption of industrial and agricultural products by increasing purchasing power, to reduce and relieve unemployment, to improve standards of labor, and otherwise to rehabilitate industry and to conserve natural resources."[2]

The Act set up the National Recovery Administration whose function it was to encourage business and labour groups to draw up codes of industrial practice, which it would then examine, sanction, and, if necessary, enforce in the courts. The reformist and humanitarian objects of the legislation were fairly clear; they were to

[1] M. Friedman and A. Schwarz, *op. cit.*, p. 420.
[2] As reprinted in *National Recovery Measures in the United States*, International Labour Office, (1933).

improve labour conditions and establish or confirm the collective bargaining rights of organised labour. This in itself was a notable advance in a country in which labour disputes had been frequently bloody and bitter. In return for concessions on this front employers were to be allowed, subject to governmental review, to co-operate among themselves to eliminate "unfair competition". In other words, the anti-trust laws were to be side-stepped.

The political and intellectual antecedents of NRA are complex.[1] From the ranks of organised labour and its representatives in Congress came pressure to prevent employers from lowering labour standards of pay and hours in response to depression. Roosevelt found himself faced with Congressional demands in the form of the Black-Connery Bill for a prohibition of inter-state trade in goods produced by men working longer than thirty hours a week: in other words, with proposals for reducing unemployment by work-sharing methods.

During the war and throughout the 'twenties there had been a rapid growth in the number and scope of trade associations. Some business leaders, notably Gerard Swope, president of General Electric, and Henry Harriman, of the United States Chamber of Commerce, believed that the anti-trust laws should be modified to allow trade associations to establish codes of behaviour which would stabilise prices and employment, co-ordinate investment plans, protect employees, and eliminate wasteful competition.[2] As a result of depression the traditional American antagonism to big business as such had softened. Conditions seemed ripe for a move towards government sponsorship of business collectivism.

### Progressivism and Institutionalism

There were, however, deeper intellectual roots to this approach. Roosevelt drew upon a number of the -isms and ideologies that had formed on the middle-left of American political and intellectual life in the previous forty years: agrarian populism, urban progressivism, the "new nationalism", institutionalism and pragmatism.[3] As we have noted already, there is no British equivalent to agrarian populism, with its antagonism towards any organised creditor interests. The demands of the Labour Party for the nationalisation of the banking system do not fall into the same category; they were largely political in motive, and were not identified with protection

[1] The best accounts can be found in A. Schlesinger, *op. cit.*, Vol. II; R. Tugwell, *The Democratic President* (1957), pp. 280-92.
[2] See J. Dorfman, *The Economic Mind in American Civilisation* (1959), Vol. V, pp. 632-6; D. R. Fusfeld, *The Economic Thought of F. D. Roosevelt and the Origins of the New Deal* (1956), pp. 200-1.
[3] See W. A. Leuchtenburg, *op. cit.*, pp. 32-6.

of the rural debtor classes. But there are certain rough parallels and links between progressivism and other British social and political movements. The progressive movement began in the early years of the twentieth century; it was largely a manifestation of the political conscience of the middle classes. The movement was based on protest against the condition of the urban masses, poverty, corruption in local politics, inequalities of wealth, and the concentration of economic power. By the turn of the century the traditional American assumption of equality of opportunity became increasingly difficult to maintain in the face of the growth of large corporations and the existence of an urban proletariat. America had clearly become a class society, and her politics took on the language of class, even if it was, to begin with, the genteel tones of *noblesse oblige*. The British counterpart to the kind of reforms which progressives called for can perhaps be found in the Liberal welfare legislation before 1914, also introduced under bourgeois auspices.[1] But the progressives had to wait until the New Deal before a similar impulse for reform brought the equivalent of Lloyd George's old age pensions, unemployment insurance, and protection for trade unions.

It has been argued that Roosevelt's programme was largely derived from the Progressive tradition.[2] In the early years of the New Deal, however, and particularly in the case of NRA, the individualism and opposition to big business inherent in this tradition, and carried into practice by the anti-trust laws at the turn of the century, was not greatly in evidence. Some of the members of Roosevelt's original "brain-trust", notably Rexford Tugwell, Adolf Berle and Raymond Moley, were more impressed by the advantages of a planned industrial order composed of large units than with the virtues of atomistic competition. The inspiration of this approach derives from what is known as the "new nationalism", and the writings of the American institutionalist school of economists, of which Tugwell and Berle were members.

Institutionalism was an amorphous body of ideas loosely drawn from the writings of Thorstein Veblen and the German historical school. Above all, it was a literature of radical dissent from what were regarded as the methods and findings of orthodox economics. It bears roughly the same relationship to the mainstream of economic theory as did the writings of the Webbs and W. J. Ashley in Britain.[3] Typically, the institutionalist writers rejected the orthodox neo-classical view of the economic system as a smoothly-functioning

---

[1] A detailed study of parallels and connections can be found in A. Mann, "British Social Thought and American Reformers of the Progressive Era", *Mississippi Valley Historical Review*, March 1956.

[2] D. R. Fusfeld, *op. cit.*

[3] See p. 158 above.

machine; they preferred to look upon society as an evolutionary organism characterised by conflicts and tensions which could only be overcome by institutional adaption and social reform. They also rejected the hedonist assumptions of economic theory, with its bias in favour of the individual decision-maker as the basic unit of analysis. They wished to see greater concentration on collectivities and institutions, and a greater awareness of the fact that social habits and cultural forms were historically and socially determined. In place of the abstract, deductive methods of orthodoxy they wished to see more weight given to concrete, inductive, historical, statistical and descriptive studies. They frequently expressed a profound distrust and dislike for *laissez-faire* and the competitive market process: social and economic change could best be achieved by conscious, pragmatic, learning-by-doing, methods of intervention and control. Another important element in the institutionalist approach was the emphasis given to technology: they were impressed by the possibility of applying social engineering and scientific management techniques to the problems of the economy as a whole.

Nationalism could be linked with this programme on several levels. The importance attached to the history of particular institutions and societies could lead to a stress on the uniqueness of national experience. In the American case this was frequently associated with a romantic conception of rural life, a warm appreciation for the richness and spaciousness of the American natural endowment, and a desire to develop and conserve natural resources. From this a step could be taken towards the view that, with her wide variety of resources, it was possible for America to be self-sufficient. Free trade like *laissez-faire* was associated with orthodox economics.

The writings of Berle and Tugwell fit well within this broad body of ideas. In 1932, Berle, together with Gardner Means, published *The Modern Corporation and Private Property*. In it they drew attention to the growth in size of business corporations and indicated various ways in which this development had outdated much of the theory of competitive adjustment, and the social attitudes based upon it. Markets no longer functioned anonymously; they were capable of being "administered" by a few dominant producers. With increasing size had come the separation of ownership and control; it was no longer possible to speak of profit as the motive, guide, and reward for individual initiative. These developments also raised in acute form the problems of the relationship between the state and the private corporation. Berle and Means recognised the need for some form of extra social control, but in the long run they looked to the ethical regeneration of business leadership, and to the emergence of "a purely neutral technocracy balancing a variety of claims by various groups in the community and assigning to each a portion of the income stream on the basis of public policy rather than private cupidity."[1]

Tugwell also stressed the irrelevance of the competitive ideal: in the new technocratic age social and economic goals would be achieved by co-ordination rather than competition. Unlike Berle, however, he envisaged a much larger role for the government planner. He supported the case for planning by means of an analogy with the need to abolish "absolute sovereignty" among nations in order to secure peace; and believed that the techniques of scientific management at present used within firms should be applied on a nation-wide scale.[2]

It is easy to see how such ideas could be used to support some form of increased co-operation between government and business; it could, according to taste, be a prelude to extensive state intervention and planning, or develop into a system of industrial self-government sponsored and loosely regulated by the state. It is less easy to see what contribution this approach could be expected to make to recovery. Here perhaps some comparison with the British planning movement of the 'thirties may be helpful. There is an obvious similarity between the Tugwell-Berle position and its embodiment in NRA, and the views of men like Harold Macmillan and the efforts of Conservative governments to foster combination and market-sharing arrangements.[3] Indeed, the "corporatist" movement, in one form or another, can be found in most capitalist countries, democratic and fascist alike, at this time. Stability, and possibly recovery, was to be sought by structural reorganisation; by the elimination of wasteful competition and excess capacity; by the co-ordination of investment and marketing decisions. Macmillan's case for the "creation of National Councils for each industry and/or group of industries" proceeds from the same logic as the Swope plan and the NRA codes. They both envisaged that recovery would come by encouraging restrictive, or as the authors would have preferred to call it, co-operative, methods to bring production and consumption into line on an industry by industry basis.

There is, however, an important difference between the thinking which went into Macmillan's version of corporatism, and that of the NRA: the labour provisions of the NRA codes have no counterpart in the British discussions. This can partly be explained by the fact

[1] *Op. cit.*, p. 356.
[2] The contrast between Berle and Tugwell is spelled out in greater detail in A. Schlesinger, *op. cit.*, Vol. II, pp. 173-8. For a representative example of Tugwell's views at this time see "The Principle of Planning and the Institution of *Laissez-Faire*", *American Economic Review*, March 1932.
[3] Cf. pp. 215-7 above.

that such provisions were less necessary in Britain where collective bargaining was more highly developed, and where the trade union movement had proved strong enough to resist much of the pressure to lower wages. But the labour provisions of the NRA codes were designed to serve more than a reformist purpose in the minds of their proponents; they were also intended as means of protecting and possibly increasing purchasing power. They owed their inspiration to the influence on New Deal thinking of the doctrines of under-consumption. The anti-orthodox bias of institutional modes of thought made it receptive to the heretical ideas of men like J. A. Hobson and his American equivalents, William Foster and Waddil Catchings. Institutionalists were less pre-disposed to see harmony and inevitability in the workings of the economic machine; they were, consequently, more prone to believe in the possibility of an inherent tendency towards over-production and under-consumption—a tendency which could only be overcome by deliberate intervention and planning. Hobson certainly seems to have enjoyed a greater reputation among American institutionalists than he did at home.[1] In common with many New Dealers, including perhaps Roosevelt himself, Tugwell accepted Hobson's account of under-consumption-ism as the cause of depressions, and its corollary that unemployment could be cured by a revival of purchasing power.[2]

## Keynes and the NRA

Given these tendencies in early New Deal thinking, it might seem that the ground was well-prepared for an acceptance of Keynesian ideas. There were, it is true, some interesting parallels. As we have noted earlier, Keynes and the "new Liberals" had done a good deal in the "Yellow Book" to draw attention to the development of business collectivism; they had also made several suggestions for coming to terms with the new industrial order which are similar to those advanced by Berle and Means, and Tugwell.[3] The general tenor of Keynes's *The End of Laissez-Faire* was very much in keeping with the ideas of the institutionalists, and was welcomed as such by Tugwell himself.[4] It is also true, as Schlesinger has pointed out, that the nationalism inherent in the policy of devaluation, and the regulatory activities of the first New Deal, have some affinity with Keynes's own espousal of national self-sufficiency at this time.

[1] See J. Dorfman, *op. cit.*, Vol. IV, pp. 174-5, 339.
[2] See B. Sternsher, *Rexford Tugwell and the New Deal* (1964), pp. 35, 139; R. Tugwell, *The Democratic President*, p. 234; J. Dorfman, *op. cit.*, Vol. V, pp. 765-7.
[3] See e.g. *Britain's Industrial Future*, Bk. II, "Organisation of Business", the part written largely by Keynes himself.
[4] See Tugwell's review in *New Republic*, Oct. 13th 1926.

Schlesinger notes that in both cases some control over financial and trade relations with the outside world was advocated in order to make planning possible on the domestic front.[1] Moreover, the fact that it was Keynes who later made Hobson's ideas on under-consumption respectable to academic economists seems to round off the sequence of similarities. But the similarities are in fact misleading, as an examination of Keynes's criticisms of the NRA will show.

The NRA codes were supposed to be capable of preventing the fall of prices, profits, and purchasing power. The weak case for them was that by fixing minimum wages and setting limits to the number of hours worked, not only would the available employment be shared more equally, but the massive deflationary influence of the depression would be prevented from exerting its full force on prices and wages.[2] A stronger case for the codes was that they would operate as a reflationary device, raising wages and purchasing power, and ultimately, prices and profits.

The self-defeating nature of a measure which raised both prices and costs was overlooked in 1933, when, under the leadership of General Johnson, and to the accompaniment of a good deal of bally-hoo, the campaign to negotiate codes was at its height. Roosevelt seems to have believed that an infectious tide of re-employment could be launched at the cost of allowing businessmen to fix prices.[3] It soon became apparent that the NRA was being used by some businessmen as a simple cover for price-raising. Moreover, enormous problems were encountered in attempting to administer the cumbrous machinery of state intervention where detailed regulation of conditions of work, manufacture, and sale, was required. Some much-needed reforms were achieved; the codes may have prevented further deterioration; but it is difficult to see how, even given good behaviour on the part of the businessmen, they could have been expected to start an upward trend.[4]

In his open letter to Roosevelt at the end of 1933 Keynes warned against confusing reform and recovery; he could see nothing in the NRA which helped recovery, and felt that there was too much emphasis on raising prices as an end in itself, rather than as a result of an increase in purchasing power, output, and employment. He had levelled the same criticisms at British policy-makers who maintained that recovery would come as a result of restriction of supply.[5] He

[1] *Op. cit.*, Vol. II, pp. 179-80.
[2] See e.g. A. Sachs in C. Wilcox (ed.), *America's Recovery Program* (1934).
[3] See R. Tugwell, *The Democratic President*, pp. 310-13.
[4] W.A. Leuchtenburg, *op. cit.*, pp. 67-70.
[5] See e.g. *The Means to Prosperity* (1933), Ch. III, and his letter to H. Macmillan cited p. 217n. above.

H*

returned to the same theme when he visited the United States in 1934 to receive an honorary doctorate at Columbia University. The objectionable side of the NRA was its "restrictionist philosophy". What was acceptable in dealing with the problems of an over-extended agricultural sector could not be applied to industry "because of its excessive complexity and regimentation". He went on to say that: "I find most Americans divided between those who believe that higher wages are good because they increase purchasing power, and those who believe that they are bad because they raise costs. But both are right, and the net result is to cancel out. The important question is the proper adjustment of relative wage rates. Absolute wage rates are not of primary importance in a country where their effect on foreign trade has been offset by exchange devaluation."[1]

In the light of these criticisms of NRA and other schemes based on a similar extended micro-economic view of recovery problems, it is misleading to describe Keynes as a nationalist planner of the same type as Tugwell. As we have noted in an earlier connection, in the final stages of Keynes's journey towards the *General Theory* his attention became focused exclusively on the problem of raising the level of effective demand by monetary and fiscal methods. This was associated with a desire to distinguish clearly between the logic of the individual producer and the logic of managing the overall level of demand. This was the theme of his Columbia address in 1934.

"For our problem today is no longer one of how the individual firm can produce most. It is a question of introducing central controls, so as to make certain that a sufficient effective demand will be forthcoming to furnish the inducements to the individual firm to produce what it is capable of producing. This requires a new technique and quite a different kind of decision from those which face the efficient manager of an individual firm. To the individual firm, if I may use a metaphor, the earth is flat; but the men in charge of the central controls must remember that in its totality the globe of economic life is round. One man's costs are another man's income. One man's spending is another man's sales.

"Unfortunately, economists have studied the economic system as a whole almost as little as the businessman. They also have been too often accustomed to describe a flat economic earth and they have too little to teach the administrators about the good round

[1] *New York Times*, June 10th 1934. The correspondence aroused by Keynes's earlier criticisms of the New Deal is interesting: Raymond Moley claimed that Keynes's suggestions had been adopted. Irving Fisher supported Keynes's criticisms of the NRA and his proposals for increased public works spending. Willford I. King, however, felt that loan-financed public works would simply reduce private spending by an offsetting amount. See *New York Times*, Jan 1st 1934.

world as a whole. Thus practical experiment has to discover what theory has failed to indicate."[1]

It is not difficult to see that this statement was a mild rebuke, not only to his own profession, but also to the administrators of the New Deal. The whole weight of his advocacy, in his letters to Roosevelt, his interview in 1934, and his published writings, was placed on the need to use loan-financed public works to raise the level of effective demand. He believed that circumstances in America were more propitious for such a programme than elsewhere, because the multiplier effects of public expenditure were likely to be greater as a result of the smaller foreign trade sector and the consequently smaller import leakage.[2]

## Public Spending and the New Deal

The consistent weakness of the New Deal recovery programme, up to 1938 and possibly beyond, lay in the failure to grasp fully the connection between public spending and economic revival. This weakness sprang from many sources, one of which certainly was Roosevelt's pragmatic approach to economic and other questions, and his lingering attachment to fiscal orthodoxy. It is well known that Roosevelt attacked the Hoover Administration in his campaign speeches in 1932 for failing to cut back on expenditure as federal revenues fell; and that he claimed that this failure had added to the nation's difficulties by undermining public confidence. The crucial speech on this subject was made in Pittsburgh, where he pledged himself to a 25% cut in expenditure and said: "I regard reductions in Federal spending as one of the most important issues of this campaign. In my opinion it is the most direct and effective contribution that Government can make to business."[3] He also repudiated public spending as a solution to unemployment.[4]

Unfortunately for the sake of consistency, if not electoral success, he also stated that budget deficits should not be allowed to stand in the way of programmes to alleviate distress. The conflict between these two positions runs through the whole New Deal programme; it led to confusion, errors of judgment, and prevented any firm position being taken.

One of the emergency measures of the first one hundred days of Roosevelt's Administration was an Economy Bill which made reductions totalling $500 million in veterans' pensions and civil

---

[1] *New York Times*, June 6th 1934.
[2] See *New York Times*, June 10th 1934.
[3] *Public Papers and Addresses* (1938), Vol. I, pp. 796-8.
[4] *Ibid.*, p. 625.

service pay. The rationale for this measure was similar to that used by supporters of orthodoxy in Britain. Budget deficits were not simply a consequence of depression but an aggravating cause; government borrowing to finance deficits would raise interest rates and draw off funds from private business; they would undermine confidence in government credit and lead to inflation.

At the same time, however, Roosevelt embarked on massive relief schemes and created federal lending and spending agencies whose function was to underpin the crumbling debt structure. One of his earliest measures was to authorise federal grants (instead of loans) to state relief programmes—a course of action which Hoover had been unwilling to undertake. He also initiated a federal relief programme in the shape of the Civil Works Administration and the Civilian Conservation Corps, later supplemented by the Works Progress Administration and the National Youth Administration. All of these bodies supported public works of a relief type; they were required to meet the need partly served by unemployment insurance in Britain. Apart from institutions such as the Reconstruction Finance Corporation and other bodies concerned with making loans to financial institutions, or taking over the burden of existing private debt, the other main spending agency was the Public Works Administration. The funds for this agency were originally appropriated as part of the National Industrial Recovery Act, and the idea seems to have been that public works could be afforded *after* recovery had been initiated by NRA methods.[1] In fact, however, with the failure of NRA, public works spending on large capital projects came to assume a separate, though never a dominant, role.

Roosevelt was aware of the conflict between the deflationary impact of his economy programme and the inflationary intent of his monetary policy. He attempted to reconcile the two by claiming that he was "seeking an inflation which will not wholly be based on additional government debt".[2] He later became aware of a similar conflict in his pursuit of economy at the same time that he was increasing public spending on relief and public works. He tried to bridge this gap by distinguishing between "ordinary" and "emergency" expenditures. It was right to cut down on the former, and as far as the latter were concerned, he claimed that much of it was either in the nature of "sound" loans which would be self-financing over a period of years, or could be met from increased taxation.[3]

Roosevelt's fundamental conservatism in these matters is revealed

[1] See S. Harris (ed.), *The New Economics* (1947), p. 17.
[2] Letter to Colonel House, April 5th 1933, quoted in Leuchtenberg, *op. cit.*, p. 48.
[3] See Lewis H. Kimmel, *Federal Budget and Fiscal Policy 1798-1958* (1959), p. 178; B. Sternsher, *op. cit.*, pp. 134-5.

in a number of ways. He liked to have an orthodox leavening in his Administration, particularly in the key financial posts. In the early days of the New Deal this position was occupied by Lewis Douglas, Roosevelt's first Director of Bureau of the Budget, whose ideas on budgetary matters were as rigid as those of Philip Snowden in Britain. Douglas was the main supporter of the economy campaign and consistently opposed or sought to curb the activities of the spending agencies.[1] He did not resign until 1934, and even then it was against Roosevelt's wishes. Douglas's place as keeper of the orthodox conscience of the Administration was later assumed by Morgenthau as Secretary to the Treasury.

Roosevelt's attitude to public spending was an ambivalent one. A sense of sin and mismanagement attached to unbalanced budgets; he hoped that public works expenditure could be concentrated on sound, self-supporting projects; and, wherever possible, even these were pared down or delayed.[2] He recognised the need for relief expenditure, but could not entirely free himself from the notion, derived from the individualism of the progressive tradition, that such expenditure undermined personal initiative. At first he looked for revival as a result of such measures as NRA and the Agricultural Adjustment Administration; it was only after failure on this front that he turned to public works. He continued to hope that all relief expenditure could be phased out in favour of a comprehensive system of contributory social security. This was, in fact, one of later achievements of the New Deal, but it did not replace relief works. It is hardly surprising then that Roosevelt found difficulty in accepting unbalanced budgets as a conscious aim of policy. The deficits actually incurred were never planned; they were the unintended and unwanted by-product of policies designed for other purposes.[3]

It would be unfair, of course, to attribute the shortcomings of New Deal thinking in these matters entirely to Roosevelt. Professional economic analysts, particularly in the earliest and worst phases of the depression, were sharply divided over diagnosis and remedies. The public reputation of academic economists emerged somewhat impaired from the events which immediately preceded and followed the 1929 crash. Many economists had shared the general optimism concerning the possibility of perpetuating the boom conditions of the late 'twenties. Irving Fisher, one of the most highly respected members of the academic community, had the misfortune to make a number of public predictions and pronouncements on this subject in the autumn of 1929 just before the crash; the most famous of

[1] Schlesinger, *op.cit.*, Vol. II, pp. 279-81.
[2] See B. Sternsher, *op. cit.*, p. 134; Schlesinger, *op. cit.*, p. 278.
[3] See L. H. Kimmel, *op. cit.*, pp. 182-3.

these was that: "Stock prices have reached what looks like a permanently high plateau."[1] And when the boom collapsed economists—not necessarily the same ones—did not endear themselves to
the public by proclaiming that the slump was a natural purgative.
The same orthodox opinions that we have noted in the British
academic community were also well-represented in the United
States. There were plenty of Jeremiahs to argue that fiscal orthodoxy
and monetary inaction were the safest ways of dealing with depression.[2]

As the definition of "Deal" in New Deal cited earlier shows,
Roosevelt's pragmatic approach prevented him from being influenced by doctrines which preached inaction on the basis of
"economic law". By the same token, however, it also sealed him off
from the sophisticated theories of action which Keynes used to
support his case.[3] Keynes took every opportunity to make his
position clear to the President; he could even be said to have enjoyed
more direct access to Roosevelt than to politicians in power in his
own country. In 1934, for example, as a result of the intercession of
Felix Frankfurter, Keynes had a series of talks with Roosevelt and
members of his "brain trust". The tit-bits of evidence we have on
these talks indicate that very little rapport was established between
the two men. Frances Perkins reports that Roosevelt was mystified
by Keynes's "rigmarole of figures" and felt, as a result, that "he
must be a mathematician rather than a political economist".[4]
Tugwell, who acted as Keynes's host, considered the visit to be "a
mutually valuable interlude" for Roosevelt's advisers, but that in the
exchanges with the President himself Keynes's attitude was "more
that of an admiring observer than that of an instructor".[5] The thank-
you letters which both Keynes and Roosevelt wrote to their original
intermediary, Frankfurter, show little more than politeness.[6]

While it is true that in 1934 the Keynesian revolution was still in
embryo, it is necessary to ask whether the message Keynes delivered
in his open letter to Roosevelt in 1933, his Columbia address in 1934,
and presumably in his Washington conversations, was really such
a difficult one to understand and accept? As with similar questions

---

[1] Quoted in J. K. Galbraith, *The Great Crash* (1961 Penguin edn.), p. 95.
[2] See e.g. Alvin Hansen's views cited pp. 183-4 above. See also M. Friedman and A.
Schwarz, *op. cit.*, pp. 112-115; and J. Dorfman, *The Economic Mind in American Civilization*,
Vol. V, p. 658.
[3] See J. M. Burns, *op. cit.*, pp. 329-336.
[4] *The Roosevelt I Knew* (1946), pp. 225-6.
[5] *The Democratic President*, pp. 374-5.
[6] See M. Friedman, *Roosevelt and Frankfurter, Their Correspondence, 1928-1945* (1967), p.
222. It is difficult to see how Friedman can maintain (p. 13) that the "legend" that Keynes
and Roosevelt were unable to understand each other is "destroyed" by this slender
evidence. His assertion that "the ideas and doctrines of Keynes ran through the philosophy
of the New Deal" testifies to wishful thinking in this matter on his part.

raised earlier in the British context, it is impossible to give a definitive answer. Nevertheless, some of the factors relevant to an answer should be mentioned. Compared with the situation faced by British policy-makers in the late 'twenties and to a lesser extent in the 'thirties, the American problem was made easier by its very acuteness, and above all by the virtual absence of external constraints posed by foreign confidence and the balance of payments. On the other hand, the magnitude of the spending programme which would have been required to offset the decline in private consumption and investment spending was quite unprecedented. And even if Roosevelt had been thoroughly convinced that it was possible to overcome depression by these means, it is not certain, given the entrenched attitude of many in the United States towards balanced budgets and government debt, that it would have been politically feasible. It has been argued, however, that in view of the powers which Roosevelt was able to command in the first years of office, he could easily have obtained congressional acquiescence for a massive spending programme at this time.[1]

The full force of Keynes's contribution to our understanding of unemployment and depression had to wait upon the publication of the *General Theory* in 1936, and on the process of conversion that followed; but the main policy conclusions were clearly spelled out to British and American readers in Keynes's earlier writings. Although the British government made no move in their direction in the 'thirties, the Swedish Social Democrats clearly understood and acted under their influence.[2] And while there are good reasons for regarding Keynes's contribution to these matters as being unique in many respects, there was plenty of previous discussion and support among American economists for milder forms of public works proposal and contra-cyclical budgeting.

The pre-Keynesian academic debate on contra-cyclical public works proposals followed much the same course in the United States as in Britain during the 'twenties; and it derived much of its inspiration from the same source, namely the Minority Report of the Royal Commission on the Poor Laws.[3] During the 1921 depression, for example, the Report of the President's Conference on Unemployment gave fairly unanimous endorsement to the view that public works should be planned and carried out on a contra-cyclical basis. Ironically enough, Herbert Hoover, then Secretary of Commerce, was Chairman at this conference. Under the boom conditions of the

---

[1] See J. M. Burns, *op. cit.*, p. 331.
[2] See p. 209 above.
[3] See C. J. Anderson, "The Compensatory Theory of Public Works Expenditure", *Journal of Political Economy*, Sept. 1945; and B. Higgins, *Public Investment and Full Employment* (1946).

second half of the 'twenties less was heard of these proposals, and very little legislative action was taken. Interest revived again after 1929. The nearest American equivalent to the Liberal expansionist programme in Britain at this time was that associated with the two under-consumptionist writers, William Foster and Waddill Catchings. They modified the traditional case for public works by arguing in terms of the need to revive private purchasing power, rather than simply in order to offset fluctuations in private investment.[1] Nor was there any lack of support within the academic community for a policy of balancing the budget over the length of the trade cycle.[2] What this tends to suggest, therefore, is that novelty alone, or lack of cogency in the advice being offered, cannot be used to explain Roosevelt's attachment to orthodoxy in the early years of the New Deal.

Many structural and financial defects in the American economy, and many social injustices, were revealed by depression. These tended to distract the attention of New Deal policy-makers, particularly in the early years. The development of Tugwell's views provides a typical example of the learning process which many New Dealers underwent in this period. As an under-consumptionist Tugwell had little difficulty in rejecting the orthodox, wage-cutting solution. On humanitarian and economic grounds he advocated an increase in federal relief expenditures and loan-financed public works. In this respect he was ahead of Roosevelt and could see the contradictions involved in the President's attempt to pursue economy and balanced budgets, while being forced by relief expenditures into continuing deficits. Nevertheless, in 1932–3 Tugwell believed that it might be possible to finance the relief expenditures by higher taxes falling mainly on the wealthy. For as he said later, "even to those who were more realistic about the future need for relief and public works, fiscal conservatism did not seem an impossible policy".[3] In other words, as in the case of British followers of Hobson within the Labour Party, under-consumptionism merely strengthened those reformist views which already favoured redistribution of purchasing power on other grounds. In 1932 Tugwell attached greater significance to micro-economic planning as a recovery measure; the removal of disparities between retail and wholesale prices, and between agricultural and manufacturing incomes, seemed more important to him at this stage. He eventually moved on to the milder position of contra-cyclical budget balancing, but only, as his

---

[1] See e.g. *The Road to Plenty* (1928).

[2] Jacob Viner advocated this in 1931; see R. Lekachman (ed.), *Keynes' General Theory, Reports of Three Decades*, pp. 263-4. The idea was endorsed by a group of Chicago economists, including Viner, in S. E. Leland (ed.), *Balancing the Budget Federal Fiscal: Policy During Depression*, (1933).

[3] *The Democratic President*, p. 240.

recent biographer has pointed out, "after he had given up hope of seeing implementation of collectivism".[1]

Keynes himself was not inclined at this stage to be over-harsh in his criticism of the New Deal as a recovery programme. He continued to press for greater emphasis on capital expenditure, making full use of the multiplier doctrine; but he was also aware of Roosevelt's difficulties. "There was no one to whom the President could look for infallible advice. An experimental and empiric method was the only alternative to inaction." He was full of praise for the young men in Washington; they had made the United States "the outstanding economic laboratory of the world". He envied them their opportunity.[2]

By the middle of the 'thirties some consensus among those immediately concerned with policy-making in the United States seems to have formed around a theory of deficit-spending, or *ex post* rationalisation, known as "pump-priming". The basic idea behind pump-priming was that a certain volume of public spending injected into the economy would stimulate a self-perpetuating rise in private incomes and spending. Once the private forces of recovery had taken hold it would be possible for government spending to taper off. In so far as this type of thinking was based on anything more than simple analogy, it relied on a combination of the multiplier and accelerator doctrines. The multiplier explained the dependency of consumption expenditure on an initial injection of investment, and the acceleration principle explained how further investment could be induced by changes in consumption expenditure. Keynes himself lent some support to pump-priming by his use of the multiplier doctrine in advocating that federal expenditure from borrowed funds should be stepped up to $400 million per month. But he gave no support to the accelerator side of the case because he was clearly sceptical as to whether business investment was capable of coming to the rescue.[3] In any event, pump-priming was one of several casualties suffered during the depression which took place in 1937–8.

### Depression Again, 1937–8

After an erratic start the American recovery proceeded rapidly in the years between 1934 and 1937. It was based to a very large extent on a rise in consumer purchases of non-durable goods; but in 1936 private net investment became positive for the first time in over five years. Much of this investment took the form of inventory accumu-

[1] B. Sternsher, *op. cit.*, pp. 133-140; and M. Eccles, *Beckoning Frontiers* (1951) pp. 1-14.
[2] Columbia University Address as reported in the *New York Times*, June 6th 1934.
[3] See *New York Times*, June 10th 1934.

lation of a speculative or unintended kind. Partly as a result of this, and of the large injection into the economy by the government in June in the form of the repayment of the soldiers' bonus, there was a definite spurt of activity in 1936. Production, profits and prices began to rise. In spite of the fact that unemployment remained around the 6 million mark fears were expressed that the boom was getting out of hand. During the election campaign of 1936 Roosevelt had promised to balance the budget in the near future; and this promise was renewed in the following year. The soldiers' bonus had been enacted by Congress over Roosevelt's veto; at much the same time the government was deprived of anticipated receipts from a processing tax which was ruled to be unconstitutional by the Supreme Court. In June 1937 cuts were made in expenditure by the Works Progress Administration and the Public Works Administration. To replace lost revenue, new profits and social security taxes were also introduced. By August 1937 there were definite signs of a reversal in the upward trends of the previous year. The next nine months saw the most rapid decline in American economic history; production fell by 33%, national income by 13%, and unemployment mounted from 6 to 10 million.[1]

Even with the benefits of hindsight, the limitations of theory and data make analysis of the causal factors difficult. It now seems to be agreed that the reduction in the government's net contribution to spending in 1937 played an initiatory role in the collapse. Another contributory factor in the situation, according to some commentators, was the action of the Federal Reserve Board in August 1936 and March 1937, in raising member banks' reserve requirements.[2] The burden of maintaining recovery was thrown on to private investment at a time, when—owing to weaknesses in the capital market, errors of optimism in inventory policies, rising labour costs, and declining business confidence—it was ill-equipped or unwilling to shoulder it.

The onset of yet another depression before recovery from the last one was complete dealt a sharp blow to the Roosevelt Administration and to the hopes of many supporters of the New Deal. Nevertheless, the depression of 1937–8 ,and the debate to which it gave rise, marks an important turning point in the history of Keynesian ideas in the United States. One of the effects of the depression was to bring to a head the differences between those who believed that the government should undertake a more active role to bring full recovery, and those who believed that the key to recovery lay in fiscal probity by the

---

[1] The most complete study of the recession is by Kenneth D. Roose, *The Economics of Recession and Revival* (1954).
[2] See M. Friedman and A. Schwarz, *op. cit.*, pp. 525–534.

government, the restoration of business confidence, and thereby private spending.

Both groups were able to claim that the events of 1937–8 supported their position; both agreed that private investment had proved inadequate to support recovery; both agreed that pump-priming by the government had failed to start sustained recovery. Where they disagreed was over the reasons for this state of affairs, and in the policy conclusions that should be drawn from it. On the orthodox side it could be argued that renewed depression confirmed the diagnosis that the deficit-finance of previous years had not done the job expected by its more optimistic supporters. It was further claimed that unbalanced budgets and other New Deal policies had undermined business confidence. Their opponents on the other hand claimed that the depression showed that more, rather than less, determined public spending policies were required; that the switch towards orthodoxy in 1937 had led to collapse; that the private forces of recovery were not adequate to the task; and that perhaps this was the result of chronic rather than acute weaknesses in the American economy.

Those who adopted the latter interpretation were able to find reinforcement for their position in Keynes's *General Theory*. The debate which took place during and after the depression was, therefore, one of the first major confrontations between post-*General Theory* economic ideas and orthodoxy. The particular interpretation of Keynes's doctrines adopted by his American followers in this period led to a sharpening in the conflict between government and business, a conflict which was already a growing feature of the second stage of the New Deal. It is to this period, therefore, that one must look for the seeds of the extremism which has until recently been such a marked feature of American debate on the economic responsibilities of the state.

The renewal of depression did not evoke an immediate and decisive response from the Administration. Roosevelt's hesitancy on this occasion confirms all that has been said so far about his inability to conceive and carry through a consistent policy with regard to public spending. The leadership of the orthodox camp within the Administration was assumed by Morgenthau; he had been urging on Roosevelt the necessity for balancing the budget, and had good reason to believe in 1937 that Roosevelt had accepted this as an appropriate aim of policy. In 1936 Morgenthau considered that spending policies had not worked; the time had come "to strip off the bandages, throw away the crutches" and see if the economy "could stand on its own feet".[1] He considered that spending agencies like the Reconstruction Finance Corporation and the Public Works

[1] Cited in W. A. Leuchtenberg, *op. cit.*, p. 245.

Administration had diverted funds from private enterprise and created uncertainty among investors. Moreover, deficits were inflationary. Pressure on the President to balance the budget was maintained by the Treasury even as the business indicators turned downwards. The business community, it was claimed, needed reassurance. Roosevelt in his bewilderment was beginning to entertain the notion that the depression was brought on by the antagonism of businessmen towards the New Deal, but he gave his blessing to a speech made by Morgenthau in November 1937, in which he stated that it was the intention of the Administration to balance the budget.[1]

By this time, however, there was a growing band within the circle of Roosevelt's advisers advocating increased public spending along Keynesian lines. The leadership of this group was assumed by Marriner Eccles, then Chairman of the Board of Governors of the Federal Reserve System, and a vocal and determined spokesman for compensatory spending policies from the moment he joined the Administration in 1933. Eccles was a rarity: a successful banker with enlightened views. Although his views were Keynesian in spirit, they did not derive from reading Keynes.[2] Opposition to Morgenthau's approach to the depression came also from other sources within the Administration, notably from Harry Hopkins, Harold Ickes, William Douglas and Robert H. Jackson. Attached to each of these men was a group of young economists acting as their advisers; chief among these were Lauchlin Currie working for Eccles, and Leon Henderson for Hopkins. Even in Morgenthau's own department there were those who, like Herman Oliphant and Harry Dexter White, supported the public spending approach.[3]

Another factor uniting some within this group was distrust of the business and financial community; they took the view that the recession could partly be explained by business opposition to the New Deal and by the growth of monopolistic pricing practices.[4] Although, as we shall see, deficit finance and a tougher policy towards business have frequently gone hand in hand in the United States, there were possibilities for conflict and confusion between these two approaches. Roosevelt found it easier at first to accept the anti-monopoly side of the liberal New Dealers' case; his "policy" became one of allowing some spokesmen for the Administration to preach balanced budgets, while others talked fiercely about the need to control business power and influence.

For some time Roosevelt allowed the debate to go on around

[1] See J. M. Blum, *op. cit.*, pp. 395-7.
[2] See *Beckoning Frontiers*, pp. 131-2. His public papers were collected under the title *Economic Balance and a Balanced Budget* (1940).
[3] J. M. Blum, *op. cit.*, p. 387.
[4] W. A. Leuchtenberg, *op. cit.* pp. 245-251.

him, listening to all suggestions but taking no action. In his State of the Union message in January 1938, he spoke of the need to revive purchasing power but made it clear that he hoped this would arise from an increase in private investment spending. In February the pro-spending party received powerful outside support in the form of a private letter to the President from Keynes urging him to supplement passive policies of relief by an active public-spending policy. Keynes considered that the depression was due partly to "errors of optimism" on the part of private investors, and, by implication, on the part of the government too. By curtailing public spending they had placed excessive reliance on the accelerator side of a pump-priming operation. In the circumstances, Keynes considered that "the present slump could have been predicted with absolute certainty". He believed that the United States presented ample opportunities for public investment, or encouragement to private investment, in housing, in public utilities and transport. He clearly considered the Administration's rough handling of the business community to be both unwise and unnecessary. The letter closed with the following *cri de coeur*:

"I am terrified lest progressive causes in all the democratic countries should suffer injury, because you have taken too lightly the risk to their prestige which would result from a failure measured in terms of immediate prosperity. There *need* be no failure. But the maintenance of prosperity in the modern world is extremely *difficult*, and it is so easy to lose precious time."[1]

At the end of March the economic situation took a further turn for the worse, and it was this which gave the pro-spending party the chance to press home their case with Roosevelt. On April 14th Roosevelt submitted to Congress a large spending and lending programme amounting to $3.75 billion; some was for W.P.A. relief, Farm Security, and for the National Youth Administration; some was for reactivating public works spending and loans for slum clearance, highways, and flood control schemes. At the same time, measures to expand credit were taken, including lower reserve requirements for banks and the de-sterilisation of gold. The expansionist fiscal policy thus inaugurated was continued right up to the beginning of the Second World War.

The budgetary deficits which Roosevelt had promised to eliminate in 1932 continued throughout the whole of the 'thirties. In 1939 the

[1] Letter to F. D. R. February 1st, 1938, Franklin D. Roosevelt Library, New York. Keynes got little in return for his pains. Roosevelt turned the letter over to Morgenthau—the least sympathetic member of the administration to the ideas which it contained—to answer for him. See J. M. Blum, *op. cit.*, pp. 402-5.

federal deficit was larger than in any previous year except 1936. But it was only after 1938 that these deficits were accepted as beneficial by the Administration, and even then the idea was only accepted in a modest and contra-cyclical form. It is a sobering thought, therefore, that in no present-day sense of the term can the United States be said to have achieved anything near full employment in the whole decade of the 'thirties. As more recent work has shown, judged in terms of the level of demand needed to secure full employment, the expansionist effect of American fiscal policy in this period was stronger than that of 1929 in only two years—1931 and 1936. In both of these years the effect was largely due to bonus payments to veterans which were strongly opposed by the Administration in power at the time. The actual trend of the effect of fiscal policies under the New Deal was downward; the main reasons for this were that the rise in federal expenditure was partially or completely offset by contractions in expenditure on the state and local level, and by an upward shift in the tax structure. On the basis of this evidence it has been concluded that: "Fiscal policy, then, seems to have been an unsuccessful recovery device in the thirties—not because it did not work, but because it was not tried."[1]

## Secular Stagnation

In the light of what has just been said, it is not surprising that the trend of professional economic thought in the United States in the 'thirties should have been away from moderate consensus towards more pessimistic interpretations of the capacity of capitalism to survive unaided, and more radical views on the proper role of the state in economic life. The dominant form which these views took can be summarised under the term "stagnationism". Stagnationist ideas of one sort or another were characteristic of economic thought in many countries at this time, but in the United States the climate of opinion proved to be particularly hospitable to such notions. When Keynes's *General Theory* appeared, it was his theory of long period unemployment, with its emphasis on the problems of a secular decline in investment opportunities, that gained prominence in the United States.[2] One of the chief reasons for this was that Alvin Hansen, who became Keynes's leading American disciple and interpreter, developed Keynes's hints on the subject into a major thesis.[3]

[1] E. Cary Brown, "Fiscal Policy in the 'Thirties: A Reappraisal", *American Economic Review*, December 1956.

[2] For a summary of Keynes's views on this subject, see pp. 169-70 above.

[3] Even in his original, and by no means enthusiastic, review of the *General Theory*, Hansen expatiated on the stagnationist theme; see *Journal of Political Economy*, Oct. 1936, pp. 680-3. It seems likely that he had already given much thought to this question.

Hansen and other American stagnationists constructed a version of recent American history to support their position which ran roughly as follows: 1929 marked the end of a remarkable expansionist era in American economic life, which, in the nineteenth century, had been associated with an open and advancing land frontier, rapid population growth, and technical innovation. These factors ensured that there were plentiful outlets for saving, so that while prosperity might be interrupted by cyclical disturbances the underlying trend of the economy had been healthy. These expansive forces began to lose their strength before the First World War, but in the decade after the war a burst of intensive investment activity had taken place. The investment boom of the 'twenties was dependent on the backlog of housing need inherited from the war and the earlier period of population growth; the inauguration of the automobile and electrical age; the extraordinary export surplus created by American foreign investment; the heavy volume of public investment by state and local authorities in highway construction; and the rise of durable consumer goods' industries financed by instalment credit. All of these influences had combined to mask the stagnationist trend; but there was also a suggestion that they were transitional and fortuitous. The dislike felt by New Dealers for the so-called "new era" prosperity of the 'twenties encouraged the view that it was based on an "irresponsible" burst of activity, which had robbed the future and contributed to the depth of the slump by exhausting investment opportunities.[1]

The problem for the future would be to find new outlets for profitable investment to replace those no longer likely to come from an expanding population and land frontier. While in the nineteenth century capital accumulation had been both of a widening and a deepening kind, with more capital being required as output expanded, and more capital being used to produce a given output, the prognostication for the future was less clear. It could be that in a mature economy innovation would be capital-saving as well as labour-saving; that consumers' capital would become more important than producers' capital. On the other side of the coin there were worries associated with tendencies towards excessive saving in a rich, mature economy. The important savers were more and more the large corporations, many of which were bureaucratic and conservative in their policies with regard to replacement investment, tending to keep excessively high depreciation reserves. New institu-

---

[1] The most important of Hansen's writings on this subject are *Full Recovery or Stagnation?* (1938), and *Fiscal Policy and Business Cycles* (1941). See also *An Economic Program for American Democracy* (1938), by seven Harvard and Tufts economists (R. V. Gilbert, G. Hildebrand Arthur Stuart, Maxine Sweezy, Paul Sweezy, L. Tarshis, John D. Wilson); and G. Colm and F. Lehmann, *Economic Consequences of Recent American Tax Policy* (1938).

tions, and methods would have to be pioneered by the government
to channel savings into socially productive investment.

The weakness of the underlying investment situation was used to
explain the extremely poor performance of the American economy
in the 'thirties, and the failure of mere pump-priming to bring self-
sustained recovery. The induced investment caused by the expansion
of consumption was insufficient and unreliable for the job in hand;
it collapsed soon after the government's net contribution was
curtailed. A new surge of autonomous investment was needed.
Stagnationism also cast doubts on the effectiveness of counter-
cyclical ideas on public spending. A good deal more would be
required in the future than the occasional stimulus to private
investment. A permanently enlarged contribution by the state in
the form of continuous deficits would be needed to offset the deeper
tendencies at work which made it more difficult to maintain full
employment. In Hansen's words:

> "The theory that large deficits could be swiftly followed by
> substantial surpluses rested on the assumption that a vigorous
> boom would surely follow once the upswing was started—a boom
> so vigorous, indeed, that it needed to be held in restraint. Fiscal
> policy as a regulatory device was designed not merely to prime the
> pump, but equally to control the boom. The philosophy of stabil-
> isation was nourished in the traditional outlook of the nineteenth
> century epoch of expansion. It feared the boom even more than
> the depression. But now, owing to deep-seated causes inherent in
> the essential character of a non-expanding economy, secular stag-
> nation stalks across the stage, or at least shows its face. If there
> is no surging investment boom to be checked, great fluctuations
> in deficit financing must be avoided, lest any rapid reduction
> should aggravate and intensify the underlying tendency toward
> investment stagnation."[1]

Much of this was merely an extension of Keynes's hints on stagnation. But there were also native roots and branches to the stagnationist case. The existence of the American land frontier played
such an important part in American history and mythology that it
is not difficult to find dismal speculations about the implications of
its closure well before the 'thirties. The connection between closure
of the frontier and the rise of large corporations at the turn of the
century was an essential element in the progressive tradition. As was
the arrival of a period of "maturity" in which it would be necessary
for the federal government to assume a more active role in controlling the activities of large corporations and public utility com-

[1] *Full Recovery or Stagnation?*, pp. 301-2.

panies, and in husbanding scarce national resources so as to prevent unscrupulous exploitation.[1] In 1933, for example, Tugwell had contrasted the "era of economic development" which had just passed, with the "era of economic maintenance" which was to follow, and for which it was the duty of the New Deal to provide guide lines.[2] Such ideas certainly prepared the ground for Keynes.

Hansen's version of the stagnationist thesis also contained elements that were non-Keynesian in origin. As we have seen, Keynes became less and less interested in the problems of business organisation; he believed that government intervention could be concentrated on regulating the flow of community savings and investment. Hansen, on the other hand, linked the decline of investment opportunities with the increasing bureaucratisation and rigidity of the modern corporation. One of his earliest criticisms of the *General Theory* was that under-employment equilibrium would not be stable unless certain assumptions derived from the older neo-classical theory of employment concerning the rigidity of prices and wages and monopolistic practices were incorporated into the Keynesian system.[3] These hints were expanded later. In the past, with rapid growth, competition had been tolerated by producer interest groups in a way that was no longer possible now that markets were not expanding rapidly; hence the growth of monopolistic practices by businessmen and trade unions, price rigidities, and the blockage of cost-reducing innovations.[4]

We have noted already the way in which some members of the Roosevelt Administration combined a "Keynesian" pro-spending position with an attack on the business community, and on business practices which seemed to them to be hindering recovery. For them, Keynesian ideas simply provided additional ammunition in a longstanding battle. During the 1937–8 depression they argued that monopolies had destroyed the multiplier effect of public spending by raising prices; that businessmen were holding back on investment out of opposition to the New Deal, and were cutting pay-rolls rather than prices. It was, of course, still possible to support progressive policies for the break-up of holding companies and large concentrations of economic power without accepting the Keynesian case.[5]

In his private letter to Roosevelt in 1938, Keynes had warned against inflaming business sentiment unnecessarily. Not long after the announcement of his new spending programme in 1938, as a sop

---

[1] See D. R. Fusfeld, *op. cit.*, p. 242.
[2] B. Sternsher, *op. cit*, p. 47.
[3] *Journal of Political Economy*, Oct. 1936, p. 680.
[4] *Full Recovery or Stagnation?*, p. 299; *Fiscal Policy and Business Cycles*, pp. 363-4.
[5] There is now an excellent study of this subject by E. W. Hawley, *The New Deal and the Problem of Monopoly* (1966). On the points made in the text see especially pp. 296-301; and Chapters 20 and 21.

to those who regarded monopoly as *the* barrier to recovery, Roosevelt also announced his intention to set up a committee to make "a thorough study of the concentration of economic power". This body eventually emerged as the Temporary National Economic Committee. Over the next three years this committee collected a massive volume of testimony from businessmen and economists on subjects ranging from the effect of taxes and patents on business behaviour, to the question of price levels, profits and unemployment. From an anti-trust point of view it has been said that the committee was "a harmless device that could be used by each group to urge a specific line of action or no action at all".[1] For Hansen and other stagnationists it provided a valuable forum within which to conduct their campaign for their particular interpretation of Keynesianism. Indeed, one of the chief criticisms by representatives of the business community was that the TNEC monographs provided an illegitimate way of using public funds to spread an insidious gospel of gloom about the capacity of American capitalism to maintain prosperity.[2] But as a more sympathetic reader said:

> "[The investigations of the TNEC] are the product of a mood of deep despair over both the justice and efficiency of our economic arrangements. The information compiled . . . is a telling indictment in its general effect. There can be little doubt that, in the hands of a powerful party . . . this official portrait of our economy would be a powerful, perhaps decisive, political instrument of reform."[3]

This verdict is an accurate one. It can be applied to this whole phase of American debate. Stagnationism was a radical and reformist doctrine which set out to achieve far more than the acceptance of the principles of economic management by the state. Considered purely on its economic merits, it seems now to have been discredited, although it could be argued that it has only been "falsified" by the high level of military expenditure during and after the Second World War. It was quite clearly a reaction to the failure of American policy-making in the 'thirties. But as we have seen, fiscal policy failed because it was not tried; and it is doubtful if the limited evidence of this period was sufficient to conclude that the incentives for private investment were permanently weakened.[4] The real significance of

---

[1] *Ibid.*, p. 488.
[2] See e.g. *Fact and Fancy in the TNEC Monographs*, National Association of Manufacturers, (1942).
[3] M. Abramowitz in the *American Economic Review*, Supplement on TNEC, June 1942, p. 53.
[4] The leading opponent of stagnationism was G. Terborgh, *The Bogey of Economic Maturity* (1945). For Hansen's reply see his *Economic Policy and Full Employment* (1947). See also E. W. Swanson and E. P. Schmidt, *Economic Stagnation or Progress* (1946).

stagnationism lay in its political appeal. For many it was the American equivalent of the non-Marxist, left-wing movements in Europe in the 'thirties. It is obvious that the permanently enlarged public spending which stagnationists called for carries with it implications for the take-over of many functions previously performed by the private sector, as well as for the extension of state intervention into entirely new fields. It should be seen, therefore, on one level as an attempt to prevent weak booms from being prematurely smothered; and on another level as part of a long-standing debate on the ideals of American public life. In both these respects it has echoes in public debate today.[1]

[1] See pp. 300-310 below for post-war equivalents.

PART THREE:

# The Second World War and After

# CHAPTER TWELVE

# Keynesian War Economics and Post-War Plans

A prominent American economist has said that wars are common-place or routine occurrences so far as the long-term development of economic science is concerned. There is certainly a good deal of truth in his statement that "a war may ravage a continent or destroy a generation without posing new theoretical questions".[1] But wars un-doubtedly change the climate of economic debate and provide a laboratory for conducting social and economic experiments. The Second World War, both in Britain and the United States, acted as a forcing ground for ideas and for techniques of economic measure-ment and control which would have taken longer to bring to fruition under peace-time conditions. In this respect, unlike the First World War, it was responsible for a radical modification in the conduct of economic affairs after the war. But if the war itself taught few new lessons in economics, it certainly underlined several that had been written in the inter-war period.

In January 1939 Keynes was questioned in the *New Statesman* on his political and economic beliefs in the light of the emerging struggle with the totalitarian regimes. He used it as an opportunity to expatiate on the limitations of "our nineteenth-century school of Treasury officials", and on their unfitness to serve the cause of "energetic expansion".

> "Great as is my admiration for many of the qualities of our Civil Service, I am afraid that they are becoming a heavy handicap in our struggle with the totalitarian States and making ourselves safe from them. They cramp our energy, and spoil or discard our ideas."[2]

By November Keynes was engaged in his last and most successful campaign to get his ideas accepted by the Treasury. This time it was a question of gaining recognition for his views on the problems of war finance. At first it seemed that his ideas would be discarded once

[1] G. J. Stigler, "The Influence of Events and Policies on Economic Theory" as reprinted in his *Essays in the History of Economics* (1965), p. 21.
[2] *New Statesman*, Jan. 28th, 1939.

more. But the early military setbacks that brought Churchill to power in May 1940 also favoured Keynes. Within eighteen months of his condemnation of the Treasury, therefore, he found himself, contrary to all previous expectations, ensconced in the Treasury itself, and in a position to shape the course of events. From 1942 onwards he was increasingly involved in the diplomacy of external finance for Britain's war effort, and later with the problems of post-war international reconstruction; his efforts at Bretton Woods and in negotiating the American Loan at the end of the war occupied most of his energies in the last years of his life. In spite of the enormous practical importance of these activities, however, there is no doubt that his early efforts with regard to the internal problems of war finance had a greater impact on policy both at the time and subsequently.

## War Economics

War presents all the problems of an economic system operating under peace-time conditions in a simplified but acute form. They are simplified by the narrowing of aims to one overriding one: maximum mobilisation of resources to defeat the enemy. They are also simplified—though the word may seem less appropriate here— by the concentration of economic decision-making in the hands of the government. They are made more acute by the hazards of enemy action and by the fact that solutions must be found rapidly.

A useful distinction can be made between the micro and macro branches of war economics: the one concerned with the allocation of scarce physical resources and manpower among alternative civilian and military uses; and the other concerned with the regulation of the overall monetary and fiscal climate within which the allocation decisions are made. The first requires a planning apparatus for directing men and materials into those uses which both in the long and the short run will be most conducive to the build-up of military potential; this type of planning decision has to be based on a clear picture of the physical resources available and the priorities in the demands made on them. The second branch of war economics must be so conducted as to facilitate the transfer of resources to war purposes without undue strain in the form of open or repressed inflation, or recourse to a level of taxation likely to have a debilitating effect on incentives and production. At all stages, the preservation of equity of sacrifice and the minimisation of the difficulties and burdens of the post-war period have to be kept in view. The financial branch of war economics must be based on estimates of flows of aggregate income and output; from these can be calculated the impact of different taxes, and of government borrowing and spending, on the levels of consumption, saving, investment, and exports.

The macro and micro branches of war economics should be strictly complementary. Without an effective system for controlling the general level of expenditure by consumers, businesses and the government, an intolerable strain would be placed on the mechanism for allocating manpower and materials for military purposes, and on schemes for rationing civilian supplies. The same is true in reverse. Much of the work of planning the war effort was done in terms of a physical *numéraire*—available manpower or shipping space—instead of in terms of money.[1] The success of British war finance in the Second World War, as R. S. Sayers has explained, can to a large extent be judged by the fact that "those responsible for organising Britain's war effort were never forced to feel that financial policy was important".[2]

Economists and statisticians were able to make important contributions behind the scenes to both aspects of the conduct of the British war effort. But it was in relation to financial policy that the war revealed most clearly the progress that had been made in economics as a result of the work of Keynes in the inter-war period. To put the matter in slightly different terminology, it was during the Second World War that the co-ordination between macro- and micro-economic understanding, which had been so conspicuously lacking in the inter-war period, was first achieved.

One of the primary influences on British policy-makers, particularly at the beginning of the Second World War, was the memory of the failures and successes in the conduct of economic policy during and after the First World War. Apart from strategic controls over certain key sectors of the economy, for the first two years of the earlier war the government had relied heavily on the price mechanism and on private enterprise to achieve its allocation and production goals. At the beginning of the Second World War it was recognised that the logic of controls would require their extension beyond munitions production, transport, shipping and coal mining to cover the civilian use of scarce resources. Moreover, the active co-operation of organised labour would be needed to implement a manpower policy and to reduce the risk of industrial disturbance. In order to enlist this co-operation a number of concessions would have to be made in the form of price controls, rationing, and excess profits taxation. In the financial sphere, there was awareness of the need to minimise the post-war burden of dead-weight debt by improved borrowing

---

[1] See E. A. G. Robinson in D. N. Chester (ed.) *Lessons of the British War Economy* (1951), p. 40; and his *Economic Planning in the U.K.* (1967), p. 7.

[2] *Financial Policy, 1939-1945* (1956), p. 21. The opening chapter of this work contains an extremely clear picture of the whole field of war finance and economics.

I

techniques, and by devising a system of taxation which would meet
equitable criteria and avoid disincentive effects on production.

## Interest Rates

The desire to avoid the mistakes of the First World War was particularly marked in the case of interest rate policy. In the First
World War the authorities had relied extensively on the traditional
peace-time mechanism of raising Bank Rate to defend the external
value of the pound; a rudimentary system of exchange control
was devised only towards the end of the war. Monetary policy
was also saddled with most of the responsibility for acting as a
counter to domestic inflationary tendencies. As a result, the
borrowing of the government to finance the war was done on unfavourable terms, thereby imposing a heavy burden on post-war
finance. This was certainly one of the reasons why at an early stage
of the Second World War it was decided, after some wavering, to
retain the policy of cheap money that had been in force since the
conversion operation of 1932. Another reason was the experience
gained by the authorities in the field of monetary management
during the cheap money era of the 'thirties. But the decision was
also undoubtedly influenced by the trend of academic economic
thought on the rate of interest as it emerged after the Keynesian
revolution.[1]

We have noted earlier how the Keynesian revolution brought
about an integration of monetary and real variables in economic
analysis, and led to a reduction in the importance previously
attached to the money supply and the rate of interest as economic
regulators. During the 'thirties many economists came round to the
view, expressed by Keynes in his *General Theory*, that changes in the
rate of interest were likely to have only a feeble influence on the
rate of saving or investment, particularly under depression conditions. They supported the policy of keeping interest rates low, but
were not inclined to accord cheap money a major status as a recovery
measure. Empirical evidence derived from questionnaires and inter-
views with businessmen conducted by a group of Oxford economists
in 1937 appeared to confirm the idea that changes in the rate of
interest were not a significant influence on business investment
decisions.[2]

As early as April 1939 Keynes was putting the case for keeping
interest rates low during the war. If the export of capital could be

[1] On this see R. S. Sayers, *op. cit.*, Ch. V.
[2] See the essays reprinted in T. Wilson & P. W. S. Andrews (eds.) *Oxford Studies in the
Price Mechanism* (1951), Ch. I.

brought under direct control, the only justification for higher interest rates would be to strengthen the government's hand in competition with private firms for borrowing resources. Keynes believed that control of new issues rather than higher interest rates was the appropriate remedy for this situation. Nor were higher interest rates necessary, he felt, to foster personal or corporate saving; the rise of real incomes and profits as a result of the increase in economic activity connected with the war would have a more potent effect in raising the level of saving. In view of the importance, therefore, of keeping down the cost to the Exchequer of borrowing, the maintenance of low interest rates seemed to be the only sensible course of action.[1]

The Keynesian position eventually prevailed; the Second World War was fought on a three as opposed to a five per cent basis. In spite of the enormous increase in the size of the National Debt by the end of the war, the burden of interest payments did not loom as large in the calculations of post-war Chancellors as it did in the 'twenties. The Keynesian attitude to cheap money was also influential in Washington. So much so that Harrod has suggested that this, rather than the New Deal, was Keynes's main contribution to American prosperity.[2]

## How To Pay For The War

Even during what later became known as the "phoney war" period it was realised that the main problem would be to finance the build-up of government expenditure for war purposes in a way that would not be inflationary. While this build-up was slow, and while there were still unemployed resources and stocks to mop up, the problem of inflation was not acute. With the ending of the "phoney war", and with mounting concern about the relative scale of British and German war expenditure, it became clear that the early war budgets were inadequate. They failed to make sufficient demands on national resources and did not attack inflation vigorously enough. Apart from questions of equity, the main problem was to find suitable criteria by which the adequacy of budgetary measures could be assessed.

In November 1939 Keynes made a decisive contribution to the debate on this matter in articles for *The Times* which were reprinted in modified form in the following year under the title of *How to Pay*

---

[1] See Keynes's articles in *The Times*, April 17th, 18th and July 24th, 25th, 1939. At much the same time Keynes was successfully pressing his case before the Standing Committee of the Economic Advisory Council under Lord Stamp's Chairmanship, whose job it was to advise on the financial problems of rearmament; see R. S. Sayers, *op. cit.*, pp. 153-5.

[2] *Life of Keynes*, p. 493.

*for the War*. In this pamphlet he showed how the aggregate demand approach, which he had pioneered in the 'thirties as an explanation for unemployment, could be applied with equal value to the problems of full employment and inflation. More particularly he showed how this method of approach, coupled with national income accounts, could be used to measure the extent of the problems to be tackled by budgetary policy during the war. It was a decisive contribution in the sense that it provided the foundation for Kingsley Wood's budget in 1941 and all subsequent war-time budgets.

The burden of Keynes's case was that the government had so far shown itself unwilling to face up to the problem of inflationary pressure arising out of the war effort. In peace-time, with excess capacity in the system, higher employment and incomes would lead to higher consumption. In war-time, once the nation's resources were fully employed, it would be impossible to raise civilian consumption without impeding the war effort. In fact, a reduction in consumption would have to be engineered if this effort was to be adequate. The attempt by households to spend the higher incomes generated by full employment in competition with the government would merely result in higher prices and shortages, but no significant increase in consumption. Some consistent plan for drawing off purchasing power would be needed. Voluntary saving and additional taxation, Keynes believed, would either be inadequate or involve intolerable sacrifices at the expense of incentives. Unless inflation was controlled directly at source it would be necessary to extend the coverage of the wasteful and inefficient system of rationing and direct controls.

Keynes's plan consisted of a set of linked proposals at the centre of which was a scheme of compulsory saving or deferred pay. It contains all the usual marks of Keynes's ingenuity and optimism, and demonstrates his desire to combine economic expediency with social justice. *How to Pay for the War* was in many respects an ideological tract designed to prove to the working classes that borrowing and heavier taxation of the rich alone were not feasible or desirable methods of financing the war from their point of view. Inflation could only be in the interests of the *rentier*. Compulsory saving would ensure that the rewards to effort on the part of the working classes were merely postponed, not dissipated by rising prices. Moreover, the ownership of the National Debt in the form of post-war rights to deferred consumption would be more widely distributed throughout the community. With war-time inflation brought under control in this way, the scheme could be extended to include universal family allowances and subsidies to keep down the cost of basic necessities.

These would also provide a *quid pro quo* for trade union co-operation to stabilise wages.

A further subtlety of the scheme was that the release of deferred pay could be made to coincide with "the onset of the first post-war slump". In this way it could be said to be self-liquidating because it would take the place of the loans to finance public works that would otherwise be necessary. To satisfy those for whom this type of reasoning was unacceptable, Keynes proposed that the release of deferred pay should be financed by a post-war capital levy so as to avoid adding to the National Debt. It is difficult to imagine a more comprehensive set of financial proposals; they were simultaneously anti-inflationary, counter-cyclical, and designed "to snatch from the exigency of war positive social improvements".

But the real significance of Keynes's plan lay not so much in its ingenious proposals as in the system of "arithmetic" on which they were based. The conventional approach to budgeting was to estimate the gap to be filled by extra taxation by calculating the difference between expenditure on the one side and existing revenue plus "normal" borrowing on the other, where "normal" was defined as not being in excess of the flow of "voluntary" saving. In the Keynesian scheme an "inflationary gap", as it became known, was calculated by estimating the difference between the aggregate demand and supply of output at the existing price level. Instead of being narrowly concerned with the immediate budgetary components, public finance was seen as an important balancing item in a larger whole comprising the flow of national income or output and the external balance of payments.

In *How to Pay for the War* Keynes first estimated the maximum level of output obtainable assuming full employment of domestic resources; to this were added the resources which could be made available for domestic use by allowing an excess of imports over exports to be financed by drawing down gold reserves and the sale of foreign investments. This provided a figure for the "output potential" of the economy. Given this, it was possible to show by how much private consumption would have to be reduced in order to allow the target level of government expenditure to be achieved without inflation. Alternatively, the national income could be computed, and estimates made of voluntary saving and of the revenue from existing taxes; the remaining gap between aggregate demand and supply of output provided an indication of the amount by which taxes or saving (voluntary or compulsory) would have to be raised in order to avoid inflationary pressure.

When Keynes first put forward his proposals the public was not prepared to accept them. Within the Treasury the seriousness of the

situation was beginning to be recognised, and the Keynesian method
of stating the problem was also becoming familiar.[1] But there was
still resistance on grounds of practical detail and principle to Keynes's
drastic remedies. The budget introduced by Sir John Simon in 1940
relied exclusively on higher taxation and voluntary saving to counteract inflation. Keynes had already anticipated the arguments in
favour of relying on these "normal" methods in his pamphlet. He
did not feel that adequate voluntary saving would be forthcoming
to close the "gap" revealed by his estimates. If this proved to be the
case, even heavier taxation would have to be tried, and this would
retrench further on the sources of voluntary saving. The main drawback of the voluntary method, according to Keynes, was that the
volume of saving forthcoming was not independent of the degree of
inflation taking place; it could be the result of inflation rather than
the method for its control. To the extent that voluntary saving at the
existing level of prices was inadequate to prevent inflation, the
subsequent rise in prices would complete the process; but it would
be accompanied by a vicious price-spiral and the redistribution of
income in favour of profit-receivers.

Two other factors influenced Keynes's attitude in putting forward
his scheme: his dislike of detailed controls and rationing, and the
antipathy to private thrift which he had acquired in the inter-war
period.[2] Food subsidies and family allowances were later adopted,
and deferred pay became the basis of the post-war credits scheme.
But the plan as a whole was never allowed to become the main-stay
of war finance; rationing, queues, and savings drives were very much
a necessary, and dominant, feature of war-time life in Britain.

The fall of the Chamberlain government in May 1940 brought
Sir Kingsley Wood to the Chancellorship of the Exchequer. By June
Keynes had been appointed to a Consultative Council to advise the
new Chancellor; and shortly after he was given a room in the
Treasury with a roving commission. He was now in a position to
press the case for a consideration of the problems of war finance in
terms of the kind of arithmetic expounded in *How to Pay for the
War*. The difficulty was that there were no official estimates of
national income at this time; Keynes's proposals were worked out
on the basis of estimates by Irwin Rothbarth; the earlier statistical
work on these matters had all been undertaken by private investigators without official backing, notably by Colin Clark in his
*National Income and Outlay* (1937). Without these estimates inflationary
gap analysis could be little more than a speculative exercise; it was

[1] See E. A. G. Robinson, "John Maynard Keynes, 1883-1946", in R. Lekachman, (ed.),
*Keynes' General Theory*, (1964), p. 68.
[2] On the latter point see, *How to Pay for the War*, p. 10.

certainly not sufficiently well-grounded to form the basis for official policy. In the summer of 1940 Richard Stone and James Meade started work on the first official survey of national income and expenditure; their findings provided the basis for Treasury discussion of the task to be achieved in the forthcoming budget.

The Chancellor's first budget was thoroughly Keynesian in its method of presentation and in the spirit of many of the detailed proposals. The budget speech contained a full account of the problems of war finance and a rationale in terms of inflationary gap analysis for the particular measures to be taken. Among the papers accompanying the financial statement were Stone and Meade's estimates of national income and expenditure.[1] This apparently minor innovation was a major event in the history of the application of economics to policy formation. Not only was the government providing the public with the information upon which decisions were to be based, they were also publishing, for the first time, figures that were estimates and projections rather than a formal record of actual outcomes. As Richard Stone has said: "The essential fact is that the national income White Papers . . . attempt to measure as best they can the set of transactions that is significant for economic analysis, rather than to reach ideally precise estimates of those parts of economic activity for which data happen to be available."[2]

## War Economics in the United States

Keynes's influence on American economic policy in the Second World War was not confined to the question of cheap money, where it was chiefly of a rather diffused kind anyway. As soon as the United States became committed to the war, the same issues of war finance faced by Britain earlier had to be tackled. In July 1940 Keynes contributed to a *New Republic* symposium on "How to Pay for Defense".[3] He specifically directed his attention to the question of whether his plan for restricting civilian consumption by deferred pay and higher taxes was suitable to the United States. Although he considered the thinking on which his plan was based to be universally applicable, he did not feel the United States had yet reached the stage at which it would be necessary to bring it into operation. The enormous wealth-producing capacity of the United States was still not being fully utilised; a massive increase in output would be necessary to achieve full employment. The failure of the New Deal

[1] *An Analysis of the Sources of War Finance and an Estimate of the National Income and Expenditure for 1938 and 1940*, Cmd. 6261.
[2] "The Use and Development of National Income and Expenditure Estimates", in D. N. Chester (ed.), *Lessons of the British War Economy*.
[3] July 29th, 1940.

deficits to produce full employment had shown the magnitude of the task. A tripling of loan-financed expenditure on armaments in Britain had still not eliminated unemployment. The chances were that an increase in war expenditure would make possible an increase in consumption in the United States, whereas consumption and the war effort would be competitors in Britain; no special stimulus to saving would therefore be needed.

A year later, when Keynes visited Washington on business connected with lend-lease and the external financing of Britain's war effort, he made contact with a group of young economists working in the Office of Price Administration and Civilian Supply.[1] On this occasion he expressed the view that the time had now come to press for fiscal measures to curb inflation. The American economists replied in the spirit of his earlier article to the effect that output was capable of expansion without significant price increase. They backed up their case with statistical projections of the type prepared by Meade and Stone in Britain, and with full Keynesian logic. They were, in fact, more expansionist than Keynes himself—a difficult feat normally. The difference of opinion was partly due to scepticism on Keynes's part about some of the assumptions underlying the estimates. But another factor may have helped to produce a divergence: Keynes had some experience of the length of time required to convince the public of the need for action. For their part, the American economists, with all the memories of the failures of the New Deal behind them, were anxious not to apply the fiscal brake too soon. As one of their spokesmen, Walter S. Salant, stressed in a letter to Keynes, "the level of output which we reach during this defense program will in the future probably be a bench mark for comparison. . . . It would be a calamity to have this bench mark at a level which is so low that it leaves millions of people unemployed." If the choice were posed between a moderate price increase and heavy unemployment, they would prefer the former.[2]

### Economists in Government Service

Perhaps one of the most important results of the Second World War for economics lay in the recruitment of economists into the machinery of government. In the United States, notably in the latter years of the New Deal, the employment of economists by various agencies within the Administration was already a well-established practice.

---

[1] Among those whom Keynes met on this occasion were: Walter S. Salant, Don D. Humphrey, J. K. Galbraith, Raymond Goldsmith, Calvin Hoover, J. M. Clark, Richard Gilbert and John Cassels.

[2] Letter from Walter S. Salant to J. M. Keynes, June 12, 1941. The above account is based on correspondence made available to me by Mr. Salant, to whom my thanks are due.

Close relations existed between Washington officials and those universities where active research was being carried out on problems connected with immediate policy concerns. The Fiscal Policy Seminars conducted by Alvin Hansen and J. H. Williams at Harvard in the late 'thirties, for example, were frequently attended by economists working in government. And as early as 1934 the Department of Commerce had co-operated with Simon Kuznets and a group of statisticians at the University of Pennsylvania and at the National Bureau of Economic Research to produce national income estimates. But in Britain this kind of inter-change of personnel and ideas hardly existed before the Second World War. Economists were drafted into government service during the First World War, but they tended to merge imperceptibly with other temporary civil servants. After the war their services were used mainly on *ad hoc* committees and Royal Commissions. The chief exception to this, however, was the Economic Advisory Council created by MacDonald in 1930.[1]

It would be difficult to claim that the Advisory Council exercised any influence on the policies pursued during the 1931 crisis; after this date it was allowed to lapse. A standing committee of the council—the Committee on Economic Information—did, however, remain in business, charged with the responsibility for producing periodic reports on the economic situation. This committee under the chairmanship of Lord Stamp was composed of outside experts, G. D. H. Cole, H. D. Henderson, J. M. Keynes, Sir Alfred Lewis, D. H. Robertson and Sir Arthur Salter, and two Senior Civil Servants, Sir Frederick Leith-Ross and Sir Frederick Phillips, who provided the main link with the official decision-making process. Confidential reports were sent to the Prime Minister. From all accounts the committee does not appear to have been a very vigorous or successful body. Sir Arthur Salter's verdict was as follows:

"All the relevant information was at our disposal. We were able over a great range of controversial questions, to make unanimous recommendations which would, if adopted, have profoundly changed the policy of the time. In retrospect they can, I think, be seen to have anticipated much that later became orthodox in Whitehall and elsewhere. But in fact we had little practical effect. Our reports were secret, and could be, and were, rejected or ignored by any department which disliked them, without explanation in public, or even in private to ourselves."[2]

[1] See p. 124 above.
[2] *Memoirs of a Public Servant* (1961), p. 230.

I*

By the late 'thirties there were signs of disintegration. Nevertheless, the committee continued to operate until the outbreak of war, when it was given a new lease of life, only to lose its identity later by being absorbed into the more complex network of advisory bodies which was then created.[1] The next step was taken in 1939, when a body known as the Survey of Financial and Economic Plans was set up. This consisted of Lord Stamp, H. D. Henderson and Henry Clay, supplemented later by E. A. G. Robinson and J. Jewkes; its duties were to survey and co-ordinate the preparations being made for war. The initial motive seems to have been to head off suggestions being made in Parliament for the establishment of a Ministry of Economic Affairs.

The Treasury remained at the centre of economic policy-making and advice until the Churchill government took office in 1940. After this date a number of different policy committees were created based on the complex Cabinet structure introduced by the new government.[2] One of the most important of these was the Economic Policy Committee under the chairmanship of Arthur Greenwood, then Minister without Portfolio and a member of the War Cabinet. It was in conjunction with the work of this committee that a sizeable group of economists was recruited to staff the Central Economic Information Service. In January 1941 the Economic Policy Committee was disbanded and the Information Service was divided into two parts, one of which became the Central Statistical Office, while the other became the Economic Section of the Office of the War Cabinet. The latter body mainly served under the important Lord President's Committee, which, under Sir John Anderson, took charge of most of the larger questions of economic policy. Economists were also attached to other ministries or committees. One group, for example, formed part of the Prime Minister's Statistical Section, working mainly under Lord Cherwell, the Prime Minister's personal scientific adviser.[3]

The significance of this recruitment of economists during the war was that a substantial number of leading members of the academic profession, and those who later became members of that cadre, gained access to information and valuable administrative experience. The process of education worked both ways: civil servants taught economists and vice versa. It led to a substantial injection of realism into economic studies and greater respect for expert economic knowledge on the part of officials. The conferences that took place

---

[1] See J. H. Jones, *Josiah Stamp, Public Servant* (1964), pp. 296–303, 329.
[2] See D. N. Chester, "The Central Machinery for Economic Policy" in *Lessons of the British War Economy*.
[3] See the account given by G. D. A. MacDougall in *ibid*.

in Keynes's room at the Treasury have been described as "seminar classes in adult education".[1]

Co-operation between economists with different views could lead to a softening of pre-war dividing lines and greater mutual respect. Speaking of this period Robbins said that: "It has afforded an interval in which, our entanglement in the controversies of the past being suspended, we could consider old positions without that acute attachment to interested intellectual capital, which, in normal times, makes it so difficult to change one's position." In his own case, as he generously acknowledged, it led to a modification of his views on the capacity of the economic system to achieve overall stability without government intervention. "I owe much to Cambridge economists, particularly to Lord Keynes and Professor Robertson, for having awakened me from dogmatic slumbers in this very important respect."[2] Government service, it seems, came closer to the ideal that universities are supposed to represent than they often do in fact. The same thing seems to have happened in Washington during the war: Paul Samuelson has said that it became "in a real sense *the* centre of economic science".[3]

Another important result was the official backing given to the collection, refinement, and publication of national income and related statistics. From relatively humble beginnings in 1941 an important branch of economic statistics has developed, without which the application of macro-economic theory to policy problems would be practically impossible. Unlike many natural scientists, those working in the social sciences are not always in a position to conduct experiments. They are correspondingly more reliant on statistical information about social and economic behaviour that may be merely the by-product of state intervention for purposes unrelated to the scientific task in hand. This was certainly true of the early national income estimates. By proving their worth to government economic experts it was possible to obtain official backing and finance for their collection and presentation. Theoretical analysis having shown the importance of certain quantitative evidence, and war having furnished a proving ground, this information was made available for the testing and further refinement of theoretical models. The value of the national income accounts is, of course, not confined to the problems of war finance; they are of central importance in any well-designed policy for controlling the level of economic activity.

---

[1] By a Treasury colleague of Keynes as cited in E. A. G. Robinson, "John Maynard Keynes, 1883-1946", reprinted in R. Lekachman (ed.), *Keynes' General Theory: Reports of Three Decades*, (1969), p. 70.
[2] See *The Economic Problem in Peace and War* (1947), pp. 2 and 68.
[3] See "American Economics" in *The Collected Scientific Papers of Paul A. Samuelson* (1966), Vol. II, p. 1651.

A final point to note about the war-time incursion of economists into government is that when, as happened very early in the war, thoughts turned towards plans for post-war reconstruction, economists were on hand to ensure that the lessons of the war and inter-war period were not ignored.

## Post-War Planning

In both world wars the pre-war world exerted a strong, though radically different, influence on thinking about the post-war period. In 1918 nostalgia for pre-war institutions and practices was the dominant public sentiment; it was a sentiment shared by most politicians and economists. The inter-war period held no fascination for those who had come to maturity in it. Who would consciously strive to re-establish an economic order which, in Britain, in spite of the advances of the 'thirties, entailed an average level of unemployment of over 10%? Or indeed an international order in which the world economy was characterised by growing autarchy and declining levels of trade? The inter-war period seemed to epitomise everything that ought to be avoided in reconstructing a new system. In fact, one of the weaknesses of post-war planning, as revealed by later events, was that excessive concern with the mistakes of the past hindered consideration of the new problems of the post-war world until they had become acute.

The Second World War had proved conclusively that it was possible for governments to exercise considerable control over economic resources in order to fight a total war; and that in this respect democratic systems were certainly not inferior to the dictatorships—though they might have to employ similar methods at times. It was inevitable that many would feel that if such powers were capable of being utilised to prosecute war, they could also be used to eliminate unemployment in the post-war period. The war analogy had frequently been invoked but never acted on in the inter-war period. Keynes himself had recognised that it might be "politically impossible for a capitalistic democracy to organise expenditure on the scale necessary to make the grand experiment which would prove my case—except in war conditions".[1] For this reason he and his followers were anxious to capitalise on the gains of the war-time experiment.

[1] *New Republic*, July 29th 1940; see also his B.B.C. talk "Will Rearmament Cure Unemployment?" *The Listener*, June 1st 1939.

## The White Paper on Employment Policy

The formal recognition of the principles of the Keynesian revolution in Britain was a remarkably quiet affair. The publication by the Coalition Government of the famous White Paper on Employment Policy in 1944 aroused far less public interest and controversy than the Beveridge Report on Social Security had done when it appeared eighteen months earlier. The best part of the White Paper was its first sentence: "The Government accept as one of their primary aims and responsibilities the maintenance of a high and stable level of employment after the war." As *The Economist* pointed out, the remarkable feature of the White Paper was that whereas previously state intervention had been "reluctant, hesitant and pushed forward by ineluctable circumstances", now "there is a bold and conscious assumption of responsibilities and authority . . . over a whole vast terrain of policy".[1] The authors of the document themselves were fully aware that they were breaking new ground.

"Not long ago, the ideas embodied in the present proposals were unfamiliar to the general public and the subject of controversy among economists. Today, the conception of an expansionist economy and the broad principles governing its growth are widely accepted by men of affairs as well as by technical experts in all the great industrial countries. But the whole of the measures here proposed have never yet been systematically applied as part of the official economic policy of any Government. In these matters we shall be pioneers."[2]

This statement of faith can be seen as the end of a long journey, beginning perhaps with the Minority Report of the Royal Commission on the Poor Law in 1909, or with the Keynes's writings in the 'twenties. Strengthened by knowledge gained in conducting the war economy, the White Paper recorded an intention to avoid the experience of the inter-war period, and the belief that the government possessed the means for doing this. Like any document of this kind, however, it bore the marks of compromise between the various departments, ministries, and personalities in the Coalition Government. Inevitably too, it was largely directed towards overcoming problems of which there had already been experience in the inter-war period. Some of its limitations as a guide to future policy took time to discover; others were more immediately obvious.

Much of the White Paper was devoted to the problems of transition from war to peace. Here the experience of inflationary boom

[1] June 3rd 1944, p. 737.
[2] Cmd. 6527, p. 26.

followed by rapid slump in the period after the First World War was the main conditioning factor. The White Paper stated that there would be no problem of maintaining aggregate demand in the immediate period of post-war reconstruction and demobilisation; rather it would be necessary to retain rationing and controls to prevent inflation. There is evidence here of the determination of Bevin and the Labour members of the Coalition Government to prevent a recurrence of the post-1918 rush to dismantle the apparatus of war-time controls.[1] The White Paper also upheld the need to maintain cheap money throughout the reconstruction period. In its emphasis on a strong policy to achieve "a balanced distribution of labour and industry", the White Paper reflected concern for the inter-war problem of localised unemployment in areas heavily reliant on staple industries.

Without actually predicting a post-reconstruction slump the White Paper warned that it might not be very long before a deliberate policy was required to maintain the level of employment.[2] But the discussion of remedies to deal with this situation in the document was decidedly feeble. The problem of employment policy was depicted almost exclusively in terms of the need to counter fluctuations caused by the volatility of private investment and foreign demand for British goods. Apart from some vague suggestions for "encouraging large businesses to plan their own capital expenditure in conformity with a general stabilisation policy", no direct effort was to be made to overcome the instability of private investment. The two main proposals were: forward planning of public capital expenditure so as to allow its timing to be adjusted to fluctuations in private demand, and an ingenious scheme, devised by James Meade, for varying national insurance contributions in accordance with the level of unemployment. The expectation, therefore, was of cyclical fluctuations in effective demand, and the aim of policy was seen as one of offsetting or reducing the amplitude of such swings of private activity. As Beveridge pointed out: "The policy of the White Paper is a public works policy; not a policy of full employment."[3]

But the chief weakness of the White Paper lay in its treatment of the budget as a means of controlling the level of employment. The paragraphs dealing with this subject are highly confused. The main remedies proposed, contra-cyclical public investment programmes and variations in national insurance contributions, were both outside the framework of normal budgeting. As a later commentator has said, employment was treated "as a separate and, as it were,

[1] See A. Bullock, *Life and Times of Ernest Bevin* (1968), Vol. II, p. 316.
[2] *Op. cit.*, p. 10.
[3] "The Government's Employment Policy", *Economic Journal*, Sept. 1944 as reprinted in *Full Employment in a Free Society* (1944), p. 262.

occasional aspect of policy".[1] Tentative mention was made of the possibility of varying taxation in accordance with the needs of the trade cycle, but this was immediately countered by the statement that: "None of the main proposals contained in this Paper involves deliberate planning for a deficit in the National Budget in years of subnormal activity."[2] *The Economist* noted the equivocal use of the word "deliberate" here and went on to say: "In economic policy, as in war, it would be nice to combine victory with a balanced budget, but a deficit is better than a defeat."[3]

The concern of the Treasury in the inter-war years with the problem of the National Debt made its appearance felt in this part of the White Paper. If taken seriously, the following paragraph could have undermined all the positive proposals in the rest of the document:

"Both at home and abroad the handling of our monetary problems is regarded as a test of the general firmness of the policy of the Government. An undue growth of national indebtedness will have a quick result on confidence. But no less serious would be a budgetary deficit arising from a fall of revenue due to depressed industrial and commercial conditions. Therefore, in controlling the situation, especially in the difficult years after the war, the Government will have equally in mind the need to maintain the national income, and the need for a budgetary equilibrium such as will maintain the confidence in the future which is necessary for a healthy and enterprising industry."[4]

The struggle to gain acceptance of responsibility by the government for maintaining a high and stable level of employment was a much harder one in the United States than in Britain. Like all significant policy decisions in the American system, however, it was fought out in the open rather than, as in Britain, behind closed doors. We have already noted that the British White Paper shows definite marks of compromise; it will not be possible to see how that compromise was arrived at until the relevant official papers become available.[5] Nevertheless, some evidence on this subject can be culled from published memoranda written by H. D. Henderson while at the Treasury.[6] On the basis of this evidence it seems safe to say that if Keynes's views had prevailed the document would have been much bolder, and that if Henderson's memoranda had been accepted as

---

[1] J. C. R. Dow, *The Management of the British Economy, 1945-60* (1964), p. 365.
[2] *Op. cit.*, cf. paras. 72 and 74.
[3] June 3rd 1944 Similar criticisms were made by Beveridge, *op. cit.*, p. 265.
[4] *Op. cit.*, pp. 25-6.
[5] Neither of the relevant official histories by Hancock and Gowing and R. S. Sayers deals with this issue in detail.
[6] *The Inter-War Years*, H. Clay (ed.) 1955), Part IV, items 3 and 6.

the basis for policy there would have been no open commitment to full employment at all.[1] As it was, one of the motives for bringing out a document on this subject seems to have been a desire to forestall Beveridge, who was known to be in the field once more.[2]

Henderson opposed fiscal remedies for maintaining the level of income on grounds of "sound finance" and because he felt they were unlikely to be effective; public works might have a limited role to play in easing the problems of transition from war to peace. No less than the Keynesians, he believed that a post-war slump was possible; his own scheme for dealing with this was for the state to place orders with manufacturers for consumption goods produced on the war-time utility pattern. But in 1943 his position was that "employment, like happiness, will come most readily when it is not sought for its own sake".[3] He appears to have conducted a rear-guard action against the White Paper. All of the animus he felt against the claims of the "new economics" and the technique of national income projections can be seen in the attack which he made on Keynes's criticisms of the draft White Paper. He set out to show that the defects of the report were not so much timidity as capitulation to "the momentarily fashionable approach to the subject", an approach which he considered "unhistorical, unimaginative and unscientific". The basis of his position was an alternative reading of the "facts" of inter-war experience. On two occasions, 1920–21 and after the 1931 crisis, orthodox finance was responsible for adding to unemployment or retarding recovery. In neither case, however, was it decisive. The real cause of the high level of unemployment was to be found in external factors which reduced the demand for traditional British exports. Public works and unbalanced budgets could not deal with this sort of structural problem.

It is quite true that in the early days of enthusiasm for the macro-economic approach some of its advocates paid inadequate attention to the structural or micro-economic issues underlying the aggregates. It is also true that Henderson was justified in stressing the importance of the external constraints on domestic employment policy. But placing one micro-brick upon another did not enable him to reach the same vantage point as those who began by taking a global view using the new national income accounts about which he was so scornful. It is difficult not to conclude from Henderson's memoranda that he had failed to grasp the significance of the new approach.

---

[1] Henderson was also sceptical towards the British Government's whole-hearted co-operation with the United States to produce schemes which would commit Britain to the removal of trade and payments restrictions. On this his position was more justified by subsequent developments; see *ibid.*, esp. pp. 209-219. See also Sir David Waley, "The Treasury During World War Two" in the *Oxford Economic Papers, Supplement*, 1953.

[2] See W. Beveridge, *Power and Influence* (1953), pp. 328-330.

[3] *Inter-War Years*, p. 234.

This would not be remarkable except for the fact that as co-author of *Can Lloyd George Do It?* he was one of its progenitors.

## Full Employment in a Free Society

Beveridge's *Full Employment in a Free Society*, which appeared in the same year as the White Paper, was a far more radical document. Beveridge had the assistance of a group of young Keynesian economists, and the result was a report which in terms of diagnosis and remedies was closer to the spirit of the Keynesian revolution than the White Paper.[1] Without going as far as the stagnationists in America, the main emphasis in Beveridge's full employment policy was on the need to overcome the problem, not of cycles, but of a chronic tendency towards a "general deficiency of aggregate demand". To deal with this problem a policy was outlined in considerable detail. It was described as "a long-term programme of planned outlay directed by social priorities and designed to give stability and expansion to the economic system".[2] In the *General Theory* Keynes had argued in favour of a National Investment Board on the grounds that "the duty of ordering the current volume of investment cannot safely be left in private hands".[3] This proposal was endorsed by the Beveridge Report, and also, it should be added, by the Labour Party in its first post-war manifesto.[4] In addition, however, the Beveridge Report advocated an expansion of total outlay in a number of directions: private consumption expenditure through income redistribution and social security benefits; increased collective demand for essential consumer goods, with the government acting as wholesaler; public investment expenditure on housing, roads, schools, hospitals, defence, and the nationalised industries. It was a highly ambitious programme combining the aims of full employment with extensive social reform. Yet, since it was intended to socialise demand rather than production, it was claimed that the plan "by-passes the socialist-capitalist controversy".[5]

Needless to say the implications for budgetary policy explored in the Report went far beyond the timid ambivalence of the government's White Paper; the whole area of fiscal policy and deficit finance was surveyed. The White Paper had confirmed that National

---

[1] The economists concerned remained anonymous at the time: they were Joan Robinson, Barbara Wootton, Nicholas Kaldor, E. F. Schumacher, and Frank Pakenham. See also *The Economics of Full Employment* (1944) by a group of economists working at the Oxford Institute of Statistics; this too was more representative of Keynesian thinking than the White Paper.

[2] *Op. cit.*, p. 30.

[3] *General Theory*, p. 320.

[4] It had been incorporated in the party programme during the 'thirties, see pp. 343-4 below.

[5] *Op. cit.*, pp. 190-3, 205-7.

Income and Expenditure accounts were to be published annually. The Beveridge Report offered a long appendix by Nicholas Kaldor on "The Quantitative Aspects of the Full Employment Problem in Britain", which entailed making projections of the full employment level of national income four years ahead. It was, as its author has recently claimed, "the first attempt to build up comprehensive estimates from a large number of separate forecasts (and assumptions) within the framework of a consistent econometric model".[1]

### The American Employment Act

Although in point of time the British government was the first to commit itself to the maintenance of high levels of employment after the war, other countries followed her lead in fairly quick succession.[2] In the United States the equivalent to the British White Paper was the Employment Act of 1946—equivalent in some but not all respects, the crucial difference being that the Congressional form of government required a legislative embodiment of the commitment. At a very early stage of the war, in fact before the United States was actually involved as a combatant, Keynesian economists in Washington began to prepare the ground for post-war action on employment policy. We have seen already how this influenced the work of economists in the Office for Price Administration.[3] Other agencies were also in the field, notably the National Resources Planning Board, which had been instructed by Roosevelt in 1940 to collate post-war plans, and an independent body, the National Planning Association.[4] Another centre of Keynesian thinking in the government was the Fiscal Division of the Bureau of the Budget, which had gradually been evolving the kind of budgetary techniques necessary for the implementation of an employment policy. In the Treasury too, Harry Dexter White headed a team of economists working along similar lines.

Massive military expenditure had had a dramatic effect on the American economy. Within two years of her entry into the war, national income had risen by more than in the whole previous decade, and unemployment was virtually eliminated. Moreover, unlike Britain, in spite of the resources "wasted" in the war effort, American standards of living reached a new height during the war. The campaign conducted by Keynesians in Washington was a

[1] N. Kaldor, *Essays on Economic Policy* (1964).
[2] See e.g. W. J. Rose "Full Employment; the British, Canadian and Australian White Papers", *The Economic Record*, Dec. 1945.
[3] See pp. 263-4 above.
[4] See e.g. NRPB, *After Defence – What?* (1941); A. Hansen, *After the War – Full Employment* (1941); J. H. C. Pierson, *Fiscal Policy for Full Employment* (1943); NPA, *National Budgets for Full Employment* (1945).

continuation of the stagnationist debate in the latter years of the New Deal. The high level of military expenditure which had been necessary to bring the economy up to a full employment level of income was used as evidence to confirm the stagnationist case, and to underline fears of what might happen once the prop was removed. Memories of what had happened when the government's net contribution had been reduced in 1937 were still fresh. At the end of the war there would be a need and an opportunity to fill the gap created by the reduction of military expenditure with a long-term programme of social improvement that would entail a permanent increase in public expenditure. Unlike Britain, the United States would not have the stimulus provided by post-war reconstruction; hence the added importance of preparing plans for increased public spending on roads, education, low-cost housing, flood control, slum clearance, public health, and provision for the aged, etc. These were typical projects, and they were coupled frequently with proposals for a radical redistributive taxation policy. Conservatives in America were not entirely wrong, therefore, in suspecting that under the cover of a commitment to full employment, a large-scale political and social revolution was being planned. Keynesianism was too powerful a weapon of social reform to be allowed to sink to the status of a technocratic device.

The initiators of the move to gain legislative approval for the aim of maintaining full employment began work in earnest in November 1944.[1] In their efforts to give wide appeal to their Bill, and later to meet the demands of their opponents, they became involved in a lengthy semantic game. In its original form as a Senate Bill the announced purpose was "to establish a national policy and program for assuring continuing full employment in a free competitive economy". It was to be the duty of the Federal Government to pursue policies that would fulfil this aim by stimulating private and non-Federal expenditures, and, if necessary, by providing "such volume of Federal investment and expenditure as may be needed to assure continuing employment". The President was called upon to transmit to Congress an annual "National Production and Employment Budget", which was to forecast the size of the labour force and the major components determining the aggregate level of expenditure. In the light of this forecast he was enjoined to give details of a programme of action to eliminate any deficiency between the forecast and the "full employment volume of production". These proposals were linked with measures to ensure that monopolistic practices did not impede the purposes of the main purpose of the Bill. It was also

---

[1] The history of the antecedents of the Employment Act and the story of its legislative progress is told in great detail by S. Bailey, *Congress Makes A Law* (Vintage Books, 1964)

proposed that a Joint Committee of Congress be set up to receive, comment, and prepare legislation on the basis of the President's Report.

The legislative process took the form of a progressive dilution of the content of the original Bill. The anti-Keynesian pressure groups were no less well organised, and certainly better represented in Congress than the pro-Keynesian forces in the Administration and elsewhere. It did not take long for such bodies as the United States Chamber of Commerce, the National Industrial Conference Board, and the National Association of Manufacturers to get to work. Already by 1943 they had achieved a minor victory when the appropriations for the National Resources Planning Board were cut off. And if employment levels and standards of living had risen during the war so had the size of the American national debt. It grew from $43 billion in 1940 to $269 billion in 1946—and to many in the United States this was a far more significant index of the state of the nation's health. The Employment Bill provided an opportunity to continue the battle, interrupted by the war, against the "fiscal irresponsibility" and "socialistic tendencies" of the New Deal. Keynesian economists were certainly aware of this threat and were not without resources of their own, but they can perhaps be forgiven for underestimating the tenacity with which these beliefs continued to be held by prominent men in Congress and business circles.

In the course of the hearings and debates on the Employment Bill, every conceivable objection was raised against its "free-spending" philosophy: it would undermine free enterprise, kill business initiative, destroy confidence, and lead to inflation. The names of Keynes and Beveridge were invoked to condemn the Bill, sometimes linked with "other" totalitarian thinkers like Hitler and Stalin.[1] By the time the Bill emerged as the Employment Act of 1946 it was a distinctly more qualified, timid, and vague document. Compare, for example, the first sentence of the British White Paper (p. 269 above) and the original statement of purpose in the Senate Bill (p. 275 above) with the following:

"The Congress hereby declares that it is the continuing policy and responsibility of the Federal Government to use all practicable means consistent with its needs and obligations and other essential considerations of national policy with the assistance and co-operation of industry, agriculture, labor, and state and local governments, to coordinate and utilise all its plans, functions, and resources for the purpose of creating and maintaining, in a manner calculated to foster and promote free competitive enterprise and

[1] See S. Bailey, *op. cit.*, pp. 118 and 130.

the general welfare, conditions under which there will be afforded useful employment, for those able, willing, and seeking to work, and to promote maximum employment, production, and purchasing power."

It may truly be said that the United States walked backward into a commitment to promote maximum (not full) employment. This did not prevent the *New York Herald Tribune* from describing the Act as "perhaps the most serious threat to free enterprise and democracy with which the country has been confronted in the 170 years of its existence."[1]

In the Act the whole apparatus of the "National Budget" was thrown over in favour of an annual economic report by the President on the general economic situation. The Joint Committee was retained but with weakened powers. There was, however, one major innovation in the form of a Council of Economic Advisers, whose job it was to advise the President, gather information about the economy, and help prepare the annual report. This body, as it turned out, has provided protection from the effects of other weaknesses in the Act.[2]

### International Economic Planning

Running parallel to these discussions of domestic employment policy in Britain and the United States were the negotiations between the two countries on the question of rebuilding international economic relations on improved lines after the war.[3] The British government and its advisers were particularly interested in the construction of a set of rules and institutions which would minimise any possible clash between external stability and the achievement of full employment. In the United States, however, first priority was given to the commercial problems concerning multilateral, non-discriminatory trade between countries. American post-war planners were not indifferent to the financial and monetary problems connected with balance of payments adjustment and exchange rates, or to the international aspect of full employment policies; but the American situation and climate of opinion gradually forced their negotiators to proceed with greater caution and less urgency on these matters.

These differences of approach between the two countries made their presence felt as early as 1941 when the Atlantic Charter was drawn up, and more seriously when the terms of Article 7 of the

[1] June 14th 1946.
[2] On this, see pp. 333-4 below.
[3] The history of these negotiations is exhaustively covered in R. Gardner, *Sterling-Dollar Diplomacy* (1956).

Mutual Aid Agreement were settled. The disagreement was expressed in British resistance to American pressure for an unqualified commitment to eliminate trade discrimination (i.e. imperial preference) without receiving in return assurances that effective action would be taken in the United States to maintain high and stable levels of employment; there could be no trade-barrier disarmament, it was held, until fears of instability in the American economy were assuaged. A related difference of emphasis ran through the proposals for post-war financial collaboration put forward by both countries in 1943. The British plan for a Clearing Union drawn up by Keynes was considerably more expansionist in aim than the American plan for a Stabilisation Fund drawn up by Harry Dexter White.

These preliminary discussions provided a basis at least for the agreements reached at Bretton Woods in 1944, which resulted in the creation of the International Monetary Fund and the International Bank for Reconstruction and Development. Progress on a code to deal with commercial and unemployment issues was more difficult to achieve. The differences between Britain and the United States on these questions tended to grow rather than diminish at the end of the war. As the debate on the Employment Act showed, the United States was less willing to commit itself to full employment policies. Whereas in Britain the war led to a left-ward movement in politics, the opposite was the case in the United States. British fears that an American recession might jeopardise chances of maintaining full employment proved unfounded, but the bitterness engendered by the conditions attached to the Anglo-American Financial Agreement in 1946, and the subsequent collapse of the agreement in the convertibility crisis in 1947, led to the breakdown of further efforts to move toward the multilateral ideal. The failure of Congress to ratify the Charter of the International Trade Organisation signed in Havana in 1948 marked the end of this phase in post-war economic planning.

Perhaps because it seemed to fall outside the arena of party politics, many post-war planners entertained ambitious hopes of reconstructing international economic relations on semi-utopian lines. Here was a real opportunity to build a system which would avoid the inter-war conflict between Keynesian policies of full employment and classical free trade ideals. Judged by post-1918 standards some notable successes were achieved by international collaboration: the settlement of war debts was one. A great deal more thought was given to post-war economic problems than in the case of the First World War. As was noted at the time: "It is not devoid of significance that most of the points of the Atlantic Charter deal with economic problems, while Wilson's Fourteen Points are almost entirely political."[1] Nevertheless, it was in the field of international economic diplomacy that the biggest disappointments were to come, mainly because very little attention was paid by post-war planners to the problems of transition from war to peace.

British and European recovery took much longer than expected. When the International Trade Organisation collapsed, all that was left was a General Agreement on Tariffs and Trade—a much less grandiose affair, though one which has worked better than could have been anticipated at the time. Neither of the Bretton Woods twins, the IMF and the IBRD, was capable of dealing with the kind of disequilibrium situation left by the war. Both were largely put aside for use in the fairer weather for which they were designed.

One of the incidental tragedies of the failure of post-war planning in the international field was the fact that it was here that Keynes sacrificed most of the last years of his life. The last months of Keynes's life were actually spent fighting for and defending the Anglo-American loan. After this attempt to move rapidly towards multi-lateralism and convertibility had failed in 1947, a completely new start had to be made along more sober lines than those laid down by post-war planners.

[1] E. A. Goldenweiser in National Bureau of Economic Research, *Economic Research and the Development of Economic Science and Public Policy* (1946), p. 55.

# CHAPTER THIRTEEN

# The Keynesian Revolution: Fruition

### The Post War Record in Britain and the United States

Important though they were as historical landmarks, the British White Paper and the American Employment Act were chiefly paper victories. Both contained statements of intent, both established machinery for coping with employment problems, but neither proved to be adequate as blueprints for action. Equally, the more detailed plans put forward by the Beveridge team and by Keynesians in America were designed to deal with problems which mostly failed to materialise in the post-war period. The post-war planners were guilty of a mixture of excessive optimism and pessimism. The optimism took the form of an underestimation of the length of the transitional period after which, it was hoped, domestic and international economic affairs would return to normal. The pessimism was most in evidence in the widespread expectations of a severe, post-transitional slump, and in the belief that the pre-war cyclical pattern of instability would re-assert itself, with the United States acting once more as the villain of the piece.

By most criteria the transitional period in Europe lasted until the early 'fifties. The expectations of American Keynesians and of the Beveridge team, who foresaw the problem as one of dealing with a heavy slump and chronic deficiency of effective demand, were also falsified by events. Estimates of the level of unemployment that might be expected in America in the post-transitional period—if no countervailing action was taken—reached as high as 11 million: in fact, in the period 1945-6, unemployment never rose above 2½ million. Extrapolation from the pre-war record, stagnationist fears, and political aspirations, combined to bias the forecasts in a pessimistic direction.

Beveridge suggested 3% of the working population as the practicable minimum level of unemployment that could be achieved in peace-time Britain, a figure that was regarded as "an impossibly high standard of achievement" by some of his critics.[1] In fact, of course, unemployment in Britain, except in certain regions, has rarely risen

[1] See e.g. J. Jewkes, "Second Thoughts on the British White Paper on Employment Policy in National Bureau of Economic Research", *Economic Research and the Development Science and Public Policy* (1946), p. 116; and D. H. Macgregor, *Economic Thought and Policy* (1949), pp. 172-4.

above or even approached 2% throughout the whole post-war period. Inflation rather than unemployment has claimed more of the attention of British policy-makers until recently, and the same has been true, to a lesser extent, in the United States.

Over the whole post-war period the performance of the American economy has been consistently better than was feared by many foreign and domestic observers. Not only has there been no major slump, but the endogenous business cycles to which the American economy was supposed to be particularly prone have been mild by pre-war standards. The post-war recessions have lasted on average for a year; the largest decline, which took place in 1957-9, represented only a 4.3% drop in real Gross National Product. Moreover, it is not certain that the cyclical pattern of post-war American experience should be regarded as endogenous; there is evidence to suggest that instability may be the result of changes in government defence spending uncompensated by changes elsewhere in the government accounts.[1] More significantly perhaps, in the light of post-war expectations, in only one case, the first recession in 1949, were the economies of European countries seriously effected by American conditions. For the rest of the period the European and American economies have danced to different tunes.

In Britain and most other European economies the "cycles" have been of a quite different character from those of earlier periods; they have been registered as uneven movements in the *rate of growth* of output and demand, rather than as fluctuations in the *level* of output and employment. National output has continued to grow every year since the war, with the exception of 1952 when it remained static. A recent study of variations in the rate of growth of output has concluded that they can be explained in terms of variations in the pressure of aggregate demand, which, in turn, can partly be attributed to changes in government policy. Whilst, therefore, autonomous and external fluctuations in demand have continued to affect the performance of the British economy, post-war cycles have to a large extent been "self-inflicted" by the action of government itself in trying to manage the economy.[2]

In the light of this experience one might conclude that the Keynesian revolution in policy has either been supremely successful or that, for other unexplained reasons, it has proved unnecessary. The first alternative is much closer to the truth; but it should be borne in mind that the Keynesian revolution is not simply a matter of employment policy, still less of counter-cyclical action. It is best thought of

---

[1] On this see the case argued by P. Samuelson, *Stability and Growth in the American Economy*, Wicksell Lectures, 1962.

[2] J. C. R. Dow, *The Management of the British Economy 1945-60* (1964), Ch. XV.

as a rational approach to the problems of economic management in general, based on a conscious assessment of the outcomes of alternative lines of action. It was only after considerable further experience of policy-making in the new post-war situation that complete victory for the Keynesian revolution in this sense could be announced in either Britain or the United States. Furthermore, in the course of acquiring this experience additional problems have arisen which have made it necessary to modify and refine both the aims and methods of economic management. A brief discussion of some features of economic policy-making in the post-Keynesian world we now inhabit is left to a postscript to this study. The question to be considered here is how policy-makers in Britain and the United States approached and entered that world.

### Britain: *Labour in Power*

In spite of the use made of Keynesian techniques of overall financial control during the war, the Labour Government only gradually came to accept the use of such methods in peace-time. In the early post-war years heavy reliance was placed on physical controls to deal with problems of demobilisation and reconstruction. Much of the apparatus inherited from the war, of controls over imports, building, the allocation of scarce materials, prices, and the distribution of consumers' goods, was retained. The Coalition White Paper committed both parties to the retention of controls during the transitional period, but there is little doubt that the use of physical planning methods as a peace-time device was more congenial to the socialist philosophy of public ownership and direction, particularly as it had emerged from the debates on planning in the 'thirties. This time, however, the background was one of reconstruction and inflationary pressure rather than recovery from depression. Financial controls of a Keynesian type did not bear the whole strain during the war; and a good case could be made for the use of controls to cope with shortages and the balance of payments situation immediately after the war.[1] Nevertheless, it would appear that many of the ideas of Labour planners were based on political analyses of capitalism that were pre-Keynesian, and possibly even anti-Keynesian, in emphasis and origins. The tendency of this type of thinking was to delay acceptance of fiscal (and monetary) policy as an active tool of management, or rather perhaps, in Dow's words, it made it "more difficult to sort out what were the essential, and what the less important, economic functions of the state in the post-war

---

[1] See e.g. I. M. D. Little, "Fiscal Policy" in G. D. N. Worswick and P. H. Ady (eds.), *The British Economy 1945-1950*, (1952), pp. 168-9.

world".[1] Once more an uneasy relationship existed between macro-
and micro-economic thinking, similar to that noted on earlier
occasions when discussing British and American recovery policies
in the 'thirties.[2]

The budgets introduced by Hugh Dalton, the first Labour
Chancellor of the Exchequer after 1945, were retrograde so far as the
use of national income accounting methods was concerned. The
Treasury under Dalton continued to operate in a secondary role
outside the machinery of economic planning; the manpower gap was
given greater prominence than inflationary gap analysis. Dalton
seems not to have learnt or been sympathetic to the terminology of
national income accounting, and there is plenty of evidence in his
published pronouncements to suggest that he never really got beyond
accepting the by then old-fashioned idea of balancing the budget over
the length of the cycle.[3] In his last two budgets presented in 1947
Dalton did recognise that inflation was the main problem to be
tackled, and tackled not merely by using controls to suppress it,
but by budgetary "disinflation"—a word coined by *The Economist*
at this time to describe the new target for Keynesian methods.
Although Dalton aimed at and achieved a disinflationary budget
surplus, he remained sceptical as to the possibility of using inflationary gap techniques to estimate the size of the problem.[4]

In view of Dalton's dubious status as a "Keynesian" Chancellor,
it is somewhat ironic that he should so frequently be criticised for his
"ultra-Keynesian" position—in the pejorative sense—with regard to
cheap money. For the first two years after the war Dalton conducted
a determined campaign to keep interest rates down to and below the
fairly low level maintained throughout the war. Several motives inspired this campaign. There was first of all the desire to keep down the
cost of government borrowing, and to reduce the interest-burden of
existing debt to the Exchequer. This was particularly important during
a period of heavy expenditure on reconstruction, and while ambitious
nationalisation schemes were being undertaken. It was also hoped that
low interest rates would have a favourable effect on the balance of payments by reducing the interest-cost on sterling balances held in London.
Fear of post-war collapse and willingness to encourage movement towards the "euthanasia of the *rentier*" may also have played a part.[5]

---

[1] J. C. R. Dow, *op. cit.*, p. 11. See also S. H. Beer, *Modern British Politics*, pp. 189-194.
There were also some pro-Keynesian currents at work among Labour intellectuals; see
pp. 351-2 below.
[2] See pp. 217-8, 231-5 above.
[3] See pp. 346-7 below for a brief discussion of Dalton's views as an economist.
[4] See J. C. R. Dow, *op. cit.*, p. 28n.
[5] Dalton claimed that he had Keynes's full support; see his letter to *The Economist*, 3rd
Feb. 1951, and *High Tide and After* (1962), pp. 161, 183 and 231. Keynes died in April 1946,
before Dalton's campaign reached its peak.

Dalton came in for a good deal of criticism for his aims and handling of the cheap money policy, notably from the financial press. In
retrospect it seems that a justifiable approach was carried too far too
quickly, and that the inflationary potential of the policy, though not
by itself very great, was underestimated.[1] The real lesson of the cheap
money episode from the point of view of this study is that it further
demonstrates, not so much excessive attachment to one aspect of
Keynesianism, as the lack of emphasis placed by the Labour Government in this period on techniques of overall management.

1947 was a disastrous year for the Labour planners. In February
an extremely severe winter led to coal shortages and the breakdown
of electricity supplies; for a month or so, as a result of the closure of
factories, unemployment rose above the two million mark. In August
there was a balance of payments crisis connected with the run-down
of the American loan at double the anticipated rate, and with the
undertaking to establish sterling convertibility which was part of the
original loan agreement negotiated in the previous year. The
convertibility experiment lasted only six weeks before it was finally
abandoned as a result of the depletion of British gold and dollar
reserves. What was later recognised to be a world dollar shortage had
for a brief period been funnelled through the sterling channel. The
episode marks the beginning of the more sober and realistic appraisal
of the problems of restoring the international economic and monetary
system which eventually resulted in the Marshall Aid programme.

Coming close on each other, the fuel and convertibility crises were
a damaging blow to *simpliste* notions of economic planning through
quantitative controls and targets. The government's response was to
institute improvements in the planning process and to tighten up
certain controls, notably over imports. A new interdepartmental
planning body, attached to the Lord President's Office, was set up
under Sir Edwin Plowden. Later in the year these responsibilities
were transferred to a new Ministry of Economic Affairs, whose first
incumbent was Sir Stafford Cripps. A few months later, when Cripps
succeeded Dalton as Chancellor, he took with him to the Treasury
all the co-ordinating functions newly vested in him and his economic
planning staff. For the first time since early in the war the balance of
official economic power and expertise within the governmental
machine was shifted back to the Treasury.[2]

With Cripps as Chancellor, a new phase in post-war economic
policy-making began. The transition from war to peace had been
accomplished, and production, if not productivity, was above pre-

---

[1] See C. M. Kennedy, "Monetary Policy" in Worswick and Ady, (eds.) *The British
Economy, 1945-50.*
[2] The Economic Section remained with the Cabinet Office until 1953.

war levels; the nature and extent of the problem of full recovery had been established. Inflation and domestic consumption would have to be kept in check while resources were freed to allow for an expansion of exports and investment. The policy of disinflation through budgetary surpluses, which had been inaugurated by Dalton, was continued with conviction by his successor for the next three years. Cripps was more at home with Keynesian terminology and methods than Dalton; his budgets were more firmly set within a framework of detailed analysis of likely future trends in the economy as presented in the annual *Economic Survey*. Under Cripps a balance was established between physical and financial planning. Short-term budgetary objectives and long-term aims were brought together.[1]

In spite of the continued application of various controls, and the determined use of budgetary methods to restrain and rearrange the pattern of aggregate demand, it was soon found that operating the economy at full employment led to persistent upward pressure on wages and prices. During the war it had been recognised that a successful planning effort required close co-operation with the trade unions, backed up by reserve powers for directing labour. With Bevin at the Ministry of Labour, and with extensive controls over profits and prices in the form of rationing, utility schemes, and food subsidies, this side of the war effort had been carried out relatively smoothly without great use of the reserve powers. Given the understandable attachment of trade unionists to free collective bargaining, it was inevitable that in peace-time conditions this aspect of planning would become more difficult to maintain, even for a Labour Government. There was still a need, however, for a manpower and wages policy which would enable the government both to meet its structural or micro-economic targets by routing labour in the right directions, and to prevent a wage-price spiral from frustrating its disinflationary macro-economic aims. The emphasis shifted therefore towards finding a basis for a voluntary agreement between the government and the unions on a national wages policy.

In February 1948 the government produced a *Statement on Personal Incomes, Costs and Prices* in which it was argued that "until more goods and services are available for the home market, there is no justification for any *general* increase of individual money incomes".[2] Exceptions could be made only in industries where productivity was rising or which were undermanned. The TUC response to this was to insist on the need to safeguard low-paid workers and established wage differentials, thereby, in effect, repulsing any government intentions

---

[1] For an account of economic planning in this period by a member of the planning staff see E. A. G. Robinson, *Economic Planning in the U.K: Some Lessons* (1967).
[2] Cmnd. 7321.

to modify the results of collective bargaining in the interests of achieving a planned distribution of manpower. But the unions were willing to co-operate to produce general wage restraint in the interests of curbing inflation. In return for restraint they demanded action by the government to reduce profits and prices, a "special contribution" in the form of a capital levy, and the removal of the ceiling on food subsidies. Much of this bargain was honoured by both sides in the next two and a half years. Cripps succeeded in getting voluntary dividend limitation from the employers, but was not so successful in stabilising, let alone reducing, prices.

This bargain between the government, the unions, and to a lesser extent the employers, was remarkable from several points of view. First of all, it worked on a purely voluntary basis: wage rates rose by only 5% over the period of restraint. Although similar in many ways to the agreement reached between the unions and the government under conditions of war, it set the pattern for the kind of "democratic planning" which had been outlined in the first *Economic Survey*. In this document the government recognised the limits of compulsion and the need for voluntary co-operation between the major producer and labour interest groups.[1] In this respect, it gave a foretaste of later attempts to implement an incomes policy, many of which, until recently perhaps, have been far less successful than this early prototype.

The co-operative principle in democratic economic planning was also recognised in the Working Parties set up in 1945, composed of representatives of the employers and unions, together with independent members, to study particular industries and recommend changes in methods or organisation, production and distribution. This scheme later led to legislation enabling Development Councils to be set up in a number of key industries.[2] Here again we have in embryo the type of thinking which in more recent revivals of the idea of planning has led to the establishment of regional development councils and "little Neddys".

The Cripps wage restraint bargain foundered on the rock of sterling devaluation in September 1949. The initial impact of devaluation was to evoke a further response from the unions in the form of an offer to freeze wages and suspend cost-of-living clauses in wage agreements. As the effects of devaluation made themselves felt in the form of rising import prices, however, it became more and more difficult for the unions to hold the line. By the end of 1950 the policy of restraint was in ruins.

---

[1] On the political implications of the episode see S. H. Beer, *op. cit.*, Ch. VII.
[2] See P. D. Henderson, "Development Councils: An Industrial Experiment", in Worswick and Ady (eds.), *The British Economy, 1945-1950*.

By early in 1949 the twin policies of budgetary disinflation and wage restraint had been remarkably successful in raising exports and production, while at the same time curbing inflation. The American recession of that year reduced dollar earnings, particularly those of the overseas sterling area, and provoked the now familiar speculative attack on sterling. By September this attack could no longer be staved off: a large devaluation of 30% was announced together with an additional dose of disinflation in the form of cuts in investment and government expenditure. Since most countries followed Britain, the main effect of devaluation was to revalue the dollar upwards. It can be seen, therefore, as the next logical step after Marshall Aid and the European Recovery Programme towards eliminating the world dollar problem.

Devaluation certainly produced a quick turn-around in the trade and reserve figures, but the benefits were shortlived: in the middle of 1950 commodity prices began to rise steeply as a result of the Korean War boom. To the deterioration in the British balance of payments situation which this brought about was added the problem of rising government expenditure on rearmament. It became more difficult to manage the economy by aiming at an overall budgetary surplus, with cuts falling heavily on domestic consumption. Controls over the allocation of strategic raw materials and over some prices were reintroduced. The unfortunate task of framing a budget under these conditions fell to Hugh Gaitskell, perhaps the first entirely self-conscious Keynesian to occupy the Chancellorship.

### The Conservatives in Power

The balance of payments situation continued to deteriorate right up to the general election in October 1951 when the Conservatives returned to power. The change of government provided the first real test—since the White Paper on Employment Policy—of acceptance by both major parties of the broad Keynesian principles of peace-time economic management as they had evolved in the intervening years. Although several isolated Conservative voices had been raised against national income accounting and Keynesian budgeting, it was soon made clear that, just as the Conservatives accepted the welfare measures introduced by their predecessors, so too would the continuity in fiscal management be maintained. The publication of forecasts in the *Economic Survey* was discontinued, but R. A. Butler, the first Conservative Chancellor, went out of his way in presenting his first budget in 1952 to reassure his critics that he had made use of "the whole machinery of economic forecasting . . . available to my predecessors in office".[1] The basic continuity in budgetary thinking was

[1] Cited in J. C. R. Dow, *op. cit.*, p. 71n.

epitomised by the coinage of the term "Butskellism" at this time.

In 1952 a recession occurred in some export and consumer goods' industries; it was partly the result of a fall in United States and Australian purchases of British goods, and partly due to domestic inventory adjustments made necessary by the hectic stockpiling activity of the previous year. Fortunately, so far as the balance of payments was concerned, the fall in exports was more than compensated by a fall in import prices. A fairly neutral budget in 1952 was followed by one in which a small net boost was given to consumer spending. Although the fall in industrial production in 1952—Gross Domestic Product failed to rise—does not appear to have been anticipated by policy-makers, the budgets of 1952-3 represent a modest milestone in the history of the Keynesian revolution: for the first time in the post-war period budgetary policy was consciously used to stimulate rather than restrain the economy.

Here, conveniently at the century's mid-point, the British part of the Keynesian story might end on a note of bi-partisan harmony—of apparent victory for a set of ideas whose evolution in the inter-war and war years has been traced in earlier chapters. Unfortunately, it is not quite as simple as this: the Conservatives, like the Labour Party when it first took office, were prey to certain ideas of a pre-Keynesian kind. Unlike the Labour Party, however, these ideas took some time to manifest themselves.

One of the main issues of party contest in the early 'fifties turned on the relative merits of controls and "planning" versus the price mechanism and "freedom". These skirmishes, it could be argued, were largely irrelevant to the underlying problems of managing the British economy—though not entirely without damaging consequences. There was, in fact, substantial agreement between the parties on the general desirability of removing many controls, though there were differences over priorities and the pace at which de-control should proceed. The process of dismantling controls was well under way by 1950; it began with Harold Wilson's "bonfire controls" in November 1948. The trend was reversed during the crisis years of 1950-52, when both Labour and Conservative Governments were forced to tighten many direct controls. After 1952 economic conditions were favourable to a resumption of the process of decontrol, though some food rationing remained as late as 1954, and some controls over the allocation of materials were in force until the latter half of the 'fifties.[1]

Apart from the abolition of controls in this period, one of the chief claims made by Conservative spokesmen was that they had re-

[1] See P. D. Henderson, "Government and Industry", in Worswick and Ady (eds.) *The British Economy in the 1950's* (1962), pp. 327-336.

activated monetary policy as a tool of economic management. There was a good deal of truth in this claim, even though there were already signs of an end to "neutral" monetary policies under Gaitskell. Beginning in November 1951 Bank Rate became mobile once more. A series of attempts were made in the following years to restrict, reduce, and redirect the volume of bank advances, and to vary hire purchase regulations in support of alternating policies of credit restriction or ease. With the disappearance of import controls and the gradual return to convertibility at this time, the external value of the pound began to loom large in the calculations of Conservative Chancellors. Monetary policy, therefore, was pressed more and more into the service of both internal and external stability, with changes in Bank Rate being used to attract foreign balances into London and as a signal for changes in the direction of domestic monetary policy. If the matter had rested here, with monetary policies being used in support of fiscal policy as part of a balanced package, no more would need to be said. But this was not the case.

For ideological reasons Conservative policy-makers in the 'fifties consistently over-estimated the powers of monetary policy as a controlling device. Many Conservatives regarded the revival of monetary policy as the natural complement to the removal of physical controls; it was believed to be a free market or pricing device which operated in a flexible, rapid and non-discretionary fashion. It could be presented as the antithesis of Labour ideas on detailed planning and discriminatory intervention. Less grandiose considerations also helped to encourage an optimistic view of the potency of monetary measures; during inflation the use of fiscal policy to control aggregate demand might require an upward movement of income taxes—a policy likely to conflict with Conservative electoral promises and hopes.

The circumstances of the early years of the "new" monetary policy lent credence to these Conservative articles of faith. As a result of the stimulus given to consumer spending in the 1953 budget, fairly rapid expansion took place in the period 1953-54. A favourable movement in the terms of trade prevented the expansion from imposing significant strain on the balance of payments. *Post hoc, ergo propter hoc* reasoning led to the conclusion that success could largely be attributed to the "new" monetary policy. By 1955 nearly exclusive reliance was placed on "the resources of a flexible monetary policy" to control boom conditions which had partly been encouraged by an unwise expansionary budget aimed at the electorate rather than at the needs of the economy. On this occasion monetary policy proved ineffective. A supplementary autumn budget had to be introduced, taking back most of the concessions made in April.

By itself this episode did not shake Conservative faith in monetary

K

policy. In September 1957 a more doctrinaire interpretation of the aims and methods of monetary policy was put forward by Peter Thorneycroft when inaugurating a new period of credit restriction to deal with the post-Suez exchange crisis. A package of measures was introduced which included a rise in the Bank Rate to 7%. Thorneycroft's rationale attracted as much attention as the measures themselves. The Chancellor considered that doubts as to the external value of the pound were based on the failure to stop the rise in prices at home. He also clearly indicated that a stable price level was to be given priority over other aims of policy, including the level of employment. The onus for maintaining full employment was to be shifted, implicitly at least, onto the unions; if *they* showed restraint, unemployment would be kept at a minimum. In addition to stressing "sound currency" as a policy aim, a new emphasis was placed on defeating inflation by exercising strict control over the quantity of money. Alongside this revival of the quantity theory of money there were hints of the revival of another exploded doctrine, namely the "Treasury View".[1] Fortunately, however, so strongly did Thorneycroft and his junior ministers, Enoch Powell and Nigel Birch, hold to these dogmas that they felt it necessary to resign when their Cabinet colleagues, with greater instinct for political and economic survival, refused to accept their proposals for putting a rigid ceiling on all government expenditure.

The main criticism of Conservative ideas on economic management, as judged by the experience of the 'fifties, must be that there was an increasing divergence between ideals and reality which could only be made good by the development of a mystique about monetary weapons in particular, and non-discretionary market discipline in general. To resolve growing doubts as to the *modus operandi* of monetary policy and its effectiveness as a stabilising device, the Radcliffe Committee was appointed in 1957 to inquire into the whole subject. As a result of its Report on the Workings of the Monetary System published in 1959, we now possess a clearer and more sober picture of the precise contribution and limitations which monetary policy can make to economic management. It certainly does not have the almost magical qualities attributed to it by many Conservative Ministers, and, it must be added, by some of their expert advisers. Monetary weapons alone are incapable of managing the level of demand. Changes in interest rates and in the availability of credit are not an important influence on some of the most important categories of expenditure. Nor has monetary policy been flexible and general in

---

[1] Credit for this rediscovery has been given to Enoch Powell, then a junior minister at the Treasury; see C. M. Kennedy in Worswick and Ady (eds.), *The British Economy in the 1950's*, p. 318.

its operation; it proved difficult to reduce bank advances quickly, and some types of borrower were hit hard by credit restrictions while others were left relatively untouched. During a prolonged credit squeeze there are as many leakages—due to the availability of money-substitutes—in a developed monetary system as there are loopholes in a regime of strict controls; both types of system encourage their own forms of evasion and inefficiency. As the Radcliffe Committee pointed out, "directional effects are in some degree unavoidable" and may, if ignored, be undesired and harmful. Conservative Chancellors frequently issued detailed guidance to bank managers as to which classes of borrower should be favoured or discouraged. Changes in hire-purchase regulations turn out to be one of the most effective of monetary controls, yet it is clear that these are, and perhaps need to be, discriminatory in their operation.

Ministerial exhortations were just as much a feature of Conservative as of Labour rule, but less effort was made to achieve success on the crucial wages front. The Conservatives, it seems, were unwilling to make the necessary concessions to the trade unions to achieve a genuine wages-policy bargain;[1] they preferred to confine themselves to manipulation of the general economic situation, while resorting to pleas for voluntary restraint and hoping that private initiative would coincide with the public interest. In 1957 a new tack was tried with the appointment of a Council on Prices, Productivity and Incomes consisting of "three wise men" operating outside the ordinary political and administrative sphere. The hope seems to have been that greater pressure could be brought to bear on the unions to restrain wages if the public interest in these matters was expounded by an independent body.

Conservative economic management in this period was characterized by what has been described as "backdoor intervention".[2] This underlines what was said earlier about the basic irrelevance of the party division over "planning" and "freedom". Both parties found themselves pursuing similar ends, while artificially magnifying the differences between the respective means adopted. This is not to say that there have been no differences over the ends of economic policy or over priorities among these ends. Thorneycroft's point of view would not have get very far under a Labour Government. But the important fact is that he went too far for his Conservative colleagues. On the other side too, taking recent experience into account, who can say now that a Labour Government is unwilling to sacrifice domestic employment to external stability?

---

[1] The party differences on this and other matters are discussed by S. H. Beer, *op. cit.*, pp. 362-70.

[2] By G. D. N. Worswick in *British Economy in the 1950's*, pp. 73-4.

A related aspect of Conservative thinking in the 'fifties that deserves comment was the bias in favour of "automatism". This type of thinking was influential throughout the period, but it reached its zenith with the resuscitation of the quantity theory of money under Thorneycroft. This episode was a throwback to pre-1931 gold standard ideas; the motive appears to have been a desire to evade the responsibilities of political decision-making.[1] Once more though, the real lesson lies in the fact that Thorneycroft could not carry his colleagues with him on this issue.

Ideological differences between the parties are certainly capable of influencing policy choices and styles of conduct in policy matters. The dictates of political expediency and of pressure groupings will also affect what is done and when it is done. While the Labour Party is likely to suffer from excessive optimism as to what planning can achieve, the Conservatives are prone to the opposite delusion. It may be a significant sign of convergence, however, that the early steps towards a reinstatement of planning in the early 'sixties were taken by a Conservative Government.

By the end of the 'fifties the agenda of British economic debate was firmly established. Most of the issues we continue to face had been raised, and most of the expedients open to modern governments had been tried *seriatim* and in varying combinations. General unemployment on the inter-war pattern was replaced by an unevenly rising price level as one of the continuous features of the post-war situation. After 1952 inflation could no longer be treated as a simple excess demand phenomenon, though disagreement on the relative importance of cost-push and demand-pull factors still persists. With general unemployment virtually abolished, the need for specific solutions to deal with regional unemployment and other signs of structural imbalance stood out more clearly. The necessity for some kind of incomes policy to supplement fiscal and monetary policies was widely acknowledged, though only recently has a frontal but still not entirely successful attack on this knotty problem been made.

Inflation and the failure to contain wage increases within the margin provided by increasing productivity are, of course, connected with the recurrent weakness of the British balance of payments. Given Britain's responsibilities as an international banking centre and the size of her foreign defence commitments, the state of foreign confidence and of the current account imposes a major constraint on domestic policies aimed at improving a sluggish rate of growth. The balance of payments and the defence of a particular exchange

[1] Joan Robinson's comment seems entirely fair in this context: "The enormous ideological attraction of the Quantity Theory of Money . . . is due to the fact that it conceals the problem of political choice under an apparently impersonal mechanism." *Economic Philosophy* (1962), p. 98.

rate have been the usual reasons for the changes of direction in British fiscal and monetary policy—changes which have created the typical "stop-go" cycle. These cycles in turn have impaired the growth of the economy by making long-term expansion in productive capacity difficult to sustain. Without economic growth an incomes policy becomes simply another negative restraint, and is consequently more difficult to secure. British economic policy-making can be described as a recurrent attempt to break out of this frustrating, if not actively vicious, circle of causation.

## The United States

The Congressional battle over the Employment Act, itself a continuation of early struggles within and against the New Deal, provided a foretaste of the difficulties that have since been encountered in bringing the Keynesian revolution to a successful conclusion in the United States. Engagements which were fought and won earlier in Britain have come to be fought on a continuing basis in the United States. Victory has only been partial until recently.

In spite of this, however, the post-war record represents a considerable improvement on the 'thirties. How far the improved record has been due to wise management, greater natural resilience, or to fortuitous factors arising out of the continuing high level of military expenditure, is not an easy matter to resolve. Post-war studies of American fiscal policy since the war seem to show that while the doubts and hesitations which surrounded the Employment Act, the mythology attached to balanced budgets, "fiscal responsibility" and the rest, have never been entirely absent, they have also never led to policies which were seriously in the "wrong" direction. This is not to say, however, that the "correct" action has never been impeded or tardy, or that it has never been taken for the "wrong" reasons.[1]

There have been many obstacles of an intellectual and political variety to the implementation of discretionary stabilisation policies in the United States. The overriding importance attached by many American businessmen and powerful Chairmen of Congressional Committees to the balanced budget as an end of good government and as a criterion of sound economic management is well-known. The tenacity with which this view is held in spite of the overwhelming weight of testimony as to its arbitrariness and possible damaging consequences as an aim of policy has created a major gulf

[1] See A. E. Holmans, *United States Fiscal Policy, 1945-1959* (1961), W. Lewis, *Federal Fiscal Policy in the Postwar Recessions* (1962); E. Cary Brown, "Federal Fiscal Policy in the Postwar Period" in R. Freeman, ed. *Postwar Economic Trends in the United States*, (1960).

between its proponents and the vast majority of professional economists in the United States.

The political roots of the balanced budget dogma in the American system are not hard to find. They are part and parcel of the suspicion that a profligate executive will encroach on the political and economic prerogatives of the legislature and of the business community. It can be shown, however, that under certain circumstances pursuit of annual balance in the budget will actually frustrate the cause of retrenchment and debt-reduction. It can be shown that, far from damaging the interests of the business community, deficit spending may be the only way of preventing the erosion of profits during recessions. It can be shown that the concept of a "neutral" federal budget, which somehow leaves the private sector of the economy untouched, has either no existence in reality outside of the most severe theoretical models, or would require extensive discretionary action to achieve and maintain. It can be shown that the "burden" of an increasing debt on "our grandchildren" does not exist, or rather, if it does, then it is quite different in character from the "burden" usually talked about. All to no avail. One consequence of the direct relationship between the citizen and his government which the American system of government enshrines is that illegitimate arguments based on the analogy of ordinary household prudence carry additional force.

An ingenious explanation of business opposition to deficit finance has been put forward by Sydney Alexander; he maintains that it is a *cri de coeur* based on the belief (realisation?) that acceptance of deficit spending entails a loss of status in the eyes of the public; it implies that leadership and initiative in maintaining American prosperity have passed from the businessman to the government official and the "expert".[1] Strangely enough, this view is not incompatible with pressure from the business community for government protection and assistance, nor, more strangely still, with the actual existence of deficits.

Were it not for the fact that the American constitution, with its rigid separation of powers, provides ample opportunity to frustrate and obfuscate decisive discretionary action by the executive, much of this debate could be consigned to the folk-lorist. Budgets in the United States are put together by a number of agencies within the executive branch—the Bureau of the Budget, the Treasury and the Council of Economic Advisers. The resulting tax and appropriation proposals are then submitted by the President to Congress for its approval. Tax proposals may refer to an indefinite or to a specified

---

[1] "Opposition to Deficit Spending for the Prevention of Unemployment" in *Income, Employment and Public Policy; Essays in Honour of Alvin H. Hansen* (1948).

period of operation; and all such proposals are subjected to extensive Committee hearings in both Houses of Congress, with representations from interested parties being made at all stages. A different set of Committees look into appropriations. While the executive retains greater powers over the phasing of expenditure, the time-lag in the enactment of tax proposals can be up to nine months.[1] The jealousy with which Congress regards its fiscal powers, the division of responsibility at all levels, the openings (and necessity) for private political side-dealing, make discretionary fiscal action difficult. To an outsider, the wonder is that it is even possible to conceive.

### Automatic Stabilisation

The difficulties involved in co-ordinating professional diagnosis, Presidential resolve, and Congressional approval have led to considerable emphasis being placed on automatic, as opposed to discretionary, stabilising devices. Any budgetary system in which tax receipts and government expenditures rise or fall as incomes as a whole change has a measure of built-in flexibility which operates in a stabilising direction. During a period of falling incomes and unemployment the budget naturally moves into a deficit, thereby attenuating the forces of decline. The process works in reverse as incomes rise, with the tendency to move into a surplus acting as a brake. On the tax side, the stabilising effect depends largely on the width of the tax base, the progressiveness of the tax scale, and on the proportion of tax receipts derived from items which vary markedly with changes in the level of national income. On the expenditure side, the automatic stabilising effect is greater the larger the proportion of total government expenditure spent on items that tend to rise or fall in the same direction as the economy. The typical items in this category are unemployment compensation, welfare payments, and subsidies paid to agriculture on a sliding-scale (price or income) basis. Broadly speaking, the strength of these automatic devices depends on the size of the total budget in relation to other actual or desired levels of national income.

As a result of the war there was a considerable increase in the proportion of national income passing through the government accounts, a widening of the coverage of the progressive tax system to include larger numbers of people, and a rise in the "progressiveness" of tax scales. All of these developments made it more feasible as well as politically attractive to rely on automatic stabilising devices. The errors of the post-war predictions acted in the same

[1] For a useful summary account of American procedures see A. E. Holmans, *op. cit.*, Ch. 1.

direction.[1] It could be argued that if the art of forecasting future trends was in such a crude state, the effectiveness of discretionary action was likely to be impaired, and could even be de-stabilising. Once the initial tax and expenditure structure had been settled by reference to the aim of achieving a balanced budget at a high level of employment, a built-in set of stabilisers operates without sophisticated forecasting procedures. Rules and mechanisms rather than discretionary authority are allowed to determine the course of events.

Not long after the war the Committee for Economic Development, a body composed of moderate businessmen and economists, produced a well-articulated fiscal programme for a "stabilising budget policy" based mainly on built-in flexibility.[2] As modified and strengthened, this programme provided the basis for compromise and consensus among a wide range of professional opinion in the late 'forties and early 'fifties. At the same time, however, attention was drawn to some of the weaknesses of the CED emphasis on automatism, and the remaining or implicit discretionary elements within the programme[3] At a later stage in the development of post-war policy-making more serious doubts as to the adequacy of the programme were entertained. In particular, the question was raised as to whether the automatic stabilisers, while continuing to modify the severity and duration of recessions, had not also inhibited the forces of recovery and impeded growth. As with the inter-war system of unemployment benefits in Britain, it was argued that the good was becoming an enemy of the best. As Walter Heller noted in 1957: "More progress might be made in overcoming the [rigidities] of the taxing process if reliance on fiscal automaticity and monetary manipulation did not remove some of the pressure for action."[4] For a time, though, the automatic stability approach provided a resting place; it was certainly an advance on annually balanced budgets as an aim of policy.

The fondness for automatism within the Conservative Party in

---

[1] The main source of error lay in the failure to take adequate account of the run-down of personal inventories of durable consumer goods, and of the enormous increase in liquid assets at the disposal of the public. As a result, estimates of the relationship between private consumption and income were seriously off target; see M. Sapir, "Review of Economic Forecasts for the Transition Period", in *Studies in Income and Wealth*, Vol. II, (1949). For economists the episode was a sobering one. It demonstrated that much more work was needed to improve forecasting models and estimating techniques. It reinforced the need for more detailed research into some of the variables determining consumer behaviour which lay dormant in Keynes's discussion of the problem. But while in the long run the failure of the forecasts was a stimulus to further research, in the short run it proved an embarrassment to the supporters of full employment programmes based on discretionary action.

[2] See *Taxes and the Budget: A Program for Prosperity in a Free Economy* (1947).

[3] See P. A. Samuelson, "Principles and Rules in Modern Fiscal Policy", in *Money, Trade and Economic Growth: Essays in Honour of J. H. Williams* (1951).

[4] W. Heller, "C.E.D's Stabilizing Budget Policy after Ten Years", *American Economic Review*, Sept. 1957.

Britain, and the way in which this was related to faith in the flexible stabilising powers of monetary policy, was mentioned earlier. A similar combination of beliefs, with similar ideological roots, can be found among the American proponents of automatism. But the contrasts should be noted also. The argument about rules versus authority has a long tradition in American discussions of monetary institutions and policy. The suspicion of centralised authority in the United States, and the "legalism" of American political life, which has led to attempts to define and curb the actions of authority by a system of pre-determined legal or quasi-legal rules of conduct, have no exact counterpart in British political thinking. This is largely due to the absence of a written constitution and the greater effectiveness of non-legal methods of influencing outcomes in Britain's more homogeneous culture and unified political system. Moreover, the discussion of the relative advantages of fiscal and monetary action in the United States was influenced in favour of monetary controls by the political and administrative difficulties of implementing tax changes—difficulties which again have no real counterpart in the British parliamentary system with its party discipline and clear dominance of executive functions.

## American Fiscal Policy Since the War: The Truman Administration

As in Britain, the early post-war years in the United States were taken up with the problem of containing inflationary pressures which had been pent up during the war. By 1946 fears of an imminent slump ceased to exercise much influence on policy thinking. The United States faced the problem of inflation with fewer direct controls than were possessed by British policy-makers, but also with no balance of payments worries. Congressional agitation to bring taxes down from the high war-time levels was resisted, and federal expenditure was reduced as a counter-inflationary move. It was not until the post-war re-stocking boom had run its course in 1948 that the intentions and machinery of the Employment Act were put to the test.

The response of the Truman Administration to the recession which began in this year and continued into the next was not particularly reassuring to the supporters of the Act. A tax cut proposed by a hostile Congress largely on political grounds became law only over the objections of the Administration, who believed that inflation rather than recession was the problem to be countered. The tax-cut, together with the additional appropriations required for military purposes connected with the Berlin blockade, proved fortuitously to be the right kind of medicine. In no sense can the

K*

confused arguments used to justify these actions be taken as evidence
that a conscious anti-recession policy was being pursued with any
vigour. There was still far too much talk about balanced budgets
on all sides for comfort; and it was only with considerable reluctance
that the President in mid-1949 came to accept the inevitable deficit
for that year as a necessity. It has been pointed out, however, that
even this was more than had been possible under the New Deal.[1]

During the Korean War which began in June 1950 the emphasis
shifted back once more to the problem of containing inflation—
where it was to remain for the next two years. It proved difficult but
not impossible under conditions of war to raise taxes in order to
offset some of the inflationary pressure arising out of rearmament
expenditure. Once more though, fortuitous factors connected with
the decline in domestic consumption relative to disposable income
after 1951 made the task of the Administration easier. In Britain there
was much greater willingness to deal with the situation created
by the Korean boom by means of direct controls and increases in
taxation; and there was relatively little disagreement between the
major parties on this course of action.[2] Although the episode has been
described as one in which there was a successful application of anti-
inflationary fiscal methods in the United States, it was still possible
to believe that the outcome would not have been so propitious if
Keynesian and orthodox ("paying for the war") logic had not
happened to coincide.

## The Eisenhower Administration

The change-over from a Democratic to a Republican President in
1953 provided a real test as to the acceptance by both parties of the
basic philosophy of the Employment Act. This was much more the
case than with the change from a Labour to a Conservative Government in Britain. The last Republican President before Eisenhower
had been Herbert Hoover; and the Employment Act can hardly
be described as bi-partisan in the same sense that the British White
Paper was. "Keynesianism" was still regarded by many Republicans
as a Democratic Party doctrine, irrevocably associated with the New
Deal.

During his campaign Eisenhower made full use of traditional
Republican slogans; he would eliminate the budget deficit, bring
taxes down, reduce the overall size of the budget, and wage war on
inflation. The early measures of the new Administration, aided by

---

[1] W. A. Lewis, *op. cit.*, p. 117.
[2] For a comparison of the responses in Britain and the U.S.A. at this tie seme A. E.
Holmans, *op. cit.*, pp. 192-4.

the fall in military expenditure, were fully in line with these slogans. The first crop of Cabinet appointments were all men with business experience, orthodox in their economic pronouncements and hostile to the concept of "big" government. It was not even certain that the Council of Economic Advisors, which had come under Congressional fire at the end of the Truman Administration, would have its appropriations, and therefore its licence to exist, renewed.

The last point was the first to be settled when Eisenhower recruited a new Council of Economic Advisers under the chairmanship of Arthur Burns. It seemed to be significant of a new line in economic policy that he should favour an economist who was non-Keynesian, if not actually anti-Keynesian, in his thinking. Burns was noted as a specialist in business cycles along the lines established by Wesley Mitchell and the National Bureau of Economic Research, which entailed careful study of the historical record of cyclical activity. At the end of the war Burns had written a thoughtful critique of Keynesian thinking in which he refused to accept many features of the Keynesian theory ("a speculative analysis of uncertain value"), and was dubious as to whether governments would be able to honour their commitment to maintain full employment.[1] In office, he accepted the responsibility of the government to prevent large-scale collapse by means of fiscal and monetary weapons. True to his background though, Burns's thinking remained fairly firmly within the contra-cyclical mould. But coming as he did to office at a time when the future of the Council of Economic Advisers was in doubt, and when the activities of Senator Joseph McCarthy made the government service distinctly less attractive to many academic economists, Burns exerted a moderating and educative influence on the potentially retrogressive forces at work within the Eisenhower Administration.[2]

Half-way through the first year of the Eisenhower Administration it became clear that a recession was in prospect, hastened or perhaps even initiated by the cut-back in defence expenditure after Korea. Under pressure from the Democratic opposition, the Administration reassured the public that they were determined to use their fiscal, monetary and other powers to combat recession. A tax reduction proposed earlier for old-fashioned political and budgetary reasons was hurried to the fore as a counter-recessionary device; a restrictive monetary policy was quickly reversed; and a host of supporting measures, including a speed-up of expenditure programmes, was undertaken. Although criticisms have been made of the timidity and

[1] *Economic Research and the Keynesian Thinking of Our Times*, (1946). See also, Burns's exchange with Hansen in the *Review of Economics and Statistics*, Nov. 1947.
[2] E. S. Flash, *Economic Advice and Presidential Leadership* (1965), Ch. IV.

opportunism of the Administration's response, and of the premature withdrawal of support during recovery, there is no doubt that the episode shows clear signs of *de facto* Republican acceptance of fiscal management responsibilities. Automatic rather than discretionary fiscal action may have been more important in offsetting the decline in activity, but as Paul Samuelson has pointed out, "no responsible person in either political party came forward . . . to suggest that the built-in stabilisers of our system be vitiated by the perverse discretionary action of raising tax rates in order to avoid budget unbalance".[1] It could certainly be maintained that the Republican response in 1953–4 was neither better nor worse than the handling by the Democratic Administration of the 1948–9 recession.[2]

### Retrogression and New Causes for Concern

As was true to a lesser extent under the Conservatives in Britain, however, the upswing of economic activity in the mid-fifties led to a revival of outmoded forms of traditional wisdom. In the United States the most common form of this wisdom turned on the concept of balanced budgets. As sermons by Eisenhower and his Secretary of the Treasury, George Humphrey, on the virtues of restricting federal expenditure, and on the disasters of budget deficits, became more frequent, the gap between professional and political economic opinion widened.[3] Although another recession was more or less successfully weathered in 1957–9, the actual performance of the American economy provided increasing cause for concern. Retrogression in economic thinking seemed to be matched by retrograde tendencies at work in the economy itself. The increasing emphasis on the self-sustaining capacity of America's private enterprise system, and on the dangers of inflation, seemed to be accompanied by growing complacency about the level of unemployment. Many American economists began to feel that the situation called for a re-affirmation of the Keynesian ideals expressed in the Employment Act.[4]

Between 1947 and 1953 the average rate of unemployment in the United States was 4%; between 1954 and 1963 this figure had risen to

[1] "The Economics of Eisenhower: A Symposium", *Review of Economics and Statistics*, November 1956, p. 372. See also E. Cary Brown, *op. cit.*, pp. 164-70.
[2] See A. E. Holmans, "The Eisenhower Adminstration and the Recession, 1953-5, *Oxford Economic Papers*, Feb. 1958, p. 53.
[3] It was merely one facet of the anti-intellectualism which seemed to cling to the Eisenhower era. After 1956 Arthur Burns's moderating influence on the economic pronouncements of the Administration was absent. Humphrey's presence at the Treasury had driven out most of the economists from that department much earlier.
[4] In 1962, for example, *New Republic* mounted a symposium entitled "Time for a Keynes?" For a strong revival of the charges made by Keynes in the inter-war period, see J. M. Culbertson, *Full Employment or Stagnation?* (1964).

$5\frac{1}{2}\%$, with a peak level approaching $7\%$. The recovery phase of each succeeding recession was weaker and left behind it a large number of unemployed. Recovery from the 1957–9 recession was hardly complete when another dip occurred in 1960. A number of basic questions were raised: Had a state of under-employment equilibrium been reached which required the firm application of Keynesian techniques for raising the level of effective demand? Or were there reasons to believe that the unemployment was of a new type and therefore less amenable to such techniques? Was it, for instance, brought about by changes in the structural characteristics of the American economy which the labour market was less able to absorb? Was it the result of an accelerated rate of technical innovation, automation, and changes in the age and educational composition of the work-force?[1] In view of the high incidence of unemployment in certain areas and industries, and among certain groups within the population, notably non-whites and the poorly-educated, the problem of unemployment could be seen as part of a far wider problem of poverty, social tension, and cultural deprivation.[2]

Attention was also focused on what was regarded as an unsatisfactory growth rate when compared with the Soviet Union, Japan, and most European countries—only Britain was below the United States in the growth league table. Left and right in the political spectrum could be united by the promise of having more resources to devote to the space and arms race and to welfare services; by the prospect of rising standards of living for all, and by an expanding job market for a growing population. Here too, faster economic growth was connected with fundamental issues concerning the quality of American life and values. The Russian sputnik had made it necessary to look at the American educational system. Were enough public resources being devoted to it? What contribution could extra investment in education make to faster growth? Was Galbraith right in his belief that private affluence amid public squalor was the prime characteristic of the American version of the capitalist system?[3] If so, how should growth and/or a reallocation of social priorities towards public and away from private needs be accomplished?[4]

At the same time other factors made the problem of managing the American economy more difficult. In the late 'fifties a new kind of conflict between high levels of employment and rising prices had

[1] For a useful selection of views from a vast literature see S. Lebergott. (ed.), *Men Without Work* (1964) and A. M. Ross (ed.) *Unemployment and the American Economy* (1962.)

[2] Two influential works on poverty have been M. Harrington, *The Other America* (1962) and G. Myrdal, *Challenge to Affluence* (1964).

[3] *The Affluent Society* (1958).

[4] For representative samples of the literature produced by this debate see G. M. Gutmann (ed.) *Economic Growth, An American Problem*, (1964) and E. S. Phelps (ed.) *The Goal of Economic Growth*, (1962).

arisen, making the choice between the two more divisive. Prices continued to rise even when there was considerable slack in the economy. Moreover, after 1958 the state of the United States balance of payments began to loom large as a constraint on domestic fiscal and monetary policies. The surplus on current account was no longer sufficiently large to bear the strain of an enlarged overseas aid, defence, and investment programme. Gold outflows and rising short-term liabilities forced American policy-makers to consider the the state of foreign confidence, thereby placing them in a similar position to that occupied by their British counterparts for the whole of the post-war period.

## The Kennedy-Johnson Administration

There seems little doubt that future historians will regard the debate on economic and social priorities which took place towards the end of the 'fifties and the early 'sixties as one of the most sustained and far-reaching upheavals in American intellectual and political history. It was against this background that John F. Kennedy was elected in 1960 on a promise of "getting the country moving again" after a period of torpor and passivity. In keeping with the broad Democratic tradition, he claimed that he would make more active use of the powers of the federal government. On the economic front he pledged himself to a reduction in the level of unemployment and to a higher rate of growth.

Presidential terms of office provide a more significant way of dividing American history than do, say, the reigns of monarchs or the periods of office of different Prime Ministers to the historian of modern Britain. And while the shortcomings of writing economic history in terms of four-year periods are more apparent than they would be when writing political history, the enormous powers which the American presidency confer on an individual make the division an important one to any history of economic policy-making. The change-over from Eisenhower to Kennedy illustrates the way in which the balance between the elements of continuity and novelty in policy formulation can gradually but decisively be shifted.

From the outset there was one very important agency at work within the Kennedy Administration making for a change of direction in economic policy—expert economic advice. Enough has been written by and about the "new frontiersmen" to make detailed comment here unnecessary.[1] Coming after an Administration which

[1] Apart from the two major accounts of the Kennedy Presidency by A. M. Schlesinger and T. C. Sorensen, more germane to this book are J. Tobin, *The Intellectual Revolution in U.S. Economic Policy-Making* (1966) and Walter H. Heller, *New Dimensions of Political Economy* (1966).

was not exactly renowned for its intellectual adventurousness, Kennedy's promise of an active use of the powers of his office to deal with America's problems attracted enthusiastic support from many intellectuals, and not least from professional economists. It has been said that a training in economics inculcates a conservative outlook; that the student acquires a healthy scepticism towards enlarged schemes of social improvement.[1] It is also worth bearing in mind that economists are attracted to situations in which it seems likely that there will be opportunities for implementing their ideas. This was certainly the case under Kennedy.[2] A large number of distinguished academic economists descended on Washington to serve the new Administration in one capacity or another.[3]

One of Kennedy's earliest appointments was that of Walter Heller to the post of Chairman of the Council of Economic Advisers. Heller was explicitly entrusted with the job of returning "to the spirit as well as the letter of the Employment Act".[4] A special task force under the leadership of Paul Samuelson was also appointed to make an appraisal of the current recession and to recommend steps to deal with it. The report submitted by this group made an important distinction between the immediate recession and the more fundamental problem of underlying sluggishness in the economy. Measures designed to deal with the former should merely be a preliminary step towards, and not a substitute for, more thorough-going remedies to deal with the latter.

True to its origins this report was thoroughly Keynesian in its orientation. The balance of payments was a constraint, but "it would be unthinkable for a present-day American government to deliberately countenance high unemployment as a mechanism for adjusting to the balance of payments deficit". Similarly with inflation: if prices and wages showed a tendency to rise before a satisfactory level of employment was reached, there should be no curtailment of expansionary monetary and fiscal policies; rather they should be supplemented by a direct attack on the cost-push problem. As a "first line of defence" they recommended the following: a speed-up of existing expenditure programmes, including any increases in defence expenditure that could be justified on their own merits; an expansion of welfare programmes including an extension of the

---

[1] See G. J. Stigler, "The Politics of Political Economists" in his *Essays in the History of Economics* (1964).

[2] It was true also for a time under the Labour Government in Britain after 1963. Some contrasts between the role of the economic adviser in the British and American systems of government are considered pp. 331-6 below.

[3] Of the many who could be named the following are probably best known: Walter Heller, Paul Samuelson, J. K. Galbraith, James Tobin, James Duesenberry, Otto Eckstein Arthur Okun, Gardner Ackley, Seymour Harris, Robert Solow, Kermit Gordon, Gerhard Colm, Walter Salant, Joseph Pechman and Charles Schultze.

[4] See E. S. Flash, *op. cit.*, p. 175.

existing, hard-pressed, unemployment compensation system; an increase in public works programmes in a number of areas; and encouragement to housing through the Federal Housing Administration.

In view of the balance of payments situation, the Samuelson task force advised that less use could be made of easy credit conditions; this would bring down short-term interest rates but might cause an outflow of foreign funds. Nevertheless, they recommended that an effort should be made through debt-management policies to bring down long-term interest rates—the rates most likely to influence investment spending. As a second line of defence they advised recourse to a temporary tax cut, partly on the grounds that it was the kind of stimulus most likely to be acceptable to orthodox opinion in Congress and abroad. On the whole it was a conservative document, especially in its sensitivity to conventional budgetary feelings; but it contained in essence much that was done later.[1]

In the first year of his presidency Kennedy adopted most of the first line of defence measures suggested by the task force, adding to them a large variety of programmes of a structural or reformist nature to deal with specific anomalies, shortcomings, and bottlenecks. Like Roosevelt, Kennedy found it easier at the outset to achieve reformist aims than to move towards the major economic goals outlined in his election addresses. As Schlesinger says, the early measures constituted "a programme of welfare, perhaps a programme to end the recession, but not a programme of economic expansion".[2] Although most of his economic advisers were in favour of a temporary tax cut, neither Kennedy nor his Secretary to the Treasury, Douglas Dillon, were prepared initially to take this step. Kennedy was willing to allow a deficit to develop within the budgetary framework set by his predecessor, but he would not countenance any measure which entailed deliberate deficit finance. In this quarter at least, continuity was maintained. The most the President was willing to do at this stage was to pledge himself "to a Federal revenue system that balanced the budget over the years of the cycle".

Kennedy's economic understanding may not have developed sufficiently by 1961 for him to have accepted, even privately, deliberate deficit finance. There were, in addition, strong political reasons for proceeding with caution. In spite of the underlying reality of budget deficits, the Eisenhower Administration had succeeeded in covering its affairs in a mantle of fiscal righteousness. Kennedy felt vulnerable to the charge of fiscal irresponsibility; he had called for

---

[1] The report appeared under the title "Economic Frontiers" in M. B. Schnapper (ed.) *New Frontiers of the Kennedy Administration*, (1961).
[2] *A Thousand Days* (1965), p. 548.

sacrifices and could not reconcile this with tax-cuts. He did not wish to jeopardise the rest of his legislative programme by arousing Congressional suspicions. It was fortunate, therefore, that political circumstance, in the form of the Berlin crisis in the summer of 1961, played into Kennedy's hands. It enabled him, with good conscience, to increase the annual rate of expenditure on defence by $3 billion. As we now know this bonus was nearly nullified by a proposal to raise taxes to cover the extra defence spending. In persuading the President to withdraw the tax-increase proposals, his economic advisers scored a significant minor victory in the battle for economic rationality. But they could not prevent him from announcing that he intended to balance the 1962–3 budget.

By the end of 1962, however, there was a convergence of economic advice and Presidential pronouncement; the gap between ideology and rationality, between appearance and reality, was being closed. It took another two years, and, perforce, another President, to bring Congressional and business opinion to something approaching the same state of understanding. This can roughly be said to have occurred when Congressional approval was obtained for a permanent tax-cut in 1964, when the budget was still unbalanced, and under conditions that in previous years would have been regarded as showing clear signs of recovery. Instead of being regarded as the royal road to ruin, deficits were embraced as a deliberate stimulus to higher levels of employment and rates of growth. For his part in this episode it has been said of Kennedy that "he was unquestionably the first Keynesian President".[1]

## What has been achieved?

The victory that has been scored for Keynesian principles under Kennedy and Johnson has been celebrated on all sides. But what exactly has been achieved and is it likely to be permanent? There have been so many victories turned sour in the history of the pursuit of Keynesian objectives in the United States that scepticism seems to be the safest course. The enthusiasm of Kennedy's admirers and advisers is understandable; but have they allowed themselves to be swayed by their hopes, perhaps even by their own eloquence? The general tenour of comment is so "up-tempo" that there may be some danger of reality being obscured by the enormous public relations task necessary to achieve the tax-cut. To the British

[1] A. M. Schlesinger, *op. cit.*, p. 549. The decisive intellectual turning point in a story which is packed with turning points of one sort or another is generally regarded as having taken place in a speech made by Kennedy at the Yale Commencement in June 1962. This speech has been described by Heller (*op. cit.*, p. 37) as "the most literate and sophisticated dissertation on economics ever delivered by a President".

observer, less used to a political system in which legal forms are so important, and where so much business is conducted in open forum, it may seem that excessive attention is paid to slogans, and even to the qualifying phrases in official statements and handouts. And after all, even if it is all true and permanent, does it not simply place the United States where most European countries have been for many years?

The first answer to these questions is that the tax-cut actually worked—and more importantly perhaps, has been seen to work—in more or less the fashion predicted by the experts. In the five years after the modest beginning of the Kennedy programme in 1961, and before escalation of the war in Vietnam late in 1965 began to exercise a new, and potentially inflationary, boost, the American economy enjoyed its longest post-war boom. Unemployment was brought down from over 7% to 4 %, and the annual growth rate was raised from below 3% to over 5%. The post-war pattern of recessions seems to have been broken. And all this was achieved with a very modest rise in the price level because of the simultaneous increase in productivity. As a result, both profits and real wages have risen sharply. To round off what has been correctly described as a text-book success, the budget moved into surplus in 1965. The only critics have been those reformers and liberal expansionists who favoured increased federal spending on poverty, welfare, and cultural programmes, rather than tax-cuts as a means of stimulating the economy.[1]

But Keynesians in the United States are fully aware of the dubious, if temporarily beneficial, features of a success story which for most people is based simply on *post hoc, ergo propter hoc* reasoning. They are also aware of some of the dangerous concessions that were made to the ideology of balanced budgets in order to overcome that ideology.[2] In 1962, for example, the tax-cut was justified on the grounds that it was the best way of ensuring a balanced budget in the near future—an argument which could prove embarrassing at some future date since it implies that virtue attaches to balanced budgets *per se*. Economic logic alone would require agnosticism on the question of whether deficits and surpluses over any given period should exactly offset each other. In political economy, as Paul Samuelson has pointed out, "two wrongs *may* come nearer to a right *than one alone*".[3] Real and permanent success can only come from a

---

[1] As an example of this point of view see R. Lekachman, *The Age of Keynes* (1967), pp. 248-255.
[2] See W. Heller, *New Dimension of Political Economy*, p. 30-41 and K. Gordon, "Reflections on Public Spending", *Public Policy*, Vol. XV., 1966.
[3] "Economic Policy for 1962", *Review of Economics and Statistics*, February 1962, p. 6.

genuine intellectual revolution which replaces old fetishes not with new ones, but with a genuinely rational approach to the problems of economic management. In the nature of things the successful completion of an intellectual revolution is more difficult to establish; it requires an educational process to bring politicians and leaders of public opinion to a state of understanding approaching that of the professional economic community. In the United States system of government this requires not merely the conversion of an inner élite, as in Britain, but a massive turn-around in the views of the public, its Congressional representatives, and business leaders.

It would certainly seem as though there has been a "narrowing of the intellectual gap between professional economists and men of affairs" in recent years.[1] Rarely in the history of economics can economists, the custodians of the "dismal science", have enjoyed so much public esteem and trust as they have in the United States in recent years. It may even survive the first occasion on which economists advise that in the interests of economic health taxes and interest rates will have to be raised. Twenty years after his death Keynes's picture was featured on the cover of *Time* magazine. A few weeks later *Business Week* weighed in with its own contribution, in which it was stated that the prestige of economists had been raised "to an all-time high" by the last five years of expansion.[2] It would be expecting too much of economists not to preen themselves a little. Intellectual victories of this kind are rare anywhere, let alone in the United States.

Although to Kennedy and Johnson must go the credit for political courage and tenacity in putting the expansionary programme over, the palm must go to their economic advisers for devising the necessary measures, and for waging a sustained campaign on their behalf. In one respect, of course, the tools were not new; they were part of the Keynesian inheritance. But American economists have perhaps been excessively modest in their claims on this point. There were special obstacles to the acceptance of an expansionary fiscal policy in the United States. In overcoming these, American economists have done more than wipe the slate clean; they have forged tools of economic management and devised new standards of economic performance that have carried our understanding of these matters further forward. There are few countries where official statements of policy have been on such a consistently high level of sophistication as they have in the United States since 1961. The Kennedy-Johnson team of advisers has clarified the issues which many

[1] W. Heller, *op. cit.*, p. 1, and J. Tobin, *op. cit.*, pp. 1-2.
[2] See *Time*, December 31st 1965 and *Business Week*, Feb. 5th 1966.

countries, not merely the United States, will have to face in the second half of the twentieth century.

Some of the intellectual obstacles that had to be overcome have their counterpart in the inter-war discussions. James Tobin has drawn attention to three of these: the cyclical view, the structural interpretation of unemployment, and the balanced budget dogma. The idea of the cycle as an inherent feature of American capitalism limits stabilisation policy to the task of moderating excessive tendencies for activity to depart from a statically-defined middle position. This type of thinking leads also to what Tobin has called the "first derivative obsession": as long as the direction of movement seems to be satisfactory, less attention need be paid to a comparison of the levels actually achieved with what could be achieved with full employment and a higher rate of growth. Structural explanations of the American unemployment problem were put forward by various groups: by those who regarded it as a regrettable but unavoidable by-product of rapid technological progress, and by those who saw it as providing grounds for large-scale reform coupled with federal spending programmes in special areas and on specially deprived sections of the population. In both cases it tended to obscure the macro-economic problem arising out of a deficiency of aggregate demand. The obstacle posed by balanced budgets is more obvious and has been dealt with already.

All of these obstacles have gradually been overcome. The structural diagnosis acquired great strength from its appeal to ordinary common-sense. Structural change, in the form of shifts in the allocation of resources, adaptation to new methods, and changes in the demographic composition of the labour force, occurs constantly in a dynamic economy. There was no lack of ingenious *ad hoc* explanations as to why this or that group was differentially affected by unemployment. One by one these explanations were scrutinised and found wanting. None of them was capable of bearing the burden of showing why the labour market had become less and less capable of adjusting to technical and demographic change.[1] The Council of Economic Advisers was able to demonstrate that the structural component in the higher unemployment figures was extremely small; that it provided no grounds for believing that the Council's target rate of 4% unemployment could not be reached without special labour market policies such as manpower re-training schemes. They fully accepted that once this interim target was reached by ordinary Keynesian methods, it would become necessary to institute such policies in order to reduce unemployment further

---

[1] For a review of the evidence see Robert M. Solow, *The Nature and Sources of Unemployment in the United States*, Wicksell Lectures 1964.

without adding to price and cost pressures. Their arguments were not incompatible with measures to improve labour mobility and to cushion the effects of unemployment on those sharply effected; still less were they thought of as alternatives to more direct methods of dealing with the cost-push problem. But they were meant to establish better perspectives and priorities. Only with the economy working at full stretch would it be possible to see where new employment opportunities would have to be created by other methods.

Taking the target of 4% unemployment as given, and assuming a $3\frac{1}{2}$% annual rate of growth in real GNP, the Council was able to calculate the gap between actual and potential GNP at full employment. This gap provided an estimate of the loss of output and government revenues which could be attributed to unemployment; and it underlined the need to keep demand expanding each year to prevent the gap from widening. It was a marked advance on cyclical assessments of policy tasks and achievements. As with the inflationary gap analysis used during the war, the new "performance gap" had to be stated in fairly precise quantitative terms in order to be useful for policy-formation purposes. The improvement in forecasting techniques since the war was therefore a necessary preliminary to the restatement of policy aims in terms of future growth possibilities.[1]

Related to the concept of a performance gap at full employment was the idea that a growing economy with an unchanged tax structure and level of government expenditure tends to exert a "fiscal drag" on the system. The growth of the economy itself automatically produces a movement towards a budgetary surplus (or reduction of deficit), which, if uncorrected, acts as a deflationary influence. To assess the direction and magnitude of the fiscal policy needed to keep the economy on target required a new measure of budgetary surpluses or deficits—one which would enable a distinction to be made between the actual outcome and the desired budgetary outcome at full employment growth. Such a measure showed by how much, for example, taxes would need to be reduced or federal expenditures increased, in order to offset the automatic tendencies towards a full employment surplus. The basic idea was to draw attention to the desired state of the economy rather than the actual trend in the state of the government's finances.

The clarification which has been achieved does not, of course, support policies of annual tax-reduction alone. The American debate has now shifted to the more interesting question of how the fiscal dividends from growth and full employment should be used. It could be for the purposes of expanding private and public investment in the interests of even faster growth; it could be to reduce taxes and

[1] See W. Heller, *op. cit.*, pp. 61-2.

thereby pass on to the consumer the fruits of American growth. To the Galbraith-Hansen school of thought, neither of these alternatives is acceptable; they would prefer to see fiscal dividends ploughed back in the form of federal programmes to tackle poverty and improve the quality of the American social and cultural environment. In both cases, however, there is a sense in which, in contrast to Britain, the American debate has moved on to more significant questions.

# CHAPTER FOURTEEN

# Postscript: Economics and Policy in the Post-Keynesian Era

Unlike the United States, there has been no recent dramatic triumph in British economic policy to celebrate. Quite the reverse. In neither country, however, can economic policy-making be said to have emerged onto a sunlit plateau. That would not be consistent with the nature of the problems being tackled: it would require a society in which the economic and other goals were fixed, perfectly compatible with one another, and agreed on by all sections of the population. Mere acceptance of responsibility for economic management, of course, is no guarantee of success in carrying out those responsibilities. Many of the tools of management have proved to be inadequate; and where successes have been registered this has served to raise the standards by which we judge success in related fields. Are there any lessons of a general kind to be drawn from the British and American experience of economic policy-making in the post-war period?

In both countries there have been cases where ideology has impeded economic understanding and action. But there is also evidence to suggest that ideology can be overcome if the tools of economic analysis and the appropriate tests are sufficiently precise to show that reality and intention are too far apart for political and economic comfort. The acceptance of Keynesian economics as a technocratic device does not reduce economic policy-making itself to a technocratic pursuit; there is no end of ideology in sight. What it should do, however, by removing certain myths, is to clear the way for more significant debate on the value-choices still facing modern industrial societies.

It was feared by some that possession of Keynesian techniques would create new hazards in the form of political trade cycles; economic management would become a modern form of gerrymandering as politicians strove to create short-term economic conditions favourable to electoral success. While there have been cases which appear to confirm this view, many British politicians will testify to the fact that in the main the opposite has been true, namely that additional responsibilities in the economic sphere have increased the possibilities and penalties for failure. There have been occasions on which, it seems likely, they would gladly have exchanged their present exposed position for one in which economic conditions were still believed to be as uncontrollable as the British climate. This may account for the periodic attempts to revive doctrines which imply that the economic system is simply an automatic mechanism which only needs freedom from intervention to produce the most expedient and just results.

Like it or not, we have entered into an era not merely of extensive state involvement in economic affairs but of continuous and detailed economic management. In most cases it is no longer so much a question of whether the state should or should not possess certain powers, but how those powers can best be used to achieve consciously chosen ends. The powers involved are not necessarily those pertaining to centralised control and direction. More frequently they are of a negative kind—they entail decisions as to how certain functions should be ordered so as *not* to frustrate the attainment of other goals. Moreover, one of the main political consequences of the managed economy is that, as governments extend their responsibilities, it becomes more and more important for them to obtain the advice, consent and participation of the main producer groups.[1]

### Post-Keynesian Economic Management

Many important lessons of a more technical kind have been learnt about the tools of economic management, their uses and limitations. Nowhere perhaps is this more true than in the case of fiscal policy. We have come a long way since the *General Theory* and the inter-war discussions of public works policies. In this respect the British White Paper on Employment Policy, with its almost exclusive emphasis on contra-cyclical variations in public investment, marks the end of an era rather than the beginning of significant debate in Britain on fiscal policy.[2]

Over the post-war period in Britain there have been frequent attempts to exert control over the level of public investment as part of a general strategy for reducing the pressure of demand, notably during crises; but these efforts have never been made to bear the brunt of the tasks of management. There are good reasons for this, which apply also to the United States. Public investment and public spending generally, especially on defence and welfare services, represent fairly fixed commitments of a long-term nature; they are

---

[1] See S. H. Beer, *Modern British Politics* (1965), pp. 319-339.
[2] In the United States, for reasons given in the previous chapters, contra-cyclical ideas have had a stronger hold.

difficult to scale down quickly enough in order to deal with the kinds of fluctuations that have occurred since the war.[1] Many would feel too that the state of our social overhead capital is not such that we can afford to make it the scapegoat when things go wrong elsewhere. The case for public investment and for an improvement in the quality and scope of the services provided by the public sector should not turn exclusively on the exigencies of short-term economic management. It is fortunate perhaps that those Keynesians who advocated a massive expansion of the public sector after the war—partly on the grounds that it would guarantee full employment—were wide of the mark in their predictions. Under conditions of full and over-full employment they would have undermined their own cause by furnishing support for cuts in public expenditure. By a round-about route Keynesianism would have led back to the kind of conclusion reached by the May Committee in 1931.

Post-war stabilisation policy in Britain has mainly been conducted in terms of tax changes designed, for example, to stimulate private investment, and, more importantly from a quantitative point of view, to influence consumer spending by altering the level of disposable income. Changes in hire purchase regulations, interest rates, and the availability of credit, have mostly played second fiddle to tax changes as methods of controlling the level of demand. Here at least British Chancellors of the Exchequer are in a much more powerful position than American Presidents.[2] Party discipline in Parliament enables tax changes to be introduced in the budget and implemented immediately; additional flexibility has been acquired since 1961 by the introduction of powers to vary indirect taxation on a discretionary basis.[3]

Although several proposals have been put forward to give the American President modest discretionary or standby powers to vary taxes, Congress has so far been unwilling to forfeit its prerogatives in fiscal matters.[4] While traditionally it is more difficult for politicians to raise rather than lower taxes, it is heartening that in neither Britain nor the United States has the fear that *for this reason* Keynesian policies would be biased in favour of inflation proved to be true over the long haul.[5]

---

[1] On this see J. C. R. Dow, *The Management of the British Economy* (1964), Ch. VIII.

[2] A fact to which Kennedy himself drew envious attention, see A. M. Schlesinger, *A Thousand Days* (1966), p. 853.

[3] The outcome of more recent innovations in the form of the Selective Employment Tax is still problematical.

[4] See W. Heller, *New Dimensions in Political Economy* (1966), pp. 99-104. The political haggling which took place during the 1968 world gold crisis over President Johnson's request for an increase in taxes shows how dangerous the absence of Presidential discretionary powers can be.

[5] It is more true of Britain perhaps than the United States, owing to the difficulty of making any kind of tax change under the American system. On this point see J. C. R. Dow, *op. cit.*, pp. 212-13 and A. E. Holmans, *United States Fiscal Policy, 1945-59* (1961), Ch. XV.

Flexibility of response to changes in economic conditions is vital to modern fiscal policy. Much of the thinking of the inter-war and immediate post-war period was concerned with the cruder problems of countering massive deflationary or inflationary forces. Maintenance of full employment without inflation poses far more delicate problems of magnitude and timing than does the achievement of full employment in the first place. The "right" policy administered at the "wrong" time or in the "wrong" dosage can by itself be a source of instability. Hence the view that having rid ourselves of "natural" cycles we have been saddled with others of our own creation. But while it is sometimes important to take speedy corrective action, it is also possible for policy to become excessively concerned with short-term results to the detriment of long-term performance. The American example in recent years shows how important it is to draw up new standards of performance from time to time, in order to show the relationship between short-term policy action and the achievement of long-term goals. While sterling and balance of payments crises continue to plague British policy-makers it will be difficult to emulate the American example.[1]

It has been pointed out on many occasions that stabilisation policies are only as good as the information on which they are based; and reliable and up-to-date information about the present or recent past is just as important as accurate forecasts of the future. Nobody would deny that the art of economic forecasting is still at an early stage of development, though it has certainly improved considerably on early post-war efforts. Indeed, one of the most important developments in economics since the war has been in the field of econometrics, that branch of economics devoted to theory testing by means of mathematical models into which estimated numerical parameters can be inserted.

Keynes himself was unsympathetic towards this type of mathematical and statistical exercise, and the British government has so far been less willing to commit itself to the formal procedures of econometric forecasting than other governments—the Netherlands for example.[2] Nevertheless, advances are being made in this field, and they may eventually abolish the casual, if inspired, empiricism of men like Keynes. Greater sophistication in the use of procedures to test theory against a highly complex reality is already one of the marks of modern economics. It has led to a considerable reconciliation

---

[1] For comment on this problem see I. M. D. Little, "Fiscal Policy" in Worswick and Ady (eds.), *The British Economy in the 1950's* (1962), pp. 274-8, and J. C. R. Dow, *op. cit.*, Ch. XVI.

[2] For an unfavourable comparison of British methods with those employed in the Netherlands see R. L. Marris, "The Position of Economics and Economists in the Government Machine", *Economic Journal*, December 1954.

between "pure" theory and applied economics; and it is no longer quite so easy to divide economists in terms of their allegiance to one or other of these complementary pursuits. It may be that the offspring Keynes himself disowned will prove to be his most important legacy to economics.

Ignoring the future of econometrics, however, it is worth bearing in mind Dow's conclusion after examining the post-war economic record in Britain, that, although some policy mistakes can be imputed to faulty forecasts, "this by no means implies that policy would have been better if there had been no forecasts of a formal sort".[1]

It is sometimes claimed that we have entered a post-Keynesian era in which the accepted Keynesian nostrums are inappropriate or inadequate. Ever since the 'thirties critics have maintained that Keynesian economics is relevant only to the short-term problems of a world of heavy unemployment; that it is of limited value to one in which inflation and the long-term problems of economic growth in developed and underdeveloped countries are uppermost in men's minds. Keynes's *How to Pay for the War* and the comparative successes of war and post-war economic management have scotched some of these views, certainly as far as demand-inflation is concerned. But is Keynesian economics relevant to the problem of cost-inflation which many regard as the new and unsolved problem of the 'sixties? Does it provide any clues to the problem of achieving a faster rate of economic growth? What relevance, if any, does it have to the age-old problems of how best to allocate scarce resources and distribute the social dividend?

The maintenance of high levels of employment for long periods has brought with it new difficulties as well as leaving us free to consider problems that were previously thrust into the background or ignored. We face questions which Keynes either assumed away or did not foresee in his writings. This is hardly surprising after over thirty years. It would be disturbing if the situation were otherwise.[2] The most important change in the agenda of economic debate in the years since the Second World War falls outside the scope of this study. It concerns the problems of the underdeveloped world, for which solutions are now more insistently demanded than in the past. For political, economic, and moral reasons the enquiry into the causes and remedies for the poverty of the majority of the world's population now occupies a large proportion of the attention of economists in all

---

[1] *Op. cit.*, p. 143.
[2] Witness the situation in the international monetary field, where we are still struggling unsuccessfully to implement solutions that were clearly spelled out by Keynes at Bretton Woods in 1944, and in writings that go back to 1933 and possibly earlier.

countries. In one sense, of course, these problems are far from novel. Long-term economic development formed the centre-piece of classical economic analysis from Adam Smith to John Stuart Mill. And while Keynesian economics sheds light on certain limited features of the underdevelopment problem, it has by no means made the classical (or even the neo-classical) approach to such questions irrelevant or outmoded. Indeed, the intractability of the problem not only compels humility but has led to a more sympathetic reappraisal of classical insights.[1]

But while we have undoubtedly moved on in many respects, or have been forced to look elsewhere for guidance, it is also possible to exaggerate the *post*-Keynesian nature of the present discontents of developed nations such as Britain and the United States.

### Cost-Inflation and Incomes Policy

In recent years it has been argued that a new type of inflation has made its presence felt in developed capitalist societies like Britain and the United States; that the main source of upward pressure on the price level is no longer of the conventional Keynesian, demand-pull type, but derives directly from wage and cost movements. Cost-inflation, it is claimed, is less amenable to—or even immune from— Keynesian techniques for manipulating the level of aggregate demand; wages and prices, the argument goes, have continued to rise well before full capacity output is reached. Policies to reduce demand have resulted in falling output and rising unemployment without stopping the rise in prices.

Whether or not this is adequate evidence for the autonomous existence of cost-inflation or whether it merely shows that inflation can only be avoided by tolerating higher levels of unemployment, or running the economy at a lower pressure of demand, need not be discussed here. It is sufficient to say that interest is concentrated more and more on the processes by which wages and prices are fixed, with the object of seeing whether by some kind of incomes and prices policy, working with or without aggregate demand techniques, this problem can be brought under control. The effect of this has been that governments have had to descend from the macro-economic heights of the economy in order to exert direct influence on the wage and price-fixing institutions of particular industries. In some cases this has taken the form of dramatic interventions in key industries, such as Kennedy's successful confrontation with the steel companies in 1962, while in others it has taken the form of setting overall

---

[1] See L. Robbins, *The Theory of Economic Development in the History of Economic Thought* (1968) for a survey of classical and other contributions.

guidelines or norms within which wage and salary settlements are supposed to take place.

While it is true that these questions currently occupy a high place on the policy agenda, it is not clear that they represent a departure from the broad Keynesian framework. In the same way that present-day fiscal policy has had to be a good deal more sophisticated and flexible than the inter-war discussions of public works spending would suggest, we now find that in order to achieve a satisfactory reconciliation of conflicting policy-aims, direct planning and control of the way in which incomes and prices are settled is necessary. It may be that the situation is the result of running a modern economy at high levels of employment for longer periods than have been achieved before, *combined with* our existing wage-fixing and price-setting institutions. But it cannot be claimed that in seeking to control incomes and prices more directly we are changing the aims of economic policy or bringing a fundamentally new range of variables into the calculation.

In the narrower sense of a wages-policy the problem has been with us for a long time. It is certainly not a problem that has been ignored by economists, least of all Keynesian economists. If one wished to make a debating point, it could be argued that Keynes's criticisms of the return to gold in 1925 and of the May Report in 1931 were based on demonstrations that both of these involved a wages policy which was precisely the opposite of what was needed at the time. Less contentiously, it can be shown that economists were aware of the possible connection between high employment and wage-inflation during the 'thirties. The present-day position on incomes policy of what might be described as "right-wing Keynesians"—that it will not work so long as aggregate demand is too high and is unnecessary once aggregate demand is reduced—was prefigured in Pigou's review of the *General Theory* in 1936.

"Wage earners may exercise a continuous pressure directed to keep rates of real wages above what is compatible with maximum possible employment. So far as they do this, enhancements in money demand for labour will not be able to raise employment permanently to the boom level, because they will be offset by rising money wages. Thus, even if Mr. Keynes's full employment were established, wage earners would still have a choice between policies that promote respectively higher real wage rates *plus* more employment."[1]

[1] *Economica*, May 1936, p. 131. "Left-wing Keynesians", like Joan Robinson, drew attention to the problem at much the same time; see her *Essays in the Theory of Employment* (1936), Ch. 1. Wages policy was a feature of economic policy during the Second World War and after; see pp. 285-7 above.

The citation of historical evidence to show that the problem is not a new one does not mean that there are any simple solutions. The dilemma posed by high levels of employment and rising prices is only partly an economic one. Economists can demonstrate the conflict of aims, and may be able to produce quantitative estimates of the price that must be paid in terms of higher unemployment to achieve a stable price level; but they cannot make the decision as to whether the price is worth paying. An incomes policy may be thought of as a more acceptable way out of the dilemma, but at most it only modifies the way in which the underlying moral-political issue is posed. If there is to be an overall limit to wage increases, the problem of deciding which groups within the population shall move forward relative to others becomes acute; it can only be shirked by those who believe that the present system of income relationships, which is the result of differences in starting points and in the bargaining strengths of different groups, represents some kind of ideal.[1]

## Economic Growth as an Aim of Policy

The desire to avoid or blur the unpleasant choice at the margin between different priorities among policy aims, and between groups differentially affected by different policy-combinations, is one reason for the popularity that faster economic growth as an explicit policy objective has acquired in some political circles in recent years. It is, of course, a naïve hope. Growth is not a gift. Over the long haul it can only be achieved by paying a price in terms of current satisfactions foregone. Nevertheless, there are a variety of good reasons why it may be sensible to stimulate growth, if this can be done without compromising other ends. Is the current debate on the feasibility and desirability of doing this an "un-Keynesian" concern?

Some would have no doubt in answering this question affirmatively. When Keynes's *General Theory* appeared, Gustav Cassel, a famous Swedish economist of the day, could hardly contain the anger he felt when faced with what he believed was an attack on the source of all progress, namely thrift or saving.

> "[Keynes's conception of social economy] may perhaps correspond to the conditions of a dying civilization, where private initiative and enterprise are approaching a state of complete paralysation, and where the interest of the individual concentrates upon securing means of existence for the future without doing or risking anything. It is to be hoped that the generation now growing up will definitely reject such ideas of existence, and, conscious of the

[1] On this see J. Robinson, *Economics, An Awkward Corner* (1967).

unlimited possibilities of progress, devote its efforts to never-ceasing endeavours to raise the general standard of living."[1]

Few critics matched Cassell in his inability or unwillingness to understand the meaning Keynes attached to saving. But many, including Andrew Shonfield recently, would sympathise with Schumpeter's more sophisticated view that "those who look for the essence of capitalism in the phenomena that attend the incessant recreation of this apparatus and the incessant revolution that goes with it must . . . be excused if they hold that Keynes' theory abstracts from the essence of the capitalist process."[2]

It is certainly true that many of the key variables affecting growth —"the existing quality and quantity of available labour, the existing quality and quantity of available equipment, the existing technique"— were taken as given by Keynes.[3] Investment was mainly considered in terms of its short-run output and employment generating character-istics via the multiplier theory, and not in terms of its effects on the quality and quantity of productive capacity. But it is interesting to note that it was Roy Harrod, starting from the Keynesian base, who supplied one of the earliest and most general formulations of the dynamic principles by which these two aspects of investment can be reconciled.[4] Harrod's theory provides the foundations for one large branch of the theory of economic growth, which, without distortion, may be called *Keynesian* macro-dynamics.

Speculation about what Marshall called "the high theme of economic progress" was by no means foreign to Keynes himself. The *General Theory* contains a long-term theory of employment which embodies many of his views on economic growth. It is often over-looked simply because it was largely used by Keynesians to support a stagnationist position. But a theory of secular stagnation is the mirror image of a theory of secular growth.

Keynes's reasons for fearing stagnation were based on the view that in mature economics there was an increasing tendency, as a result of weakened incentives, for private investment to fall short of the capacity to save. Like any well-formulated prediction this position was qualified by a statement of the initial conditions that would have to be satisfied. Much of what has been regarded as pessimistic in Keynes's theory derives from his assumption that there was an acute (not chronic) tendency towards over-saving under existing conditions; and that the incentives for investment were likely to be diminished by what in the 'thirties appeared to be a long-

---

[1] "Keynes's *General Theory*", *International Labour Review*, Oct. 1937, p. 445.
[2] *History of Economic Analysis* (1961), p. 1175; see also A. Shonfield, *Modern Capitalism*, (1965), pp. 63-5.
[3] *General Theory*, p. 245.
[4] See his "An Essay in Dynamic Theory", *Economic Journal*, March 1939.

term decline in the rate of growth of population. An increasing population, he believed, was largely responsible for the buoyant demand for capital in nineteenth-century Britain. The transition from an increasing to a declining population could have a serious depressing effect on investment. Moreover, while he saw no reason why there should be a decline in the rate of technical innovation in the future, he was less certain about the effect of innovation on the amount of capital required to produce a given output. Many inventions were capable of reducing the demand for capital per unit of output, or, in other words, of shortening the average length of the period of production. The pessimistic conclusion would follow only if the assumptions were fulfilled; namely if "there is no drastic change in the distribution of wealth or in any other factor affecting the proportion of income that is saved; and further that there is no large change in the rate of interest sufficient to modify substantially the length of the average period of production".[1]

In fact, of course, not only has the tendency toward population decline been reversed, but there have also been several factors at work which have offset the higher savings expected by Keynes. Technical invention and other improvements in the quality of productive resources, including labour, have counteracted the effects of capital accumulation on the rate of return. But it is clear that Keynes was certainly alive to the problem of growth. Indeed, his faith in the power of lower long-term interest rates to call forth a substantial deepening of the capital structure would place him among the optimists in the debate on growth today.

Putting such large-scale speculations on one side, it is obvious that as a practical objective of policy faster economic growth can only be approached by first crossing the terrain marked out by Keynes's short-term theory of employment. It is certainly not inconceivable for an economy to experience economic growth while suffering from heavy unemployment—the inter-war period provides ample evidence of this. But if we are thinking of growth as a policy aim, most governments are likely to want it only if it is accompanied by fairly high and stable levels of employment.

Another way of putting the same point is to say that, having more or less succeeded in curbing variations in the rate of utilisation of existing capacity, we now look to growth in that capacity for further rises in our standard of living.[2] Here again we have a contrast

---

[1] "Some Economic Consequences of a Declining Population", *Eugenics Review*, April 1937, pp. 13-17.
[2] There is, of course, a school of thought which holds that economic growth, as commonly talked about and measured, is not worth having. For an able exposition of this point of view see E. J. Mishan, *The Costs of Economic Growth* (1967).

with earlier views on these matters. It is not simply that growth, like employment, is now considered to be amenable—how amenable is another matter—to conscious influence, whereas at one time it was thought to be simply a matter of removing obstacles (Smith and Ricardo), or of climate, natural resources and "character" (Marshall). It is also that in contrast with the views of say, Schumpeter, cyclical instability and growth are no longer thought to be inseparable. The elimination of a certain type of cycle in Britain, namely "stop-go" policy cycles, is considered by many to be essential to the attainment of higher growth; and the same holds true of those who wish to reverse the order of priorities by arguing that economic growth is the prerequisite for ending "stop-go".

Although nothing could be simpler than the arithmetic of compound interest which accounts for much of the attraction of faster growth, there is no commonly-accepted theory to explain why some nations grow faster than others. For the most part economists have to be content with stating certain boundary conditions and exploring the influence of individual strategic factors. It seems fairly clear though that in advanced economies there are close links between the Keynesian aims of high levels of employment and faster growth. By ensuring that existing capacity is fully and regularly utilised, wasteful slack can be eliminated; the extra output thus realised can be used to increase future productive capacity without retrenching on current consumption. There may also be indirect connections between high employment and growth in the form of an increased volume of net investment embodying technical improvements, and thereby making possible faster rates of productivity increase. Gains made in this way, however, are likely to be of a once-for-all variety; they may not guarantee permanently higher rates of growth. To achieve this under conditions of full employment will require deferment of consumption in order to release resources for investment in human and industrial capital.[1]

The policy issues associated with growth merge with the more familiar issues of economic management. Economic growth is likely to be impaired, or of secondary importance, while there is either excessive pressure on existing capacity leading to inflation, or if low rates of utilisation bring unemployment. Only if such difficulties can be overcome will the decks be cleared for higher growth as policy objective. The experience of Britain and the United States in recent years illustrates this point. In the early 'sixties both countries were fairly low in the growth league table. Under Kennedy, American unemployment was reduced *and* a higher rate of growth achieved.

---

[1] See J. Tobin, "Economic Growth as an Objective of Government Policy", *American Economic Review*, May 1964.

In Britain, however, failure to solve the short-term problems of stop-go, rising prices, and balance of payments difficulties, has resulted in the abandonment of efforts to resuscitate medium-term planning for faster growth.

## Micro-economics and Public Policy

The development of a new branch of economics designed to deal with the problems of aggregate output and employment was undoubtedly the single most important event in the history of economic thought and policy in the inter-war and post-war period. Hence the attention that has been paid to it in this book. But the arrival on the scene of macro-economics in no way banished traditional micro-economic problems. It is true that Keynes showed the illegitimacy of extending some parts of the logic of individual market behaviour to macro-economic questions, notably with respect to individual thrift and the effect of wage-cuts on employment. But Keynes himself believed that once full employment was established the neo-classical system comes into its own again. Indeed, he seems to have been remarkably satisfied with the theory developed by Marshall to explain this important feature of economic life. The following passage indicates the hold which this aspect of nineteenth century economic liberalism continued to have on Keynes.

"If we suppose the volume of output to be given, i.e. to be determined by forces outside the classical scheme of thought, then there is no objection to be raised against the classical analysis of the manner in which private self-interest will determine what in particular is produced, in what proportions the factors of production will be combined to produce it, and how the value of the final produce will be distributed between them . . . Thus, apart from the necessity of central controls to bring about an adjustment between the propensity to consume and the inducement to invest, there is no more reason to socialise economic life than there was before . . . I see no reason to suppose that the existing system seriously misemploys the factors of production which are in use . . . It is in determining the volume, not the direction, of actual employment that existing system has broken down."[1]

Several criticisms can be made of this statement. There is, first of all, the objection to its complacency. Is the price mechanism really so efficient or equitable in its operation? If the entire neo-classical framework is regarded as one designed to enshrine *laissez-faire*, then Keynes's demonstration of its weaknesses must be applauded—

[1] *General Theory*, p. 378-9.

but there will also be regret for his failure to complete the process of demolition.[1]

A more pragmatic line of criticism would be to point out that "volume" and "direction" cannot be separated easily in practice; the attainment of macro-economic objectives entails modification of the micro-economic characteristics of the economic system. As we have noted already, a successful prices and incomes policy cannot be operated on the basis of the belief that existing wage and income differentials are "ideal", or that wages and prices are formulated under competitive conditions in which all buyers and sellers are subjected to the same constraints. Stability in the level and rate of expansion of aggregate demand can be achieved by various combinations of consumption and investment levels; and a further permutation can be made by distinguishing between public and private consumption and investment. Taxes, subsidies, hire-purchase restrictions, monetary controls, and government expenditure patterns are not neutral with respect to their effects on distribution. A policy for faster growth which entails raising the level of investment must also decide, implicitly or explicitly, which savers and investors to encourage, and whether the social rate of return is higher on private or public investment.

Economic policies, including *laissez-faire*, are essentially discriminatory; they discriminate between groups within the population and between industries and economic regions. Progress in the formulation of economic policy comes from making the process of discrimination more explicit, sensitive, effective and self-conscious, in order to establish clearly what is being done and why.

A further reason for rejecting Keynes's statement arises out of developments in the economics of resource allocation that were taking place during Keynes's life, but which have only begun to make an impact on policy in recent years. Far from being driven out of court by the "new" economics, the inter-war period was one in which notable improvements were made in the theoretical structure of the "old" economics.

In Marshall's version of the theory of demand and supply, the existence of monopoly was recognised but largely kept separate from the "normal" case of price-determination under competitive conditions. The existence or possibility of increasing returns to scale threatens the determinacy and stability of competitive equilibrium: if unit costs fall when output is increased, what is to prevent a single firm from engulfing all others, thereby becoming a monopolist? Marshall's way of getting round this difficulty, by means of his

[1] The chief representative of this school of thought is Joan Robinson; see *Economic Philosophy* (1962), pp. 85-6.

distinction between external and internal economies of scale and the concept of the "representative firm", lost much of its appeal as increasing returns and the decay of competition began to loom large as features of the contemporary scene. In the 'twenties, therefore, beginning with an important article by Piero Sraffa in 1926,[1] a major debate took place which eventually led to a radically new theory (or set of theories) of the firm acting under market conditions that varied from perfect competition at one extreme (rather than as the "normal" case) to monopoly at the other.[2] The two names most closely assoc-iated with the later stages of this revolution were those of Joan Robinson, for her *Economics of Imperfect Competition*, and E. H. Cham-berlin, for his *Theory of Monopolistic Competition*, both published in 1933.

While the dethronement of perfect competition was a major event in the long history of the theory of value, and one which in some sense brought micro-economics into closer touch with reality, its significance for policy-making in the industrial field was negligible, or at most indirect.[3] It can best be thought of as the result of a process of regeneration which was internal to the academic community, rather than as a response to demands made by external circumstance; it was a successful extension of neo-classical marginalism to deal with theoretical anomalies that had long been recognised. This remains true even though the increasing size of firms may have lent greater urgency to the search for new solutions.

These remarks are not intended as a criticism. The construction of a positive science of micro-economics designed to provide better explanations for the structure of different industries, and for the behaviour of firms and consumers, must always be one of the major responsibilities of economists. The only criticism one might make of the theories of the firm and of the consumer advanced in this period is that the effort put into theoretical refinement was not matched by attempts to test theory against empirical evidence. This deficiency is now being remedied. Not only are a number of new hypotheses about business behaviour being tested, but the whole field of industrial economics, descriptive and analytical, has been enlivened in Britain by the existence of such bodies as the Monopolies Commision, the Restrictive Practices Court, and the Prices and Incomes Board. The need to formulate policy or pass judgment on what kinds of industrial practice are or are not in the public interest may not be essential to theoretical work in this field, but it certainly seems to have helped to concentrate the collective mind of the economics profession.

[1] "The Laws of Returns Under Competitive Conditions", *Economic Journal*, Dec. 1926.
[2] See G. L. S. Shackle, *The Years of High Theory* (1967), Chs. III-VI.
[3] See p. 214 above.

It is with respect to the welfare, rather than positive, aspects of micro-economics that the most significant developments for policy-making have taken place. Since its foundation as a systematic branch of economics the aim of welfare economics has been to furnish criteria for assessing the relative efficiency of various institutions, regimes, or policies.[1] Here too there was considerable debate on fundamental issues of theory in the inter-war period, but the outcome was not particularly encouraging to those who hoped to formulate perfectly general and objective criteria for judging economic outcomes.

Perhaps the most interesting controversy was over the economics of socialist states. On one side it was maintained that a regime in which the means of production were owned by the state would be incapable of performing the myriad calculations necessary to ensure an efficient allocation of resources. In reply, an attempt was made to show how the problem could be solved by a combination of rules for the guidance of managers of state enterprise, and a system of trial and error, the essential idea of which was to simulate the workings of ideal competitive markets under capitalism.[2] The main achievement of this debate was to spell out in detail the theoretical conditions that would have to be met in order to achieve an economically optimal allocation of resources. The value of such exercises was in focusing attention on possible defects in the pricing mechanism as a system of ensuring an efficient allocation of resources—the defects of the mechanism as a means of distributing incomes are more easily recognised. For every instance of a divergence of actual from ideal conditions, there is a *prima facie* case at least for state intervention, or some other arrangement, to eliminate, minimise, or compensate for the effect of the divergence. In this way we have returned to the kind of piece-meal social engineering which was the aim of Pigou when he first wrote his *Wealth and Welfare* in 1912.

With this brief sketch of earlier trends in theoretical welfare economics as background, it is now possible to consider recent developments in this field. There is little doubt that a major change has taken place in the orientation of the economics of resource allocation which has helped to make it an invaluable tool for those who make the vital decisions that govern resource allocation. The change can be characterised by saying that whereas in the past economists have sought mainly to interpret the world, now they are working on ways in which it can be changed. The emphasis has

---

[1] See p. 38 above.
[2] F. A. Hayek, (ed.) *Collectivist Economic Planning*, (1935), and B. Lippincott, (ed.) *On the Economic Theory of Socialism*, (1938).

shifted away from abstract systems which trace the consequences of certain assumptions about the rational pursuit of economic ends, towards concrete procedures for evaluating alternative ends, and assessing the most rational means of achieving them. Economists have made use of the concept of "economic man" for a long time in their efforts to explain economic behaviour, so to speak, from the outside. They have come in for a good deal of criticism, much of it misguided, for so doing. The aim of the new theories and methods of decision-making is to show how rationality can be achieved in practice rather than merely postulated.

While many of these techniques are capable of being used in any large undertaking, private or public, their application to governmental decision-making provides the greatest challenge and interest to the economist.[1] It is not difficult to see why so much attention is now being paid to ways of improving the standard of decision-making in the public sector. There has been a marked increase in the magnitude, complexity, and extent of government intervention and participation in the economy since the war. In 1936 Keynes could see "no more reason to socialise economic life than there was before". But the plain fact of the matter is that economic life today *is* more "socialised". In Britain, public expenditure comprises 40% of gross national product; the public sector, which includes the nationalised industries, employs directly over 25% of the nation's manpower, and indirectly, through industries that rely heavily on its custom, a great deal more; the public authorities own about 40% of the nation's capital assets; and, more significantly, are responsible for nearly 45% of the nation's annual fixed investment. It has been estimated that over 60% of the nation's scientific and technological research is financed by government agencies. All of the most vital services that make up the social and economic infra-structure of the nation are publicly controlled and operated: railways, coal, electricity, gas, roads, airways, postal services, telecommunications, the health service, and education. In trying to co-ordinate a business as big as this, where the consequences of misallocation are so great, only the best methods of financial control and objective appraisal are good enough.

The public sector is not simply a gigantic business organisation to be run exclusively on commercial lines. But neither are the crucial decisions about public enterprises and expenditure a simple matter of "politics", a word like "social" or "moral" sometimes invoked to put a premature end to rational discussion. Indeed, it is precisely because

[1] For a short introduction, see A. Williams, *Output Budgeting and the Contributions of Micro-economics to Efficiency in Government*, C.A.S. Occasional Paper, No. 4 (1967). For a comprehensive survey, see A. R. Prest and R. Turvey, "Theories of Cost-Benefit Analysis" *Economic Journal*, Dec. 1945.

of the mixture of commercial and extra-economic considerations that the problems of public decision-making are of such interest to the welfare economist. A few examples from a large and growing field should illustrate the nature of that interest and its connection with the traditional concerns of economists.

According to what criteria should the pricing and investment policies of the nationalised industries be determined? How should the performance of their managers be assessed? What sort of rate of return on capital should be expected? What combination of "public service" and "profit" should be aimed at? Interest in this type of problem can be traced back to the nineteenth century, but now the literature on this question is more regularly applied to practical decisions.

One of Marshall and Pigou's achievements in this field was to highlight cases where, owing to the existence of "externalities", the pricing system gives inaccurate signals for the guidance of resource allocation. An "externality" exists when the actions or decisions of one person lead to additional costs or benefits being imposed on others, but where those extra costs and benefits are not taken into account by the original decision-maker. Wherever such a situation arises, the marginal *social* costs or benefits of an action exceed the marginal *private* costs or benefits. In its unmodified state the price system is incapable of taking account of these extra social costs and benefits. It does not, therefore, give a true picture of the opportunity costs to society of decisions which involve external effects.

In advanced societies such external effects are becoming more common. The favourite example is the use of the private motor vehicle in congested urban centres.[1] The costs taken into account by the private motorist in deciding to operate a car in city centres do not cover all of the costs imposed on others in terms of slower traffic movement, increased accident risk, noise, dirt and fumes. The situation could be dealt with by a simple fiat banning all "non-essential" private traffic at peak hours, or by a combination of improvements in traffic engineering, parking charges, and a pricing system designed to reimpose on the car-user the full costs of his journey. By the same token, in deciding whether to invest public money in a new underground railway line, or whether to operate commuter services at a loss, the rate of return should be calculated by taking into account the external benefits in terms of reduced surface congestion costs, as well as the ordinary revenue derived from operating the new service. A new type of investment calculation, cost-benefit analysis, has been worked out for use in assessing the rate of

[1] See e.g., Ministry of Transport, *Road Pricing: The Economic and Technical Possibilities*, (1964), and E. J. Mishan, *op. cit.*

return on public investments where the social costs and benefits may be diffused or intangible. Similar methods of appraisal have been put forward to deal with decisions that have to be made on education, health, defence, and scientific research—all cases where the "output" has no simple market price but where it is possible to impute values to some of the major items.

The new aids to decision-making have multiplied rapidly. Some are relatively new in origin. Many of the methods which make up Operations Research, for example, derive from the last world war, and the classic examples of their use are still to be found in the defence field. But the basic idea of finding optimal solutions is an old one, certainly to economists. By virtue of long exposure to the problems of choice, efficiency, profit-maximisation and marginal adjustments, many economists have found the new frontier a familiar, not to say congenial, environment.

The new quantitative methods for appraising the efficiency of government activities mark an important step forward in the process of bringing economics to bear on policy-formation. They also raise a number of problems concerning the relationship of technical expertise to political decision-making in democratic systems of government. There are many who view the trend towards quantification with alarm; they see it as a threat to participation by the ordinary citizen or MP in the process of decision-making. Will it lead to a regime controlled more and more by the expert, by Burke's dreaded "sophisters, economists and calculators"? Will decisions be made exclusively on the basis of the partial evidence that is susceptible to quantification, while important qualitative, aesthetic and moral considerations are ignored?

It is difficult to say anything precise on either side of this issue without examining specific cases. What can be said, however, is that in Britain many of the fears are either highly premature or based on a misunderstanding of the provenance of quantitative techniques. It is apparently still necessary to re-iterate Marshall's statement that "economics is not a body of concrete truth, but an engine for the discovery of truth".

Economists do have a commitment to rationality in human affairs, but this should not be confused with the much narrower idea of the rational pursuit of material interests; it means that there should be consistency in the ranking of alternatives, but the alternatives need not be "economic" ones—if such indeed exist. Many of the ends effected by particular courses of action are difficult to state in quantitative terms. For example, it is not easy to place a money value on the lives likely to be saved by improved roads. In such cases it may be possible to impute a value by taking life insurance figures.

This will hardly satisfy the theologian but it does help to make explicit the conventional judgments that are made when taking decisions. Even in cases where quantification seems impossible, for example where hydro-electric schemes mar the beauty of a landscape, it is still a useful exercise to show the costs involved in preserving or destroying a particular amenity. Far from overlooking aesthetic or moral considerations, cost-benefit thinking may be the only way of ensuring that they are brought into the calculation. It is not "vulgar materialism" to set a price on such matters: "vulgar materialism" results from setting too low a price.

Moreover, it is a fallacy to conclude that because some variables are imperfectly quantifiable it is not worth quantifying others. Arguments against a particular method can frequently be turned into arguments in favour of more work being done in this field. The conclusion that we do not know enough about the relevant factors at work is itself a useful piece of information to the decision-maker. Many "non-economic" variables must be taken into account in making economic decisions; the methods and findings of other social sciences will have to be brought into the reckoning. Systematic decision-making procedures, therefore, do not give economics an overriding status; rather, they create opportunities for the application of other types of research. The "wrong" decisions can be made under any system, but it is only possible to learn from failures when decisions are based on explicit assumptions and criteria.

Many of the fears expressed about the use of quantitative methods are similar to those which influence attitudes towards any technical change, and towards automation and computers in particular. But those who have actually tried to construct a computer that will perform the functions of human intelligence are most likely to appreciate the qualities of the human brain. The same is true of economists who work in the cost-benefit and operations research field. The dangers which can arise out of indiscriminate or inappropriate use of these techniques are most likely to be avoided by those who have studied them carefully. The best security against misuse, therefore, is to incorporate larger numbers of those with knowledge of these techniques into the governmental policy-making machinery.

### The Age of the Official Economic Adviser

The main concern of this study has been with the relationship between economic thought and policy in the first half of the twentieth century. For most of the period up to the Second World War a gulf existed between academic economics and the kind of thinking that went on behind the scenes when framing economic policy decisions. This gulf, it is true, was sometimes bridged at strategic points by personal contacts between representatives of the two worlds, and by the occasional committee of experts brought in to study particular problems. Those economists who wished to make a contribution to policy questions by way of analysis or advice did so mainly by writing books, pamphlets, memoranda for official inquiries, and newspaper articles; they addressed themselves to their fellow economists or to the general public, and relied on the arts of public persuasion and the general diffusion of knowledge to make their influence felt.

Keynes's career up to 1939 is an archetypal one in this respect. It accounts for his famous statement about the relationship between the thinking of "practical men" or "madmen in authority", and that of the "defunct economist" or "some academic scribbler of a few years back".[1] The important point here is the time-lag. Keynes himself was able to cut down the time-lag in the case of his own work by being invited to take a seat in the Treasury parlour during the war; many others have since followed his example. As a result, the nature of the relationship between thought and policy has been transformed in the last twenty years or so. The self-appointed adviser and analyst working through the public media of communication continues to operate, but he has been powerfully supplemented by the economic adviser working within the machinery of government itself.

Large numbers of economists have now acquired sufficient experience of government service for a bulky literature on the economics and politics of professional economic advice to have appeared. With the development of quantitative methods of forecasting and appraisal, it is even becoming possible to speak of a *theory* of economic policy.[2] Moreover, governments have become not merely consumers of economic expertise but also active centres for economic research.[3] The fact that this situation has arisen is one of the fruits of the developments dealt with in this study. The implications of this change in the status of economics are enormous; they will certainly transform the way in which the story of the second half of the twentieth century is told. Without in any sense trying to anticipate this story, a few points can be made about the role of the official adviser today on the basis of contrasts between the British and American situations.

[1] See p. 20 above.
[2] See e.g. J. Tinbergen, *Economic Policy: Principles and Design* (1956).
[3] The Treasury evidence to the Heyworth Committee on Social Studies gives some idea of the range of official interest in academic research in Britain; see the *Memoranda of Evidence*, paras 57-66. As an indication of the change that has taken place, it is difficult to imagine similar document being produced by the Treasury at any time during the inter-war period.

## Anglo-American Contrasts

The complexity, and uncertainties of the American Congressional legislative process, and its adverse effect on clear policy-formation and implementation, have frequently been the object of unfavourable comparison with the simpler and firmer British system of cabinet government. Keynes himself said on one occasion that the Americans did not *have* a government in the ordinary (British) sense of the word.[1] But this is not a British verdict only. At the end of his exhaustive study of the legislative history of the 1946 Employment Act, Stephen Bailey concluded that:

> "In the absence of a responsible political system we run the grave risk of public cynicism and frustration, and of neglecting policies which could anticipate and to some extent preclude serious economic crises. The story of the Employment Act of 1946 suggests a need for more responsible policy-making in our national legislature. It also suggests that until we move in that direction, national economic policies will continue to be formulated by a kaleidoscopic and largely irresponsible interplay of ideas, interests, institutions and individuals."[2]

Although the outcome has perhaps not been quite as gloomy as these remarks would suggest, the record of American economic policy-making since the war certainly illustrates how difficult it is to overcome the entrenched conservative influences and interests at work in Congress. In view of these adverse judgments it can do no harm to point out some of the virtues of the American "open" and diffused system when compared with the "élitist" and centralised British system.

One of the great virtues of the American system derives from the existence of such Congressional committees as the Joint Economic Committee and the Senate Committee on Banking and Finance. These Committees have their share of cranks and backwoodsmen as members, but they also gather expert evidence on economic questions which is far more varied and up-to-date than that which is available to the ordinary British MP from journalistic and other sources. Apart from their educative function, the Committee hearings provide a more or less open forum for economists to display their wares; it encourages them to keep in touch with the larger issues of national economic policy even though their main job may be university teaching and research. Compared with such Committee hearings British Parliamentary debates on economic questions are mere undergraduate affairs.

[1] To a group of American economists, as communicated privately by Walter S. Salant.
[2] *Congress Makes a Law* (1964), p. 240.

On matters involving the employment of economists as official advisers, the American system also scores highly. Here again Keynes saw the signs correctly. In 1941 he paid the following tribute to the economists he had met in Washington:

". . . I have been greatly struck during my visit by the quality of the younger economists and civil servants in the Administration. I am sure that the best hope for good government of America is to be found there. The war will be a great sifter and will bring the right people to the top. We have a few good people in London, but nothing like the *numbers* who you can produce here."[1]

Any British observer of the current Washington scene would make the same observation today. Under the American system a large number of departments and agencies find it worthwhile to employ their own staff of economic analysts and advisers; and any one of several agencies could sport more than the total number of economists in the government service in Britain. The comparison is not entirely fair. Apart from the simple matter of the difference in scale of the two operations, there is the fact that the separation of powers makes it necessary for competing agencies in the American system to employ their own staff of experts. In spite of these qualifications, however, many British economists would compare their own situation unfavourably with that of their counterparts in Washington. Battles for the recognition of professional economic expertise that would be inconceivable in America were still being fought in Britain until recently. The unfavourable comparison could be extended to include the amount of resources devoted to the sponsorship of fundamental economic research through various governmental or quasi-governmental agencies in the United States. Even if it were only a question of numbers, ignoring the high degree of "professionalism" to be found among American economists, there is a good deal of truth expressed in J. R. Sargent's witticism on the subject, namely that "nothing succeeds like excess".[2]

Although the status of economists brought into the machinery of government in Britain during the war was confirmed by the 1944 White Paper on Employment Policy,[3] there seems to have been a period of stagnation and perhaps even of decline under the Conservative Governments of the 'fifties. A study by P. D. Henderson published in 1962 revealed that of the meagre dozen or so economists employed in government most were to be found in the Treasury and

[1] Letter to Walter A. Salant, July 27th 1941.
[2] "Are American Economists Better?", *Oxford Economic Papers*, March 1963, p. 3.
[3] "The Government intend to establish on a permanent basis a small central staff qualified to measure and analyse economic trends and submit appreciations of them to the Ministers concerned." Cmd. 6527.

the Ministry of Agriculture. This meant that there were no economists at this time in the Foreign Office, the Ministry of Aviation, and the Commonwealth Relations Office, even though all of these departments had economic sections and responsibilities. Even more surprising was the fact that the Ministries of Labour, Transport, Housing, the Board of Trade and the Inland Revenue Department did not have economic sections at all.[1] And what was true of economics was doubly so for the other social sciences.[2]

The situation has improved considerably in recent years. In 1962 the National Economic Development Council was set up with a staff of twenty economists. Since then the numbers involved in government work in one capacity or another have grown steadily, particularly under the Labour Government and with the establishment of such new bodies as the Department of Economic Affairs, the Ministry of Overseas Development and the Prices and Incomes Board. Well-established departments like the Board of Trade and the Ministry of Transport now have economic staffs or make use of economic consultants.

Pressure has certainly mounted "to increase the number of economists who are civil servants, and the number of civil servants who are economists".[3] In setting up a Centre for Administrative Studies in 1954, designed to train civil servants in economics, management, and other specialist skills, partial recognition at least was accorded to this point of view. The case for employing large numbers of economists in government, and for giving some recognition to an economics training when recruiting into the career service, has usually been linked with criticisms of the record of specific departments, and of the British tradition of the all-flexible amateur administrator.[4] It is interesting to note, therefore, that the Fulton Committee on the Civil Service seems to have gone a long way towards accepting these criticisms. In its proposals for developing greater "professionalism" in the service, it has recommended the development of a new group of economic and financial administrators; and the majority of the committee agreed that more account should be taken of the relevance of graduates' university courses to the job they are being recruited to do.[5]

One of the most important differences between the British and American systems arises out of the fact that the Council of Economic Advisers, with its primary responsibility to the President, has no real

[1] See "The Use of Economists in British Administration", *Oxford Economic Papers*, Feb. 1961.

[2] On this point see the *Report of the Heyworth Committee on Social Studies* (1965), para. 61.

[3] P. D. Henderson, *op. cit.*, p. 25.

[4] *Ibid*; see also H. Thomas (ed.) *The Civil Service* (1968).

[5] *Report of the Committee of Inquiry into the Civil Service* (1966-68), p. 105, paras 7 & 8.

equivalent in Britain. In Britain, the chief equivalent function is performed by the Economic Section of the Treasury, though in its role as adviser in drawing up budget proposals it deals with matters which in the United States are partly also the responsibility of the Bureau of the Budget. The members of the Treasury Economic Section, or for that matter any economic advisers, permanent or temporary, working in the British government machine, are first and foremost civil servants; they operate anonymously and are not easily identified with specific policy recommendations. They also enjoy security of tenure within a department which has day-to-day business to transact.

By contrast, the Council of Economic Advisers is attached to the chief executive and has no departmental duties. This position, as Walter Heller has explained, puts at the President's disposal "a catholic, not a parochial, approach to economic policy—an undivided, rather than a competing, loyalty".[1] It also means that the Council depends on the personal favour of the President to make its influence felt. Since, however, the President makes his own appointments to the Council, subject to Senate confirmation, this should not pose a major problem. Deafness to advice is the prerogative of political decision-makers in any system, but there is little point in choosing advisers that you do not intend to listen to at least some of the time.

In setting up the Council one of the intentions was to create an advisory body that would be open to Congressional scrutiny.[2] Compared with their British counterparts, the members of the Council operate in a political gold-fish bowl. By the same token, however, they have greater opportunities to explain and defend their policy recommendations. The danger of the American system, of course, is that the economist may compromise his reputation for objective economic expertise by becoming too closely allied with policies which are politically controversial. But since policy advice on major economic questions cannot confine itself to "pure" economic possibilities and outcomes it seems better that the advocacy should take place in the open rather than behind closed doors. The dangers are in any case reduced in the American system by constant interchange between government and university. Walter Heller has said that this interchange provides a good substitute "for the British career-service tradition as insurance of objectivity".[3]

Unlike their American counterparts, British economic advisers have been handed few public bouquets in recent years. Since the

[1] *New Dimensions of Political Economy* (1966), p. 52.
[2] See E. S. Flash, *Economic Advice and Presidential Leadership* (1965), pp. 16-17.
[3] *Op. cit.*, p. 24. See also J. Tobin, *National Economic Policy* (1966), pp. 204-5.

Labour Government has employed more economists than its predecessors, it was perhaps inevitable that its advisers should come in
for a share of the blame for the frustrations and failures of British
policy-making of late. Most of the criticism has been directed at the
small number of quasi-political appointments that were made with
the object of providing the government with an alternative source
of advice operating outside the normal civil service constraints.[1] A
partial movement was made, therefore, towards the American
system. In so far as the difficulties are substantive rather than due to
personalities, they may have arisen precisely because the move has
only been partial.

Criticism of measures which are identified with particular advisers
by repute only is bound to be confused and possibly unfair. The
present position of "political economists" in the British system is
anomalous; they exist in a kind of limbo region between open politics
on the one side and civil service anonymity on the other. The idea of
securing alternative advice on a free-floating basis was a good one,
but it would have been better on all sides if there were some forum,
like the Joint Economic Committee in the United States, in which
the adviser could be asked to defend his position. Issue would be more
fairly joined. Those who accept such jobs would have to choose
between the comparative coolness of university life or a regular civil
service appointment, and the excitement and heat of the political
kitchen. In practice, however, it is likely that some kind of inter-
mediate temperature could be established. As in other matters, the
fears associated with the loss of anonymity and secrecy could prove
to have an irrational foundation. Economic policy-making, of course,
is only one of several areas in which wider public participation and
direct accountability would improve the quality of British public
life.

One recent critic, Michael Postan, has said: "It may well be that
the very quality of post-war economics, the greater sophistication of
its theoretical constructions, its much refined statistical and
econometric methods, have put it out of touch with real economic
situations."[2] The paradox here is surely unintentional. It is the
purpose of "refined statistical and econometric methods" to ensure
that "theoretical constructions" correspond with "real economic
situations". If the criticism is to be substantiated it will have to be on
the grounds that the refined methods are not refined enough. What
Postan actually means and goes on to say is that other branches
of economics need to be made more sophisticated, and that skills

---

[1] For a fairly representative example of the criticism see G. Hallett, "The Role of
Economists as Government Advisers", *Westminster Bank Review*, May 1967.
[2] M. M. Postan, "A Plague of Economists?", *Encounter*, Jan. 1968.

economists have never claimed to possess—concerning technology, industrial consultancy, sociology and business management—are needed to supplement economic analysis. Quite true. The fallacy which lurks beneath the surface of such criticisms, however, is the notion that macro- and micro-economics can be easily separated. One of the lessons borne out by the experience of the inter-war period, and of the Kennedy-Johnson era in policy-making, is that micro-analysis, and intervention to deal with specific, structural problems, cannot act as a substitute for a solution of the basic macro-problems of an economy.

It may be that micro-economic decision-making procedures, and the application of general economic intelligence to every-day problems, make as much contribution to rational discussion about economic policy as any of the more dramatic and sophisticated procedures of macro-economics and econometrics. Economists are divided among themselves as to where the emphasis should be placed, but there is agreement on the value of an economics training even in those cases where only the humbler forms of expertise can be utilised. As Paul Samuelson has said: "Common-sense economics may indeed be all that anyone must use in the end. But it takes the most uncommon sense and wisdom to know just which part of the filing case of muddled notions that men call common-sense is relevant to a particular problem."[1] Although recent critics have raised doubts as to the nature of the economic expertise needed, and as to the way economists are at present employed within the governmental machine in Britain, no one has seriously suggested that questions of national economic policy can be left entirely to non-economists.

What unites economists today is not so much allegiance to a particular paradigm or ideology as commitment to explicitness and rationality in the broadest sense. There could be no more interesting testimony to this than the growing convergence between economics as practised in capitalist countries and the preoccupations of economic planners in European countries with communist regimes.[2] Alfred Marshall considered "deliberateness" to be the developing characteristic of his age; he regarded the English businessman as the harbinger of progress in this respect, the archetypal representative of all the humane and rational economic tendencies of the day.

---

[1] See his _Problems of the American Economy: An Economist's View_, Stamp Memorial Lecture, 1961, pp. 15-16. For a similar verdict by a British economist with experience of government service see I. M. D. Little, "The Economist in Whitehall", _Lloyds Bank Review_, April 1957, p. 35.
[2] For an interesting account of how this convergence has arisen see R. L. Meek, _The Rise and Fall of the Concept of the Economic Machine_ (1965), and his _Economics and Ideology_ (1967), pp. 194-5; 217-22.

During the inter-war period, as Keynes pointed out, it became more difficult to believe that the captains of industry were capable of fulfilling all the necessary functions of economic initiative and rational forethought—or rather, that when they did so there was no guarantee that the result would be socially beneficial. But there is no doubt that every modern industrial society requires these functions to be carried out by some group or other, preferably in accordance with the most effective and enlightened methods available at the time. For a variety of reasons—some of which, it is hoped, this study has illuminated—governments have now assumed many of these responsibilities. Economic knowledge, and the means by which it is furthered, provide one of the indispensable ways in which these responsibilities can be fulfilled.

# Keynes and the British Left in the Inter-War Period

The relationship between academic economics and socialism has been touched on at various points in this study, particularly when considering the debate between individualism and collectivism in the latter half of the nineteenth century, and in dealing with the events leading up to the 1931 crisis. The theme is obviously an important one in view of the fact that socialism, in its various forms, represented for most of the period under consideration the main alternative to the existing economic and social system. Although some leading economists have had socialist sympathies, and there has frequently been agreement between academic economists and socialists on particular issues, the relationship between the two traditions has often been thought of as antagonistic. That this no longer seems to be the case is one of the interesting by-products of the events and theoretical developments considered in this study. Few socialists today, except possibly hard-line Marxists, look on economics as an apologetic discipline. On the level of party politics, there is some recent evidence to show that a Labour Government is more anxious to have, and perhaps more likely to obtain, the professional services of economists. For their part, economists as a body no longer feel it necessary to sustain a viewpoint on socialist versus capitalist economics, though there is a good deal of professional interest in the techniques of Soviet economic planning and the operation of the public sector in mixed economics. One of the major reasons for this rapprochement lies, of course, in the work of Keynes, and in the technocratic developments in economics since the Keynesian revolution.

Keynes' party instincts were never very strong. Like many others in the inter-war period he was conscious of the irrelevance of party divisions in economic affairs. He encouraged or collaborated with any person or group who seemed to be working along the right lines to solve problems that were, in his view, mainly of an intellectual character. While he could feel respect for individual politicans, his view of them as a breed is perhaps summed up by his definition of politics as "the survival of the unfit". In the 'twenties he found a congenial political home in the advanced wing of the Liberals, though he clearly felt that they might soon be unable to offer a roof and floor to anyone. He disliked what he termed "state socialism" as an all-embracing creed; it was "little better than a dusty survival of a plan to meet the problems of fifty years ago, based on a mis-understanding of what someone had said one hundred years ago".[1] He also found the emphasis on class warfare in some circles of the Labour Party uncongenial—if there had to be class war he would choose to be on the side of the "educated bourgeoisie".[2] Neverthe-less, in 1926 he advocated closer co-operation between the Liberal and Labour Parties to strengthen the resistance of progressive forces against the dead-hand of Conservatism.[3]

After 1931, with the Liberals virtually spent as a political force, circumstances were more propitious for a closer relationship between Keynes and the Labour Party. Harrod, in his biography, speaks of Keynes's hope that "he might galvanise the Labour Party into constructive opposition on the basis of a programme of expan-sion", but adds that "Labour did not take its defeat as an oppor-tunity for showing its mettle and devising a realistic programme to cope with the facts as they were in the worst phase of the slump, but tended to move away towards its age-old panaceas."[4]

It is true that the effect of the downfall of the Labour Government was to fortify socialist belief. Beatrice Webb reported the mood of Labour's Annual Conference in October 1931 as one of "dour determination never again to undertake the government of the country as the caretaker of the existing order of society". There was a sense of relief as well as bitterness at having "got rid of the rotten stuff from the movement".[5] In the stocktaking period there was a good deal of talk about a "bankers' ramp", and of the need for any future Labour Government to protect itself against the capitalist conspiracy by confiscatory measures, but there was also some hard, middle-of-the-road thinking.

The Labour Government had failed because it had applied "capitalist" solutions. In opposition once more the party was forced to work out a practical alternative to orthodoxy. Harrod's account seriously underestimates the willingness in some Labour circles to find a place for Keynes and his ideas in their programme, and also the extent to which Keynes, in his isolation, approached the Labour viewpoint.

Harrod cites an article in the *Political Quarterly* as evidence of

[1] *Essays in Persuasion*, p. 316.
[2] *Ibid.*, p. 324.
[3] *Ibid.*, pp. 339-345.
[4] *Life of Keynes* (1963), p. 439.
[5] *Diaries, 1924-1932* (1948), p. 292.

Keynes's "difficulties in regard to socialism". The article in question is more than a rehearsal of "difficulties"; he was advising the Labour Party to give priority to measures which were economically sound, so as to provide a firm foundation for the subsequent realisation of socialist ideals. The ex-leaders had been "totally out of sympathy with those who have new notions of what is economically sound, whether the innovator has been right or wrong". Fortunately, the new concept of what was economically sound was not in conflict with the reformist ideas of the Party. "I am convinced that those things which are urgently called for on practical grounds, such as the central control of investment and the distribution of income in such a way as to provide purchasing power for the enormous potential output of modern productive technique, will also tend to produce a better kind of society on ideal grounds."[1]

In an interesting reply, A. L. Rowse acknowledged that "the implications to be drawn from [Keynes's] economic writings are more compatible with socialism than any other political system." But he accused Keynes of ambivalence and political naïvety in his attitude to socialism both as a moral doctrine and as a mass movement. Keynes had fallen victim to the rationalist fallacy in believing that it was possible to treat political decisions in the economic sphere as intellectual problems alone. The experts had not agreed on the solution to the intellectual problems of 1931, and Keynes had consistently failed in his efforts to influence events because he was not supported by a political movement. The dilemma which Keynes had constructed was not inherent in socialism; it had been solved by getting rid of the old guard. Rowse ended on an optimistic note by claiming that the Labour Party was now "a much more hopeful field for the propagation of his views and a more likely instrument for putting them into effect". He reminded Keynes that "the right policy for him is to seek to put himself in relation with the political environment which alone can make his views effective".[2]

It was natural that Labour's Annual Conference in 1931 should be largely taken up with the problems of banking and finance. A policy report on these questions was drawn up for presentation to the 1932 conference; it contained four proposals.

(1) That the aim of British monetary policy should be to stabilise wholesale prices and to seek international agreement to stabilise exchange rates.

---

[1] "Dilemma of Modern Socialism", *Political Quarterly*, April-June 1932.
[2] "Mr. Keynes on Socialism: A Reply", *Political Quarterly*, 1932, pp. 409-415. This became quite a hobby-horse for Rowse in this period; see his "Socialism and Mr. Keynes", *Nineteenth Century*, Sept. 1932 and *Mr. Keynes and the Labour Movement* (1936), an enthusiastic review and exposition of the *General Theory*.

(2) That the Bank of England should be brought under public ownership and control.

(3) That a National Investment Board should be set up to control the direction of investment.

(4) That emergency powers should be taken to prevent the banking community from sabotaging any future Labour Government.

Keynes's review of this document (not mentioned by Harrod) claimed that it was "convincing and acceptable proof of the continued vitality of the Labour Party"; it contained a "moderate and quite practicable monetary policy for adoption by the only organised body of opinion outside the National Government". The first proposal in favour of a managed currency clearly showed the influence of his own writings and of the Macmillan Report. Keynes was in favour of changes in the constitution of the Bank of England, but wanted it to retain greater independence. His attitude to nationalisation of the joint stock banks, excluded here but reinstated in the Party's programme later, was far more tolerant than is implied in Harrod's account: "Keynes's moderate statesmanship did not appeal to them; the *New Statesman* carried a foolish article suggesting the nationalisation of the Joint Stock Banks—as though that could do any good at this juncture!"[1] What Keynes actually said on this subject was as follows:

". . . in the first place, the control of the Big Five, otherwise than through the Bank of England, is not necessary for the purpose of handling the vital controls, whilst as a piece of socialism it belongs to a late stage of socialisation and is not one of the indispensable first measures. In the second place, I would lay ten to one that, were it a plank in the Labour platform, it would nevertheless be dropped as soon as the party assumed office. . . . The proposal to nationalise the Big Five is first-class if conceived as a piece of irritation policy, but it is not at this stage serious business."

Keynes gave a warm welcome to the proposal to establish a National Investment Board. This again was one of his own ideas, but he felt that the drafters of the report had not gone far enough; the main duty of the Board would be to control the volume and not simply the direction of investment.

"The task of the National Investment Board, as I conceive it, is, therefore, first, the maintenance of equilibrium between the total flow of new investment on the one hand, and on the other hand the total resources available for investment at the price level which

[1] *Op. cit.*, p. 439.

we are now endeavouring to maintain, i.e. so as to avoid both inflation and deflation; and secondly a division of the aggregate of new lending between foreign and domestic borrowers which is appropriate to the foreign-exchange level best united to the stability of domestic prices. . . . The grappling with these central controls is the rightly conceived Socialism of the future."[1]

Keynes did not remain in sympathy with the official utterances of the Labour opposition for long, especially when they reverted to what he called "moss-grown, demi-semi, Fabian Marxism". But then he also believed that out-of-dateness was the leading characteristic of most men actually holding office in the 'thirties. In the case of the Prime Minister, Chamberlain, he believed that blindness was his chief strength:

"If he could see even a little, if he became faintly cognisant of the turmoil of ideas and projects and schemes to save the country that are tormenting the rest of us, his superbly brazen self-confidence would be fatally impaired."[2]

Keynes seems to have believed that the best elements in the Conservative and Labour Parties were essentially liberals. If a label has to be attached to Keynes's political position in the 'thirties it is probably best to describe him as a liberal socialist.[3]

Given Keynes's attitude to political parties and his contempt for the common herd, it is not difficult to see why he failed to build up much of a following in the Labour movement as a whole. His relations with the serious economic thinkers in the movement before and after the publication of the *General Theory* require more explanation. As early as 1926 Beatrice Webb had noted that there was "no other man who might discover how to control the wealth of nations in the public interest"; she felt that he might achieve "a big scheme of social engineering".[4] Hugh Dalton might dismiss Keynes's advocacy of public works in 1929 as "mere Lloyd George finance", yet Bevin and Keynes shared much in common in their work for the Macmillan Committee, and Mosley drew inspiration from Keynes in preparing his famous memorandum.[5]

But while there was room for individual points of contact, there

[1] *New Statesman*, Sept. 24th 1932.
[2] *New Statesman*, Jan. 28th 1939.
[3] See e.g. *ibid*., p. 123. "The question is whether we are prepared to move out of the nineteenth century *laissez-faire* state into an era of liberal socialism, by which I mean a system where we can act as an organised community for common purposes and to promote social and economic justice, whilst respecting and protecting the individual—his freedom of choice, his faith, his mind and its expression, his enterprise and his property."
[4] *Diaries, 1924-1933*, pp. 112-3.
[5] See pp. 122-3 above.

was also a genuine clash of intellectual traditions. This becomes clear in the case of G. D. H. Cole, a socialist and an economist, whose policy conclusions were similar in some respects to those of Keynes. He too was feeling his way towards a new kind of economics which would encompass mass unemployment rather than leave it as the outcome of frictions and partial defects in the operation of the system. But the style of argument differs. Keynes belonged to the liberal, rationalist tradition, whereas Cole's allegiance was to the body of ideas which had opposed this tradition throughout the nineteenth century. Like other socialist thinkers who were not Fabians, and some who were, Cole inherited the antipathy to academic economics which had led Ruskin, Toynbee, and Morris to attack political economy earlier. They did so on the grounds that it ignored important moral aspects of economic behaviour, and for its apparent in-difference to "value-in-use" as opposed to market value. In approaching the problem of unemployment Cole followed the heretical line of Hobson, a fellow-disciple in the Ruskin tradition.[1]

Cole later welcomed the *General Theory* in a review entitled "Mr. Keynes Beats the Band"; he judged it to be the most important book published in economics since Marx's *Das Kapital* or Ricardo's *Principles*. Its main virtue was that it gave "the critics of economic orthodoxy solid ground on which they can set their feet".[2] At a later stage, however, Cole felt it necessary to distance himself from the new orthodoxy created by Keynes, and proclaim the continued inde-pendence of socialist economics. He disliked Keynes's emphasis on global divisions of the total product, believing that a more dis-aggregated approach in theory, and a large public sector in practice, would be needed if state intervention was to be effective.[3]

There were economists in the inter-war period of an orthodox, non-Keynesian turn of mind who were also avowed socialists: two such, Hugh Dalton and E. M. F. Durbin, both significantly enough attached to the London School of Economics, can be taken as examples. In both cases their economics and their belief in socialism seem to have been kept in water-tight compartments, providing proof, if needed, of the fact that political and economic beliefs do not necessarily coalesce into neat ideological bundles.

Dalton was an expert on public finance and the author of a well-known text-book on the subject. The only issues on which Dalton's professional views can be considered "radical" in any sense were on such questions as income redistribution, inheritance taxation, and more especially, on the subject of a capital levy to repay war debt.

[1] Perhaps the most interesting example of this aspect of Cole's work can be found in his "Towards a New Economic Theory" in *Economic Tracts for the Times* (1932).

[2] *New Statesman*, Feb. 15th 1936.

[3] *Socialist Economist* (1950), especially Ch. II.

In most of these matters, however, he was following a path well-trodden by previous, mainly orthodox, writers in this field, notably by his mentors, Pigou and Cannan. In the first edition of his *Public Finance* written in 1922, there is a brief discussion of public works as a remedy for unemployment. In the light of Bowley's proposals in 1909, and subsequent professional support by Pigou and Robertson, Dalton's conclusions can only be described as tepid and uninformative. After saying that public works schemes might "steady" the demand for labour he concluded that "such a policy cannot do much to reduce unemployment, the chief causes of which are connected with fluctuations in the value of money and in the yield of crops and with the failure of large sections of the business world to form reasonably correct estimates of future conditions or to learn from past experience of the trade cycle."[1] By 1936, in the ninth edition, he was prepared to support countercyclical public works; and a chapter was added giving cautious support to contracyclical budget balancing. It is notable that the discussion is entirely in terms of inflation and deflation, of rising or falling prices rather than incomes, and that there is no mention of the multiplier.[2] He appears to have vacillated between a fairly orthodox monetary view of the trade cycle, and faith in the ultimate powers of socialist planning. Thus in an essay written in 1934 we find him saying that "there are strong reasons for believing that, with a comparatively stable price level, production and employment are also likely to be comparatively stable", followed later by the view that: "I believe that freedom from the plague of recurrent booms and slumps can be found only in a Planned Economy."[3]

Evan Durbin is a more interesting case: a young man in the 'thirties teaching economics at the London School, who later became Dalton's Parliamentary Private Secretary, moving on to a junior ministerial post before his premature death in 1948, Durbin is chiefly known for his contributions to the debate on economic planning.[4] At an earlier stage of his career, however, he wrote a study of theories of trade depression attacking the under-consumptionist position of Hobson and others, and attempting a synthesis of the views of Hayek and Keynes (of the *Treatise*).[5] The result was strongly Hayekian in flavour and markedly pessimistic in its conclusions. He believed that expansionist solutions, whether of a monetary or fiscal type, actually made the situation worse; they could do nothing to touch the real source of depression—an over-extended capital structure—and

[1] *Op. cit.*, p. 176.
[2] *Op. cit.*, pp. 235-8 and Chapter XXVI.
[3] See H. Dalton (ed.) *Unbalanced Budgets* (1934), pp. 439.
[4] See his collected essays in *Problems of Economic Planning* (1949).
[5] *Purchasing Power and Trade Depression, A Critique of Under-Consumption Theories* (1934).

would merely perpetuate the cycle: "If pursued with sufficient vigour during the period of depression it will start the recovery but it will sow the seeds for the next boom. If pursued at any other time it will merely accentuate the process of cyclical fluctuation." The only solutions were either to increase voluntary saving, which effectively meant lowering wages and redistributing income in favour of the rich, or reducing excess capacity in the capital goods industries. The first alternative was undesirable on egalitarian grounds and the second was bound to be harsh and painful. With obvious reluctance he felt it necessary to disabuse members of the Labour movement of their optimistic faith in reflationary measures. The only solution was "to accept the hard discipline of uncompromising realism".[1] It is tempting to argue that with opinions like this it is no wonder that he turned to a planned economy as the way out.

Another source of the failure of communication between Keynes and the left-wing intelligentsia—before the publication of the *General Theory* at least—was the swing towards Marxian diagnoses of the defects of the capitalist system which took place during the depression. Keynes was notoriously tone-deaf as far as Marx was concerned. Only this can account for his inability to see even remote parallels between his own work and that of Marx on the subject of the capitalist breakdown, though this is not to say that there are any *simple* parallels. Keynes remained convinced that Marxism was simply a product of Ricardian orthodoxy, "so much so, that, if Ricardian economics were to fall, an essential prop to the intellectual foundations of Marxism would fall with it".[2]

It does not require much imagination to see how developments in this period could be interpreted as confirmation of the Marxian prediction that capitalism would eventually destroy itself by a series of deepening crises. Was there not a permanent reserve-army of unemployed? Was it not true that attempts were being made to depress wages, unemployment benefits, and the standard of living of the workers, in a vain attempt to prevent the decline of profits? While many remained committed to the view that the problems of capitalism were still soluble within the context of democracy, others, having observed the rise of Fascism and the fall of democratic socialism in France and Germany, came to the conclusion that the survival of democracy and capitalism were incompatible aims. Piece-meal tinkering was no use; the entrenched interests of the defenders of capitalism would always prevent the implementation of any real solution. Society would have to be completely reconstructed

---

[1] *Ibid.*, especially Chapter VI.
[2] *New Republic*, Feb. 10th 1935; see also his letter to Bernard Shaw quoted in Harrod, *op. cit.*, p. 462.

along Communist lines, if necessary, by revolution. The theme of alienation and extremism in British political life in the 'thirties is well-documented elsewhere, and was, of course, connected with the peace movement and other issues of foreign policy which fall outside the scope of this study.[1] The only point that is relevant here is that for those who adopted the Marxian position there was no room for the meliorist ideas of Keynes, particularly when, as was true before 1936, these were not part of a coherent theoretical system.

The most striking, though perhaps not the most typical, example of the impact of the breakdown of capitalism on British socialist thinkers in this period is provided by Sidney and Beatrice Webb, the original architects of Fabian socialism, a creed devoted to the view that socialism could be established by gradual, piece-meal change. The first sign of a change in their attitude came in 1923 when they published the *Decay of Capitalist Civilisation*. In view of what they thought was a hardening of attitudes on the part of the governing classes towards further social and economic reform, they framed an indictment of the capitalist system as a whole which was in marked contrast with their previous expositions of particular defects and institutions. By the mid-'thirties they had progressed further in this direction by completely accepting the Marxian historical prediction of the eventual collapse of capitalism. In the Minority Report of the Royal Commission on the Poor Laws in 1909 they had started the process of trying to gain acceptance for the view that unemployment was remediable within the existing framework. After two decades of continuous mass unemployment they could no longer uphold this position; they believed that they had been guilty of complacency, and had "unwittingly misled public opinion". The only hope for civilisation lay in experiments along the lines of Soviet Communism.[2]

Interest in the Soviet model in the 'thirties was not confined to Marxists and members of the Communist Party. All those anxious to extend the scope of economic planning in Britain found it necessary to take up a position on this matter, if only to differentiate the "democratic" alternative. Here again Keynes was atypical. After his first visit to Russia in 1925 he said that Communism was incapable of making "any contribution to our economic problems of intellectual interest or scientific value".[3] Commenting on the published conversation between H. G. Wells and Stalin in 1934, he re-iterated this view, claiming that as a solution to our economic difficulties communism was "an insult to our intelligence".[4]

[1] See e.g. N. Wood *Communism and British Intellectuals* (1959); J. Symons, *The Thirties* (1965).
[2] See B. Webb's account of their conversion in *Our Partnership* (1948).
[3] *Essays in Persuasion*, p. 306.
[4] *New Statesman*, Nov. 10th 1934.

The significance of communism to Keynes lay in its ascetic, religious appeal to intellectuals. Harrod states that Keynes found this depressing.[1] This is an entirely gratuitous interpretation which seems to represent Harrod's rather than Keynes's views. Keynes's actual assessment was as follows:

> "There is no-one in politics today worth sixpence outside the ranks of liberals except the post-war generation of intellectual Communists under thirty-five. Them, too, I like and respect. Perhaps in their feelings and instincts they are the nearest thing we now have to the typical nervous nonconformist English gentleman who went to the Crusades, made the Reformation, fought the Great Rebellion, won us our civil and religious liberties and humanised the working classes last century."[2]

Making every allowance for rhetoric this does not read as though Keynes found them "depressing". Once more it would seem that Harrod is guilty of trying to assimilate Keynes to the Establishment at every stage of his career. By so doing he obscures the fact that it was possible for Keynes, in despair at the inertia of conventional political leaders, to welcome signs of real concern and intellectual activity, whatever their source. For example, he had nothing but praise for the Left Book Club ("one of the finest and living movements of our time"); he expressed willingness to join Sir Stafford Cripps' breakaway group on the left of the Labour Party; and he advised Bevin and the trade union movement not to lose contact with the "splendid material of the young amateur Communists".[3]

It is true though, as we have noted earlier, that Keynes showed little interest in the planning movement, whatever its political complexion.[4] It is legitimate to describe him as antipathetic to a regime that required detailed intervention in the allocation of resources. This antipathy underlies his desire, even during the war, to minimise the scope of detailed rationing and controls. But these "moderately conservative" aspects of his position were no barrier to a socialist interpretation of Keynesianism; they could readily be detached from the general context. This fact suggests either a certain political naïvety on Keynes's part, or that, quite understandably, he did not wish to place extra barriers in the way of acceptance of his views by aligning himself too strongly with socialism. It was equally possible to interpret Keynesianism in a more limited right-wing fashion. Herein, perhaps, lies the recipe for acceptance of Keynesianism as a purely technocratic device.

[1] *Op. cit.*, p. 451.
[2] *New Statesman*, Jan. 28th 1939.
[3] *Ibid.*
[4] See p. 218 above.

Nevertheless, it is not difficult to see how enthusiastically a non-Marxist socialist could take to and develop Keynes's ideas. In the first place, Keynes provided academic support for the view that wage reductions and other attacks on the standard of living of the working classes were neither just nor expedient. His system justified an extension of the role of the state in controlling the level of investment, and provided a further rationale for the redistribution of income from high-income savers to the low-income consumers. Socialists could ignore Keynes's own view that "dangerous human activities can be canalised into comparatively harmless channels by the existence of opportunities for money-making and private wealth".[1] Here was an effective weapon for use against the Marxists on the one side and the defenders of old-style capitalism on the other; a real third alternative, the absence of which before the *General Theory* had driven many into the Communist camp.

Those who accepted the Marxian diagnosis remained impervious to the charms of Keynesianism. They pointed out that it only supported policies for removing a major defect *within* capitalism, that it did nothing to transform the basic relations between capital and labour which underlie the system and are the source of its fatal contradictions. Like all bourgeois economists, they claimed, Keynes was unwilling to see economic relationships as part of a wider set of social and political links and antagonisms. Some held that Keynesian techniques could only serve to stave off disaster, while others who took the system more seriously argued that the state, acting under the dominant influence of the capitalist class, would not have the political courage necessary to act with vigour to eliminate unemployment—except perhaps by means of war and military expenditure. There is plenty in the record of countries like Britain and the United States to suggest that this was not an idle criticism up to the Second World War. And even now, in the United States, left-Keynesians feel it necessary to campaign in advance for an extension of the public sector to take care of a possible run-down in military spending.[2]

G. D. H. Cole said that "most of the non-Marxist socialist economists swallowed Keynes whole, and became his fervent disciples".[3] There is an element of exaggeration in this view, as the tenacity with which the post-war Labour Government stuck to physical planning shows.[4] But it is certainly true that Keynes provided the means by which many British socialists could reconcile themselves to a modified form of capitalism.

[1] *General Theory*, p. 374.
[2] The most vocal exponent of this is J. K. Galbraith; see his recent work *The Industrial System* (1967).
[3] *Socialist Economics*, p. 49.
[4] See pp. 282-3 above.

An interesting example of a convert to Keynesianism is provided by John Strachey. Interesting, because Strachey was the most influential spokesman for the Marxist position during the 'thirties, and also because his conversion was a matter of head rather than heart or senility. Strachey's acceptance of the Marxist interpretation of the capitalist break-down is a clear case of someone who was driven to this conclusion by the pressure of economic and political circumstance during the depression and 1931 crisis. He had been Mosley's Parliamentary Private Secretary in the Second Labour Government and had resigned with him in 1931 when the Mosley memorandum was rejected. He became one of the founding members of Mosley's New Party, which initially furnished a rallying point for those activists who wished to create, in their own words, "a movement which would cut like a sword through the knot of the past to the meaning of the modern State". But after the failure of the New Party candidates in the 1931 election, and Mosley's swing to Fascism, Strachey became a Communist. In a powerful series of works he set out to show the theoretical weaknesses in the ideas of "capitalist economists"—among whom were numbered Robbins, Hayek, G. D. H. Cole, and Keynes —when judged by the superior insights of Marx. He rejected Lib-Lab bromides; there could be no compromise between socialism and the capitalist productive system. Nor could the former evolve out of the latter without revolution.[1]

The change in Strachey's position came gradually; it was first apparent in his *Programme for Progress* published in 1940. He had been impressed, somewhat prematurely perhaps, by Roosevelt's comparatively successful experiment in expansionist finance. As he later explained, under the influence of Douglas Jay's *The Socialist Case* (1936) and Keynes's *General Theory*, he was coming round to the idea that capitalist crises could be abolished by a socialist government working from within the system.[2] In the final stage of his conversion Strachey became one of the leading exponents of the view that:

> "so long as effective democracy exists . . . it is untrue to say that there is no possibility of applying Keynesian remedies. They will be opposed by the capitalists, certainly; but experience shows that they can be imposed by the electorate. Keynesian economic policies, joined with traditional socialist measures of public ownership and social reform, have become indispensable instruments by means of which democracy can achieve its purpose."[3]

[1] See *The Coming Struggle for Power* (1934); *The Nature of the Capitalist Crisis* (1935); *The Theory and Practice of Socialism* (1937); and *What Are We To Do?* (1938).
[2] See N. Wood, *op. cit.*, pp. 186-8.
[3] See *Contemporary Capitalism* (1956), p. 239.

# Index

Abramowitz, M., 250
Academic economics (*see also under* Keynes), 332–3
Age of Official Economic Adviser, 329–30
Ackley, Gardner, 303
Acworth, W. M., 58
Ady, P. H., 282, 284, 286, 288, 290, 291, 314
*Affluent Society, The* (J. K. Galbraith), 301
*After Defence—What?* (NRPB), 274
*After Seven Years* (R. Moley), 225
*After the War—Full Employment* (A. Hansen), 274
*Age of Keynes, The* (R. Lekachman), 221, 306
*Age of Marshall, The* (N. Jha), 23
*Age of Roosevelt, The* (A. M. Schlesinger), 222, 223
Aldcroft, D. H., 68
Alexander, Sydney, 294
Allen, G. C., 207, 213
Allen, Thomas, 137
Alten, W. M., 221
American Loan to Britain (1946), the, 256, 279
*America's Recovery Program* (A. Sachs and C. Wilcox), 233
Amery, L. S., 119, 121
*Analysis of the Sources of War Finance, etc., 1938 and 1940* (White Paper), 263
Anderson, C. J., 124, 239
Anderson, Sir John (Lord Waverley), 266
Andrews, P. W. S., 251
Anglo-American contrasts, *see under* Great Britain *and* United States
Anglo-American Financial Agreement (1946), 278
Archibald, G. C., 196
Ashley, W. J., 58, 229
Ashton, T. S., 77
Ashworth, W., 100

*Aspects of British Economic History 1918–1925* (A. C. Pigou), 78
Atlantic Charter, the, 277, 278
Attwood, Thomas, 226
Austria, 116, 194
    Austrian influence on Hayek and Robbins, 193

Bagehot, Walter, 50
Bailey, Stephen, 275, 276, 331
*Balancing the Budget Federal Fiscal: Policy During Depression* (S. E. Leland), 240
Baldwin, Stanley (Earl Baldwin), 110, 112, 118
Balfour, A. J. (Earl Balfour), 63, 64
Balfour, Sir Arthur, 124
Balfour Committee on Industry and Trade, 214, 216
Bank of England (*see also* Gold Standard), 76–7, 80, 81, 83, 91, 93, 116, 124, 141
    Labour's pressure for state control of, 92–3, 228, 344
Bank of France, 117
Bank of International Settlements, 116
*Banking Policy and the Price Level* (D. H. Robertson), 159
Bassett, R., 117, 133, 140, 143
Baumol, W. J., 179
Becker, G., 179
*Beckoning Frontiers* (M. Eccles), 241, 244
Beer, S. H., 198, 204, 212, 213, 283, 286, 291, 312
Benham, F., 131, 150
Berle, Adolf, 214, 229, 230, 231, 232
Berlin: blockade 1948, 297; crisis 1961, 305
Besant, Annie, 48
Beveridge, William (Lord Beveridge), 53, 54
    approach to unemployment problem, 55–7, 58, 103, 196–7

Beveridge William—*contd.*
full employment in a free society,
273–4
at London School of Economics, 151,
152, 195, 196
convert to Keynesianism, 197
Report on Social Security (1942),
269, 274, 280
Unemployment Insurance, Chair-
man of Committee on, 210–11
Bevin, Ernest, 88, 104, 111, 124, 135,
270, 345
advocates abandonment of gold
standard, 137
affinity with Keynes, 345, 350
Labour Minister, 285
*Life and Times of Ernest Bevin* (A.
Bullock), 102, 135, 270
Birch, Nigel, 290
Black, R. D. C., 179
Blaug, M., 57
Blum, J. M., 225, 226, 244, 245
Blum, Leon, 200
Boer War, 59
*Bogy of Economic Maturity, The* (G.
Terborgh), 250
Booth, Charles, 29, 47–8
*Booth, Charles, Socialist Scientist* (T. S.
and M. B. Simey), 48
Boothby, Robert (Lord Boothby), 119,
198
Bowley, A. L., 54, 55, 106, 160, 347
Braae, G. P., 203
Bradbury, Lord, 83, 92, 131
Bradbury Committee on Currency and
Bank of England Note Issues
(1925), 82, 84, 86, 87, 138
Bretherton, R. F., 221
Bretton Woods conference 1944, 256,
278, 279, 315
Briggs, Asa, 107
*Britain Between the Wars: 1918–1940* (C.
L. Mowat), 140, 198
*Britain's Economic Growth, 1920–1966* (A.
J. Youngson), 81, 84, 132, 160
*Britain's Economic Prospects* (R.E. Caves),
14
*Britain's Industrial Future* (Liberal "Yel-
low Book" 1928), 100, 108, 109,
209, 214, 232
*Britannia Languens* pamphlet, 15
British Economic Association (Royal
Economic Society), 23

*British Economy 1945–1950* (G. D. N.
Worswick and P. H. Ady), 282,
284, 286, 288, 290, 291
*British Economy in the 1950's* (G. D. N.
Worswick and P. H. Ady), 291,
314
*British Industries and Their Organisation*
(G. C. Allen), 213
*British Monetary Policy* (F. Benham),
131, 150
*British Public Finances, 1880–1952* (U. K.
Hicks), 96, 99
Brown, D., 186
Brown, E. Cary, 246, 293, 300
Brown, W. A., 77
Brüning, Heinrich, 200
Buchan, F. C., 151
Budget, the (budgetary control)
as tool of economic management, 94,
126–7, 166, 283, 285
in the 'Twenties, 95–100
during World War II, 260, 262
balanced Budgets, 204–9, 294, 305
deficits in, U.S., 243–4, 245–6
Bullock, Alan, 102, 134, 137, 270
*Burden of Plenty, The* (G. Hutton), 74
Burke, Edmund, 328
Burns, Arthur, 299, 300
Burns, J. M., 238, 239
Butler, R. A. (Lord Butler)
as Chancellor, 287–8
Butskellism, 198–9, 213–8, 288
Buxton, N. K., 68

Cadman, Sir John, 124
*Call Back Yesterday* (H. Dalton,
Memoirs), 35, 153, 195
Cambridge University (Cambridge
School of Economists), 14, 23, 146–
8, 148–50, 152–3, 164, 189, 191,
196, 267
*Can Lloyd George Do It?* (J. M. Keynes
and H. D. Henderson), 110, 273
Cannan, Edwin, 102, 103, 147, 148–9,
190
Carr-Saunders, A. M., 207
Cassel, Gustav, 318–9
Cassels, John, 264
Catchings, Waddill, 232, 240
*Causes and Cures of Unemployment* (W.
Beveridge), 197
Caves, R. E., 14

*Central Banking After Bagehot* (R. S. Sayers), 91

*Challenge to Affluence* (G. Myrdal), 301

Chamberlin, E. H., 324

Chamberlain, Joseph
Chairman of Local Government Board, 53
Tariff reform and, 58, 59, 63
Imperial Preference and, 59
Tariff Commission (1903), 58
*Joseph Chamberlain* (P. Fraser), 64

Chamberlain, Neville, 64, 133, 202, 262
Chancellor, 198, 204, 206–8, 211
Prime Minister, 345
Tariff Reform and, 204
*Life of Neville Chamberlain* (K. Feiling), 132, 198, 218
*Neville Chamberlain* (Iain Macleod), 133

Cheap money, 203–4, 258

Cherwell, Lord, 266

Chester, D. N., 257, 263, 266

Churchill, Sir Winston
Chancellor, and the return to Gold Standard decision, 74–5, 83, 87, 88, 89, 90, 99, 113, 127
orthodox budgetary policies of, 121
presents "Treasury View" on unemployment, 109–10
Prime Minister (War Coalition), 256, 266

Citrine, Lord, 124

Civil Research, Committee of, 124

*Civil Service, The* (H. Thomas), 333

Clapham, J. H., 44

Clark, Colin, 262

Clark, J. M., 264

"Classical" economics, interpretation of, 169, 177–81
Say's Law and, 179–80

Clay, Sir Henry, 84, 86, 87, 88, 90, 102, 103, 122, 206, 266, 271

Coal Dispute, Court of Inquiry on, 88

Coal Mines Act 1930, 213

Coats, A. W., 60, 153, 195

Cohrssen, H. R. L., 224

Cole, G. D. H., 104, 124, 265, 346, 351, 352

*Collectivist Economic Planning* (F. A. Hayek), 192, 325

Colm, Gerhard, 247, 303

Colonial Development Bill (J. H. Thomas's), 120

*Coming Struggle for Power, The* (J. Strachey), 352

Common Market, 15
Britain's approach to, 64

*Communism and British Intellectuals* (N. Wood), 349

*Congress Makes a Law* (S. Bailey), 275, 331

Conservative Party
acceptance of welfare state, 287
1931 Crisis and, 133
governments of —
through 'Thirties, 198–218
lays foundations of mixed economy (Butskellism), 198–9, 213–8, 288
1951–63, 287–93
party dissentients, 118–9
Trade and Industry Committee, 207

"Consumers' surplus", concept of, 39–42, 44

*Contemporary Capitalism* (J. Strachey), 352

Co-operative Congress 1889, 33

Coppock, D. J., 29

Corn Laws, repeal of, 59
Anti-Corn Law League, 60

Corry, B. A., 179

*Costs of Economic Growth, The* (E. J. Mishan), 320

Crawford, A. W., 223

Credit-Anstalt Bank, 116

Cripps, Sir Stafford, 350
as Chancellor, 284–6

Crisis 1931, 24, 25, 89, 114–44, 149, 209
abandonment of Gold Standard, 137–8, 201
climax of and collapse of Labour Government, 132–5
heralds new era of economic policies, 72
Keynes and, 135–42, 201, 212
May Committee and Retrenchment, 125–32
preliminary dispositions and personalities, 117–20

*Critical Essays in Monetary Theory* (J. R. Hicks), 162, 180

Culbertson, J. M., 300

Cunliffe Committee Report on Currency and Foreign Exchange, 70, 74–8, 82, 86, 89, 91, 138, 201
Keynes's criticism of, 78–81

Cunningham, W., 58

Currie, Lauchlin, 244

*Daily Express*, 207
*Daily Mail*, 207, 223
Dalton, Hugh, 35, 148, 153, 189, 195,
    199–200, 209, 345, 346, 347
    "Keynesian" Chancellor, 283–4, 285
    Memoirs: *Call Back Yesterday*, 35, 153,
    195
Dampier-Whetham, Sir William, 206
Darwin, Charles, 32
*Das Kapital* (K. Marx), 346
Davison, R. C., 54, 101, 103, 105
De Gaulle, General, 173
*Decay of Capitalist Civilisation* (Sidney
    and Beatrice Webb), 35, 349
*Democratic President, The* (R. Tugwell),
    228, 232, 233, 238, 240
*Den 'Nya Ekononiem' i Sverige* (Karl-
    Gustav Landgren), 162, 209
Devaluation of Sterling—
    in 'Thirties, 200–3; 1949, 286
Development and Road Fund Act
    1909, 55
Development Councils, introduction of,
    286
    NEDC set up, 333
*Diaries* (B. Webb), 55, 120, 342, 345
*Diary With Letters, A* (T. Jones), 140
Dilke, Sir Charles, 63
Dillon, Douglas, 304
Dorfman, J., 221, 228, 232, 238
Douglas, Lewis, 237
Douglas, William, 244
Dow, J. C. R., 271, 281, 282, 283, 287,
    313, 314, 315
Dowie, J. A., 68
Drucker, P. F., 91
Duesenberry, James, 303
Duncan, Sir Andrew, 124
Durbin, E. M. F., 150, 346, 347


Eccles, Marriner, 241, 244
Eckstein, Otto, 303
*Economic Advice and Presidential Leadership*
    (E. S. Flash), 299, 303, 334
Economic Advisory Council, 124, 135,
    140, 141, 143, 150, 212, 259, 265
    Standing Committee of, 259, 265
Economic Affairs Ministry, establish-
    ment of, 284

*Economic Balance and a Balanced Budget*
    (M. Eccles), 244
*Economic Basis of Class Conflict, The* (L.
    Robbins), 187, 189, 192
*Economic Consequences of Mr. Churchill,*
    *The* (J. M. Keynes), 84, 146, 153
*Economic Consequences of the Peace* (J. M.
    Keynes), 78, 153, 220
*Economic Consequences of Recent American*
    *Tax Policy* (G. Colm and F.
    Lehmann), 247
*Economic Doctrines, Review of* (T. W.
    Hutchison), 41, 47, 50, 110
*Economic Essays* (A. C. Pigou), 153
*Economic Growth, An American Problem*
    (G. M. Gutmann), 301
*Economic History of England 1870–1939*
    (W. Ashworth), 100
*Economic Mind in American Civilisation,*
    *The* (J. Dorfman), 221, 228, 238
*Economic Notes on Insular Free Trade*
    (A. J. Balfour), 64
*Economic Philosophy* (J. Robinson), 146,
    292, 323
*Economic Planning in the U.K.: Some*
    *Lessons* (E. A. G. Robinson) 257, 285
*Economic Policy and Full Employment* (A.
    Hansen), 250
*Economic Policy: Principles and Design*
    (J. Tinbergen), 330
*Economic Problems in Peace and War, The*
    (L. Robbins), 267
*Economic Program for American Demo-*
    *cracy* (compiled by Harvard and
    Tufts economists), 247
*Economic Recovery of Britain 1932–4*
    (H. W. Richardson), 198
*Economic Research and the Development of*
    *Economic Science and Public Policy*
    (E. A. Goldenweiser in), 279; (J.
    Jewkes in), 280
*Economic Research and the Keynesian*
    *Thinking of our Times* (A. Burns),
    299
*Economic Scares* (E. Cannan), 149
*Economic Stabilisation in an Unbalanced*
    *World* (A. Hansen), 185
*Economic Stagnation or Progress* (E. W.
    Swanson and E. P. Schmidt), 250
*Economic Surveys, post-war Labour govern-*
    *ment's annual*, 285, 286, 287
*Economic Theory in Retrospect* (M. Blaug),
    57

*Economic Theory of Socialism, On the* (B. Lippincott), 325

*Economic Thought and Policy* (D. H. Macgregor), 280

*Economic Thought of F. D. Roosevelt and the Origins of the New Deal* (D. R. Fusfeld), 228

*Economic Tracts for the Times* (G. D. H. Cole in), 346

*Economics, An Awkward Corner* (Joan Robinson), 318

*Economics and Economic Policy in Britain 1946–1966* (T. W. Hutchison), 153

*Economics and Ideology* (R. L. Meek), 336

*Economics of Full Employment, The* (Oxford Institute of Statistics), 273

*Economics of Imperfect Competition* (Joan Robinson), 324

*Economics of Recession and Revival* (K. D. Roose), 242

*Economics of the Recovery Program* (D. Brown), 186

*Economics of Welfare* (A. C. Pigou), 57

*Economists and the Public* (W. H. Hutt), 190, 194

*Economist's Protest, An* (E. Cannan), 149

Edgeworth, F. Y., 39

Eisenhower Administration, 298–300, 301, 304

Employment Policy White Paper 1944, *see under* Great Britain

*End of Laissez-Faire, The* (Keynes' lectures), 108, 156, 214, 232

*English History 1914–1945* (A. J. P. Taylor), 119

Eshag, E., 146, 147

*Essay on the Nature and Significance of Economic Science* (L. Robbins), 191

*Essays in Biography* (J. M. Keynes), 178, 179

*Essays in Economic Method* (R. L. Smyth), 34

*Essays in Monetary Theory* (D. H. Robertson), 78, 205

*Essays in Persuasion* (J. M. Keynes), 73, 82, 110, 119, 142, 144, 148, 163, 201, 342

*Essays in the Economics of Socialism and Capitalism 1885–1932* (R. L. Smyth), 31, 36

*Essays in the History of Economics* (G. J. Stigler), 21, 175, 255, 303

*Essays in the Theory of Employment* (Joan Robinson), 317

*Essays in World Economics* (J. R. Hicks), 43

*Essays on Economic Policy* (N. Kaldor), 274

*Essays on Money and Interest* (D. H. Robertson), 160

*Essays on Philosophy, Politics and Economics* (F. A. Hayek), 193

European Recovery Programme, 287

Excess Profits Duty, 99

Exchange Equalisation Account, 201, 202, 225

*History and Mechanism of the Exchange Equalisation Account 1932–9* (L. Waight), 201

*Fabian Essays*, 48

*Fabian Socialism and English Politics 1884–1918* (A. M. McBriar), 36

Fabians, the, and Fabian Society, 35, 36, 52, 349

*Fact and Fancy in the TNEC Monographs* (National Association of Manufacturers), 250

*Federal Budget and Fiscal Policy 1798–1958* (L. H. Kimmel), 236

*Federal Fiscal Policy in the Post-War Recessions* (W. A. Lewis), 293

Federation of British Industries, 78, 118

Feiling, K., 132, 198, 218

Feinstein, C. H., 68

Fellner, W., 160

*Finance of British Government 1920–1936* (U. K. Hicks), 99, 203

*Financial Policy 1939–1945* (R. S. Sayers), 257, 258

*First Year of the Gold Standard, The* (T. E. Gregory), 149

*Fiscal Policy and Business Cycles* (A. Hansen), 247, 249

*Fiscal Policy for Full Employment* (J. H. C. Pierson), 274

Fisher, Irving, 147, 224, 235, 237

Flash, E. S., 299, 303, 334

Ford, A. G., 77

Foster, William, 232, 240

Foxwell, W. J., 31

France, 13, 200, 348

Frankfurter, Felix, 238

Fraser, L. M., 221

Free trade, 28, 59, 60, 139, 150–1, 278

Freeman, R., 293

Friedman, M., 224, 225, 227, 242

*From Marshall to Keynes* (E. Eshag), 146

*From the Morgenthau Diaries* (J. M. Blum), 225

*Full Employment in a Free Society* (W. Beveridge), 197, 270, 273–4

*Full Employment or Stagnation?* (J. M. Culbertson), 300

*Full Recovery or Stagnation?* (A. Hansen), 182, 247, 248, 249

Fulton Committee on the Civil Service, 333

Fusfeld, D. R., 228, 229, 249

*Future of Industrial Man, The* (P. F. Drucker), 91


Gaitskell, Hugh, 207
　as Chancellor, 287, 289

Galbraith, J. K., 114, 238, 264, 301, 303, 310, 351

Gardner, R., 277

Geddes Committee, 99, 104

General Electric Company (U.S.), 228

General Strike 1926, 89

*General Theory of Employment, Interest and Money* (J. M. Keynes) (*see also under* Keynes), 20, 25, 56, 70, 89, 90, 140, 144–5, 152, 153, 155, 156, 158, 160–6, 217, 218, 234, 239, 243, 246, 249, 258, 273, 312, 317, 318, 319, 322, 345, 348, 351, 352

Germany, 13, 14, 62, 63, 72, 181, 193
　Depression, the, and unemployment, 115, 116
　Historical School, 194, 195, 229
　National Socialism, rise of, 116, 193, 200, 209, 221, 348
　war reparations (World War I), 79

Gifford, C. H. R., 164

Gilbert, R. V., 247, 264

Gladstone, William Ewart, 96

*Goal of Economic Growth, The* (E. S. Phelps), 301

Gold and Silver, Royal Commission on (1886–7), 49

Gold Standard
　Britain's return to (1925–31), 71, 74–5, 81–93, 113, 118; and abandon-

Gold Standard—*contd.*
　ment of, 116, 135, 137–8, 201, 205
　consequences of return to gold, 90–3, 150
　Cunliffe Committee and, 74–8
　Keynes' attitude to, 78–81
　U.S. abandons, 201, 202

Goldenweiser, E. A., 279

Goldsmith, Raymond, 264

Gordon, Kermit, 303, 306

Gowing, M. M., 271

Great Britain
　Anglo-American contrasts, 13–14, 313, 331–7
　cost inflation and incomes policy, 316–8
　Prices and Incomes Board, 324
　decline in international industrial leadership, 59, 68
　Gold Standard, return to and abandonment of, *see* Gold Standard
　government and economic policies, 16–7, 21–2, 31, 34, 45, 69, 92, 94, 116
　"decline of *laissez faire*", 16–7, 30, 43, 58, 60, 213–4
　extension of state control, 71, 73, 92–3
　'Thirties, the, and managed economy, 198–218
　　balanced budgets, 204–9
　　cheap money, 203–4
　　devaluation, 200–3
　　housing boom, 203
　　industrial reorganisation and planning, 212–8
　　recovery, 200
　　unemployment policy, 210–12
　growth record and comparisons with other countries, 15, 68–9
　major international financial centre, 13, 28, 115, 292
　post-World War II record, 280–93
　　bi-partisan policies, 288, 291–2
　　control and decontrol, 288–9
　　inflation and disinflation, 283, 285, 292
　　sterling devaluation (1949), 286
　pre-World War I stability, 23, 24, 28–9, 44, 46, 95
　public expenditure as percentage of Gross National Product, 326

Great Britain—*contd.*
　public works as solution to unem-
　　ployment, 104–13, 160, 164–6,
　　312
　welfare state, the, 95, 97–8, 199, 206
　World War II, 256–68
　　economists in government service,
　　　264–6
　　lend-lease, 264
　　post-war planning, 268–74
　　　Employment Policy White
　　　　Paper (1944), 269–73, 274,
　　　　280, 287, 298, 312, 332
*Great Crash, The* (J. K. Galbraith), 114,
　238
*Great Depression, The* (L. Robbins), 149,
　185, 186, 187, 192, 193
Greenwood, Arthur, 266
"Greenwood" Housing Act 1930, 203
Gregory, T. E., 82, 149, 150, 151
Grigg, P. J., 83, 92, 128, 141
*Growth of Public Expenditure in the U.K.*
　(A. T. Peacock and J. Wiseman),
　96, 99
Guillebaud, C. W., 207
Gutmann, G. M., 301

Haberler, G., 173, 177, 179, 183
Haldane, Lord, 124
Hall, R. L., 207, 221
Hallett, G., 335
Hancock, K. J., 87, 99, 105
Hancock, W. K., 271
Handfield-Jones, S. J., 29
Hansen, Alvin, 182, 183, 185, 238,
　265, 274, 298, 299, 306, 310
　disciple of Keynes, 246–50
Hargraves, E. L., 221
*Harmonielehre*, doctrine of, 31
Harriman, Henry, 228
Harrington, M., 301
Harris, Seymour, 170, 182, 236, 303
Harrod, R. F., 79, 107, 113, 140, 156,
　157, 161, 166, 167, 193, 196, 207,
　221, 223, 259, 319, 342, 343, 344,
　348, 350
Harvard, University of, 177, 265
Hawley, E. W., 249
Hawtrey, R. G., 110, 147, 148, 152, 224
Hayek, F. A., 58, 159, 162, 184, 188,
　190–1, 192, 193, 195–6, 217, 325,
　347, 352

Heller, Walter H., 296, 302, 303, 305,
　306, 307, 309, 313, 334
Henderson, Arthur, 134
Henderson, Leon, 244
Henderson, H. D., 74, 110, 124, 140,
　212, 265, 266, 271, 272
Henderson, P. D., 286, 333
Hewins, W. A. S., first director of
　L.S.E., 58
Heyworth Committee on Social Studies
　Report of, 330, 333
Hicks, J. R., 43, 151, 162, 180
Hicks, U. K., 96, 99, 100, 203
Higgins, B., 239
*High Tide and After* (H. Dalton), 283
Hildebrand, G., 247
*History of Economic Analysis* (J. Schum-
　peter), 58, 147, 319
Hobson, J. A., 46, 47, 120, 123, 178,
　188, 197, 217, 240, 346, 347
　influence in United States, 232, 233
　treatment of unemployment, 51–2,
　56
Hodgson, H. V., 115, 202
Holmans, A. E., 293, 295, 298, 300,
　313
Hoover, Calvin, 264
Hoover, Herbert
　Administration of, 219, 225, 235,
　　236, 298
　Secretary of Commerce, 239
Hopkins, Harry, 245
Hopkins, Sir Richard, 111, 112, 125,
　136
House, Colonel, 236
*House of Commons Debates:* (1924) 124;
　(1925) 84, 89; (1929) 109; (1930)
　123; (1931) 126; (1933) 207;
　(1935) 211, 217; (1937) 212
*How to Pay for the War* (Keynes'
　pamphlet), 259–63, 315
*How to Tackle Unemployment* (Liberal
　pamphlet, 1930), 119
Hume, L. J., 78
Humphrey, Don D., 264
Humphrey, George, 300
Hutchison, T. W., 38, 41, 43, 47, 50,
　153
Hutt, W. H., 190, 194, 195
Hutton, G., 74

Ickes, Harold, 244
Imperial Preference, 59, 64, 278

Import Duties Advisory Council, 212, 213

*Income, Employment and Public Policy: Essays in Honour of Alvin H. Hansen* (S. Alexander), 294

Incomes policy, 292, 324

*Indian Currency and Finance* (J. M. Keynes), 147

*Industrial Reconstruction and the Control of Competition* (A. F. Lucas), 213

Industrial Reorganisation (Enabling) Bill 1935, 217

*Industrial Retardation in Britain 1880–1914* (A. L. Levine), 29

*Industrial System, The New*, (J. K. Galbraith), 351

*Industry and Trade* (R. Boothby, H. Macmillan and O. Stanley), 118

*Industry and Trade* (A. Marshall), 29, 33, 41, 43

Industry and Trade, Report of Commission on, 106

*Intellectual Revolution in U.S. Economic Policy-Making* (J. Tobin), 302

International Bank for Reconstruction and Development, 278

International Economic Planning, 277–9

Mutual Aid Agreement (Britain–U.S.), 278

*International Gold Standard Reinterpreted 1914–1934*, 77

International Labour Office, 106, 227

International Monetary Fund, 202, 278, 279

International Trade Organisation, Charter of, 1948, 278, 279

*Inter-War Years, The* (H. Clay), 271, 272

*Is Unemployment Inevitable?* (A. L. Bowley and W. Layton), 92, 106, 107, 154

Italy, rise of fascism in, 72, 200

Jackson, Robert H., 244

Jay, Douglas, 352

Jevons, W. S., 31, 39

Jewkes, J., 266, 280

Jha, N., 23

Johnson, H. G., 170

Johnson, Lyndon B., 313 (*see also* Kennedy-Johnson Administration)

Johnston, Tom, 120, 122

Jones, J. H., 266

Jones, Jesse, 224

Jones, T., 140

*Josiah Stamp, Public Servant* (J. H. Jones), 266

Kahn, R. F., 163, 164–5, 207

Kaldor, Nicholas, 273, 274

Kennedy, C. M., 284, 290

Kennedy, John F., 302–5

academic economists and, 303

"first Keynesian President", 303, 305, 313, 321

Kennedy-Johnson Administration, 302–10, 336

Keynes, John Maynard (Lord Keynes), 14, 19–20, 24, 56, 119, 124

academic community and, 21, 144–97

analysis of his writings, 146–8: *Treatise on Money*, 156–9, 160–5, 169, 178; *General Theory*, 160–6, 167–72, 176, 177–82, 186–8, 195, 196 (*see also separate entries*)

differences with L.S.E., 189–97

opposition to Keynesianism, 148–50, 152–3

advocate of British New Deal, 15

Anglo-American Loan and, 279

" classical economics", interpretation of, 169, 177–81

Communism, views on, 249–50

1931 Crisis, his alternative policies, 135–42, 201, 212

contemporary orthodoxy and, 181–9

gold standard

approach to, 71–2, 138

disagreement with Churchill on, 83–4

opposition to return to, 81–92

views on Cunliffe Report, 78–81

influence in United States, 17, 24–5, 69–70, 177, 182, 219–51, 259, 263–4, 274, 275, 276, 280–2, 300, 303, 305–8

New Deal and, 220–50; N.R.A. and, 232–5, 241

Keynesian Revolution, the 24–5, 167–97, 214–8, 221, 238, 258, 269, 280, 310

Keynes—*contd.*
Lloyd George and, 107–9, 110
May Committee, views on, 130
post-Keynesian economics, 25, 89, 94, 310–37
Roosevelt, relations with and letters to, 221, 223–4, 235, 245, 249
tariff question and, 64, 150–1, 204
Treasury, the, World War II service at, 256, 262–3, 265–7, 330
*How to Pay for the War* pamphlet, 259–63
post-war planning, 268, 269–73
unemployment problem and, 20, 57, 94, 102, 107–13, 121, 152, 160
Mosley Memorandum on, his support for, 123
*Life of John Maynard Keynes* (R. F. Harrod), 79, 107, 167, 196, 223, 259, 342
*Keynes, Mr, and the Labour Movement* (A. L. Rowse), 343
*Keynes' General Theory: Reports of Three Decades* (R. Lekachman), 161, 164, 170, 173, 176, 177, 181, 240, 262, 267
Keynesian Revolution, *see under* Keynes
*Keynesian Revolution, The* (L. Klein), 162, 165, 182, 187
Kimmel, Lewis H., 236, 237
King, Willford I., 234
Klein, L., 162, 165, 182, 187
Korean War, 298, 299
Kuhn, Thomas, 174–6, 180, 181
Kuznets, Simon, 265

*Labour and the Nation* (Labour manifesto), 119, 123
*Labour and the New Social Order* (Labour manifesto), 104
Labour Exchange system, establishment of, 56
Labour Party
banking, proposals for state control of, 92–3, 228, 344–5
governments of—
1929–31: 103, 116, 117–8, 120–35, 352
break-up of and reasons for failure, 16, 133, 134, 143, 205, 342–3
1945–51: 282–7, 351; 1963: 303

Labour Party—*contd.*
National Investment Board proposal, 345
party conferences: (1929), 93; (1931), 342, 343–4
Landgren, Karl-Gustav, 162, 209
Lansbury, George, 120, 122
Laski, Harold, 190
*Harold Laski* (K. Martin), 195
Lassalle, Ferdinand, 32
Lauderdale, James Maitland (Earl of), 51
Layton, Walter (Lord Layton), 92, 105, 106, 107, 151
Lebergott, S., 301
*Lectures on the Industrial Revolution* (A. Toynbee), 30
Left Book Club, 350
Lehmann, F., 247
Leith-Ross, Sir Frederick, 265
Lekachman, R., 161, 164, 170, 173, 176, 177, 181, 221, 240, 262, 267
Lend-lease, 264
*Lessons of the British War Economy* (D. N. Chester), 257, 263, 266
Leuchtenberg, W. A., 222, 228, 233, 236, 243, 244
Levine, A. L., 29
Lewis, Sir Alfred, 265
Lewis, W. A., 293, 298
Liberal Industrial Inquiry, 108
Liberal Party
remedies for unemployment problem, 110, 111, 119
"Yellow Book" 1928, 100, 108, 109, 209, 214, 232
*Life and Labour of the London Poor* (C. Booth), 47
Lippincott, B., 325
Little, I. M. D., 282, 314, 336
Lloyd George, David (Earl Lloyd-George)
schemes for solving unemployment, 107–9, 110, 119, 120, 121, 162, 163, 211
unemployment and old-age pensions insurance, 229
*London Essays in Economics in Honour of Edwin Cannon* (H. Dalton), 148
London School of Economics, 52, 102, 148–9, 150, 346, 347
Beveridge at, 151, 152, 195, 196

London School of Economics—*contd.*
    differences with Keynes, 189–97
    foundation of, 58
*London School of Economics and Its*
    *Problems 1919–37* (W. Beveridge),
    58, 195, 196
Loveday, A., 74
Lucas, A. F., 213

MacDonald, J. Ramsay
    Labour leader and Prime Minister,
        117, 123–5, 265
    National Government leader, 116,
        133, 134, 141, 142–4, 202, 206
MacDougall, G. D. A., 266
MacGregor, D. H., 207, 221, 280
Machinery of Government, Committee
    on (Lord Haldane), 124
Mackinder, Halford J., 58
Macleod, Iain, 133
Macmillan, Harold, 118, 231, 233
    leader of progressive movement in
        party, 118, 216–7
Macmillan Committee on Finance and
    Industry (including Minutes of
    Evidence of), 70–1, 85, 87, 88, 93,
    102, 110, 115, 116, 122, 131, 135–
    7, 139, 141, 142, 143, 150, 153–5,
    157, 160, 163, 344, 345
    Keynes-Hopkins dialogue before,
        111–2
Macready, H. W., 61
Macro- and micro-economics, 18–9
    172, 181, 217, 218, 267, 272, 317,
    319, 336
    micro-economics and public policy,
        322–9
Malthus, T. R., 51, 178–9
*Management of the British Economy 1945–*
    *60* (J. C. R. Dow), 271, 281, 313
Mann, A., 229
Marris, R. L., 314
Marshall, Alfred, 14, 28–9, 60, 108,
    173, 190, 321, 323, 327, 328
    approach to unemployment problem,
        49–51, 57–8
    "consumers' surplus" concept, 39–
        42, 44, 45
    contributions to economics of welfare,
        37–45
    influence on Keynes, 14, 146–7, 153
    *Official Papers*, 31, 35, 39, 61, 62, 63,
        147

Marshall, Alfred—*contd.*
    "Social Question" and, 31–7
    socialism, attitude to, 32–4
    Tariff Reform, position on, 61–4
    tax-bounty system, 41–2
Marshall Aid programme, 284, 287
Martin. Kingsley, 195
Marwick, A., 199, 215
Marx, Karl, 32, 33, 346, 348
Matthews, R. C. O., 68
May, Sir George, 126
May Committee on National Expendi-
    ture, 70, 98, 116, 119, 132–5, 206,
    313, 316
    Minority Report, 129–30, 143
    retrenchment and, 125–32
McBriar, A. M., 36
McCarthy, Joseph, 299
McKenna, R. T., 83
Meade, James, 164, 165, 207, 221, 263,
    264
Means, Gardner, 214, 230, 232
*Means to Prosperity, The* (J. M. Keynes),
    166, 171, 202, 233
*Mechanism of Cheap Money 1931–39, The*
    (E. Nevin), 203
Meek, R. L., 336
*Memoirs of a Public Servant* (A. Salter),
    212, 265
*Memorials of Alfred Marshall* (A. C.
    Pigou), 28, 29, 31, 32, 33, 35, 36,
    37, 38, 43
*Men Without Work* (S. Lebergott), 301
Micro-economics, *see* Macro and micro-
    economics
*Middle Way, The* (H. Macmillan), 217
Mill, John Stuart, 24, 30, 50, 51, 61,
    169, 170, 316
Mishan, E. J., 320, 327
Mitchell, Wesley, 299
*Modern British Politics* (S. H. Beer), 198,
    283, 312
*Modern Capitalism* (A. Shonfield), 319
*Modern Corporation and Private Property,*
    *The* (A. Berle and G. Means), 230
Moley, Raymond, 224, 225, 229, 234
Mond, Sir Alfred (Lord Melchett),
    118
*Monetary History of the United States 1867–*
    *1960, A* (M. Friedman and A.
    Schwarz), 224
*Monetary Management Under the New*
    *Deal* (A. W. Crawford), 223

*Money, Credit and Commerce* (A. Marshall), 49

*Money, Savings and Investment in English Economics 1800–1850* (B. A. Corry), 179

*Money, Trade and Economic Growth* (H. G. Johnson), 170

*Money, Trade and Economic Growth: Essays in Honour of J. H. Williams* (P. A. Samuelson in), 296

Monopolies Commission, 324

Morgenthau, Henry, 224, 225, 226, 237, 243, 244–5

Morley, John (Lord Morley), 63

Morris, William, 33, 346

Mosley, Sir Oswald
  Labour Minister, 120, 122, 123
  memorandum for solution of unemployment, 122–3, 138–9, 345
  forms independent party, 122, 199, 332

Mowat, C. L., 140, 198, 215

Musson, A. E., 29

*My Apprenticeship* (B. Webb), 29, 58

*My Political Life* (L. S. Amery), 118, 121

Myint, H., 38

Myrdal, G., 301


*National Budgets for Full Employment* (N.P.A.), 274

National Debt, 97–9, 129, 136, 207, 211, 259, 260, 261, 270
  in U.S., growth of, 1940–6, 276

*National Economic Policy* (J. Tobin), 334

National Expenditure, Report of Committee on, *see* May Committee

National Government, 199, 200, 205, 344
  formation of (1931), 116, 133, 134, 142

*National Income and Outlay* (C. Clark), 262

National Investment Board, 109

National Recovery Administration, 227–35

*National Recovery Measures in the United States* (International Labour Office), 227

*Nature and Significance* (L. Robbins), 194

*Nature and Sources of Unemployment in the United States* (R. M. Solow), 308

*Nature of the Capitalist Crisis, The* (J. Strachey), 352

Netherlands, the, 314

Nevin, E., 97, 203

New Deal, *see under* United States, Roosevelt, F. D., *and* Keynes

*New Deal and the Problem of Monopoly, The* (E. W. Hawley), 249

*New Dimensions of Political Economy* (W. H. Heller), 302, 306, 313, 334

*New Economics, The* (S. Harris), 170, 182, 236

*New Economy, The* (R. Boothby), 118, 198

New Zealand, 200

*News from Nowhere* (W. Morris), 33

Next Five Years group, 215

*Next Ten Years in British Social and Economic Policy* (1929) (G. D. H. Cole), 106

Niemeyer, Sir Otto, 83

*Nineteen-Thirty-One; Political Crisis* (R. Bassett), 117

Nordwolle Company, failure of, 116

Norman, Montagu (Lord Norman), 74, 85–6, 89, 93, 122
  architect of return to Gold Standard, 85–7
  influence with Treasury, 92
  *Lord Norman* (H. Clay), 84, 103, 122


*Official Papers by Alfred Marshall*, 31, 35, 49, 61, 62, 63, 147

Okun, Arthur, 303

Oliphant, Herman, 244

Opie, R., 221

*Organization of Economic Studies in Relation to the Problems of Government* (J. Anderson), 124

*Other America, The* (M. Harrington), 301

Ottawa Agreement (1932), 204

*Our Partnership* (B. Webb), 55, 349

*Output Budgeting and the Contributions of Micro-economics to Efficiency in Government* (A. Williams), 326

*Oxford Studies in the Price Mechanism* (T. Wilson and P. W. S. Andrews), 258


Pakenham, Frank (Lord Longford), 273

*Papers in English Monetary History* (T. S. Ashton and R. S. Sayers), 77

*Parliamentary Socialism* (R. Milliband), 117

Parsons, Talcott, 32

*Past and Present of Unemployment Insurance* (Sydney Ball Lectures), 197

Peacock, A. T., 96, 99, 211

Pechman, Joseph, 303

Peel, Sir Robert, 96

Pennsylvania, University of, 265

Perkins, Frances, 238

*Personal Incomes, Costs and Prices, Statement on* (government pamphlet, 1948), 285

Phelps, E. S., 301

Phelps-Brown, E. H., 29, 207

Philips, Sir Frederick, 265

*Physiology of Industry, The* (J. A. Hobson), 51

Pierson, J. H. C., 274

Pigou, A. C., 28, 35, 43, 44, 57, 61, 78, 86, 110, 140, 147, 150, 152, 153, 317, 325, 327, 347

    contribution to welfare economics, 38

    Marshall's successor at Cambridge, 38

    views on gold, 153–4

*Planning Under Socialism* (W. Beveridge), 197

Plant, A., 150, 151

Plowden, Sir Edwin (Lord Plowden), 284

Plumptre, A. E. W., 164

Political and Economic Planning organisation, 212, 215, 217

*Politicians and the Slump* (R. Skidelsky), 117

Poor Law System, 47, 48, 53–5, 102, 104, 105

    Minority Report on, 53, 54, 55, 56, 57, 104, 239, 269, 349

*'Positive' Economics and Policy Objectives* (T. W. Hutchison), 38, 43

Postan, Michael M., 335

Post-Keynesian Era, *see under* Keynes *and* Great Britain

Post-war credits scheme, 262

*Postwar Economic Trends in the United States* (E. Cary Brown in), 293

*Post-War Unemployment Problem, The* (1929), 102

Powell, Enoch, 290

*Power and Influence* (W. Beveridge), 210, 272

*Prejudice and Judgment* (P. J. Grigg), 83, 128, 141

Pressnell, L. S., 83

Prest, A. R., 326

Prices, Productivity and Incomes, Council on (1957), 291

Prices and Incomes Board, 324

*Prices and Production* (F. A. Hayek), 184

*Principles of Economics* (A. Marshall), 23, 28, 31, 32, 33, 37, 38, 40, 41, 42, 44, 49, 50

*Principles of Political Economy* (H. Sidgwick), 31

*Problem of National Debt, The* (E. Nevin), 97

*Problem of the Unemployed, The* (J. A. Hobson), 47

*Problems of Economic Planning* (E. M. F. Durbin), 347

*Problems of the American Economy: An Economist's View* (P. Samuelson), 336

*Programme for Progress* (J. Strachey), 352

*Prosperity and Depression* (G. Haberler), 159, 183

Protection, *see* Tariff Reform and Protection

*Protective and Preferential Duties* (A. C. Pigou), 61

*Public Finance* (H. Dalton), 347

*Public Investment and Full Employment* (B. Higgins), 239

*Purchasing Power and Trade Depression, A Critique of Under-Consumption Theories* (E. M. F. Durbin), 347

*Reconstruction: A Plea for a National Policy* (H. Macmillan), 216, 217

Reeves, W. Pember, 58

*Relative Deprivation and Social Justice* (W. G. Runciman), 101, 140

Restrictive Practices Court, 324

Revenue Tariff, *see under* Tariff Reform

Ricardo, David, 50, 61, 109, 169, 170, 178, 179, 321, 346, 348

Richardson, H. W., 198, 203, 204

*Riddle of the Tariff, The* (A. C. Pigou), 61

*Rise and Fall of the Concept of the Economic Machine* (R. L. Meek), 336

Road Fund, the, 127, 130

*Road Pricing: The Economic and Technical Possibilities* (Ministry of Transport), 327

*Road to Plenty, The* (W. Foster and W. Catchings), 240

*Road to Serfdom* (F. A. Hayek), 192, 193

Robbins, Lionel (Lord Robbins), 61, 140, 149–50, 151, 184, 185, 187–8, 189, 190, 191–6, 267, 316, 352

Robertson, D. H., 74, 78, 110, 147, 159–60, 205, 265, 267, 347

Robinson, E. A. G., 164, 177, 207, 257, 262, 266, 267, 285

Robinson, Joan, 146, 164, 207, 273, 292, 317, 318, 323, 324

Roose, Kenneth D., 242

Roosevelt, Franklin Delano, 15, 200, 304, 352
  Keynes' letters to and relations with, 221, 223–4, 235, 238, 245, 249
  New Deal programme and legislation, 200, 202–11, 219–51
  *Public Papers and Addresses of*, 221, 235

*Roosevelt, Franklin D., and the New Deal 1932–1940* (W. A. Leuchtenberg), 222

*Roosevelt: The Lion and the Fox* (J. M. Burns), 222

*Roosevelt I Knew, The* (F. Perkins), 238

Roscher, W., 32

Rose, W. J., 274

Ross, A. M., 301

Rothbarth, Irwin, 262

Rowntree, Seebohm, 29

*Rowntree, Seebohm* (A. Briggs), 107

Rowse, A. L., 343

Royal Economic Society, 23

Rueff, Jacques, 173

Runciman, W. (1st Lord), 210

Runciman, W. G., 101, 140

Ruskin, John, 52, 346

Russia, 13, 72, 200, 221, 301
  Keynes's visit to, 349

Sachs, A., 233

Salant, Walter S., 264, 303, 331, 332

Salter, Sir Arthur, 212, 265

Samuelson, Paul A., 176, 177, 180, 267, 281, 296, 300, 303, 306
  *Collected Scientific Papers of Paul A. Samuelson*, 267

Sapir, M., 296

Sargent-Florence, P., 207

Sayers, R. S., 77, 83, 84, 87, 91, 257, 258, 259, 271

Say's Law, 51, 149, 168, 171, 179, 180

Schlesinger, A. M., 222, 223, 224, 228, 231, 232, 237, 302, 304, 305, 313

Schmidt, E. P., 250

Schnapper, M. B., 304

Schultze, Charles, 303

Schumacher, E. F., 273

Schumpeter, Joseph, 57, 58, 68, 183, 185–6, 188, 319, 321

Schwarz, A., 224, 225, 227, 238, 242

Schwarz, G. L., 150, 151

Selective Employment Tax, 313

Shackle, G. L. S., 18, 161, 324

Shaw, George Bernard, 36, 348

Shonfield, Andrew, 319

Shove, G. F., 38

Sidgwick, Henry, 31, 34, 37, 39

Simey, T. S. and M. B., 48

Simon, Sir John (Lord Simon), 262

Skidelsky, R., 117, 132, 140

*Slump and Recovery 1929–1937* (H. V. Hodgson), 115, 202

Smith, Adam, 15, 169, 316, 321

Smyth, R. L., 31, 34, 36, 37

Snowden, Philip (Lord Snowden), 89, 92, 93, 116
  budgetary orthodoxy of, 121–2, 124, 126, 133–4, 137, 142, 143, 205, 237
  in National Government, 205–6
  *Autobiography*, 121, 126, 205

*Socialism in England* (S. Webb), 36

*Socialist Case, The* (D. Jay), 352

*Socialist Economics* (G. D. H. Cole), 346, 351

Solow, Robert M., 303, 308

Sorensen, T. C., 302

Spencer, Herbert, 32

Sraffa, Piero, 164, 324

*Stabilised Money: A History of the Movement* (I. Fisher with H. R. L. Cohrssen), 224

*Stability and Growth in the American Economy* (P. Samuelson), 281

Stagnationism, 246–51, 275

Stalin, Josef, 349

Stamp, Josiah (Lord Stamp), 88, 124, 212, 259, 265, 266
  *Josiah Stamp, Public Servant* (J. H. Jones), 266

Standing Committee on Trusts 1919, 214

Stanley, Oliver, 118, 212

*Starving in the Midst of Plenty* (J. Wheatley), 120

*State in Relation to Labour* (W. S. Jevons), 31

*Sterling-Dollar Diplomacy* (R. Gardner), 277

Sternsher, B., 232, 236, 237, 241, 249

Stigler, G. J., 21, 175, 255, 303

Stone, Richard, 263, 264

Strachey, John, 352

*Structure of Scientific Revolutions, The* (Thomas Kuhn), 174

Stuart, Arthur, 247

*Studies in the Industrial Revolution* (L. S. Pressnell), 83

*Study of Industrial Fluctuations, A* (D. H. Robertson), 159, 160

Swanson, E. W., 250

Sweden, 15, 72, 95, 200, 209, 215
Keynes's influence in, 209, 215, 239
public works schemes, 72
Social Democratic Party, 209, 239

Sweezy, Maxine, 247

Sweezy, Paul, 247

Swope, Gerard, 228, 231

Symons, J., 349

Tariff Reform and Protection, 59–64, 118
1931 Crisis and, 134
Imperial Preference, 59, 64, 118
Ottawa Agreement (1932), 204
Protection, 203–4
revenue tariff, 138–40, 143, 150

*Tariffs: The Case Examined* (Beveridge and others), 151

Tarshis, L., 247

Tawney, R. H., 119, 124, 190

*Taxes and the Budget: A Program in a Free Economy* (Committee for Economic Development programme), 296

Taylor, A. J. P., 119
criticism of Keynes, 215

*Ten Great Economists* (J. Schumpeter), 58

Terborgh, G., 250

*Theories of Welfare Economics* (H. Myint), 38

*Theory and Practice of Socialism* (J. Strachey), 352

*Theory of Economic Development in the History of Economic Thought* (L. Robbins), 316

*Theory of Monopolistic Competition* (E. J. Chamberlin), 324

*Theory of Unemployment* (A. C. Pigou), 152

*Third Winter of Unemployment, The* (W. Layton), 105, 107

*Thirties, The* (J. Symons), 349

Thomas, Elwes, 225

Thomas, H., 333

Thomas, J. H., 120, 121, 123

Thorneycroft, Peter, as Chancellor, 290, 291, 292

*Thousand Days, A* (A. M. Schlesinger), 304, 313

Tinbergen, J., 330

Tobin, James, 302, 303, 307, 308, 321, 334

Torrens, Robert, 61

*Torrens, Robert, and the Evolution of Classical Economics* (L. Robbins), 61

Toynbee, Arnold, 30, 346

*Tract on Monetary Reform, A* (J. M. Keynes), 79, 80, 81, 85, 147, 148, 149

Trade unions
middle class fears of, 34–5
restrictive practices and apathy of, 29
Trades Union Congress
1931 crisis and, 133, 134, 135, 143, 144, 206
wage restraint policies and, 285, 286–7, 291

Transport, Ministry of (*Road Pricing: The Economic and Technical Possibilities*), 327

"Treasury View", doctrine of, *see under* Unemployment

*Treatise on Money* (J. M. Keynes), 146, 147, 153, 156–9, 160–4, 186, 225, 347

Truman Administration, 297–8, 299

Tugwell, Rexford, 228, 229, 230, 231, 233, 234, 238, 240

*Tugwell, Rexford, and the New Deal* (B. Sternsher), 232

Turvey, R., 326

*Unbalanced Budgets* (H. Dalton), 200, 209, 347

Underdeveloped countries, problems of, 315–6

*Unemployed, The* (R. C. Davison), 54, 101, 103, 105

Unemployment (in Great Britain) (*see also under* Keynes, *and* United States), 47–64, 84, 94–113
Assistance Board, 210
Beveridge's views on, 55–7, 103, 196–7
Crisis 1931 and, *see separate entry*
depression (1886), 53
depression (post 1931), economic policy and recovery, 198–218
Employment Policy White Paper (1944), *see under* Great Britain
expenditure on, 101–2, 115, 125, 134
Grants Committee, 104, 105, 130, 210
Insurance, 56, 71, 72, 98, 100–4, 113, 197, 229
inter-war period, 50, 64, 68, 69, 95
Keynes's ideas on, 20, 94, 107–13, 155–6, 160
Labour Exchange system established, 56
Marshall's approach to, 49–51
pre-1914 approaches and attitudes to, 46, 47–64, 56, 57–8
    Distress from Want of Employment, Select Committee on (1895–6), 47
public works and, 104–13, 119, 121, 155–6, 160, 164–5, 212
"Treasury View" doctrine on, 57, 109–13, 210, 211, 290
Statutory Committee on, 210–2
in 'Twenties, 100–4; in 'Thirties, 210–2, 268
*Unemployment* (A. C. Pigou), 57
*Unemployment: A Labour Policy* (S. Webb), 104
*Unemployment; A Problem of Industry* (W. Beveridge), 53, 54, 55, 56, 196
*Unemployment and Public Works* (I.L.O.), 106
*Unemployment and the American Economy* (A. M. Ross), 301
*Unemployment as a World Problem* (Harris Foundation Lectures), 163
Unemployment Insurance, Royal Commission on, 102
Unemployment Insurance Act, 1920, 53, 100
Unemployment Workman's Act, 1905, 100

United States
Anglo-American contrasts, 13–4, 313, 331–7
Black-Connery Bill, 228
Budgets in, procedures for formulating, 294–5
Committee for Economic Development, 296
Congressional Committees, advantages of, 331–2
cost inflation and incomes policy, 316–8
Council of Economic Advisers, 294, 299, 303, 308, 333, 334
depreciation of the dollar, 223–7
depressions (1931), 73, 77, 114–5, 185–6, 209, 220–41; (1937 to World War II), 220, 241–6
Employment Act 1946, 274–7, 278, 280, 293, 297, 298, 303, 331
Federal Reserve Board, 80, 116, 242, 244
Gold Standard, abolition of, 201, 202, 222
Keynes' influence in, *see under* Keynes
National Debt, 276
National Resources Planning Board, 274, 276
New Deal, the, 15, 25, 72, 200, 211, 214, 215, 218, 219–51, 275, 293, 297
    legislation under, 226, 228, 235–6, 237
National Recovery Administration, 227–8, 229, 231, 232, 236, 237
    Keynes and, 232–5
public spending and, 235–41
post-World War I boom, 68, 107, 114, 122, 219
post-World War II record, 280–2, 293–310
    automatic stabilisation, 295–7
    balance of payments problem, 302
    fiscal policy, 297–310
    retrogression and new causes for concern, 300–2
progressivism and institutionalism, 228–32
Public Works Administration, 242, 243–4
Reconstruction Finance Corporation, 236, 243

United States—*contd.*
  stagnationism, 249–51
  Temporary National Economic Com-
    mittee, 250
  Tennessee Valley Authority, 72
  unemployment statistics, 115, 219,
    242, 300–1, 306, 309
  Wall Street collapse (1929), 15, 113,
    115
  Works Progress Administration, 242,
    245
  World War II, 250, 255
    economists in government, 264–5
    lend-lease, 264
    post-war planning, 271, 274–9
    war economics, 263–4, 265
*United States Fiscal Policy 1945–59* (A. E.
  Holmans), 293, 313
U.S.S.R., *see* Russia


Veblen, Thorstein, 229
Versailles Treaty, 151
Viner, Jacob, 240


Waight, L., 201
Walker, G., 207
Wall Street collapse (1929), 15, 113, 115
Warren, George F., 223, 225
*We Can Conquer Unemployment* (Liberal
  manifesto), 109, 119
*Wealth and Welfare* (A. C. Pigou), 43, 57,
  325
Webbs, the, 72, 229, 349
  Webb, Beatrice, 29, 35, 54, 55, 57,
    58, 120, 196, 342, 345
  Webb, Sidney, 35, 36, 48, 55, 57, 104,
    196
Welfare economics and services, 16–17,
    28–46, 71
  Conservative acceptance of, 287
  Marshall, Alfred, and, 37–45
  public attitude to, 100
  social services expenditure, 97–8
Wells, H. G., 349
Whale, P. B., 77
*What Are We To Do?* (J. Strachey), 352
Wheatley, John, 120
*When Peace Comes: The Way of Industrial
  Reconstruction* (1916), Labour pam-
  phlet, 104
White, Harry Dexter, 201, 244, 274,
    278

Wicksell, Knut, 158, 161, 162
Wicksell Lectures, 281, 308
Wigforss, E., 202
Wilcox, C., 233
Williams, D., on "Montagu Norman
    and Banking Policy in the 1920s",
    74–5, 85
Williams, J. H., 265, 296
Wilson, Harold, 288
Wilson, John D., 247
Wilson, T., 258
Wilson, Woodrow, Fourteen Points of,
    278
*Winds of Change* (H. Macmillan), 118,
    217
Wiseman, J., 96, 99
Wood, Sir Kingsley, 260, 262
Wood, N., 349, 352
Wootton, Barbara (Baroness Wootton),
    207, 273
World Economic Conference (1933),
    72, 202, 210, 223
World War I, 22, 46, 278
  economic policies during, 257, 258
  government expenditure in, 96–7, 99
World War II, 15, 68, 255–68
  economists in public service, 265–8
  forcing ground for ideas, 255–79
  government expenditure in, 97
  Keynesian Revolution and war econ-
    omics, 24–5, 255–68
    interest rates, 258–9
    *How to Pay for the War* (Keynes
      pamphlet), 259–63, 315
  post-war credits scheme, 262
  post-war planning, 268–9, 269–73
  U.S. economics in, *see under* United
    States
*World's Economic Crisis, The* (Halley
  Stewart Lectures), 74, 163, 201
Worswick, G. D. N., 282, 284, 286, 288,
    290, 291, 314
Wright, A. L., 164


Yale University
  Kennedy speech at, 1962, 305
*Years of High Theory; Invention and
  Tradition in Economic Thought 1926–
  1939* (G. L. S. Shackle), 18, 161,
    324
"Yellow Book", Liberal, 100, 108, 109,
    209, 214, 232
Youngson, A. J., 81, 84, 90, 132, 160